Richard Shirley Smith

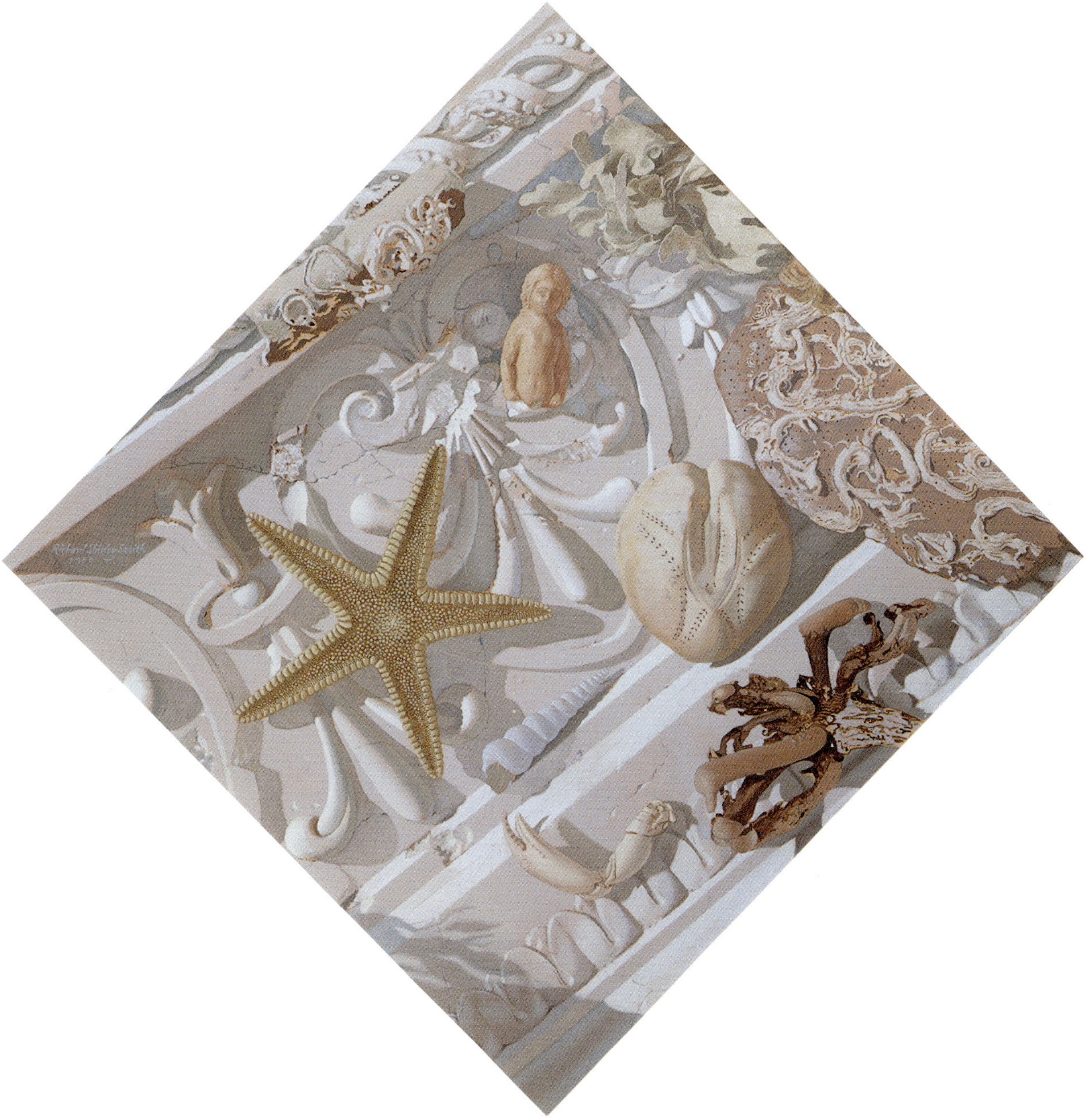

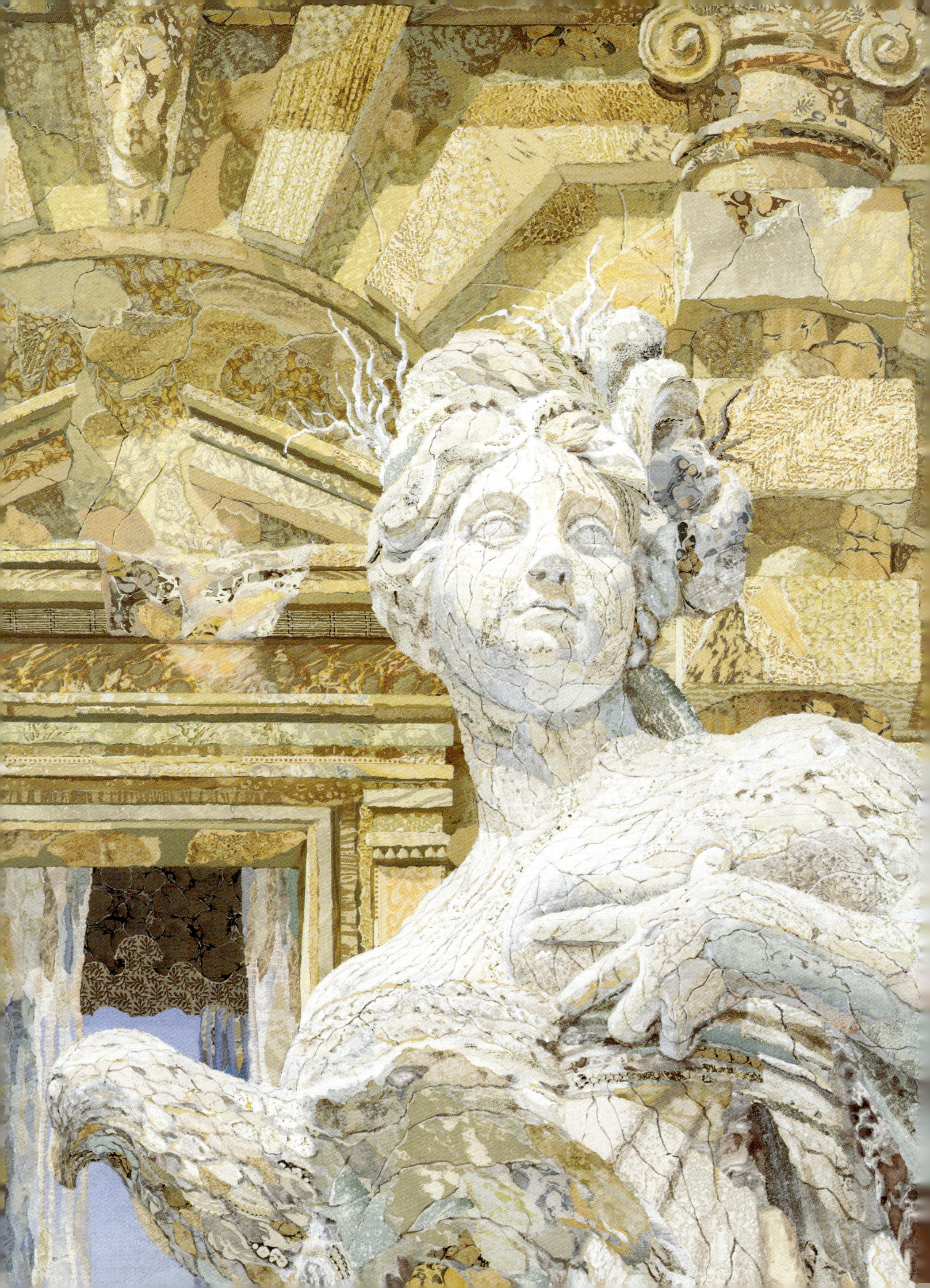

Richard Shirley Smith

The Paintings & Collages

1957 to 2000

with a preface by
Roy Strong

JOHN MURRAY

in association with
STUDIO HOUSE

Dedicated with gratitude to
Alice & Kenneth

This publication was made possible by the very generous sponsorship of
The Sheepdrove Trust
and of the
Marc Fitch Fund

First published in Great Britain 2002
by Richard Shirley Smith
and distributed by
John Murray (Publishers) Ltd
50 Albemarle Street, London, W1S 4BD

ISBN 07195 6332 1

Limited edition available from Studio House, Elcot Lane, Marlborough, Wiltshire SN8 2BA

British Library Cataloguing-in-Publication data
A catalogue record for this book is available from the British Library

Designed by Michael Mitchell and Richard Shirley Smith
Typeset by Libanus Press, Marlborough
Printed in Great Britain by
B·A·S Printers Limited, Orange Lane
Over Wallop, Stockbridge, Hampshire SO20 8JD

HALF TITLE ILLUSTRATION: Fig.1 *Classical Rock Pool*, Oil on canvas. 84 × 84cm. 1980 (*ptg.cat.90*). The relief frieze was found in a skip near the Nash houses at Regent's Park. I personally find a square canvas very directionless and dead to work on but this problem evaporates as soon as the square balances on its corner. This can be seen in hatchments in churches or on black and white Dutch floors set diagonally as they must always be. Private collection

PREVIOUS PAGE ILLUSTRATION: Fig.2 *The Sense of Touch* (*detail*), collage. 86 × 122cm. finished 1979 (*ptg.cat.72*) Collection of Michael & Caroline Mitchell

Contents

Various Essays

Appendix

Acknowledgements

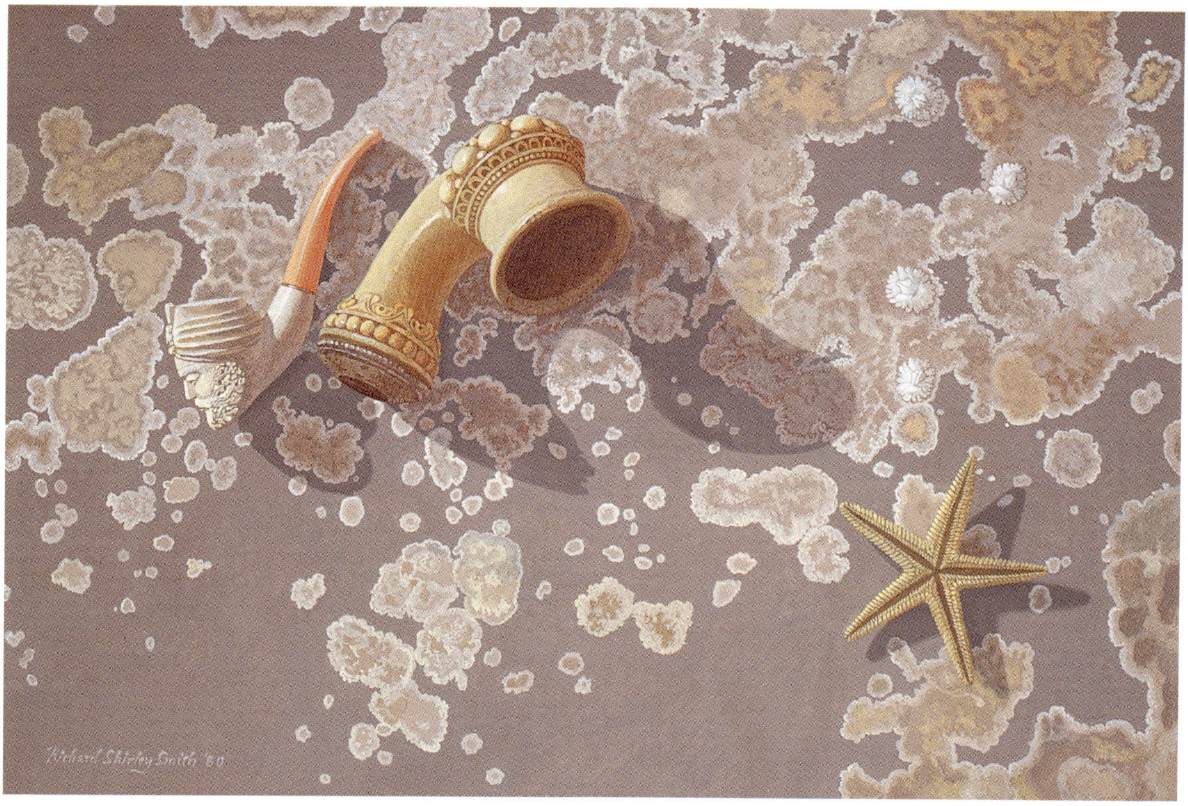

I should like to thank warmly The Sheepdrove Trust and also the Marc Fitch Fund without whose generous sponsorship this book would not have been possible. I should also like to thank Michael Mitchell & Heather Oliver at Libanus Press for valuable advice and also typesetting and layout, Rosemarie Timmis for help in checking all cross-references, Sandra Gannon for typing everything and Linda Saunders for not only reading, advising and editing but also for her poetic article. For the other perceptive articles by Sir Roy Strong, Sir Evelyn Shuckburgh, Simon Brett, Ian Lowe and Carolyn Leder, I am likewise most grateful. The publicity database was made by Amanda and Leo Shirley-Smith, and the catalogue database, upon which the book is built, was made by Tracy and Justin Shirley-Smith.

This book depends upon the photography, and I thank all the owners who have allowed me to photograph their paintings. I also acknowledge all the expert photography of Judith Aronson, George Birrell, Geremy Butler, Juliet Coombs, Sera Gay, Mike Harry, Hugh Kelly, Andrew Kolesnikow, Derry Moore, James Mortimer and John Taylor over many years. Following my 1999 solo show with Chris Beetles Ltd., Dr Beetles generously made available two dozen transparencies of remarkable size and quality which have much enhanced this book.

Every effort has been made to obtain permission and to acknowledge quotations, translations and publications and I should like to apologise for any omissions.

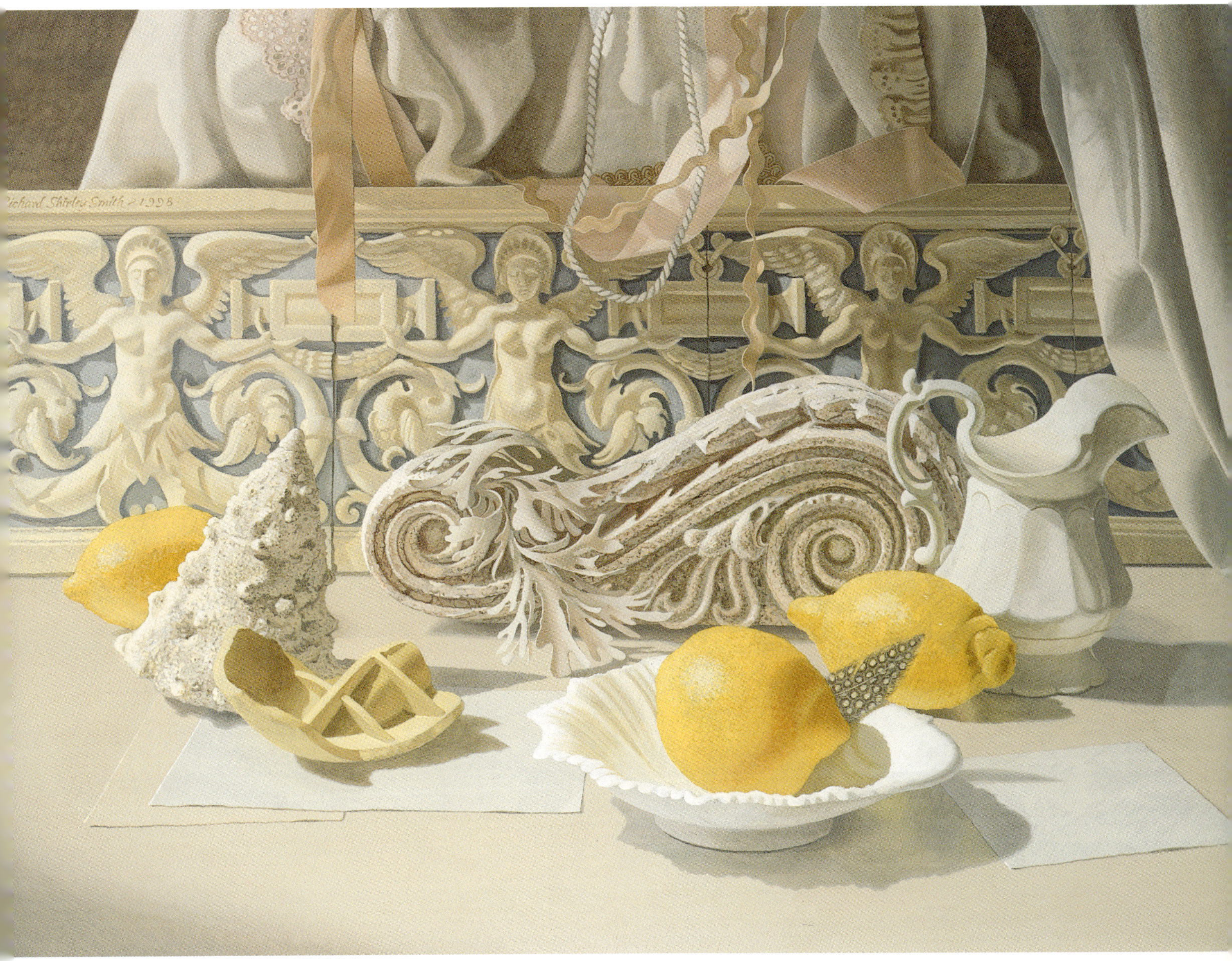

Editor's Note: The abbreviation (*ptg.cat.*) points to the list of framed works at the end of this book and (*eng.cat.*) refers to the complete catalogue of wood engravings to be found at the end of *The Wood Engravings of Richard Shirley Smith* by Iain Bain, published by the artist in 1994. All engravings are reproduced at actual size.

ABOVE: Fig.4 *Angels, Lemons & Volute,* acrylic on board. 82 × 115cm. 1998 (*ptg.cat.265*). Collection of the artist

OPPOSITE: Fig.3 *Pipes & Starfish,* acrylic on paper. 36 × 53cm. 1980 (*ptg.cat.78*). Private collection

FOLLOWING PAGE ILLUSTRATION: Fig.5 The artist designing bookplates just before the 1999 solo show with Chris Beetles at Ryder Street, St James's. The photographer, Derry Moore, managed to cause the bookplates to leap up like Lewis Carroll's playing cards. Photograph *Country Life*

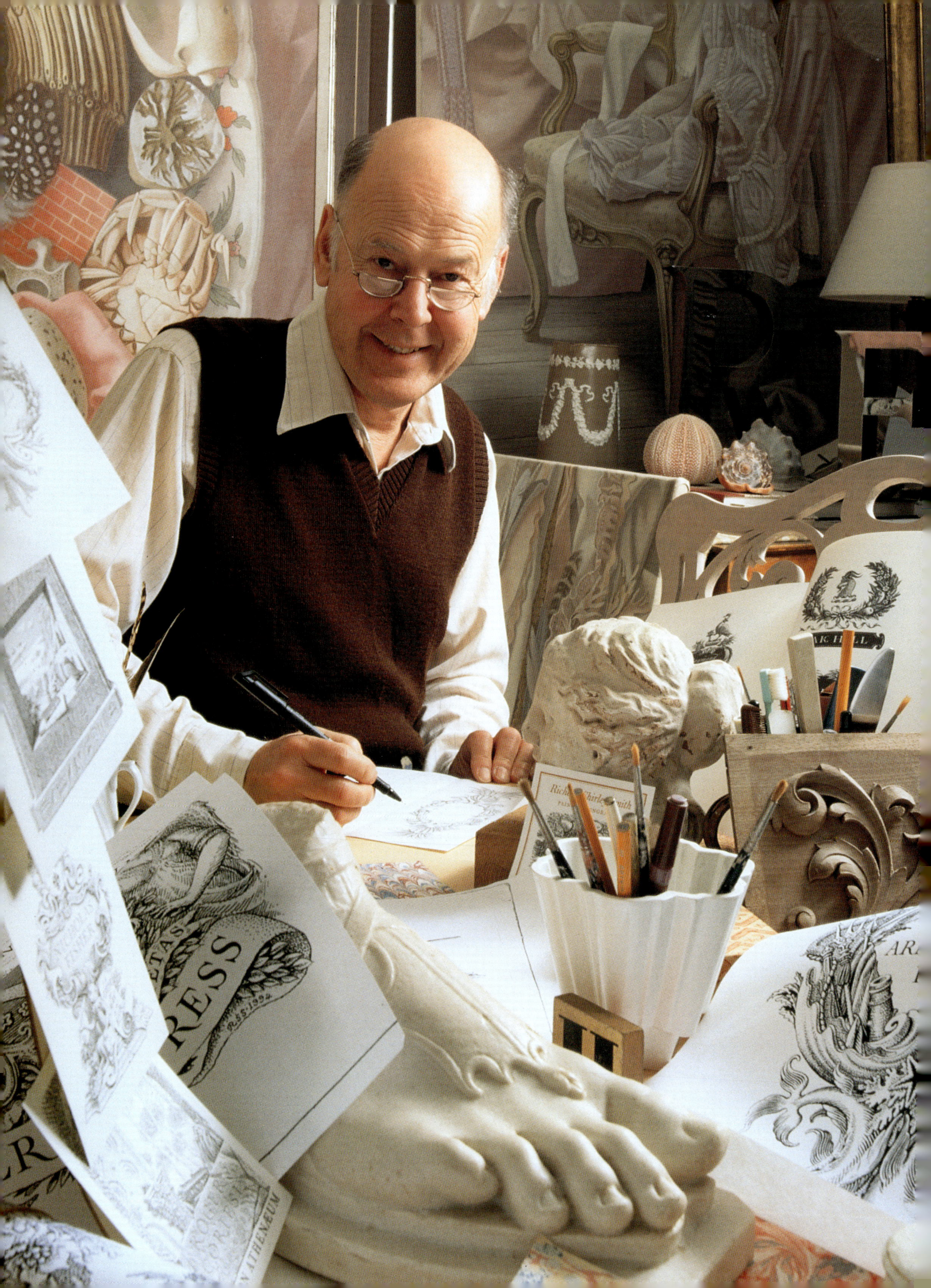

Preface

Roy Strong

Sir Roy Strong would like these words on the 1985 Retrospective at the RIBA Heinz Gallery, Portman Square, to stand as a preface to this book.

I THINK I MUST be an unacclaimed New Georgian and not a relict of the swinging Sixties after all. The enchanting exhibition of the work of Richard Shirley Smith at the RIBA Heinz Gallery reminded me of my earliest responses to the visual arts in the late 1940s, which led to an unswerving devotion to the tradition of romantic realism. In our post-modernist era, where there is at last room for aesthetic alternatives, those who bravely adhered to the discipline and vision of this tradition during the period it was out of fashion are being accorded rightful recognition.

Some of the recognition comes from a new generation of artists, such as the young Mynotts, who have had to recover the lost rigours of drawing and technique, perspective and painterly illusion, which were discarded by the colleges of art as so much worthless rubbish in the 1960s. I remember how students stood amazed before a nineteenth-century student's painstaking chalk drawing of a plaster foot in the Victoria & Albert's exhibition *Drawing, Technique and Purpose,* knowing that they were unable to do such a thing through lack of instruction.

A book which encompasses comprehensively the survival of this romantic revivalism has not yet been written. This is the stream to which Richard Shirley Smith's work belongs, one which stems back to the between-the-wars arcadia of Rex Whistler's designs and decoration, Cecil Beaton's romantic images of the Queen Mother in the style of Winterhalter, the architecture of Raymond Erith, the country-house decoration of John Fowler, Oliver Messel's stage designs, and the potent choreographic visions of Frederick Ashton. The latter indeed have never left the stage, ensuring that the romantic eye remained fed during the most barren of periods.

Most of the above were and are long-livers carrying these values through an alien era, but for artists of the generation behind them it must have taken some nerve to swim against the tide of fashion in the art schools of the late 1950s and 1960s. Perhaps that, and personal tragedy, accounts for the melancholy mood of Richard Shirley Smith's subject matter. Rex Whistler's world was an elegant one bursting with

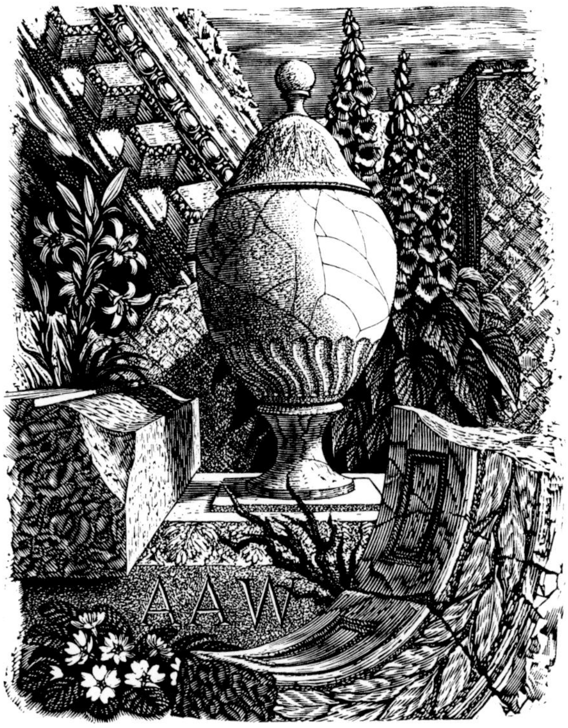

Fig.6 *Bookplate for Auberon Waugh*, an egg-shaped urn, A & Ω, wood engraving. 1978 (*eng.cat.242*)

wit and Hogarthian humour. Shirley Smith's ruins exude and revel in decay. His light, opaque palette, making use of a stunning technical illusionist virtuosity delights in every crack and chip in every surface. He loves strange juxtapositions and confrontations, creating a mythology which owes much to de Chirico and Dali but whose origins are an obsession with the architecture of the Classical and Renaissance periods. His natural use of objects as attributes and emblems with inner hidden meanings would have made him an ideal artist to respond to a programme drawn up by a humanist at the Medici court.

In *Vanity* we look into the distance and contemplate an Italian farmhouse in decay. The foreground is filled by the lower half of the statue of a classical female figure. At her feet rests a looking-glass; behind her the drawers of a chest disgorge fluttering ribbons, while a butterfly alights on the plinth. (see p.60)

The pavement in *Fatal Allegations* is scattered with tiny coffins. In *Roman Extinguisher* a lizard scales a crumbling wall to peer at a lyre and bow suspended in an alcove. This is an accumulation of private images whose decorative surfaces totally belie their sinister inner intent. So too does the subtle-pale colour range which moves through various chalky combinations of beige, grey and ochre.

Shirley Smith's wood engravings fit neatly into the world of Rex Whistler and Reynolds Stone, and are quite as fine as anything produced by either of them. The bookplates make a distinguished contribution to that genre: delightful masterpieces in miniature, deploying his usual architectural repertory of urns, altars and fragments of friezes through and over which sprout greenery and flowers. His illustrative work is typically drawn to hallucinatory and strange subject matter: skulls, a papal tiara and an hour-glass on the table, or the haunting death mask of Keats, seemingly a severed head cast upon a waving sea of bloom. (see pp.115 & 117)

Inevitably, such an artist has received commissions for murals. They are clearly highly accomplished but I do hope that this considerable talent and arresting eye will not be used just for scene painting. Richard Shirley Smith is an artist of integrity who has a disturbing visual perception to convey.

Oddly, his fundamental penchant for the mysterious and macabre makes him inappropriate for these commissions to which his technical expertise is so ideally suited. The overtones of his subject-matter are not suitable for a drawing-room or an entrance hall; hence these seem to me to give us the craftsmanship of the man but not the inner soul. The paintings and wood engravings, however, register the pulse of a complicated inner mind whose aim in life cannot be to go down in history as the purveyor of decoration devoid of serious content. Therefore the former will remain his truer monument.

In 1985 I wrote these words on a Retrospective Exhibition of the work of Richard Shirley Smith. They read, fifteen years on, as true, I trust, as they did then. My admiration has not faltered.

Roy Strong, 2000

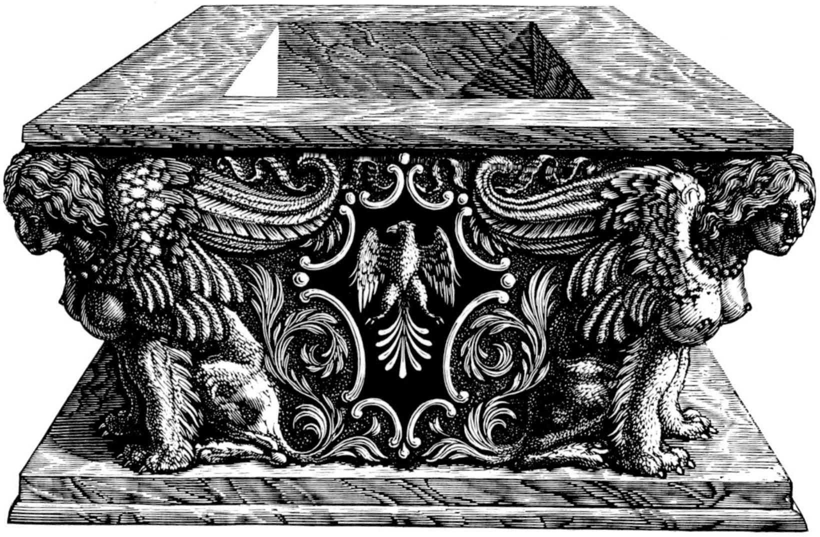

Fig.7 *Este Tomb*, from *Messer Pietro Mio*, Libanus Press, wood engraving. 1985 (*eng.cat.278*)

OPPOSITE: Fig.8 *Fatal Allegations* (*detail*), acrylic on paper. 56 × 46cm. 1976 (*ptg.cat.59*). Harlow Council

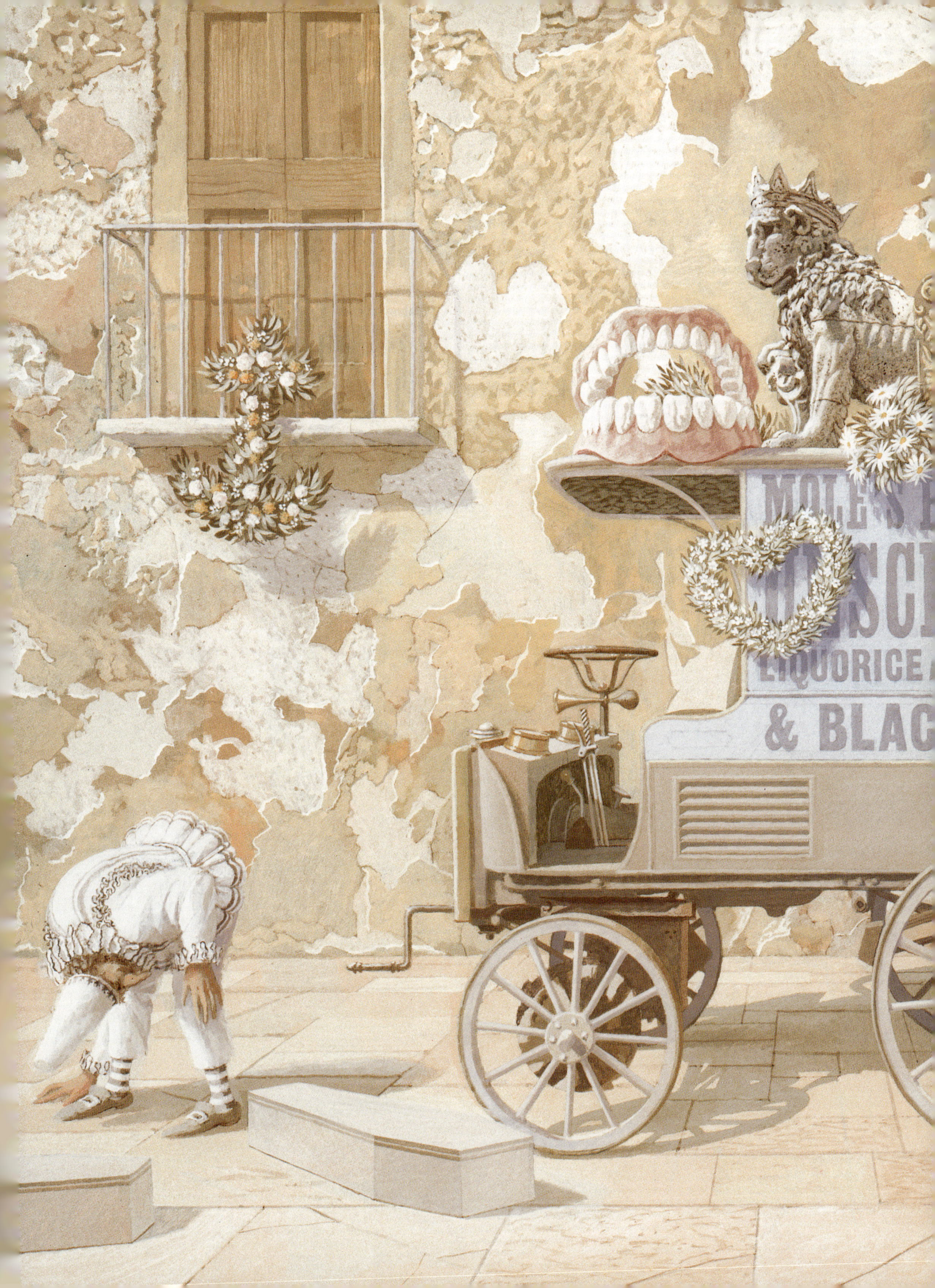
MOLE'S
LIQUORICE
& BLAC

Introduction

Richard Shirley Smith

This book is about what I paint to please myself when preparing for a solo exhibition, and a way of collecting together works that are scattered and inaccessible. Over forty years, I have made some three hundred collages and paintings for more than twenty shows, but nearly all these works are in private hands and, like my murals, never seen by students or the public. The book aims to give an idea of the variety and extent of this output by way of a catalogue raisonné.

In spite of an enduring admiration for Cubism and Surrealism, I have never at any time been much influenced by current vogues as to subject matter and style. Instead, although I owe a great debt to certain outstanding and encouraging artists, I have followed the irresistible dictates of my interests, imagination and eye, however curious or unfashionable. I discover, looking back, that there are six main subjects, often overlapping, that have always fascinated me:

Pulcinella and the *Commedia dell'Arte*
Theatrical figures in architectural settings
Surrealism
Beach-combing and objects on sand
Domestic still life
Classical fragments.

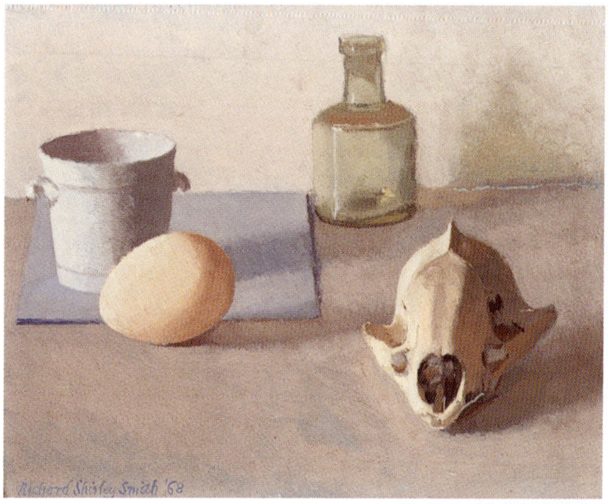

Fig.9 *Egg & Skull*, oil on board. 19 × 24cm. 1968 (*ptg.cat.10*). Collection of Michael & Caroline Mitchell

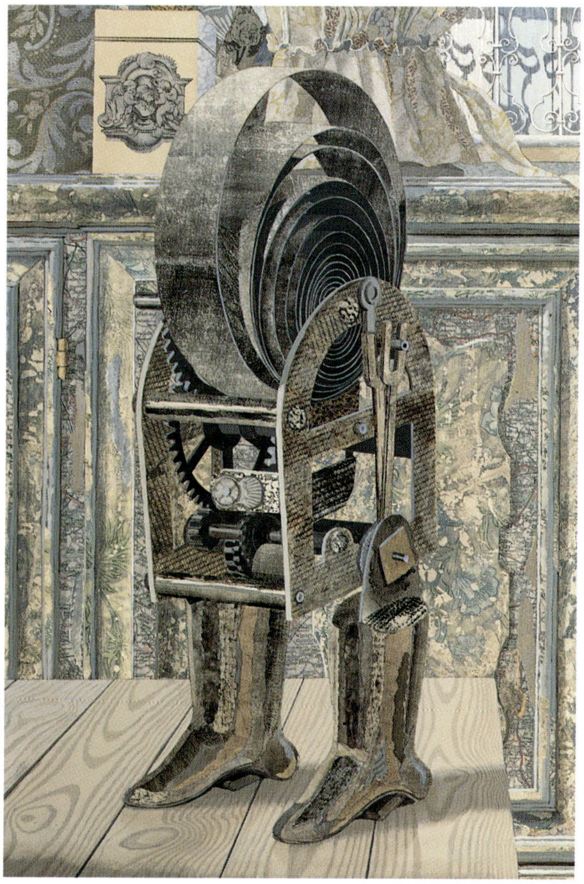

Fig.10 *Clock Walk* (*detail*), collage. 122 × 91cm. 1975 (*ptg.cat.40*). Collection of Patricia Hay-Edie

All these interests seem to have been present in my collages, which were discontinued around 1976, as well as in my paintings from very early on. The first section of the book is about the collages – how they started, and why they stopped. The paintings were made from 1975 onwards using a very straight-for-ward and unchanging acrylic technique; therefore I have grouped them into the six categories above and not treated them chronologically. Each section is introduced with a few remarks about sources and content.

The murals and paintings for illustration are mainly outside the scope of this book, although I have much enjoyed working with interior designers and publishers. The wood engravings, mostly for limited editions, poetry and bookplates, have been published and fully catalogued. However, the occasional essays collected at the end of the book include two on the wood engravings, among others that focus on murals or individual works.

By way of introduction here, I will try to sketch in the key influences – people, places, events – that shaped my career as an artist and my lasting obsessions.

I *Gerald and Joy Finzi*

At the start of Hitler's war, my father, already forty and a Harley Street heart specialist, volunteered to go to North Africa in the R.A.M.C. My mother, two sisters and grandparents moved from London to Brimpton, Berkshire. I must have been about seven when I was lucky enough to be asked by my school friends Christopher and Nigel Finzi to stay at their home at Ashmansworth on the Berkshire Downs. This was the house of the composer Gerald Finzi and his wife Joy who was an artist in many media, producing inspired wood-carvings, portrait drawings and much else. My own home had been a happy and comfortable place to return to at the end of a day, but theirs was a revelation to me even as a child. Here was a centre of civilisation and the arts where imagination, scholarship and skill were urgently employed with integrity. Whole rooms were devoted to composition, sculpture or reading and there were hundreds of exciting books. Ralph Vaughan-Williams and Sir Arthur Bliss were family friends, but luckily for me it was not only well known artists who received inspiration and encouragement but struggling beginners too. Joy was a decade ahead of the rest of the country in such matters as varieties of salad, making wholemeal bread and yoghurt and producing honey.

They showed a great kindness in encouraging me so warmly as they themselves had plenty of problems to face: Gerald's war work in the Blitz, refugees in the house, neglect of Gerald's music owing to fashion and then, as he became better known, serious illness. Christopher wrote truly: 'Joy and Gerald were a wonderful complement to each other, the whole of their union being much greater than the sum of their two individual halves'. There was always a sense of wonder at the immeasurable improbability of being alive, the complication and fabulous beauty of nature, but also an acute awareness of the fragility of life and of man's inhumanity to man. They took a delight in the lovely work occasionally achieved by artists and were concerned if talent and effort were discouraged and obstructed. Dr Howard Ferguson, who had many strings to his bow, being composer, pianist and musicologist, was Gerald Finzi's closest musical friend and years later lived near my family in Hampstead.

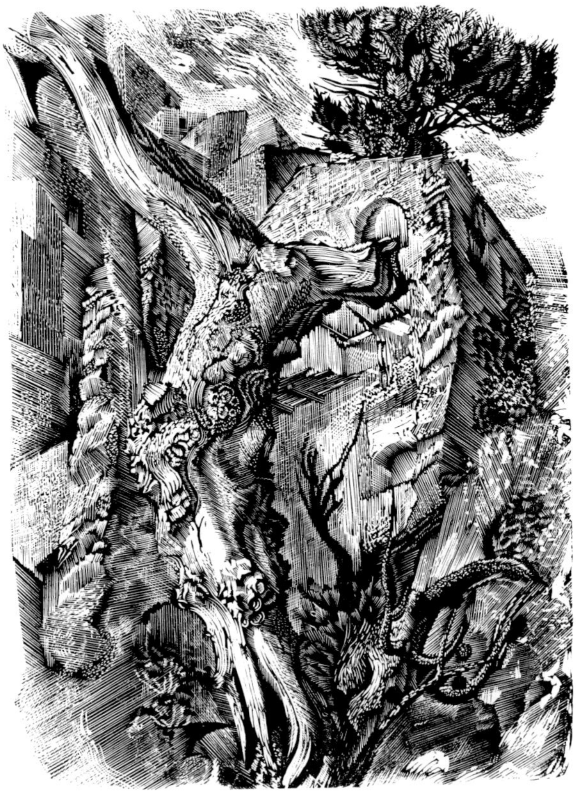

Fig.11 *The Piercéd Side* from *A Point of Departure* by Joy Finzi, Golden Head Press, wood engraving. 1961 (*eng.cat.18*)

He often received tickets for such wonders as Poulenc's *Dialogues des Carmélites*, Bartók's *Duke Bluebeard's Castle* or Debussy's *Pelléas and Mélisande*, and he kindly included me in these musical events. Unlike many musicians he loved the visual arts, too, and it was interesting for a young nobody to meet his neighbours Gerard Hoffnung and also Myra Hess, with whom he had worked on the National Gallery wartime concerts.

A few days before Gerald's tragically early death in 1956 Gerald and Joy drove with me to Great Bardfield in Essex to meet John Aldridge, a friend of theirs who was shortly to be my tutor at the Slade. This was only one of many exciting artistic expeditions Joy inspired and I was so glad that, living into her eighties, she took a great interest in my 1985 retrospective exhibition at the Ashmolean.

II Harrow and David Jones

Harrow School was an Elizabethan foundation, but I think it was only a coincidence that so many of the interests that fired me and like-minded friends were English *Renaissance* and Italian inspired. The Director of Music had in his study a wonderful set of volumes of English Elizabethan madrigals, and we loved rehearsing and perfecting those. Byrd's *Though Amaryllis Dance in Green*, Gibbons's *The Silver Swan* and Wilby's *Draw on Sweet Night* delighted us. Ronald Watkins's *Shakespeare at the Globe* project was a breakthrough at the time, as can be seen in his *Moonlight at the Globe* (Michael Joseph, 1946). It was illustrated by Maurice Percival, then the art master, a great friend to me and another enormous influence. The detailed study of *Hamlet*, *Macbeth* and *A Midsummer Night's Dream* was an unforgettable experience. Being no actor, I used to help Maurice Percival with the stage and props. Another Renaissance interest was Italic cursive handwriting which some of us pursued in the Art School, transforming our unsightly scribble into what Malvolio described as 'the sweet Roman hand'. The scribes at the Vatican wrote with exquisite sensibility.

The Art School always looked polished and civilised, with equipment clean and ready. It was decorated with artistic objects and books. No one got a chance to rush at a job at the wrong scale or with wrong materials and then dash off leaving an indelible mess of dry paint on the floor. There was always a logical way to a result: 'sort out your idea on the back of an envelope then, if it's any good, explore it a bit larger and build up steadily'. Maurice Percival had worked out exacting exercises to show how light from varying angles fell upon cones, spheres and cubes, and how cast shadow and reflected light worked. This knowledge is invaluable to a painter, and for some reason doesn't come naturally. The clever thing about this was that none of us ever said 'I can't think what to do' lest he should suggest that this was the perfect moment for one of his exercises.

Maurice was a Catholic convert and, while being charming and humorous, would always show his humility, and his kindness and respect for the underdog. He loved the purity and skill of the Italian and Flemish primitives and hated frantic and expressionist work. In the Vatican he had little time for the Sistine

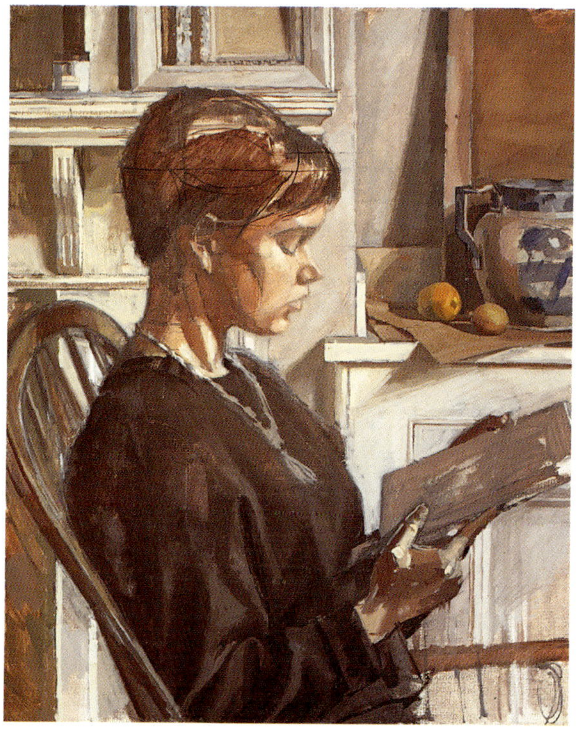

Fig.12 *Portrait of Juliet*, oil on canvas. 76 × 64cm. 1957 (*ptg.cat.1*). Painted while at the Slade School, three years before our marriage. Private collection

Ceiling and made straight for the study of Pope Nicholas V, lovingly decorated by Fra Angelico. He used to say that the rule of St Benedict provided that, if a monk got too puffed up with his painting skill, it was time he had a stint with the bees or the pigs. I remember remarking to him that I was disappointed at being passed over as a school monitor. He looked at me in astonishment: 'I can't think of anything that should make you happier'. He lived Christianity. The Housemaster's wife, Audrey Malan, was a very civilised woman, a painter, who in her youth had made a fabulous solo journey right across the Far East. The details are in her book *Eastern Visas* (Audrey Harris, Collins, 1939). She was also a friend of the poet and painter David Jones who happened to live two doors away. He was to be a very great influence in my artistic life (see my account of this friendship on page 110).

Recently, in 1996, I organised the production of *Ten Letters to Two Young Artists Working in Italy, Juliet Wood and Richard Shirley Smith,* by David Jones (Agenda Editions, 1996). This was a labour of love. These letters, richly embroidered with mythological and Christian observations, had clearly taken David some time to write, and it seemed wrong that they should be hidden away. I wanted to be able to read them and also thought the originals would be safer in the National Library of Wales, where they now are. It was lucky that Derek Shiel, who had just finished writing the substantial work *David Jones, The Maker Unmade* (Jonathan Miles and Derek Shiel, Seren, 1995), was able to edit the letters for me. His notes were so informative and entertaining that the book became a most evocative portrait of the artist at sixty-five.

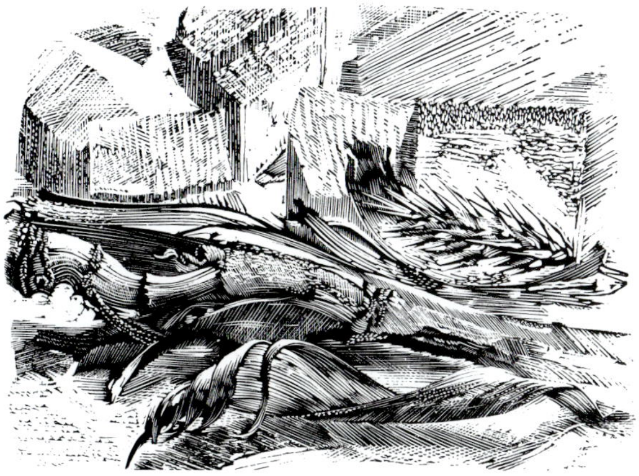

Fig.13 *Whither,* from *A Point of Departure* by Joy Finzi, Golden Head Press, wood engraving. 1961 (*eng.cat.17*)

A Dominican friend mentioned by David in one of the letters was Most Reverend Leonard Boyle O.P. We discovered that he was currently Prefect of the Vatican Library, so I wrote to ask, rather tentatively, if the library might like a copy of the limited edition of *Ten Letters.* A charming letter arrived from the Biblioteca Apostolica Vaticana, 11 September 1996: 'In spite of your fear that "it might not be sensible" I am sure the Vatican Library would be honoured to have a copy of the TEN LETTERS so please at your leisure send us one'.

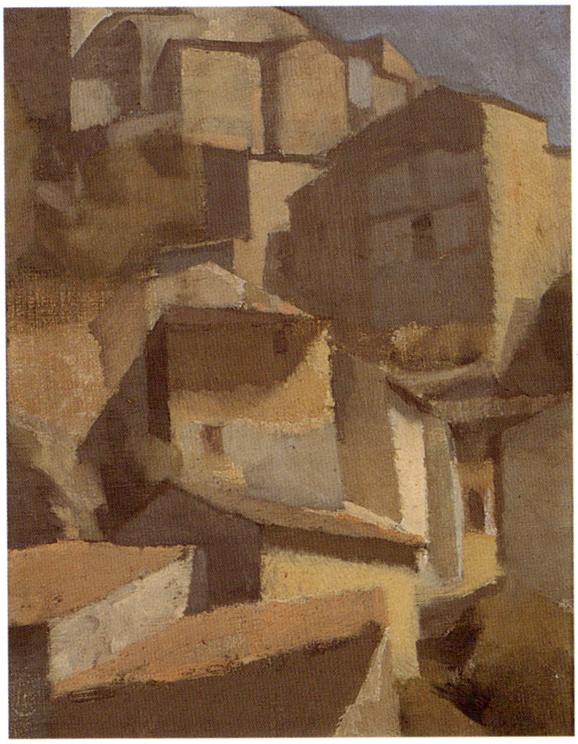

Fig.14 *Italian Farm Buildings,* oil on canvas. 30 × 24cm. 1961 (*ptg.cat.4*). An outdoor study at Anticoli Corrado. Collection of David & Juliet Hellings

III The Slade School of Fine Art

My tutor John Aldridge R.A. was a charming university-educated man and a friend of Robert Graves. He had a very special house and garden at Great Bardfield and it was always a joy to see his still lifes and landscapes in the Royal Academy's Summer Exhibition. There was much to learn at the Slade that Harrow and the Officer's Mess during National Service had by no means prepared me for. There was in my work a facile, plausible element, which I made great efforts to remedy. There were still some good strong drawings being done at the Slade then, and I worked very hard at observed drawing and painting in the life room and also in a room full of casts and plants, which I don't suppose exists any more. I was not a student who produced wonderful things, but I seemed to learn by entering and exploring every

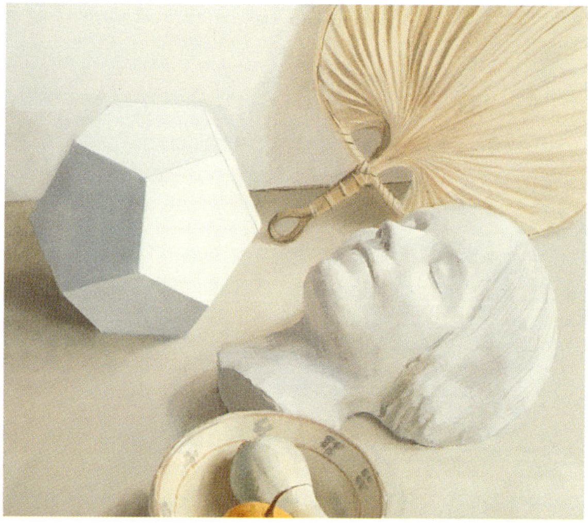

Fig.15 *Still Life with Death Mask (detail)*, oil on canvas. 46 × 36cm. 1968 (*ptg.cat.13*). Collection of Rita Carne

unpromising cul-de-sac. At least, as a professional, I don't visit them any more, knowing them as I do.

Illustrative tendencies were right off the menu there at that time. But I have always loved pictures of creatures and artefacts, and also illustrations of ideas, stories and events. None of this went down well, as can be imagined. This imaginative aspect I worked very hard on every evening. At that time I was thrilled by William Blake's work, and even now regard *Beatrice Addressing Dante from the Car, Newton, Triple Hecate* and *Pity* as the very finest of British art. Samuel Palmer's early visionary works and his note, of 1824, describing his first visit to William Blake, were a great inspiration. A remark of Samuel Palmer's which struck a chord with me concerned Palmer's dismay at his fellow artists' perverse choice of subject matter. He likened them to his dog 'who, refusing plum pudding, would lap up a vomit'. I have always swum against the tide since then and bandwagons have come and gone without me.

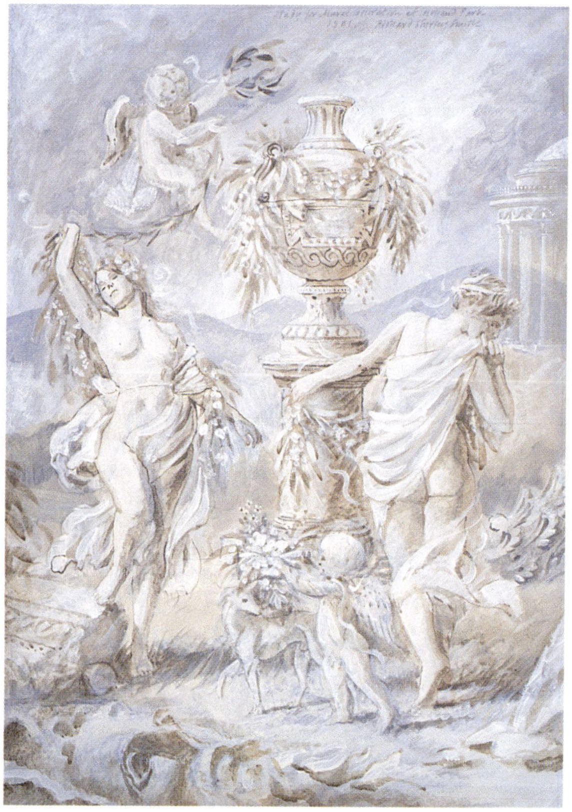

Fig.16 *Dancing Nymphs,* mural study for Holland Villas Road, acrylic on paper. 47 × 35cm. 1981 (*ptg.cat.102*). Collection of Mr & Mrs M. W. Elliott

IV Italy, Rome & Venice

After our Slade Diplomas in 1960, Juliet Wood and I married and, although we initially assumed we would then find paid work, were given an allowance by our families to study for fourteen months in Rome. We explored Rome for six months and then moved to Anticoli Corrado beyond Tivoli to paint and, in my case, to learn to engrave on wood. We stayed for a short time at the British School where we found that not all students appreciated Rome. For instance, young painters devoted to Abstract Expressionism would have preferred to be in America and probably had no interest in the fabulous historical and aesthetic riches Rome had to offer. I had the advantage of being a knowledgeable Catholic at that time, also having a great interest in antiquity and Rome in particular. I cannot begin to enumerate all we saw and can only quote Goethe's words of 1786:

> In this place the entire history of the world is ravelled up, and I feel I was born a second time, really born again, the day in which I set foot in Rome

A great inspiration was the Dominican Brother David. He was working at the Collegio Apostolico dei Penitenzieri and had been sent to Rome to show pilgrims around during the Holy Year of 1950. He regarded us as pilgrims and arranged for us to see places unreached by tourists such as the Pope's private chapel, painted

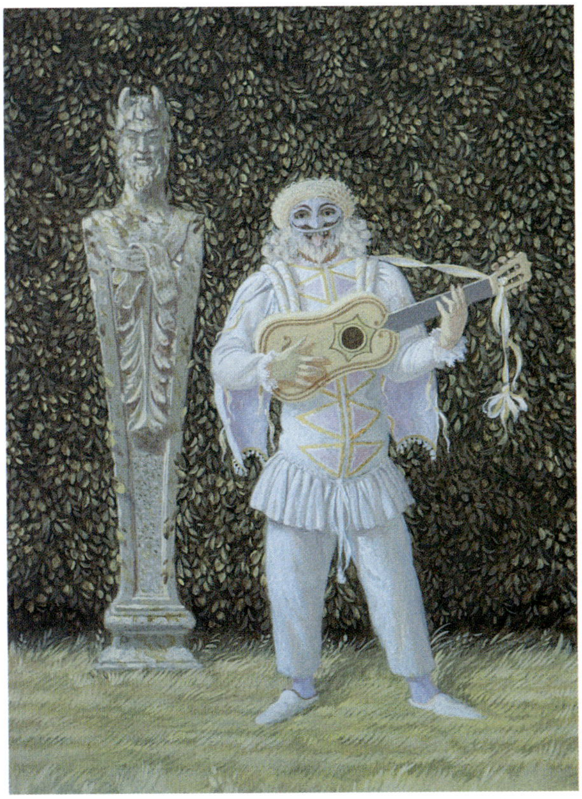

Fig.17 *Guitarist,* acrylic on paper. 33 × 24cm. 1983 (*ptg.cat.131*). In the *Commedia dell'Arte*, this character would be Scaramouche. The sculpture is a satyr herm observed at Mottisfont Abbey. Collection of Iain Bain

by Michelangelo, and the Mausoleums of the second century AD under the Crypt of St Peter's. The Collegio Apostolico faced the main portico of Sta Maria Maggiore, the finest remaining example of Constantine's great Roman basilicas. Sta Maria Minore, on the other hand, turned out to be a handy bar round the corner where wonderful expeditions were planned. Brother David even joked of changing his allegiance from St Dominic to St Martin of Tours. One memorable 'tour' was to Anagni, east of Rome, with its unusual Romanesque cathedral. Romanesque was the austere religious architecture most favoured by David Jones and his circle, and Roman Baroque, in spite of Pevsner's efforts, was as yet beyond the pale for us. I returned ten years later and photographed the architecture of Bernini, Borromini and Pietro da Cortona with great delight.

We were surprised to learn that David Jones and Brother David (Reggie Lawson in those days) had been at Ditchling in 1920 under the friendly and practical direction of Eric Gill. They had even shared a cottage which was known to Gill's daughters as *The Sorrowful Mysteries* (an allusion to the Rosary). Unsurprisingly, the girls found some of the survivors of the First World War, who came to Gill for advice, both sorrowful and mysterious. Brother David showed us the lively mosaics of birds and leaves decorating the barrel vaults of the Mausoleum of Constantine's daughter Constantia (*c.*360 AD), and he also came with us to Prenestina (birthplace of Palestrina) to see the great floor mosaic that was originally in the Temple of Fortuna Primigenia. The Romans were obsessed with Egypt, and this great flooded landscape full of exotic animals, hunters, temples and boats symbolises the mystic marriage between Isis, the Egyptian earth, and Osiris the overflowing fertilising river.

Of great interest to me was the work of the Cosmati marble workers. Two hundred years before the Renaissance these Roman marble craftsmen were foreshadowing it by going back to classical remains

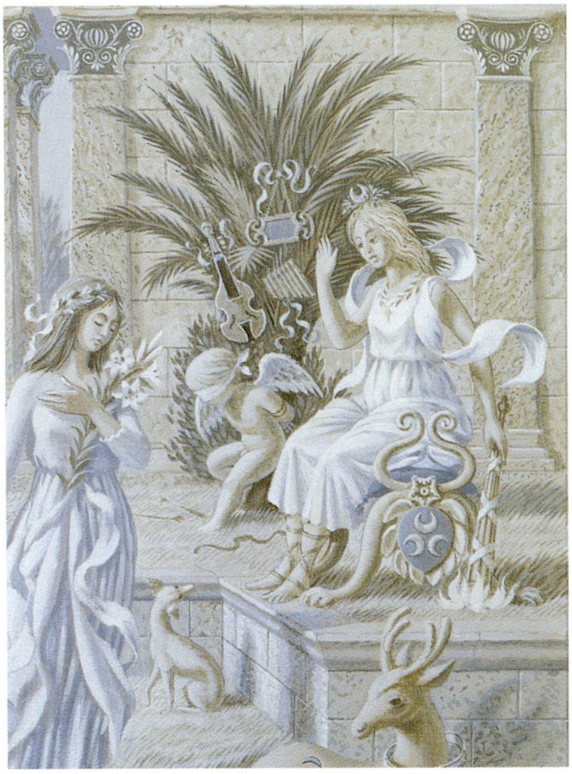

Fig.18 *Triumph of Diana,* (*detail*) acrylic on paper. 50 × 34cm. 1982 (*ptg.cat.122*). This theme, *The Chastisement of Cupid*, is from the reverse of a portrait medal of Lucrezia Borgia. Collection of Mike & Genna Eilers

and not only utilising the materials and different coloured and figured marbles but also very beautifully reusing columns, capitals and sculpture even as early as medieval times. The Cosmati comprise various families of workers, and their works are a major delight all over Rome and beyond. They would use great circular slices of green flecked Greek porphyry, or red porphyry from Egypt, and set them in pulpits,

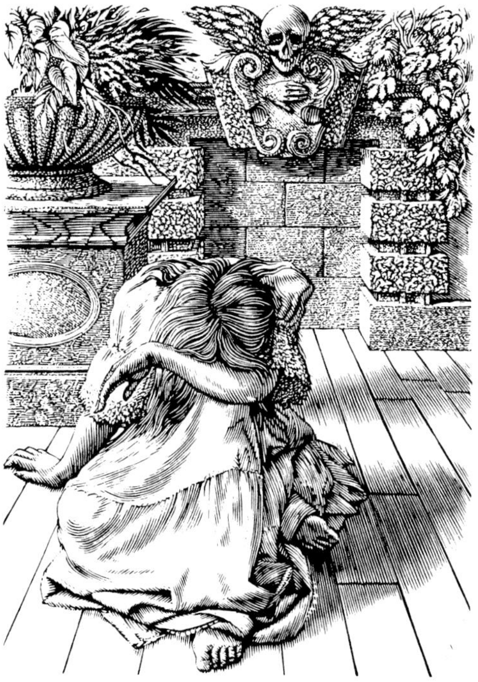

Fig.19 *The Closed Door,* for poems *The Closed Door*, James Reeves, Gruffyground Press, wood engraving. 1977 (*eng.cat.*239)

cathedra chairs, altars and the most decorative pavements, surrounding these great discs with bands of elaborately geometric marble pieces. Each Cosmati church is a heavenly variation on a theme: Sta Maria in Cosmedin, S Giorgio in Valabro, or the magnificent S Clemente. In the mid-sixteenth century Pope Julius III had a mannerist villa built on the Via Flaminia. Here, at Villa Giulia, I greatly admired the Etruscan bronze-handled mirrors decorated on the back with line engravings, where the white lines perfectly suggested the sensuous forms of the limbs of the Gods and Goddesses depicted. They reminded me of Picasso's *Vollard Suite.*

I don't think we wasted a single moment of the opportunities we were given in Italy. In a letter of 17 August 1961 David Jones comments: 'I think it's wonderful how you both get down to your painting, engraving etc. in another land and in a land of so many natural and man made beauties. Lots of people find it impossible to work under such circumstances'. He used to use the word 'exorbitant' in the sense that artists can't properly work *outside the orbit* of their first-hand experience.

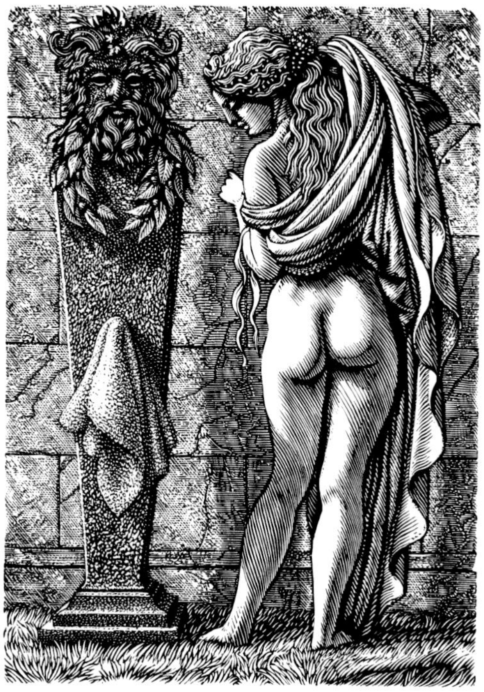

Fig.20 *Thais,* for poems *Thais*, David Burnett, The Rocket Press, wood engraving. 1984 (*eng.cat.*257)

In 1973 I published a set of four educational slide strips, *The Story of the Venetian Villas* (Visual Publications), following three photographic expeditions to the Veneto. Why was I so fascinated by these Villas, one thousand five hundred, of artistic interest alone, in all sizes and states of repair? They seemed so promising to photograph: sun and shadow falling on these marvellous artefacts, picturesquely eroded by time. They invite heavenly and decorative images of mutability.

Normally great works of art are sought in cities surrounded by garbage and exhaust fumes, whereas in the heart of the Italian countryside one can see the works of Palladio, Veronese or the sculptor Vittoria: indeed, at Maser they all three worked on the same magnificent Villa Barbaro. There have been a few occasions in my life when I have felt a particular delight and artistic privilege, and photographing Villa Barbaro was one of them. I wrote in my notes for the film strip:

> Villa Barbaro is not merely a dreary attempt to display the wealth and power of a particular family, but the collaboration of geniuses working not just for rich patrons but for friends who were themselves artists. Not only does all the splendour of the Italian Renaissance live on in these rooms from a time when Venice was a world power, but they are of human scale, have humour and are related to the practicalities of their beautiful rural surroundings.

Another great cycle of murals I enjoyed photographing was at Villa Valmarana ai Nani. In 1757 Giambattista Tiepolo painted a magnificent *Sacrifice of Iphigenia* in his grand manner, and much else in the Palazzina, while his son Domenico decorated the Guest Wing with a Gothic Pavilion, a Chinese room and charming rural scenes. I learned much from these murals.

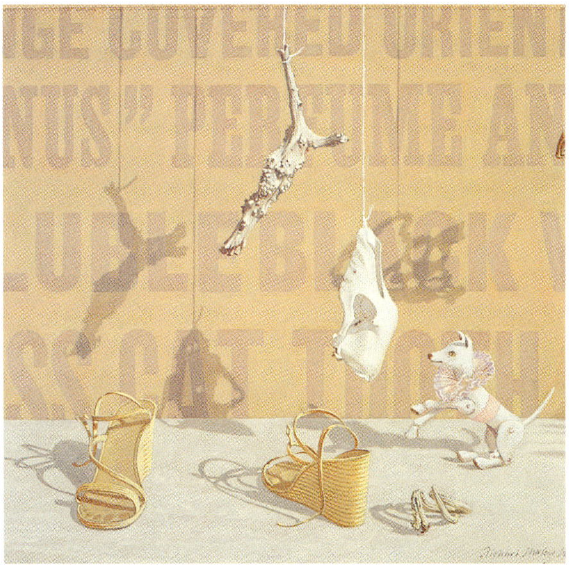

Fig.22 *Hanging Still Life (detail)*, acrylic on paper. 33 × 51cm. 1983 (*ptg.cat.128*). Collection of Nigel & Vivien Clark

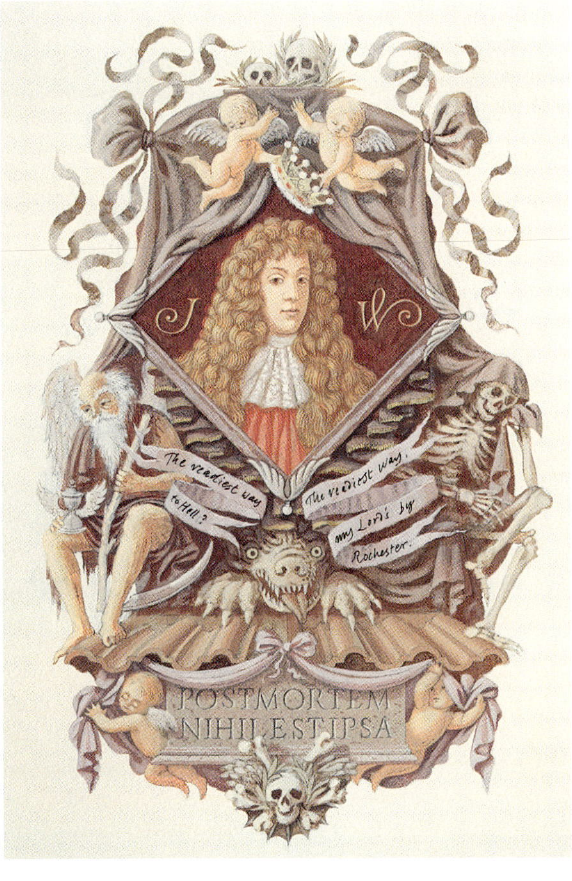

Fig.21 *Post Mortem Nihil Est*, from *Perfect & Imperfect Enjoyments* (Rochester's Poems), acrylic on paper. 40 × 28cm. 1992 (*ptg.cat.197*). The Folio Society

V *Wood Engraving*

While I was teaching myself to engrave in Anticoli Corrado near Rome in 1961, Joy Finzi came to stay. She was working on *A Point of Departure*, a group of poems expressing her bereavement, and I was inspired to make seventeen engravings to accompany – rather than illustrate – the poems. They remained unpublished for six years until Laurence Whistler suggested that Raymond Lister might like to publish them at his Golden Head Press, which he did in 1967.

I had once or twice met Janet and Reynolds Stone, the most successful wood engraver of his generation, excelling in exquisite lettering. They invited us to Litton Cheney, Dorset, and later we looked after their house and library while they were in Verona. I was reminded of how encouraging these more senior friends have been to me when I found a letter from Reynolds dated January 1968 and commenting on *The Point of Departure* engravings: '. . . I admire their flow and rhythm and freedom, as in all your work surely. Complication without confusion . . .' He had picked out exactly the qualities I value most and make great efforts to achieve.

On my return from Italy I showed these engravings to Anthony Gross who had taught etching and aquatint at the Slade. He at once recognised a huge improvement and introduced me to the Oxford

Fig.23 *Study for Three Wardrobes,* Holland Villas Road, acrylic on paper. 52 × 32cm. 1981 (*ptg.cat.111*). Wyliman Collection

University Press and Faber & Faber, where I met Berthold Wolpe, designer of the typeface *Albertus*. I did engravings for both these publishers and for Burns Oats and The Folio Society.

In 1970, at the end of my time as head of the Art Department at Marlborough College, I was asked by John Dreyfus, the typographer and agent for the Limited Editions Club of New York to do forty-two wood engravings for Stephen Spender's selection of the poems of Shelley. I think the word 'masterpiece' originally referred to the piece of work, that divides the apprentice from the professional; in which case this was my 'masterpiece' as regards engraving. John Dreyfus must have been pleased, as he wrote in *The Private Library,* (Summer, 1976):

> On looking at them again after an interval of five years, I marvel afresh at the ability with which he was able to render intricate details of architecture, landscape, seascape, flora, fauna and the human face – all with equal mastery and with astonishing control of perspective and the lighting of the different planes.

Shortly after this I began to meet experts in engraving, printing and bookplates, such as David Chambers, James Wilson, Iain Bain, Brian North Lee and, later, Michael Mitchell. They have all taken a lively part in printing, publishing or writing about my engravings.

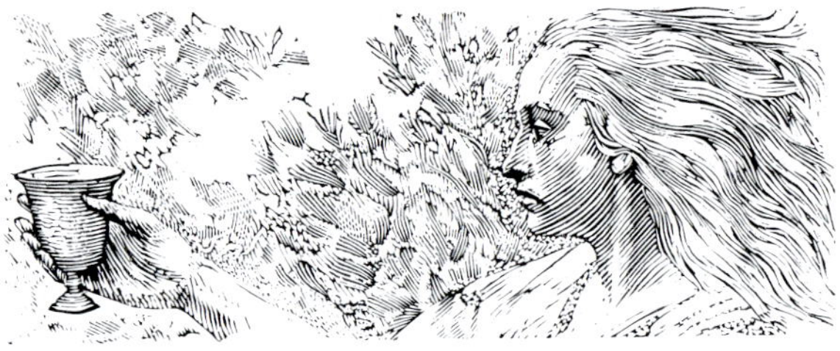

Fig.24 *Girl Offering Chalice,* from *The Poems of Percy Bysshe Shelley*, wood engraving, 1971 (*eng.cat.199*). Limited Editions Club of New York

VI *Blewbury and Trompe-l'Oeil Murals*

In 1977 I moved with my second wife Bernardine to Blewbury, South Oxfordshire. This was a village of venerable farmhouses and streams running through from the nearby downs. There was an antique shop, a framer, an art gallery and a fine printer, The Rocket Press. Here we found a good number of talented and artistic friends. At that time young composers were commissioned to write operas for the village; the world premieres being staged in the church. Richard Blackford's *Sir Gawain and the Green Knight* was in rehearsal when we arrived. In the summer there was

Shakespeare in an open-air theatre and a biennial Blewbury Festival including open studios. The nine years in Blewbury were some of the happiest in my life, and much painting and engraving went on in our small architect-designed, International-modern-style house.

The influential architect Sir Frederick Gibberd having seen an article in the *Architectural Review* (see p.41) wrote to me and bought *Fatal Allegations* (Fig.37) for his collection. I delivered the painting to his office in Percy Street and we had lunch at the White Tower Restaurant. We talked about the villas of the Veneto and even retirement. He wrote on 5 June 1977:

> How lucky you are to be able to pursue your art when you have the inclination. I have to wait until someone wants a building – ideal buildings for ideal sites are a barren pursuit: someone must want it, set a programme, and there must be an environment to influence the design and be influenced by it. However I direct my energy to garden making, setting greater and greater problems of upkeep.

He was delightful company.

One afternoon an elegant, bearded gentleman appeared at my front door. He had been recommended by Laurence Whistler to ask me to paint a clavichord he had made with a view to replacing one painted by Rex Whistler, which had been stolen (see p. 112) My visitor turned out to be Sir Evelyn Shuckburgh, recently Ambassador in Rome. Laurence wrote to me on 7 September 1978:

> I hope I convinced Evelyn that a good artist could only be hampered by having to design with reference to another, however loosely. I felt you might make it at once rich, formal, dream-like, precise, poetic and mysterious. But now *I'm* beginning to hold your brush.

Laurence's own exquisite engraved glass also has a dream-like element, for example in *Corinthian Wood* or *Way Out*, both of 1971. The dream, of course, is the clearest window into the subconscious and is therefore dear to surrealists. After seeing my first Oxford Gallery show he had written on 13 March 1976:

> There is a kind of dream which is not a bad dream. Yet slightly uneasy, and at the same time beautiful and fascinating: one wants to stay in it. That is what your pictures mean to me. It may not be what you want but there it is.

Laurence was both an inspiration and a practical help in my work.

Bill Bennette, the successful interior designer, had contacted me having tracked down my work in an Arts Council artists' information slide registry and realised the possibilities for murals. I had stopped making collages by now and had worked out a most effective way of using acrylic, which was perfect for

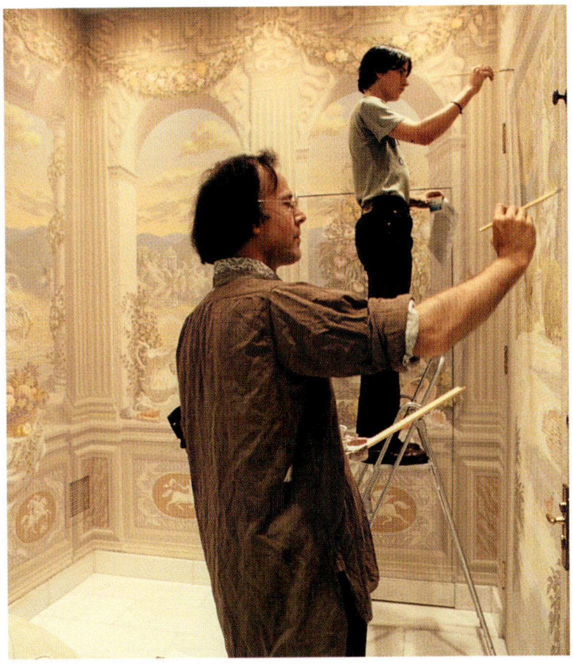

Fig.25 The artist and his son, Leo, working on the first of the murals. The Doric Villa, Regents Park, 1976

mural decoration. My first mural was in a Nash house facing Regent's Park; others followed over the years in Holland Park, Bruton Street, Eaton Square, Princes Gate and Kensington Palace Gardens (see p.135). I would work the design out on graph paper at one-fifth scale as a painting so that the client and I could see exactly what it would look like. Alterations or fresh starts could easily be made. Once agreed, it only remained to paint it on the walls at five times the size. All the creative part was done comfortably in the studio and as little time as possible was spent at the very noisy building site. I prefer to paint murals in close pale tones as I never liked dark paint on walls, which makes rooms gloomy, nor living with murals that keep catching the eye with strong contrasts. Also the acrylic distorts more, as it dries, in the darker tones than in the paler ones.

It was exciting to paint on large beautifully prepared canvas-covered walls and also to be surrounded by the painting as I worked. It was good to have young friends and ex-students working on the same project, as I was otherwise used to working alone. Another new feature was that while everything I had ever done had been paid for in a few hundred pounds at best; murals had to be a few thousand pounds. Much of this has gone to make up a small pension for which I now have Bill Bennette to thank.

VII *The Ashmolean Retrospective 1985*

About two years before my fiftieth birthday, I somehow knew that, having finished so many works, a retrospective would be essential if my career was to keep momentum. I was much encouraged by Ian Lowe at the Ashmolean and by Anne Stevens, who was working voluntarily at the Museum mainly on British printmaking (see p.120). Bill Bennette found generous sponsorship for printing from the Landseer Property Corporation, and Jane Preger was a great help at the R.I.B.A. Heinz Gallery when the exhibition moved there after Oxford. Henry Ford and Brian North Lee wrote most effectively on the paintings and engravings respectively in the catalogue. Otherwise I organised everything, designing catalogue, poster, cards and doing all correspondence, then selecting, transporting and hanging both exhibitions with my son Justin, who luckily was free at the time. I also prompted some useful press articles and, although it was an enormous effort, it seemed the right thing to have done (see review p.119). After the retrospective the Ashmolean acquired proofs of all my existing engravings for their Print Room.

1985 was a good year. David Chambers had published his Cuckoo Hill Press *Selected Engravings,* and Sir Laurence Whistler in his introduction stressed 'the fantastic and the poetical'. Sir Roy Strong's review

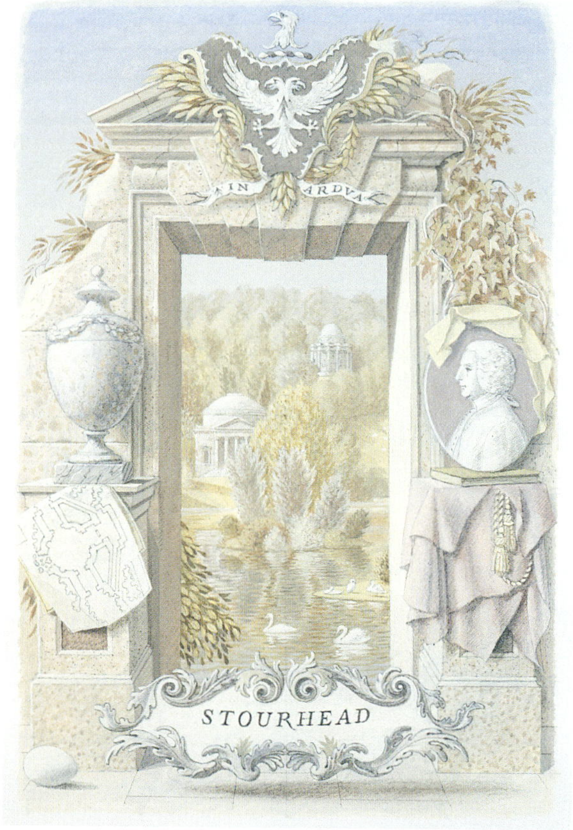

Fig.26 *Stourhead*, acrylic on paper. 40 × 29cm. 1989 (*ptg.cat.174*). This is an illustration for the forthcoming *Building Towers, Forming Gardens* by Christopher Thacker, St Barnabas Press. Wyliman Collection

of the retrospective in the *Financial Times* came to similar conclusions (p.ix). Also in this year Michael Mitchell's fine limited edition of the letters between Lucrezia Borgia and Pietro Bembo came out, entitled *Messer Pietro Mio*. Hugh Shankland of Durham University had expertly translated them, and my engravings were printed on damped handmade paper.

VIII *Credo*

'I do feel you must be in good heart and spirits to have produced such a body of work. And – aren't volutes fine subjects? I remember being first introduced to them at the age of 15 in architectural drawing lessons and being shown their particular perfection'. So wrote John Ward on 16 May 1999 after receiving my Chris Beetles exhibition catalogue.

I first met John at the Maas Gallery where he used to exhibit his fine portraits and drawings. He has the humility and interest in detail of the true artist and has been a continuing encouragement to me.

No one could accuse me of being avant-garde or a Social Realist, and there is humour and fantasy in my work. What, then, am I really serious about? A harmonious composition is one thing. Just as a memorable song often has a tune made up of carefully contrived notes, pitches and durations, so a satisfactory painted composition must be made of patches of

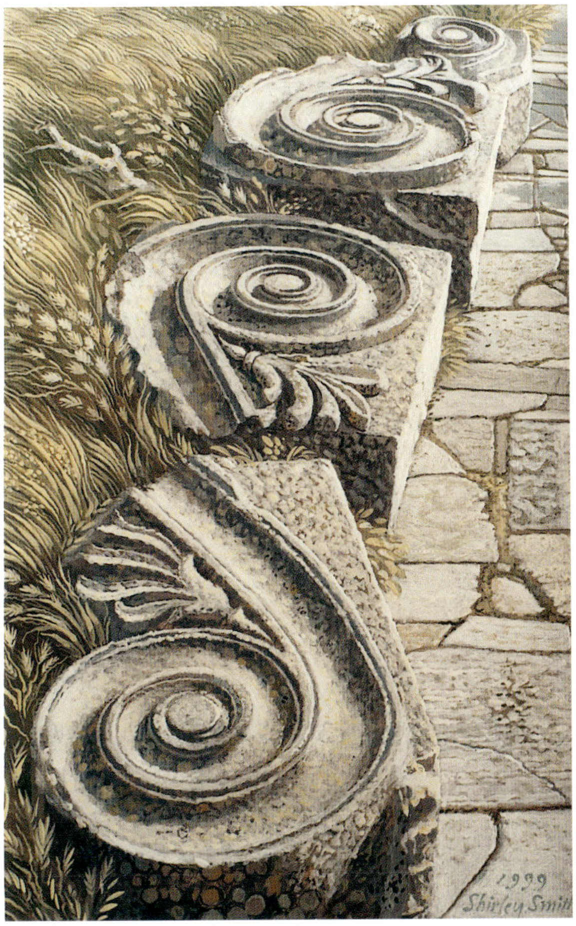

Fig.27 *Volutes at Ephesus*, acrylic on board. 30 × 19cm. 1999 (*ptg.cat.276*). Private collection

tone and colour deployed just as carefully, whatever the subject matter. David Jones described this as its 'abstract quality'. Also, genuine art must reflect life, death, damage and decay. Beauty is never more apparent than when confronted by a beast, as Rowlandson illustrates so well.

It has been said that my work takes part in two threads in English art. The first would be following in the tradition of such artists as Rex Whistler or Eric Ravilious, characterful painters who were not afraid of the 'Decorative' or the 'Romantic' and who enjoyed commissions for murals, bookplates and illustrations for books. The second thread might be the rather muted English response to Surrealism, as seen in the work of Paul Nash or Edward Wadsworth.

John Russell Taylor ends his article for my 1992 Maas Gallery exhibition with words that seem too flattering but express what I would like my work to be: 'There is humour in Shirley Smith's surrealistic juxtapositions of unmatched objects, but there is also an undertone of deeper feeling, an ability to switch and combine registers for which the only word is Mozartian'. Clearly a number of remarkable artists have taken trouble to encourage me and pass on a tradition. I feel a great obligation not to fail them and to pass on this tradition in turn. Iain Bain, who has written about my engravings, tells me that I have absorbed a tradition and reinterpreted it.

What essentially have I absorbed from these painters and engravers?

A love and knowledge of their craft and the patience to perfect it.

Awareness of the fabulous works of the past, preventing any ignorant pride.

Love of beauty based on the observation of nature.

A view of art as the monument by which civilisations are judged and as a communication with future generations.

The importance of a fertile imagination resulting in works no one else could have done.

Carlo Menotti was very emphatic that by 'wearing a false nose or painting our hair green' we may be able to surprise people for a short time but not deceive anyone as to our real identity. He believed that true originality could only be achieved by a relentless process of self-discovery in our art. In my case this could only have come about through a long sequence of paintings, murals and engravings undertaken or selected not for profit so much as because they are subjects that inspire me. They have all been done to the best of my ability and, I am assured, have my individual 'finger prints all over them'.

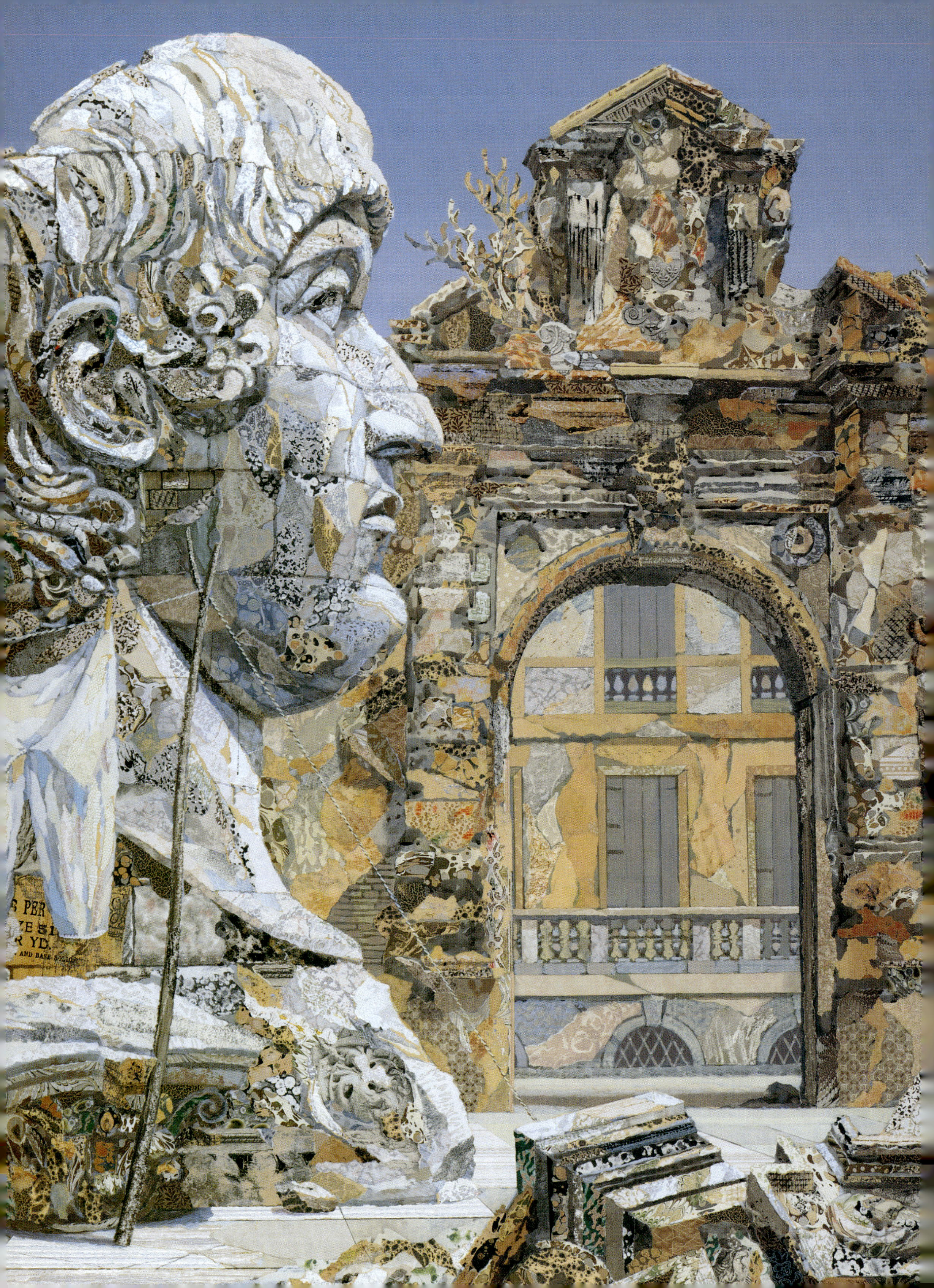

ONE

Collages

. . . the embers of the fire, or clouds or mud or other similar objects from which you will find most admirable ideas . . . because from a confusion of shapes the spirit is quickened to new inventions.

LEONARDO DA VINCI

It is only after making an effort of will to represent with minute care a grassblade, a stone, a branch, the face of an old wall that I am overcome by the irresistible urge to create something imaginary.

ODILON REDON

AT THE SLADE AND afterwards I used to work hard on carefully composed and observed oil paintings (Fig.9) but these 'spoke with a quiet voice', so much so that when one of them got into the Royal Academy Summer Exhibition it was half an hour before I could find it myself. I was familiar with Malraux's *Voices of Silence*, but this was ridiculous! I needed a stronger medium to express 'ideas' rather than the appearance of objects. William Blake disliked oil paint because it was perfect for copying appearances of mortal things rather than expressing visions. So, as Redon in the quote above progressed from observation to imagination, I found collage much more liberating.

I think the idea started when I was learning lithography. To improve a composition, I would tear up some prints and reassemble them in a better design. Other papers such as wallpapers, marbled papers or old maps were added, but never cheap, fading newspapers. At first I allowed and encouraged the various textures and colours of papers to suggest subject matter and composition but gradually the papers became a rich and vivid clothing for images already worked out. This became too time-consuming. I gradually moved to acrylic, which I found my own way of using both in paintings and on a large scale in the murals that, in the mid-seventies I was asked to undertake. Acrylic has great advantages: no smell, quick-drying, waterproof, but the best thing is that I can straight away wash over transparently and adjust the tone or colour of a detailed area already painted. Thus I can start the painting with some detail, which is not possible with oil, watercolour or gouache. The disadvantage is that acrylic drops in tone when it dries. This I can solve by keeping labelled mixtures wet in containers even for a year.

OPPOSITE: Fig.28 *Pulcinella visits Rome (detail)*, collage. 1972. 97 × 122cm. (*ptg.cat.30*). Private collection

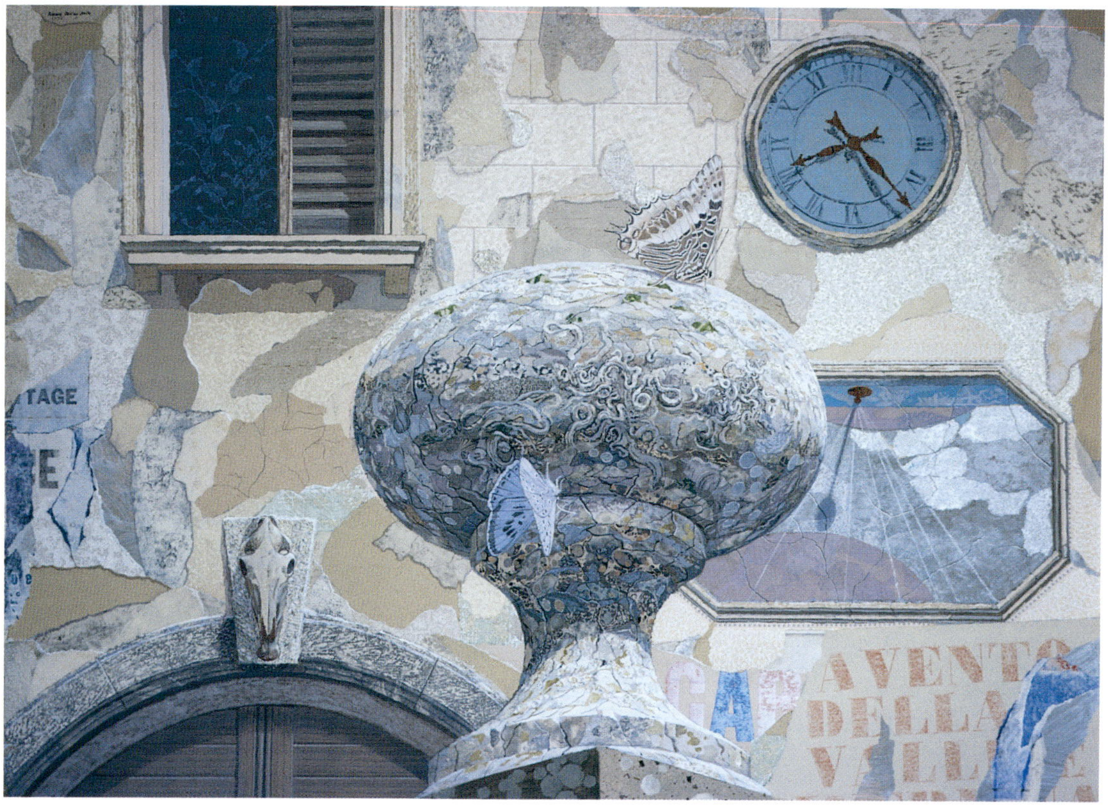

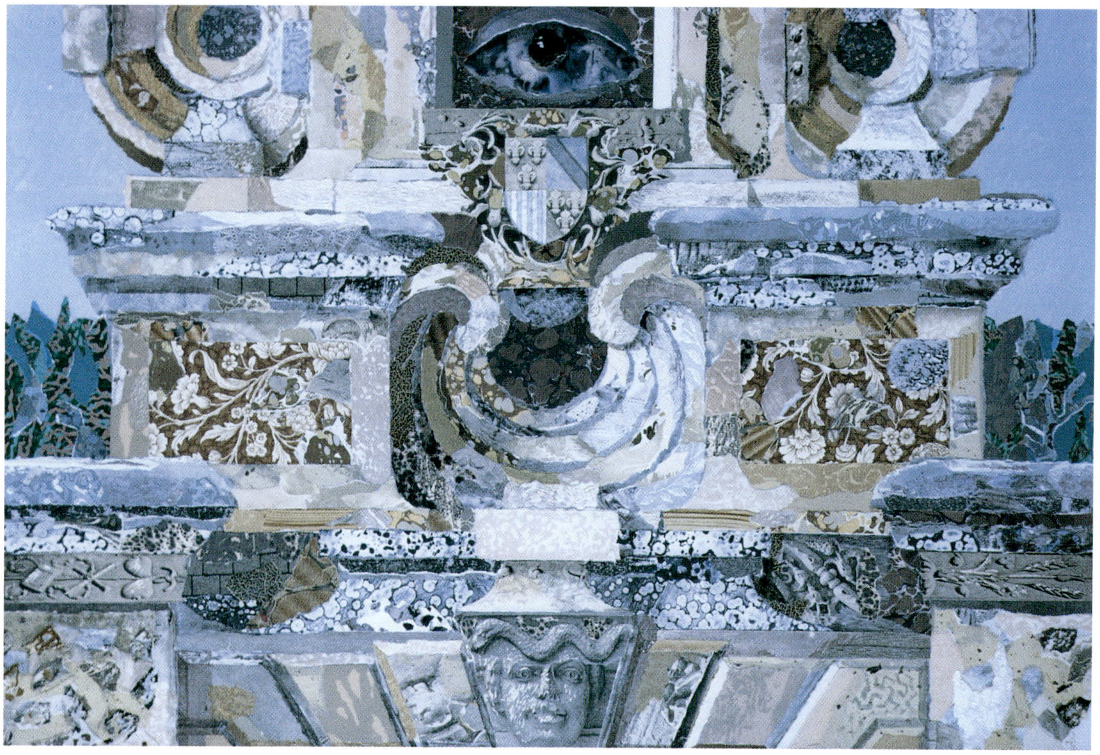

ABOVE: Fig.29 *Euclid's Stables*, collage. 86 × 122cm. 1972 (*ptg.cat.28*).
The geometry of this architecture was observed in some stable buildings in a Venetian Villa. Private collection

BELOW: Fig.30 *Cyclops Villa* (*detail*), collage. 91 × 71cm. 1970 (*ptg.cat.25*). Collection of John & Kathy Evans

OPPOSITE: Fig.31 *The Sense of Touch* (*detail*), collage. 86 × 122cm. 1979 (*ptg.cat.72*).
This rather surrealist image derives from ancient shop or pub signs. Collection of Michael & Caroline Mitchell

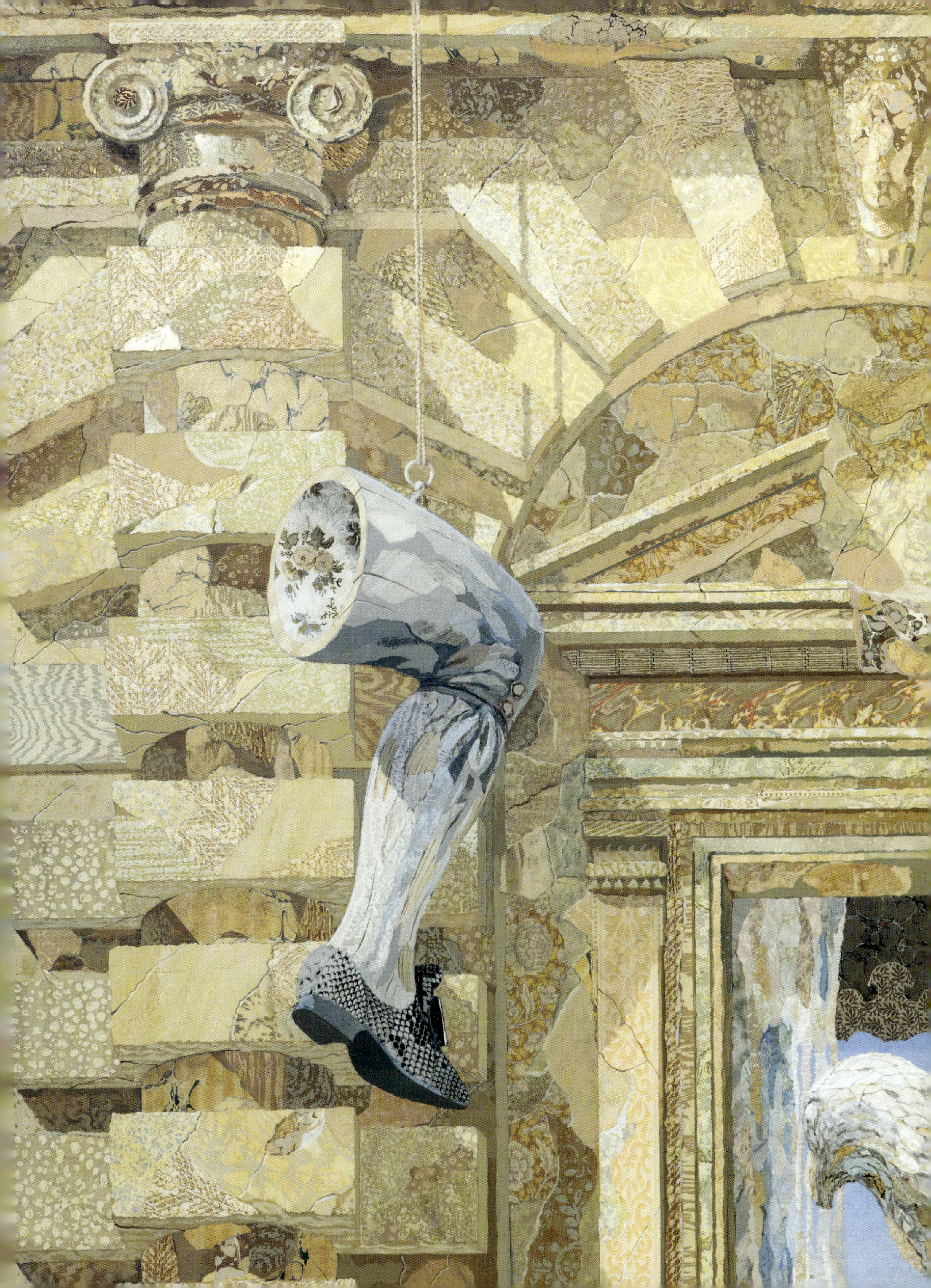

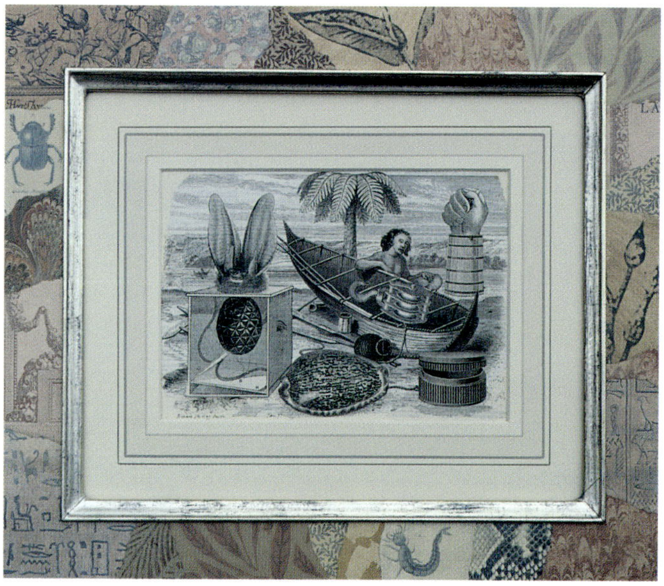

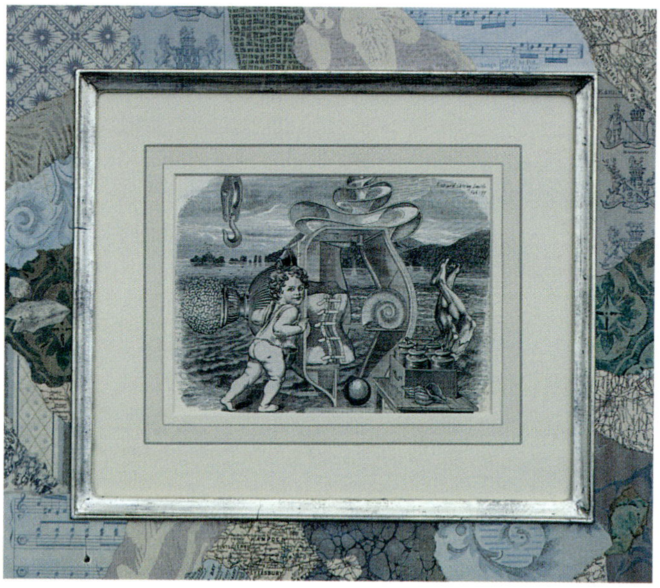

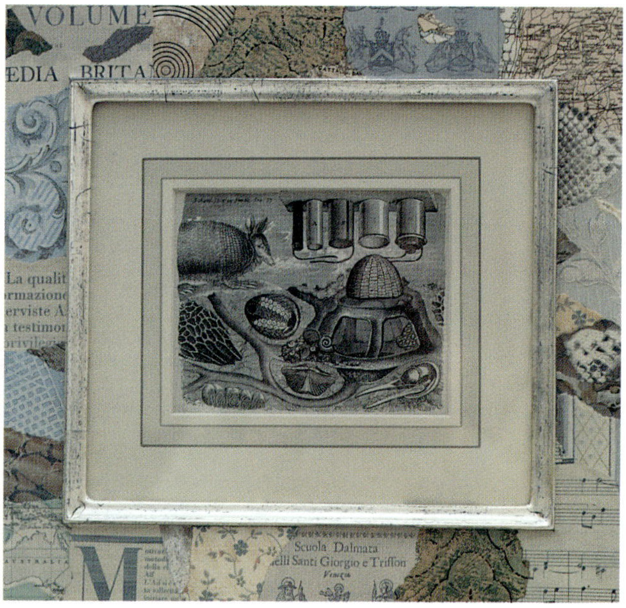

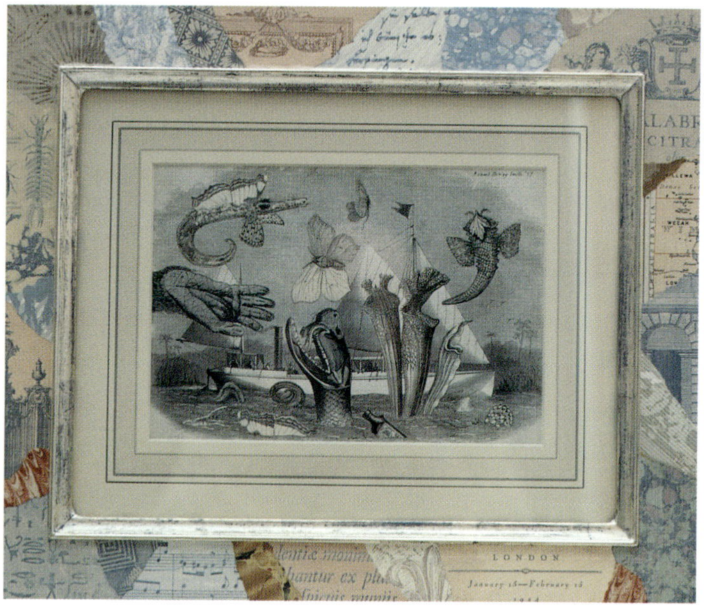

Hommage à Max Ernst. Four montages of Victorian engravings in collaged frames. The reference here is to Max Ernst's surrealistic novel in collage *Une Semaine de Bonté* (Paris, 1934)

ABOVE LEFT: Fig.32 *Pandora's Box*, montage. 13 × 18cm. 1978 (*ptg.cat.68*). Collection of Robert & Susan Stirling
ABOVE RIGHT: Fig.33 *The Bathing Machine*, montage. 13 × 18cm. 1978 (*ptg.cat.69*). Private collection
BELOW LEFT: Fig.34 *Armadillo Experiment*, montage. 13 × 18cm. 1978 (*ptg.cat.70*). Collection of Justin & Tracy Shirley-Smith
BELOW RIGHT: Fig.35 *Air Attack*, montage. 13 × 18cm. 1978 (*ptg.cat.71*). Collection of Robert & Susan Stirling

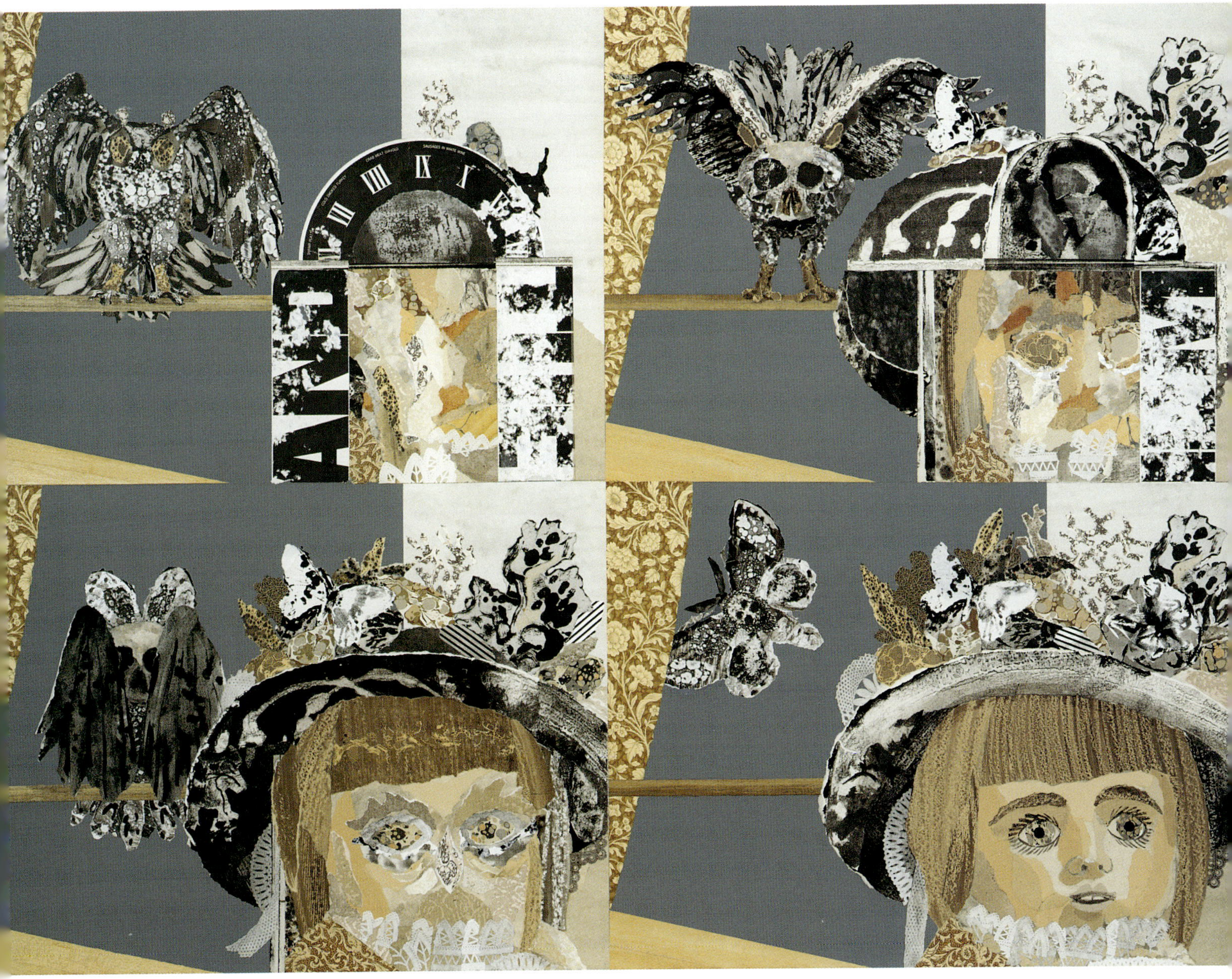

Fig.36 *Metamorphosis*, collage. 92 × 122cm. 1969 (*ptg.cat.19*). A strip cartoon records the successive changes. René Magritte's *L'homme au journal* uses a similar cartoon format but without changes actually taking place. Collection of Michael & Caroline Mitchell

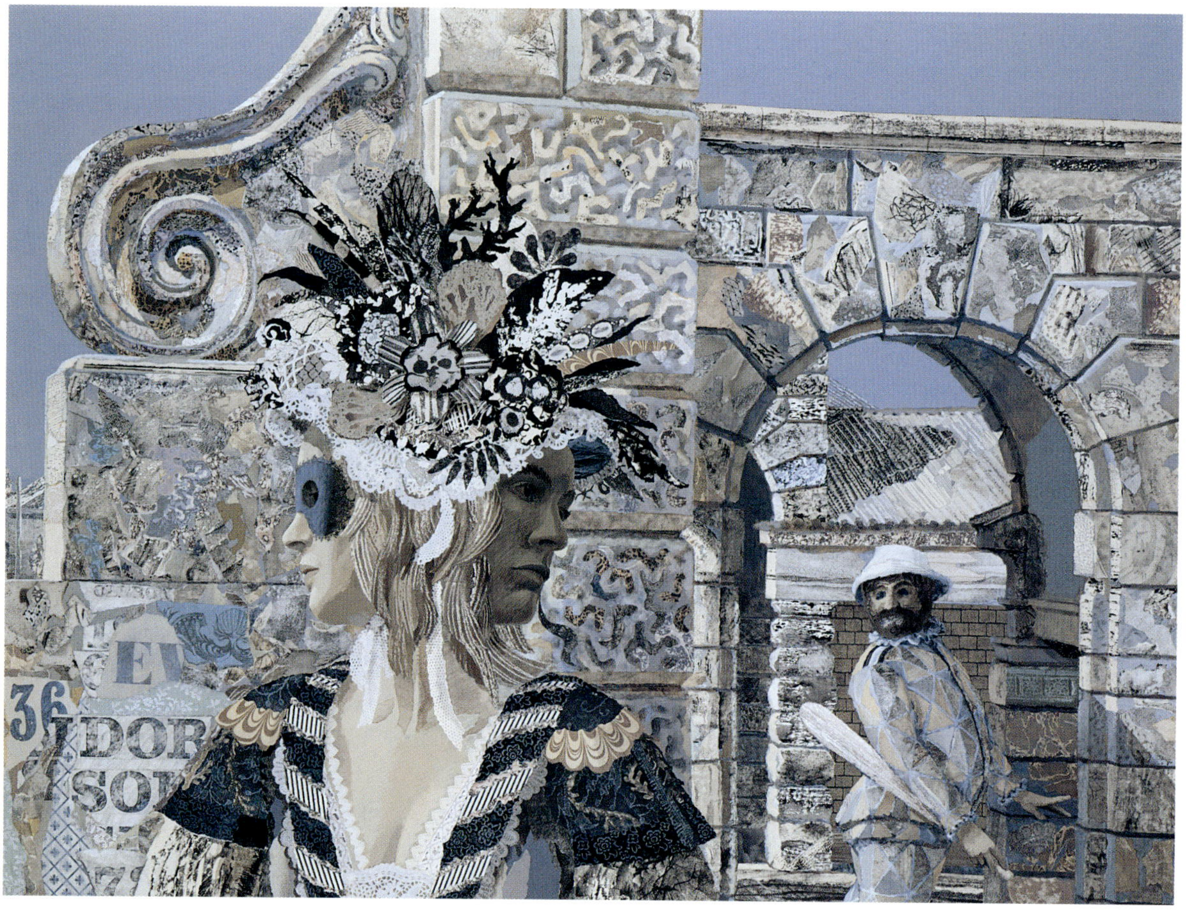

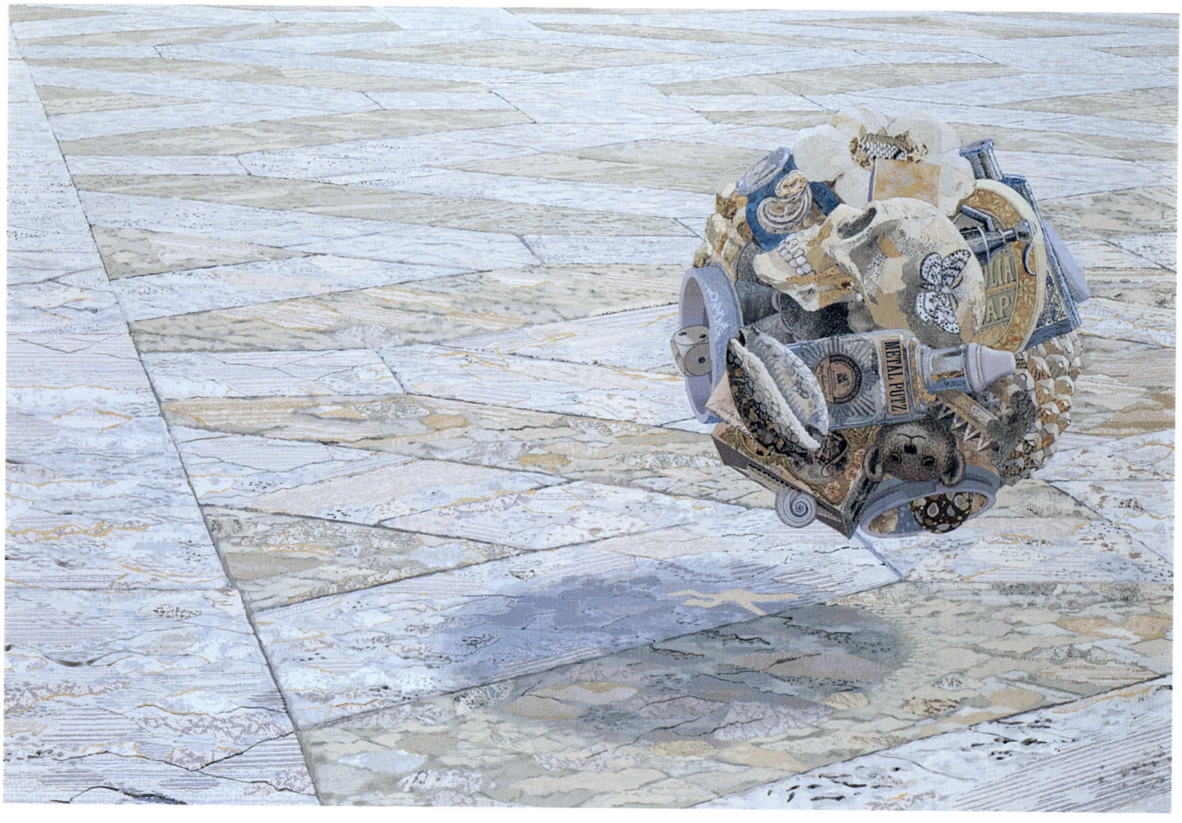
METAL PUTZ

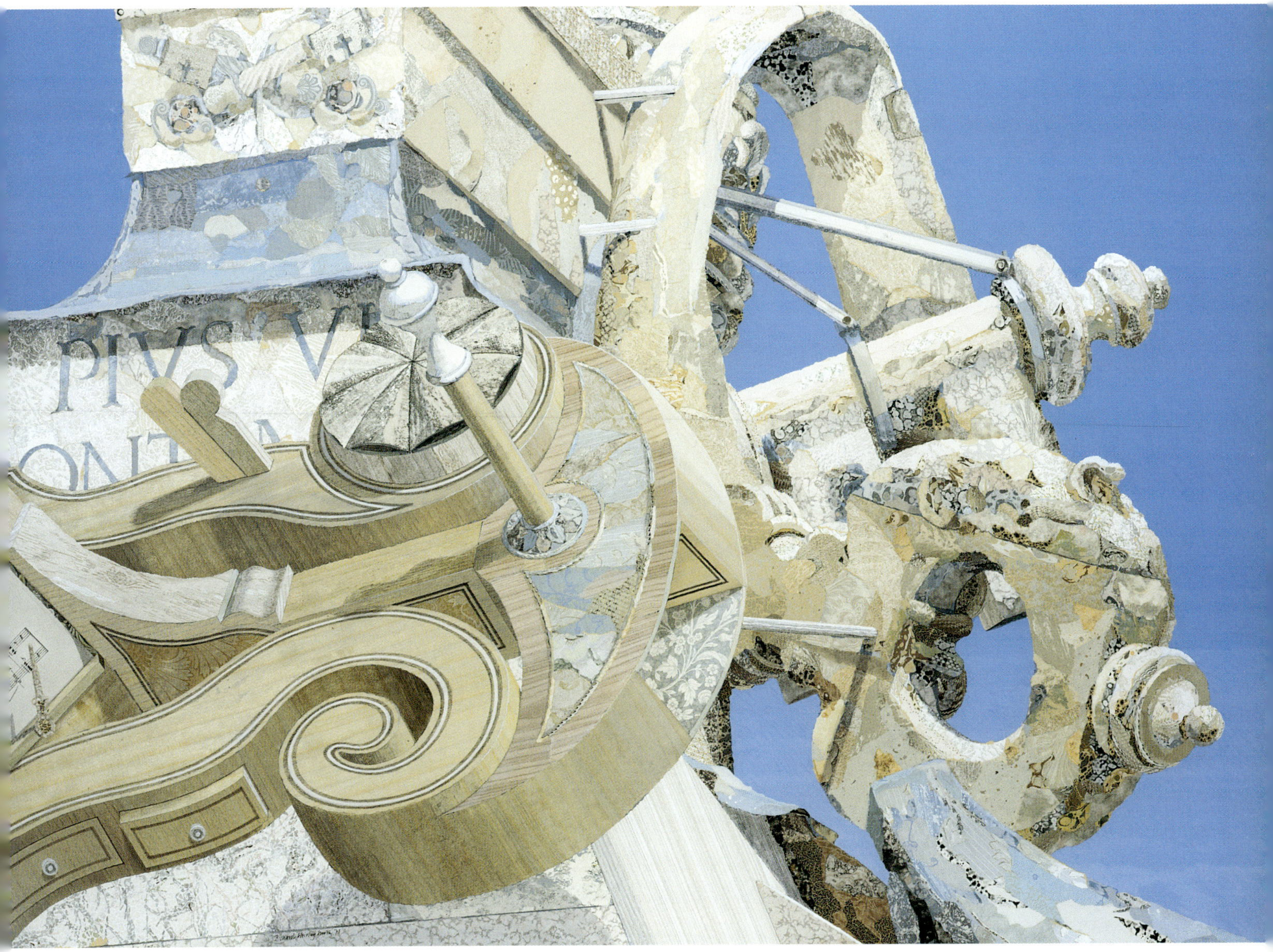

ABOVE: Fig.39 *Behind the Keys*, collage. 86 × 124cm. 1973 (*ptg.cat.33*). Photographing on the roof of the nave of St Peter's, Rome, is like being behind a gigantic marble stage set on top of a mountain. Collection of Peter & Claire Bates

OPPOSITE ABOVE: Fig.37 *Lady at Venetian Villa,* collage. 86 × 120cm. 1973 (*ptg.cat.32*). The lady wears a mask behind her head with a two-faced or 'Janus' effect. Arlecchino strutting by with his slapstick imagines she is looking at him. The mannerist Venetian villa is Villa della Torre at Fumane, Verona. Private collection

OPPOSITE BELOW: Fig.38 *Death in Venice*, collage. 69 × 102cm. 1976 *(ptg.cat.62)*. A variation on Magritte's painting *Le Voyageur*. The American phrase 'a bunch of junk' springs to mind. The pavement is from S Giorgio Maggiore, Venice. Private collection

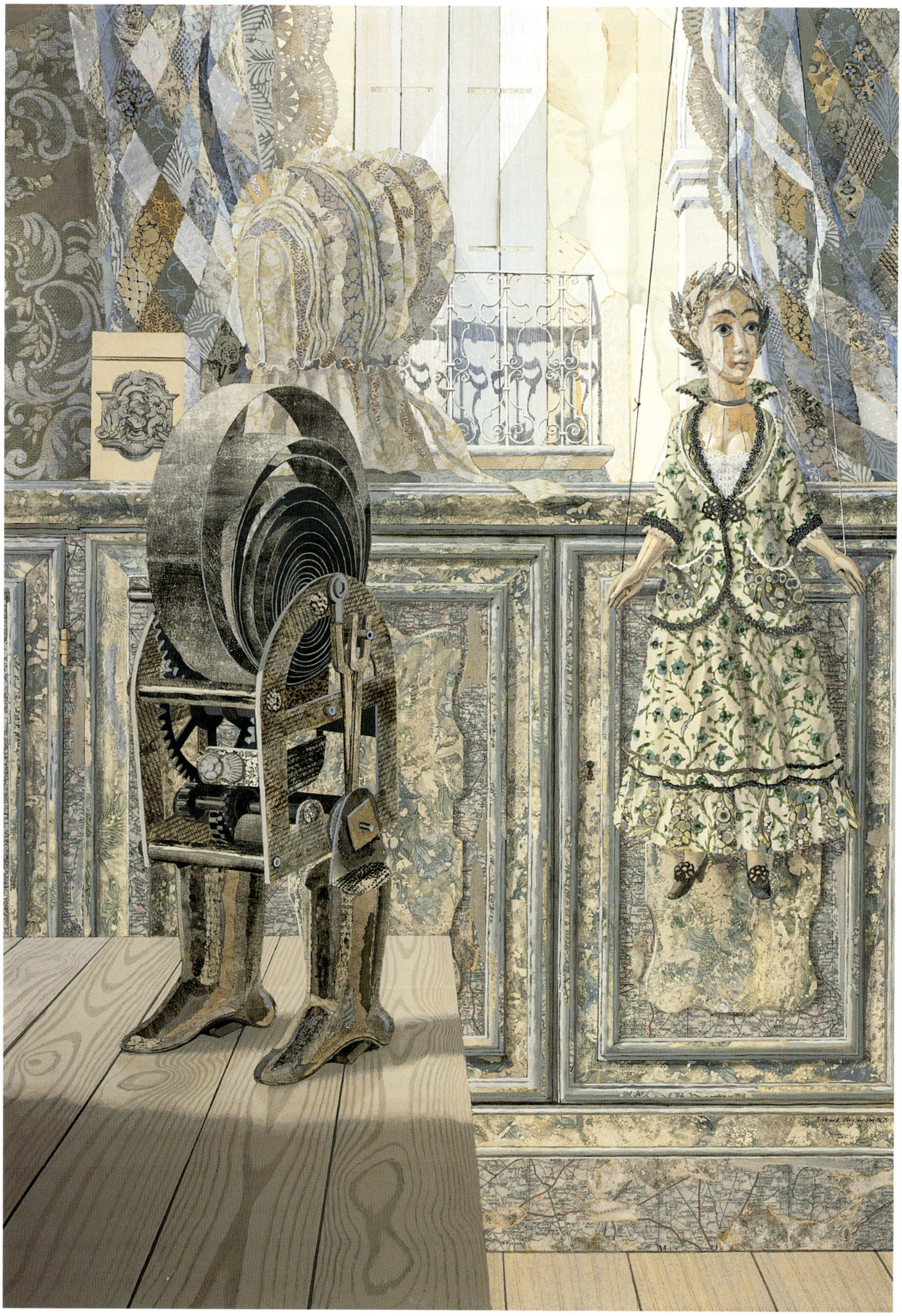

ABOVE: Fig.40 *Clock Walk*, collage. 122 × 91cm. 1975 (*ptg.cat.40*). Collection of Patricia Hay-Edie

OPPOSITE: Fig.41 *Palinurus Pontifex*, collage. 122 × 91cm. 1972 (*ptg.cat.31*). Palinurus was Aeneas's ill-fated helmsman and *Palinuridae* are spiny lobsters or sea crayfish. Pontifex means bridge-builder and has papal allusions. Collection of Peter & Claire Bates

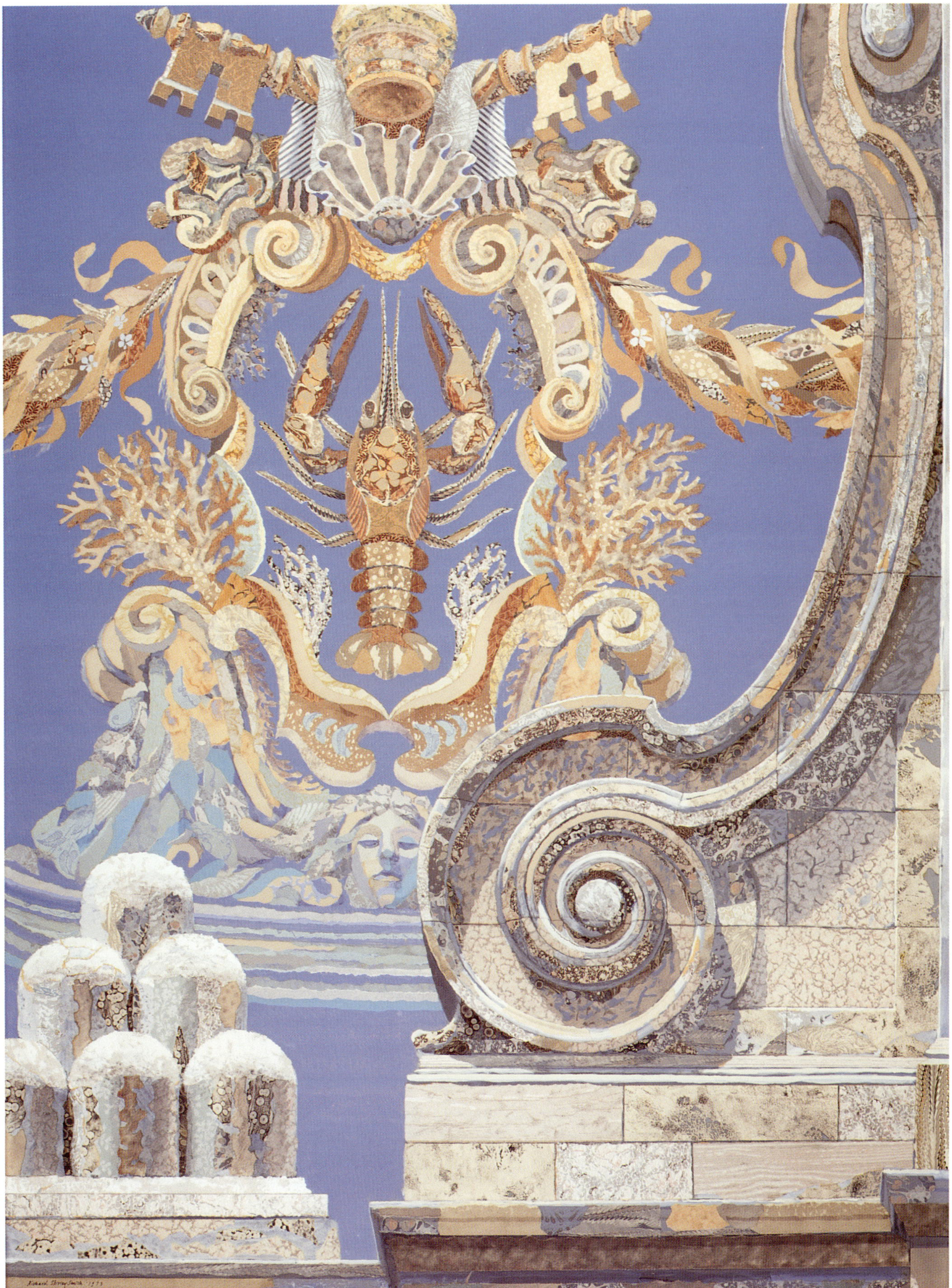

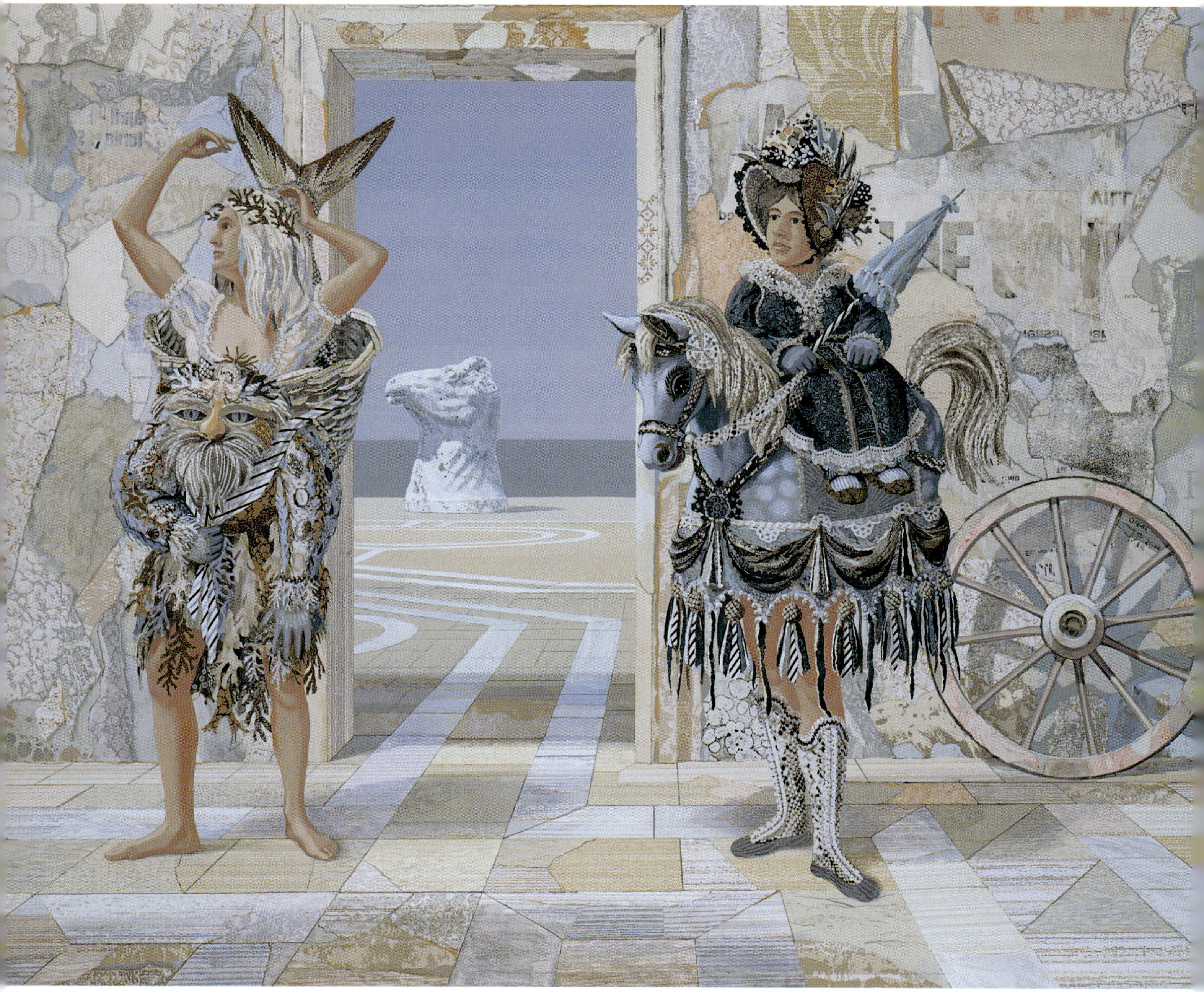

ABOVE: Fig.42 *Mermaid & Dwarf,* collage and acrylic. 91 × 117cm. 1975 (*ptg.cat.44*). Two dancers at a Masque in deceptive fantasy costume. One appears to be an old fisherman with a mermaid in a basket, and the other a dwarf on a horse. These theatrical costumes were inspired by early seventeenth-century masque designs such as those by Inigo Jones for Charles I or Daniel Rabel for Louis XIII of France. Collection of Alison Brown

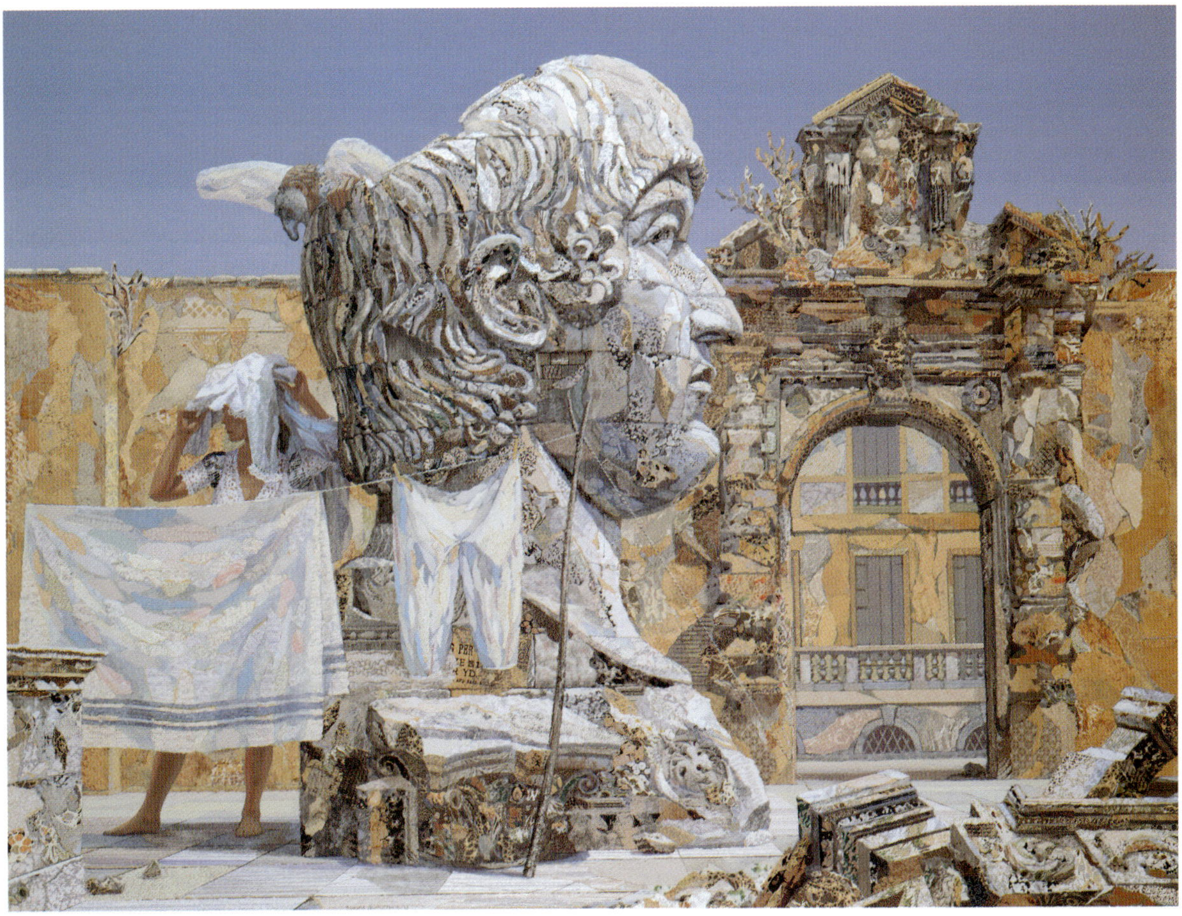

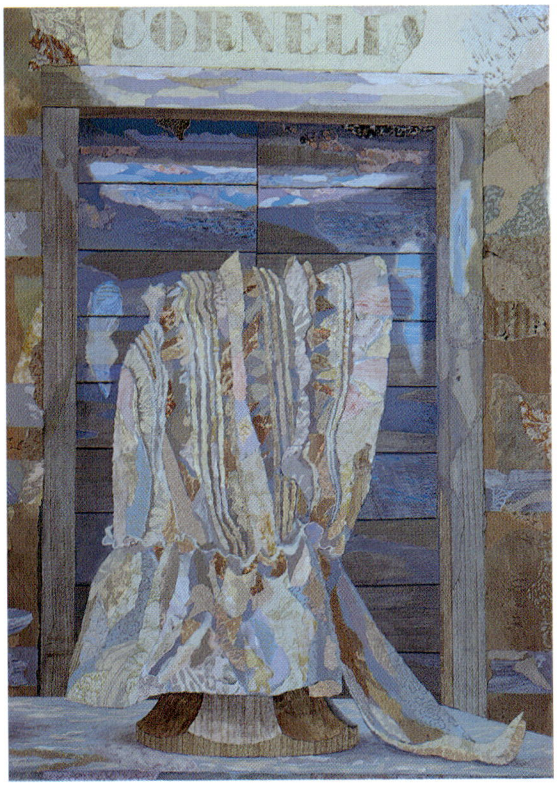

ABOVE: Fig.43 *Pulcinella visits Rome,* collage. 97 × 122cm. 1972 (*ptg.cat.30*). The head is drawn from a bronze colossus from the Conservatori Museum, Rome. It is thought to represent one of Constantine's sons. The arch was inspired by a large dilapidated portal in the Palazzo Barberini in Rome. Private collection

LEFT: Fig.44 *Effigy & Bonnet* (*detail*), collage. 86 × 120cm. 1972 (*ptg.cat.29*). Private collection

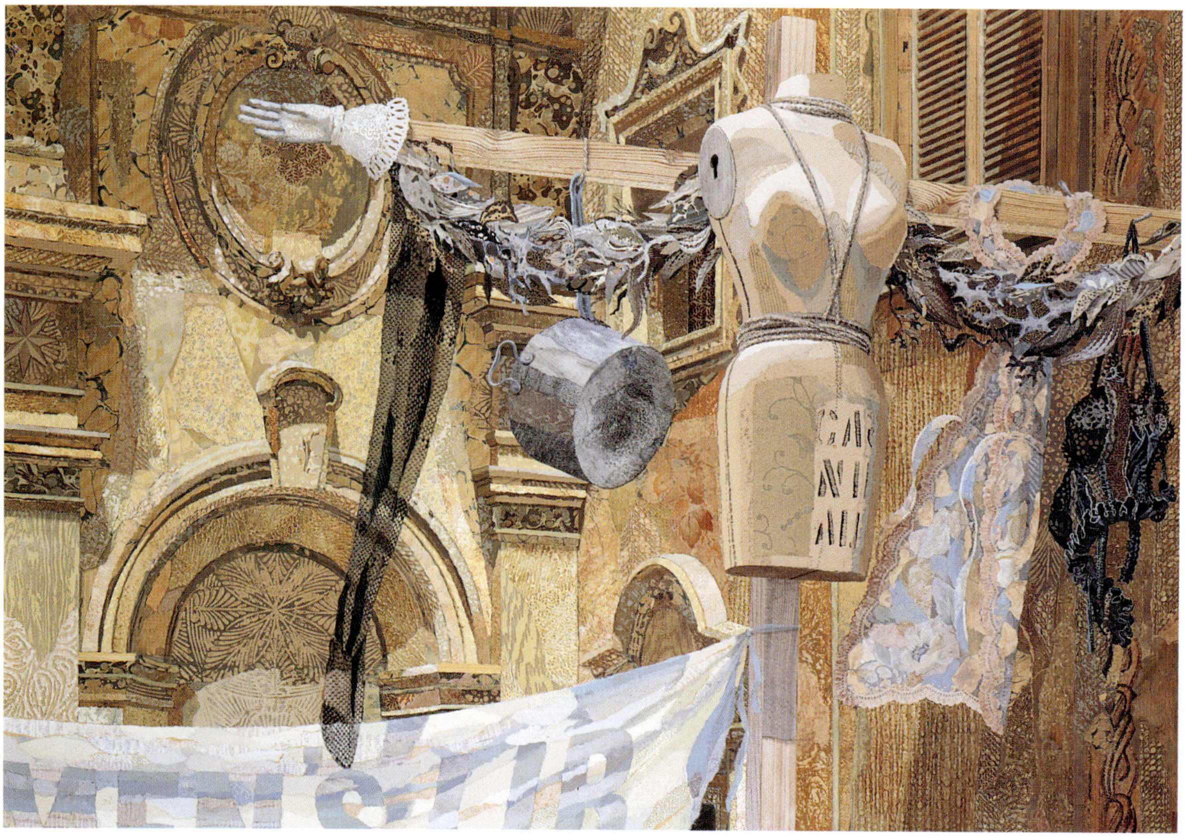

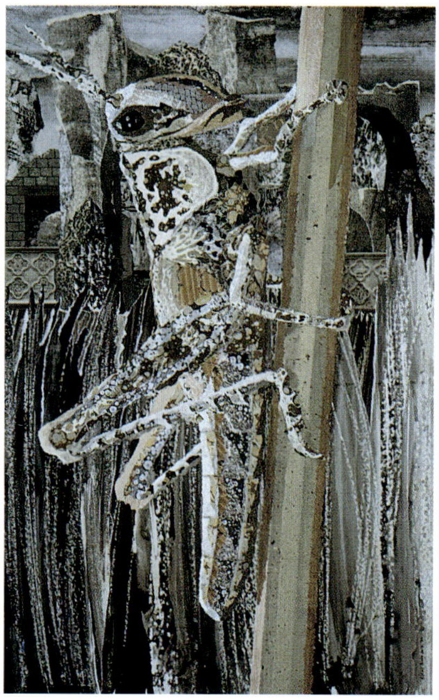

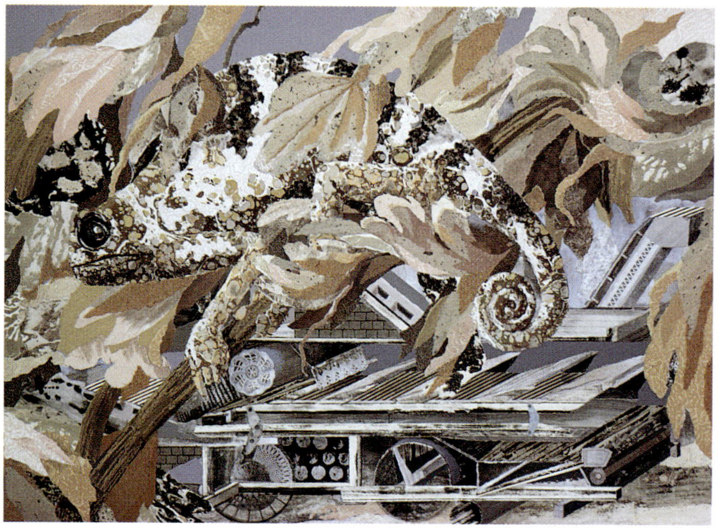

TOP: Fig.45 *Demonstration,* collage. 74 × 107cm. 1973 (*ptg.cat.34*). The idea came from a banner displayed at an early Women's Liberation demonstration. Collection of Richard & Frances Latcham

ABOVE: Fig.47 *Chameleon,* collage. 81 × 108cm. 1970 (*ptg.cat.22*). Collection of Jeremy Lemmon

LEFT: Fig.46 *Grasshopper,* collage. *approx.* 88 × 62cm. 1970 (*ptg.cat.21*). Private collection

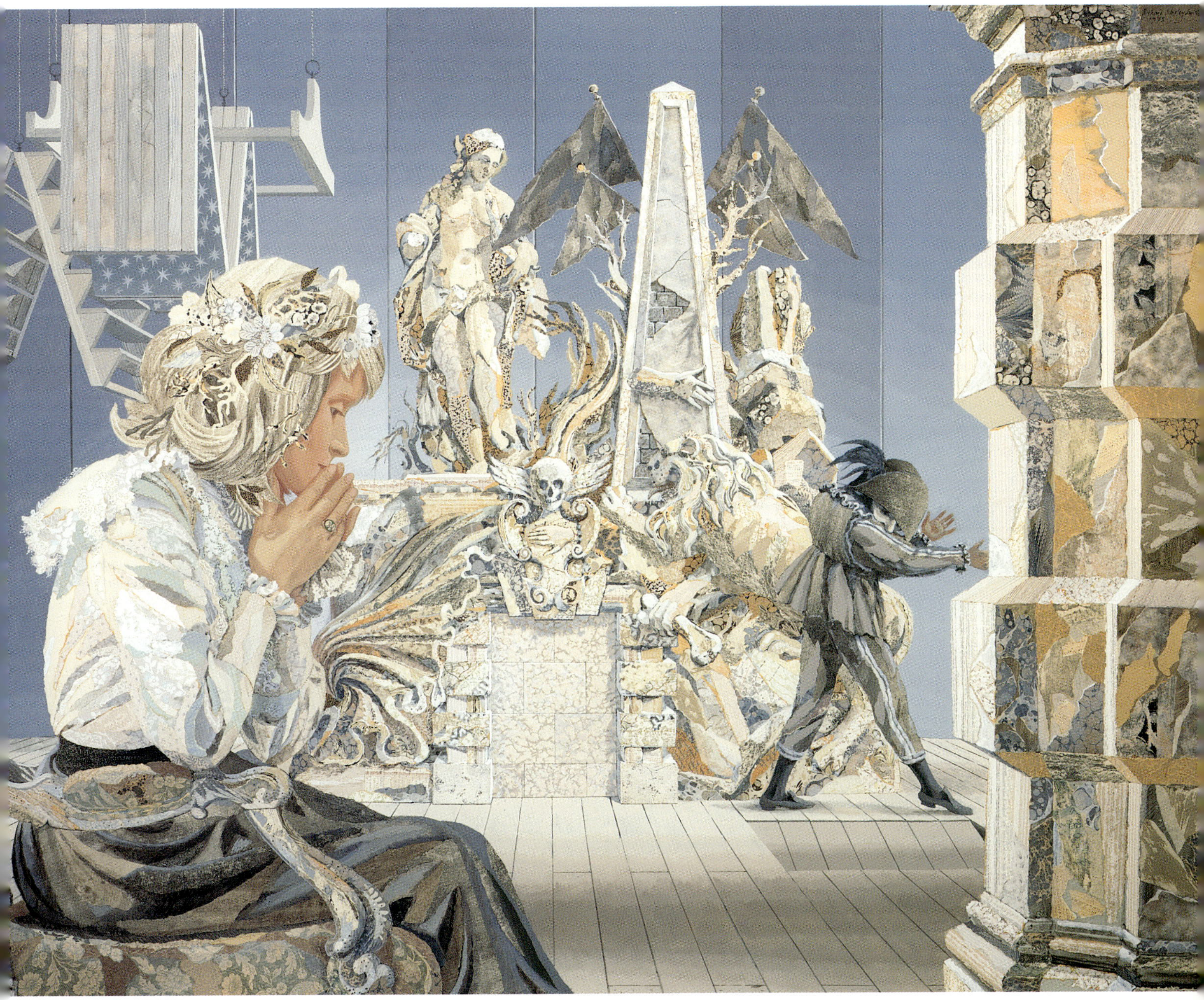

ABOVE: Fig 48 *Castrum Doloris*, collage and acrylic. 91 × 122cm. 1975 (*ptg.cat.39*). The *Castrum Doloris* was a temporary funerary monument in a church constructed by the same artists and craftsmen who would create stage sets. The *Commedia dell'Arte* character is that of The Captain, a bragging *Miles Gloriosus*. The folding platforms and stairs suspended on the left are typical seventeenth-century Italian stage machinery. Collection of Patricia Hay-Edie

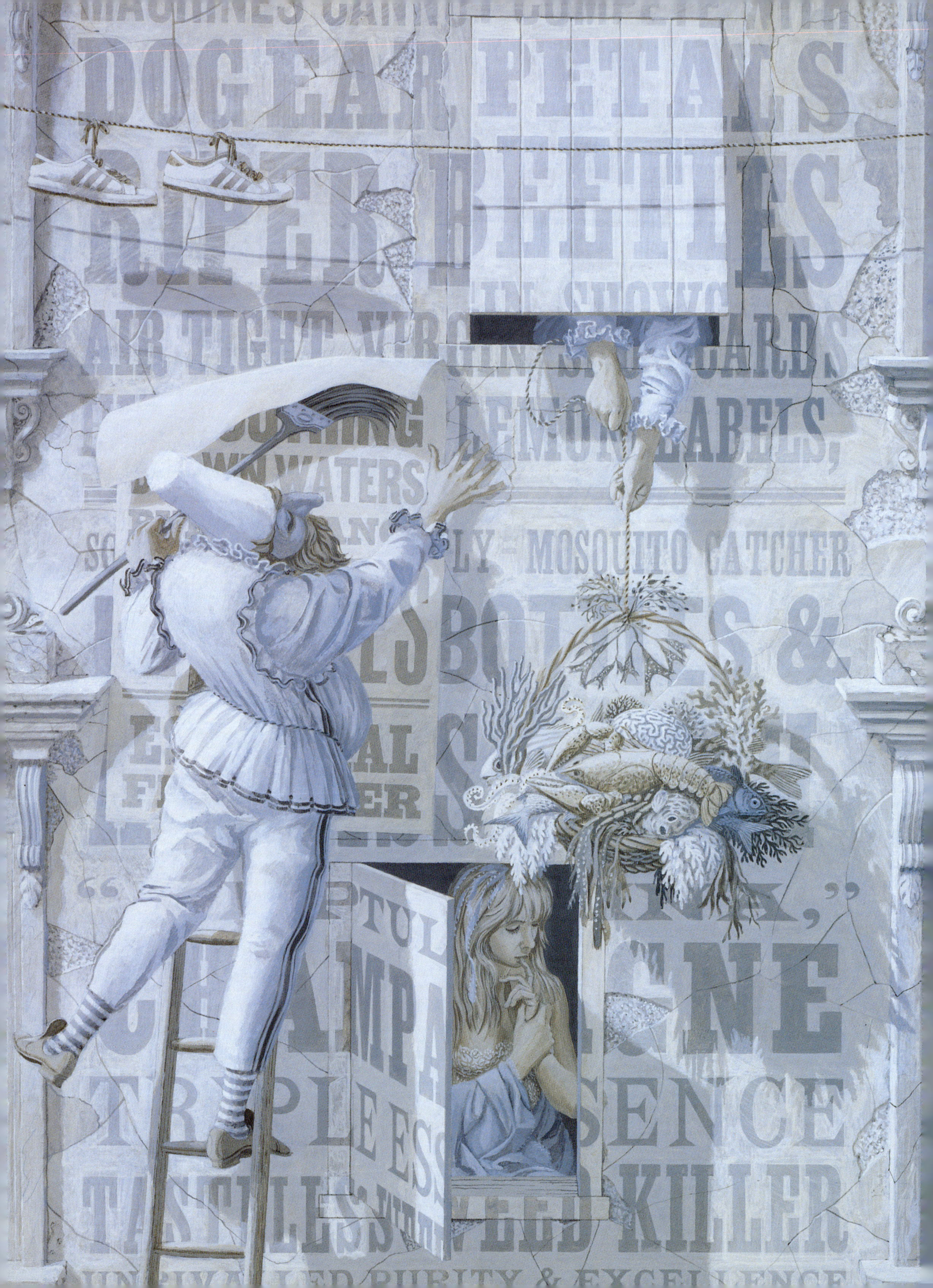

DOG EAR
BEETLES
AIR TIGHT
LEMON LABELS,
MOSQUITO CATCHER
SENCE
KILLER

TWO

Pulcinella and the Commedia dell'Arte

Pulcinella had two fathers, inheriting the worst traits from each.
He was in the habit of finding things before their owners knew they had lost them.

TRADITIONAL

THE COMMEDIA DELL'ARTE was a popular, comic form of travelling theatre that started in Italy in the later sixteenth century and spread round Europe. There were standard masked characters such as Pulcinella, Arlechino, Pantalone (the *Magnifico*), The Captain (a *miles gloriosus*) and then the inamorata Franceschina. A rough account of the plot would be pinned up and the characters would freely improvise. If one actor 'dried' another might contrive to drop something and bend down to pick it up while someone else might take advantage with his slapstick. While the audience was laughing they would get their act together, so to speak. They were specialists in music, dance, acrobatics and ribaldry with strings of sausages and suggestive prancing, so well illustrated in Jacques Callot's *Balli di Sfessania* etchings.

The aged Domenico Tiepolo, tucked away in his Venetian Villa Zianigo, began his set of one hundred and four substantial drawings entitled *Divertimento per li regazzi* (*c.*1797) in the very last days of the thousand-year-old Serenissima or Venetian Republic. These large drawings in wash and expressive pen line are enormously entertaining and show the family of Pulcinella from birth to deathbed up to all kinds of amazing activities. The set has been split up and scattered but can be studied in *Domenico Tiepolo, The Punchinello Drawings* by Adelheid Gealt (British Museum Publications, 1986). Some of the drawings have the most durable and serene compositions, which could be used just as they are for a grand mural such as Domenico might have painted with his very famous father Giambattista Tiepolo. Others comprise just a few strange animals and figures dotted about. I so much enjoy this theme and its variations that I just contrive more variations of my own as paintings.

OPPOSITE: Fig.49 *Pulcinella Fishmonger*, acrylic on paper. 60 × 45cm. 1975 (*ptg.cat.42*)
The Victorian billboard effect was arrived at by making montages of advertising typography cut from pharmaceutical magazines *c.*1895. I enjoyed describing the projected shadows and working out the perspective of lettering upon shutters. The rather surreal advertisements concocted are entertaining too: 'Champagne Triple Essence tasteless weed killer of unrivalled purity and excellence'. What fortunate weeds they must have been! Collection of Peter & Claire Bates

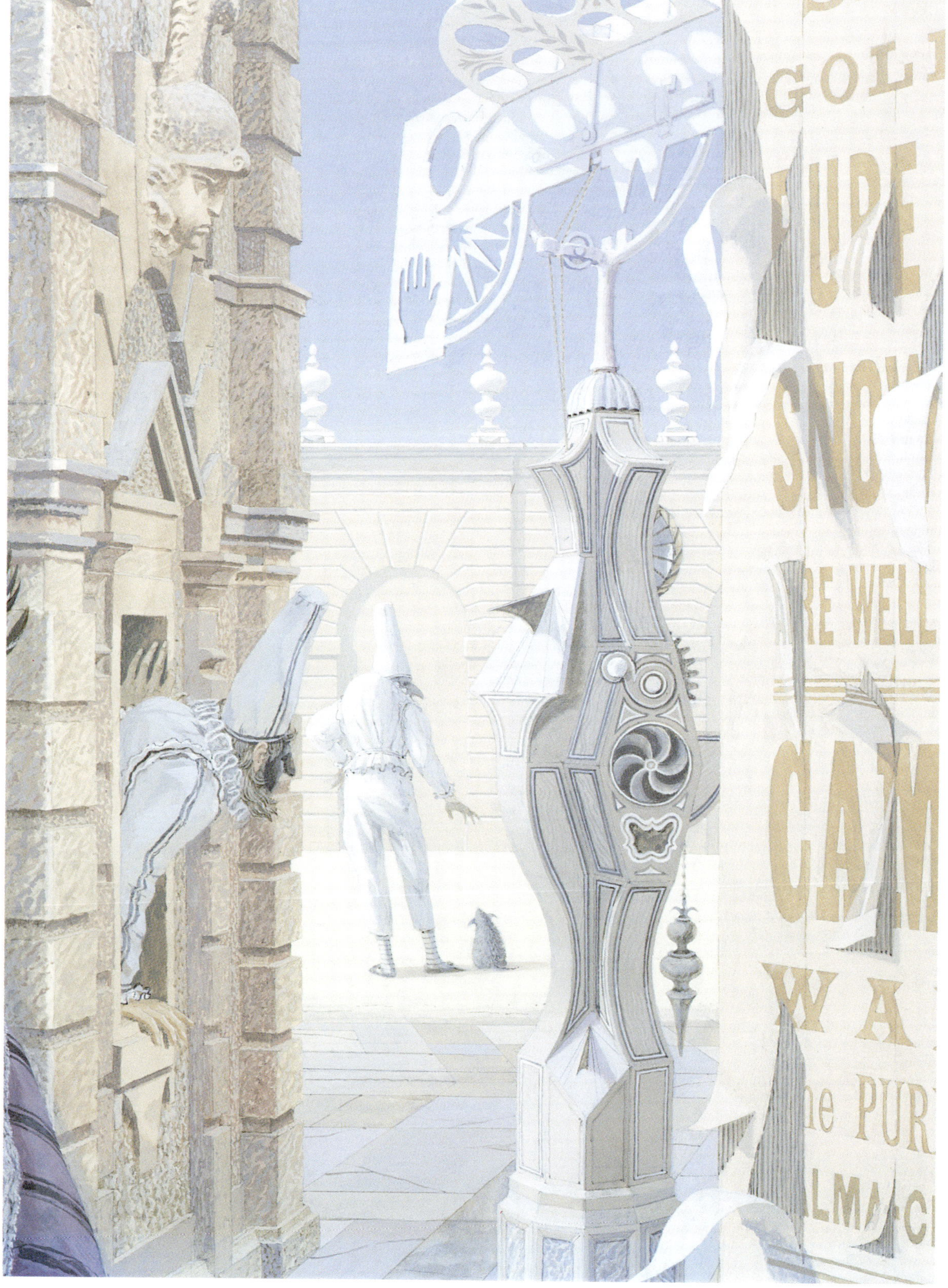
GOL
PURE
SNOW
RE WELL
CAM
WA
he PUR

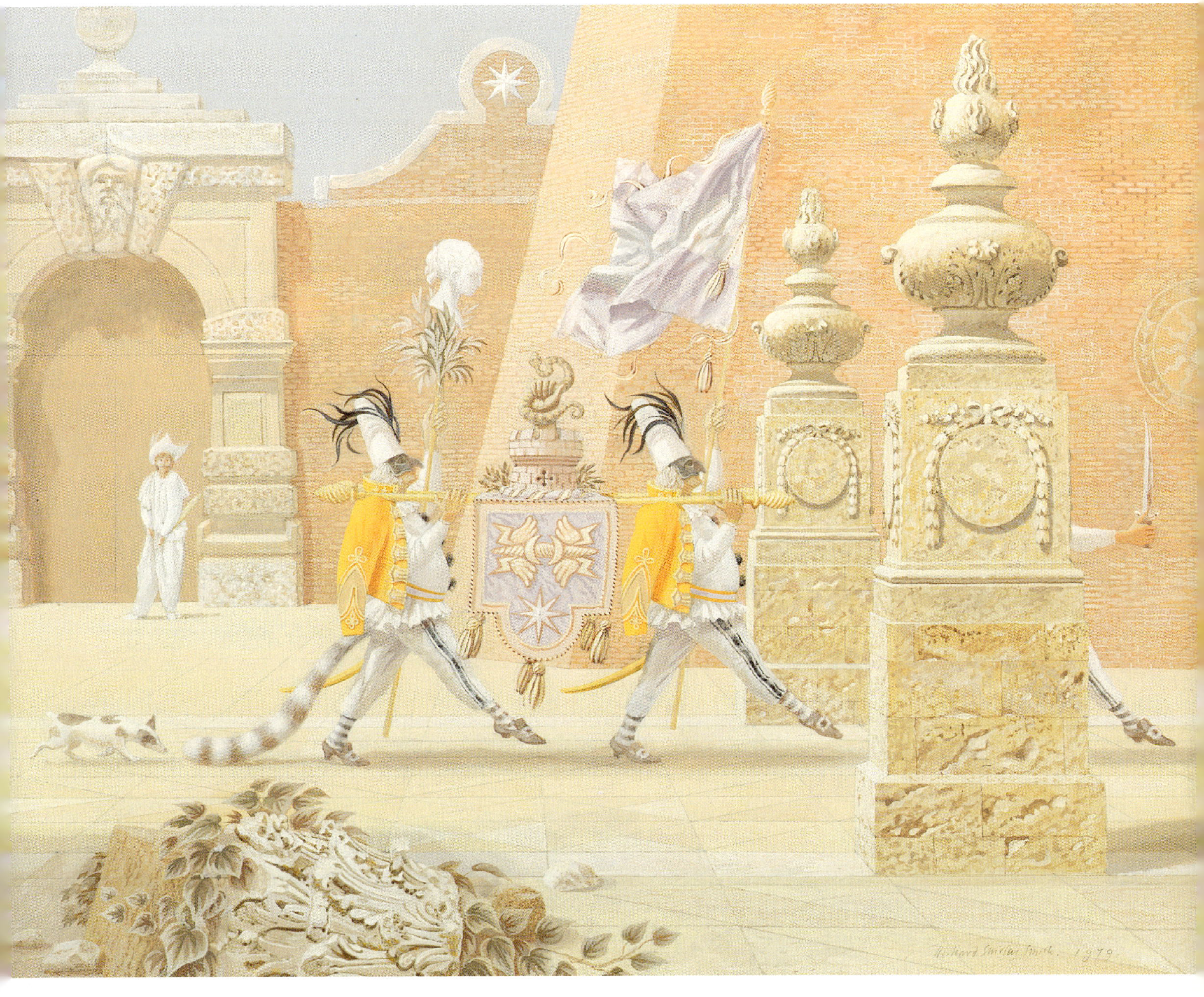

ABOVE: Fig.51 *Pulcinella on Parade*, acrylic on paper. 38 × 51cm. 1979 (*ptg.cat.87*). It is thought that the name 'Pulcinella' may be inspired by '*il pollo*', a chicken, because of his strutting walk and high-pitched voice: hence the plumes of cock's feathers. The portal, from which Scapino watches the scene, is at Villa del Bene at Dolce, Verona. Little good results from Scapino's observations. The elaborate piers on the right are from Blenheim Palace. Collection of M. P. O'Flaherty

OPPOSITE: Fig.50 *Alicia* (*detail*), acrylic on paper. 43 × 64cm. 1975 (*ptg.cat.36*). Here we have Pulcinella the dog owner. Collection of Michael & Joanna Brown

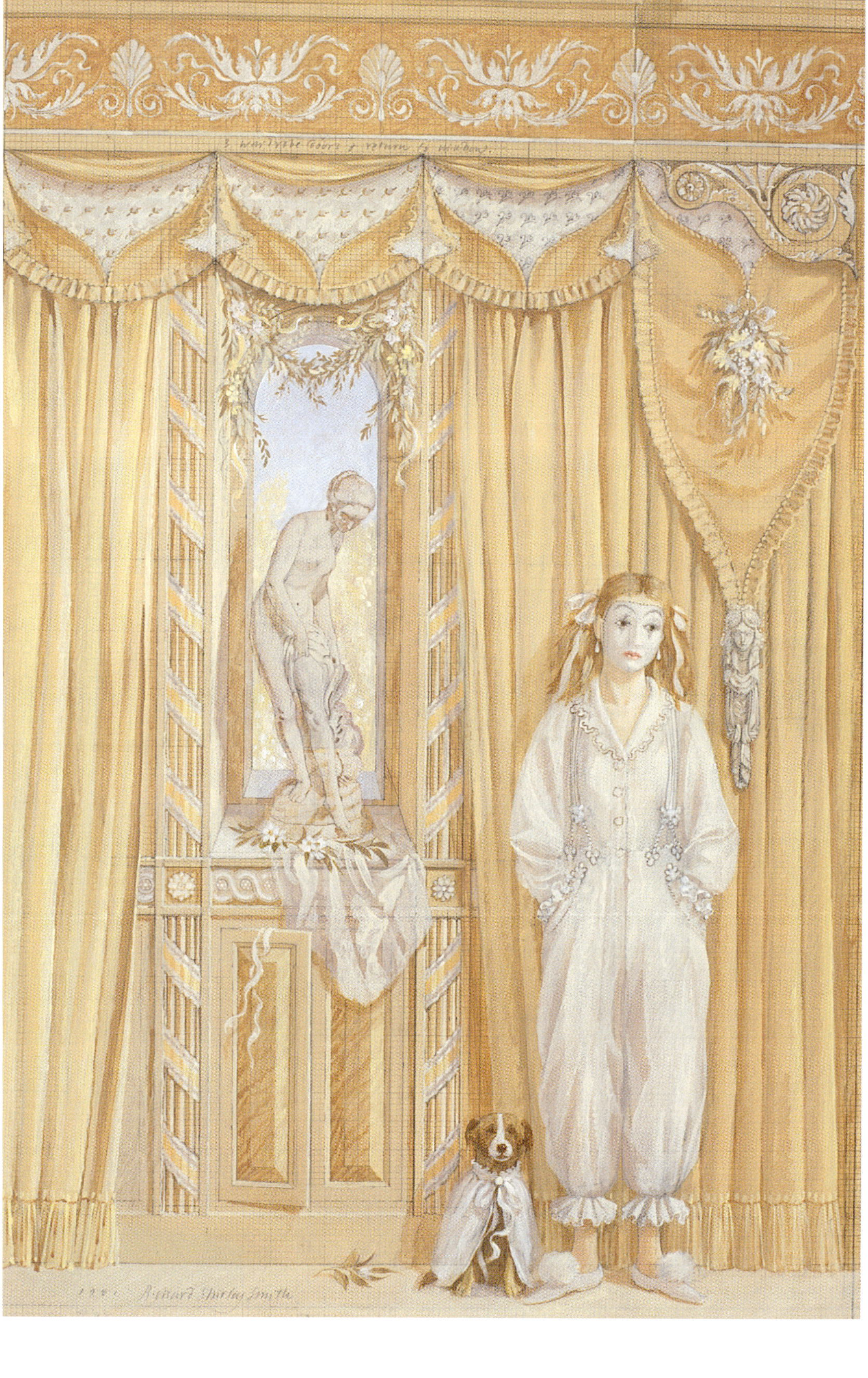

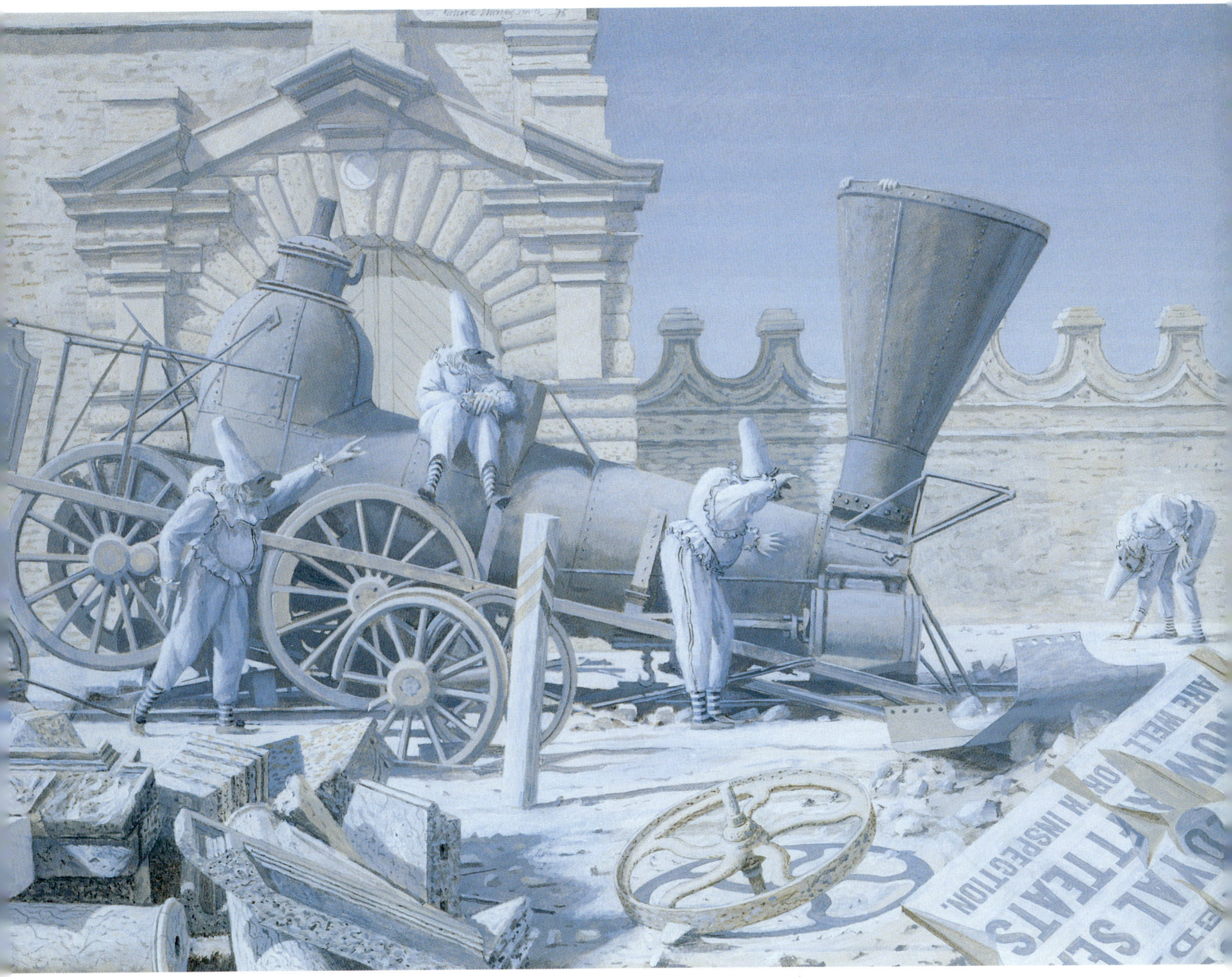

ABOVE: Fig.53 *Pulcinella Engine Driver*, acrylic on paper, 37 × 51cm. 1975 (*ptg.cat.43*). The theme relates to the old song, 'Where was the engine driver when the boiler burst?' Fingers can be seen gripping the rim of the funnel. The mannerist portal is from the Veneto. Collection of Patricia Hay-Edie

OPPOSITE: Fig.52 *Dressing-room with Girl & Dog,* acrylic on paper. 63 × 39cm. 1981 (*ptg.cat.110*). The girl in clown's costume stands in front of the mural I painted in a dressing-room in Holland Park. Collection of Frances Halligan

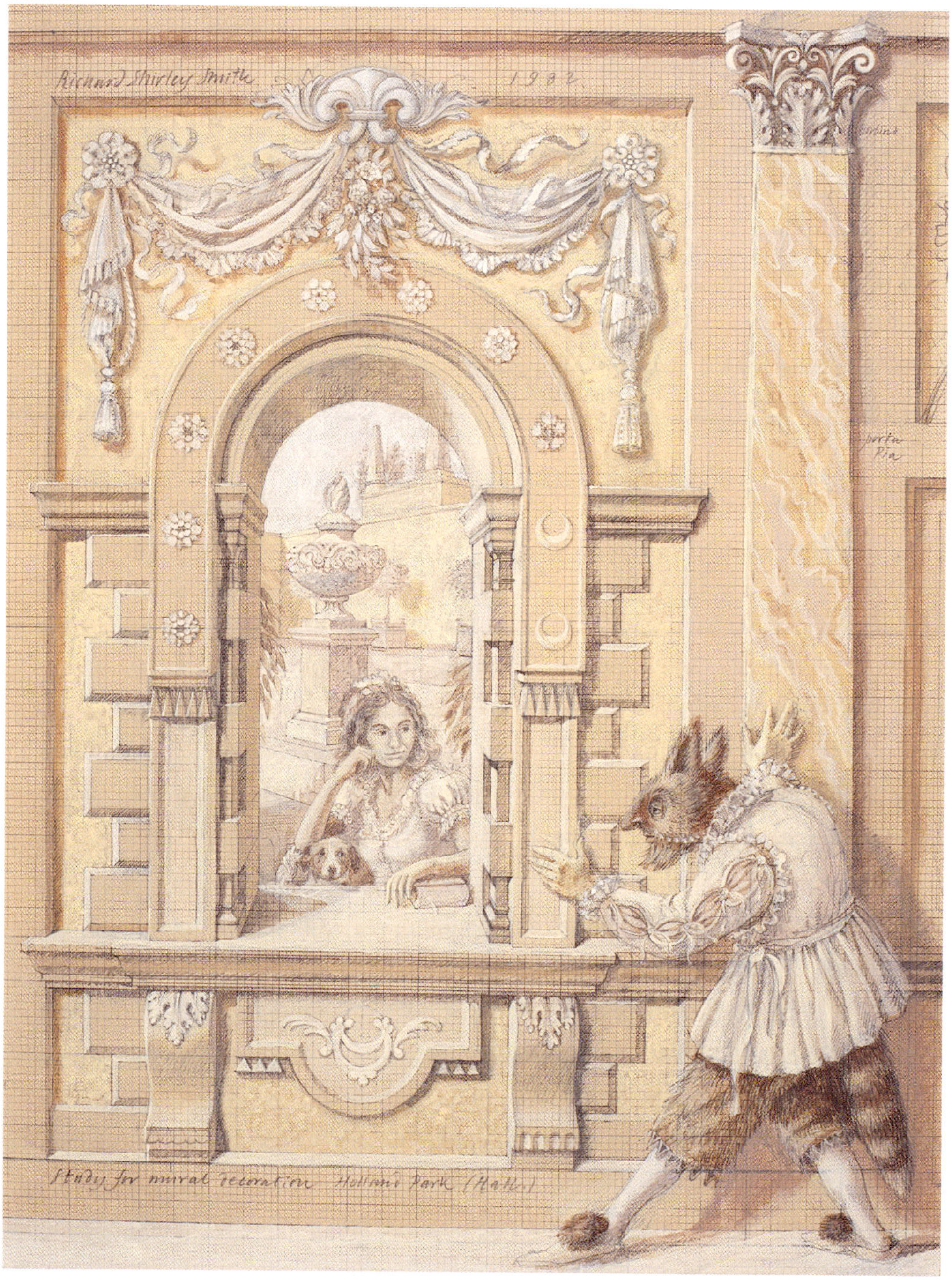

ABOVE: Fig.54 *Window Study with Dog*, acrylic on graph paper. 44 × 34cm. 1982 (*ptg.cat.118*)
This started as a cartoon for a hall mural; figures were added later. I have incorporated some architectural elements from Michelangelo's ornaments on the Porta Pia in Rome. Collection of Nicholas & Adrienne Engert

OPPOSITE: Fig.55 *Oliphant Chuckabutti Zoo*, acrylic on paper. 58 × 43cm. 1992 (*ptg.cat.199*). The poster reads: 'In the world of mules there are no rules', although 'Do not bend down behind the back legs' might have been a wise one. *Corpus canis* means dog's body, of course. I love the fortuitous shapes created when layers of paper are torn from hoardings. I saw these from the Underground train at Sloane Square. Having my camera with me, I got off, photographed them and took the following train. The zebra is a quagga, an extinct South African species of zebra. Collection of Mike & Genna Eilers

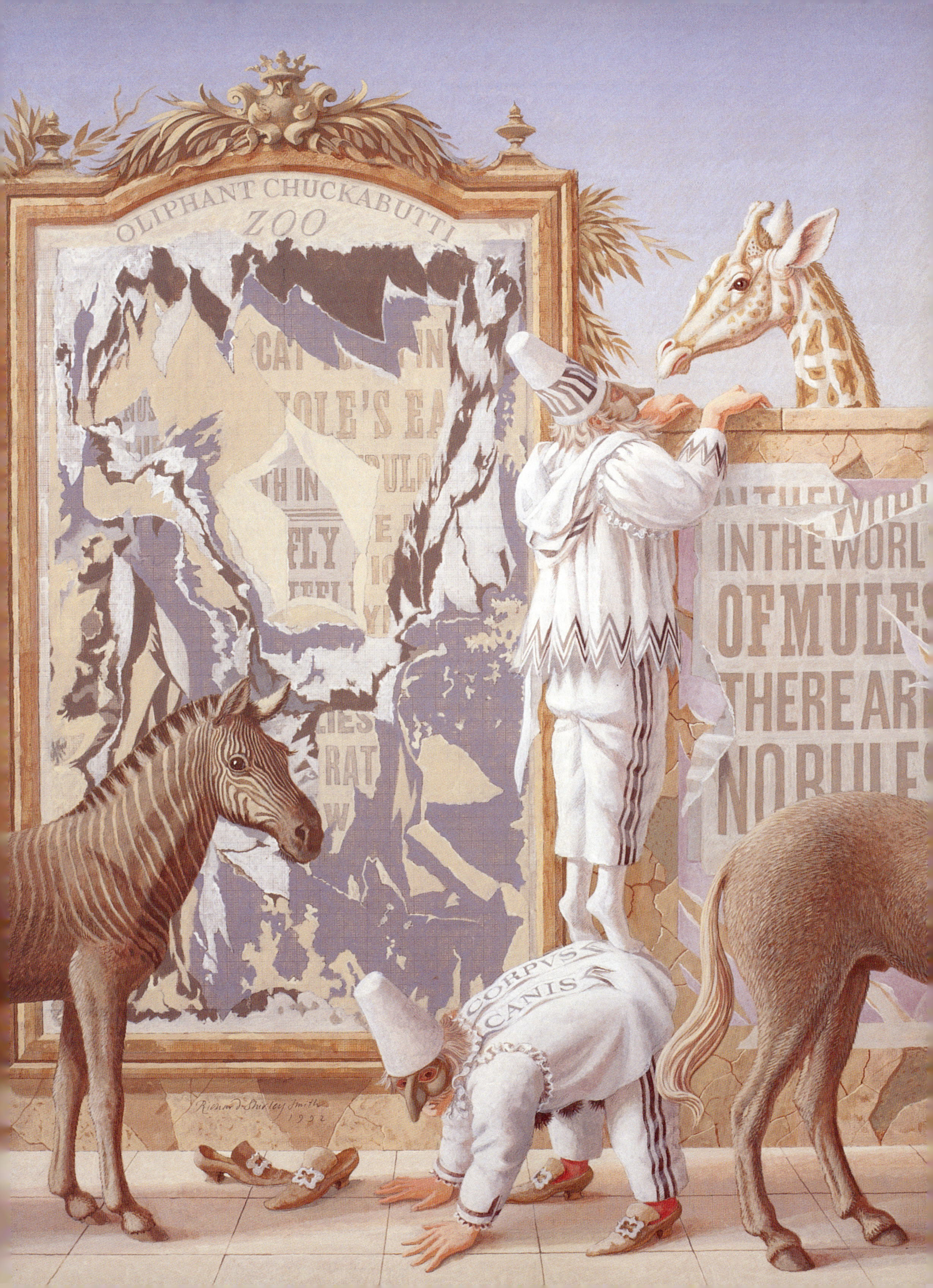
OLIPHANT CHUCKABUTTI
ZOO
INTHEWORL
OFMULES
THEREAR
CORPVS
CANIS
Richard Shirley Smith
1992

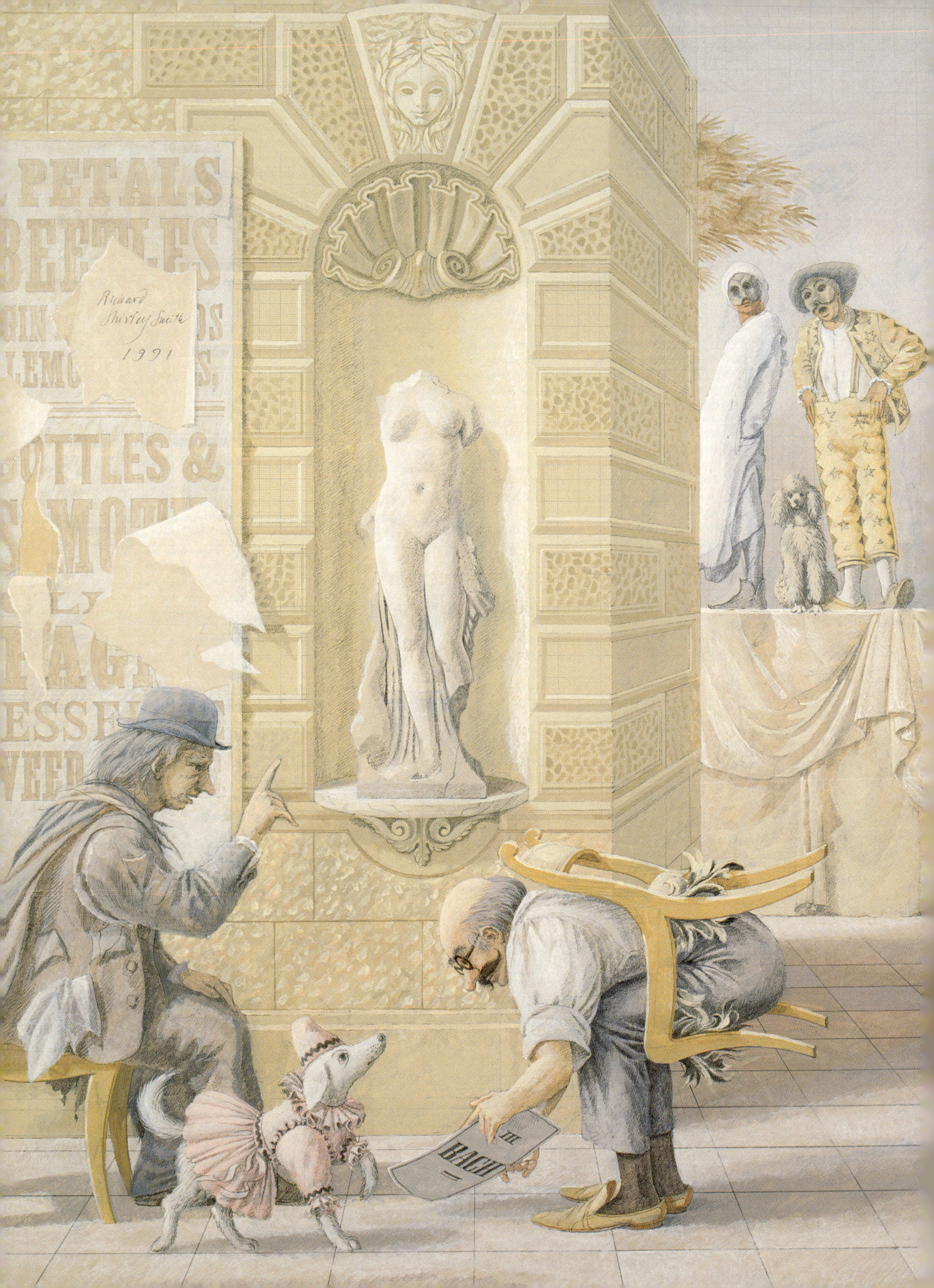
PETALS
BEETLES
Richard Shirley Smith
1991
BACH

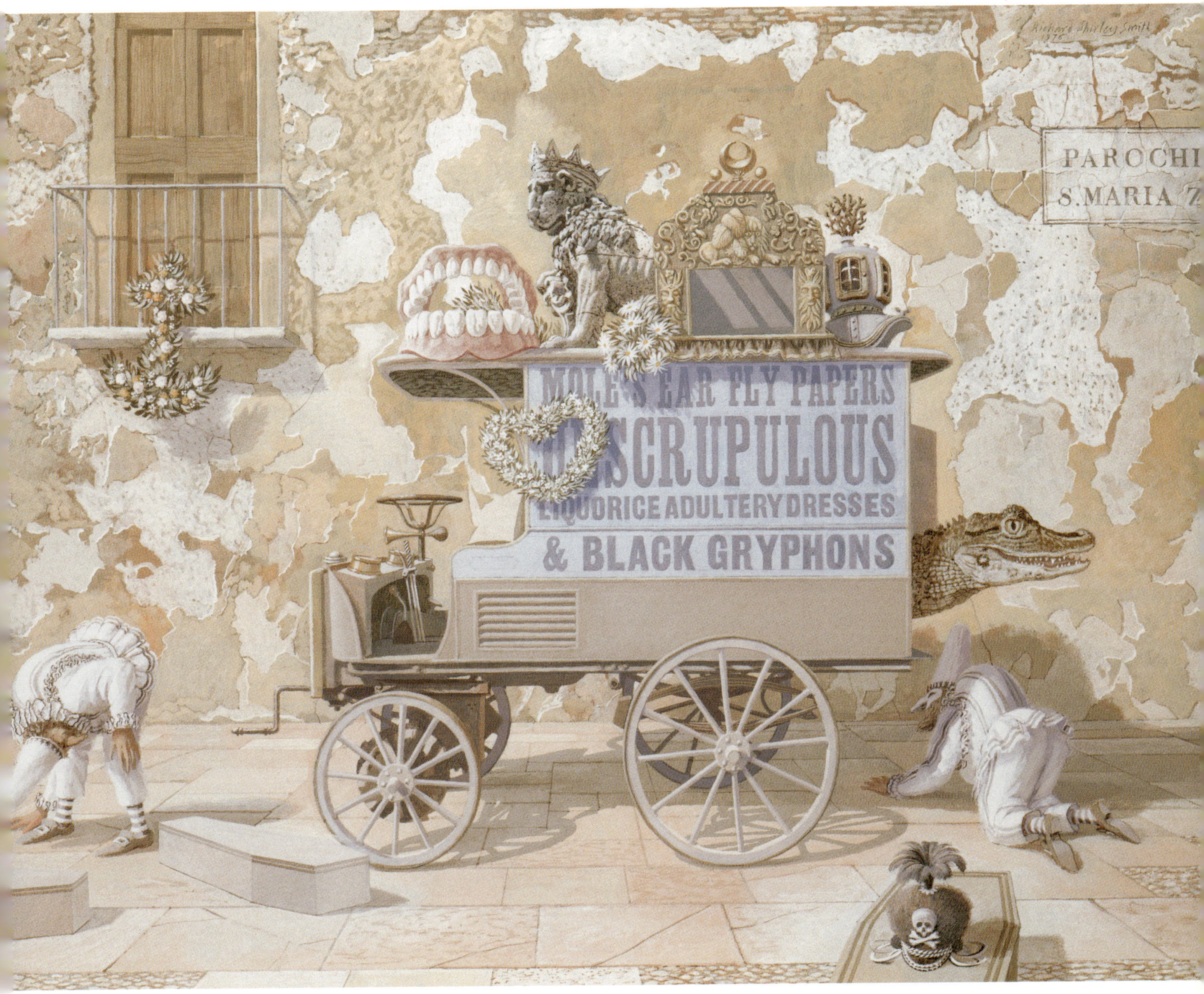

ABOVE: Fig.57 *Fatal Allegations*, acrylic on paper. 56 × 46cm. 1976 (*ptg.cat.59*). In this quasi-Venetian scene everything seems to refer to death or water. The Frederick Gibberd collection of modern British watercolours & drawings, Harlow Council

OPPOSITE: Fig.56 *Clown with Chair*, acrylic on paper. 62 × 46cm. 1991-5 (*ptg.cat.224*). One of the features of the *Commedia dell'Arte* is that humiliating or indecent events are often witnessed by the least discreet characters, as here. I have never been able to take artists seriously if they are devoid of humour. The aspiring human spirit trapped in the body of a beast must produce comedy sooner or later, as Eric Gill pointed out. Collection of Mike & Genna Eilers

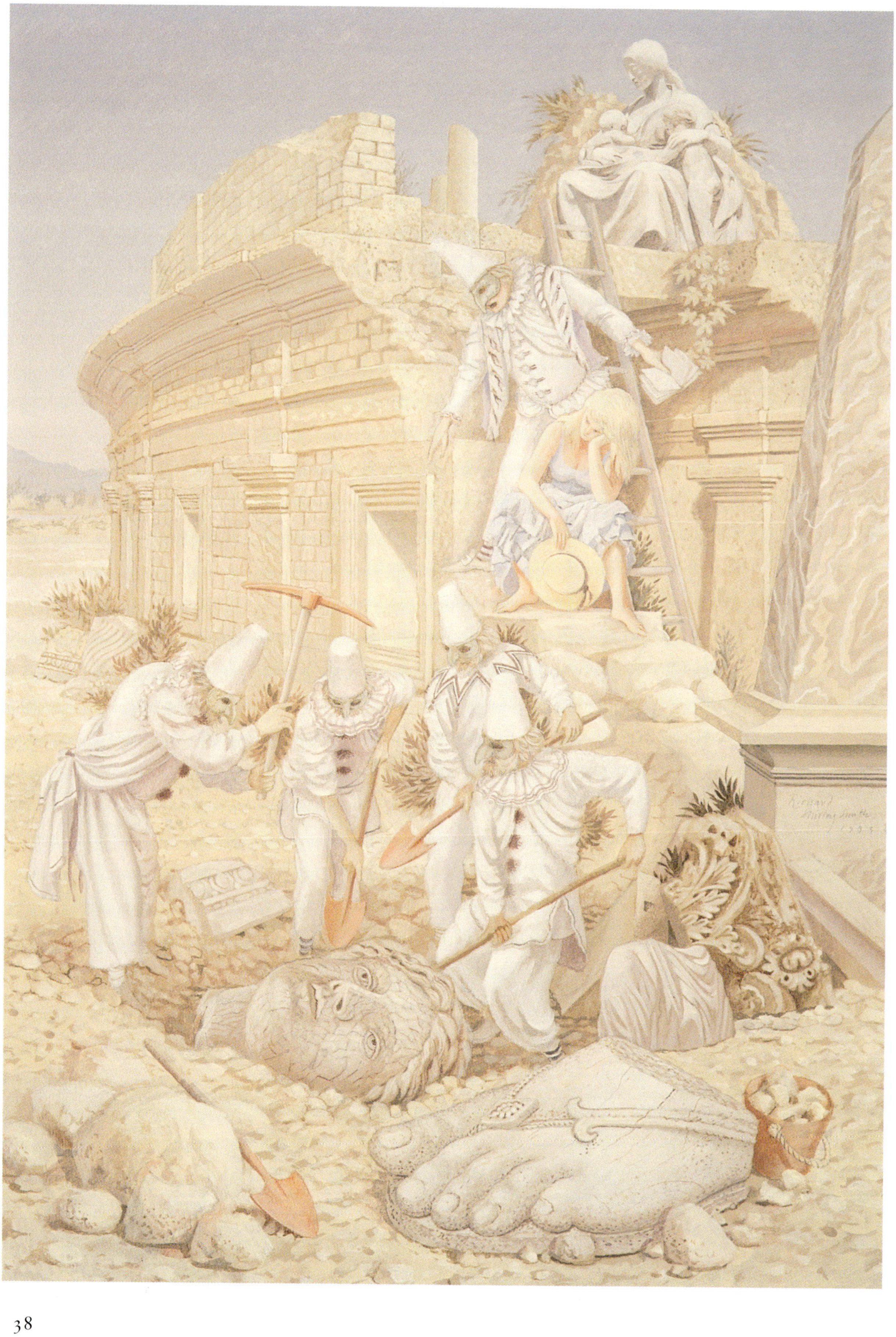

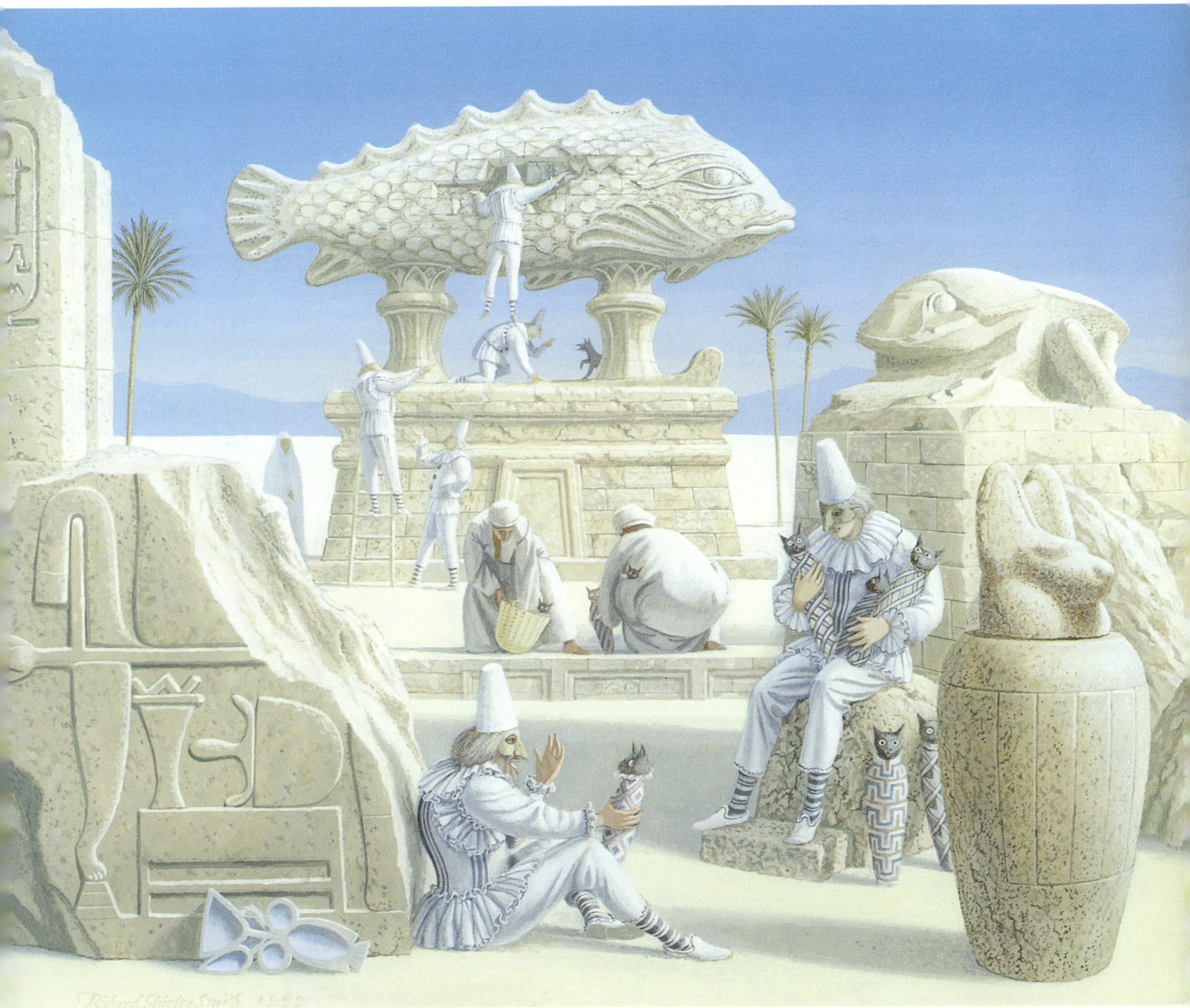

ABOVE: Fig.59 *Pulcinella Visits Egypt*, acrylic on paper. 53 × 67cm. 1999 (*ptg.cat.279*). Everything is authentic except the fish. Pulcinella is collecting mummified cats to take home to Italy. Collection of Alison Brown

OPPOSITE: Fig.58 *Pulcinella Archaeologist*, acrylic on paper. 72 × 51cm. 1992-3 (*ptg.cat.209*). Pulcinella and his troupe have taken up archaeology in the south of France and experience some beginner's luck. The gigantic foot was observed at Chatsworth. Collection of Richard Blackford

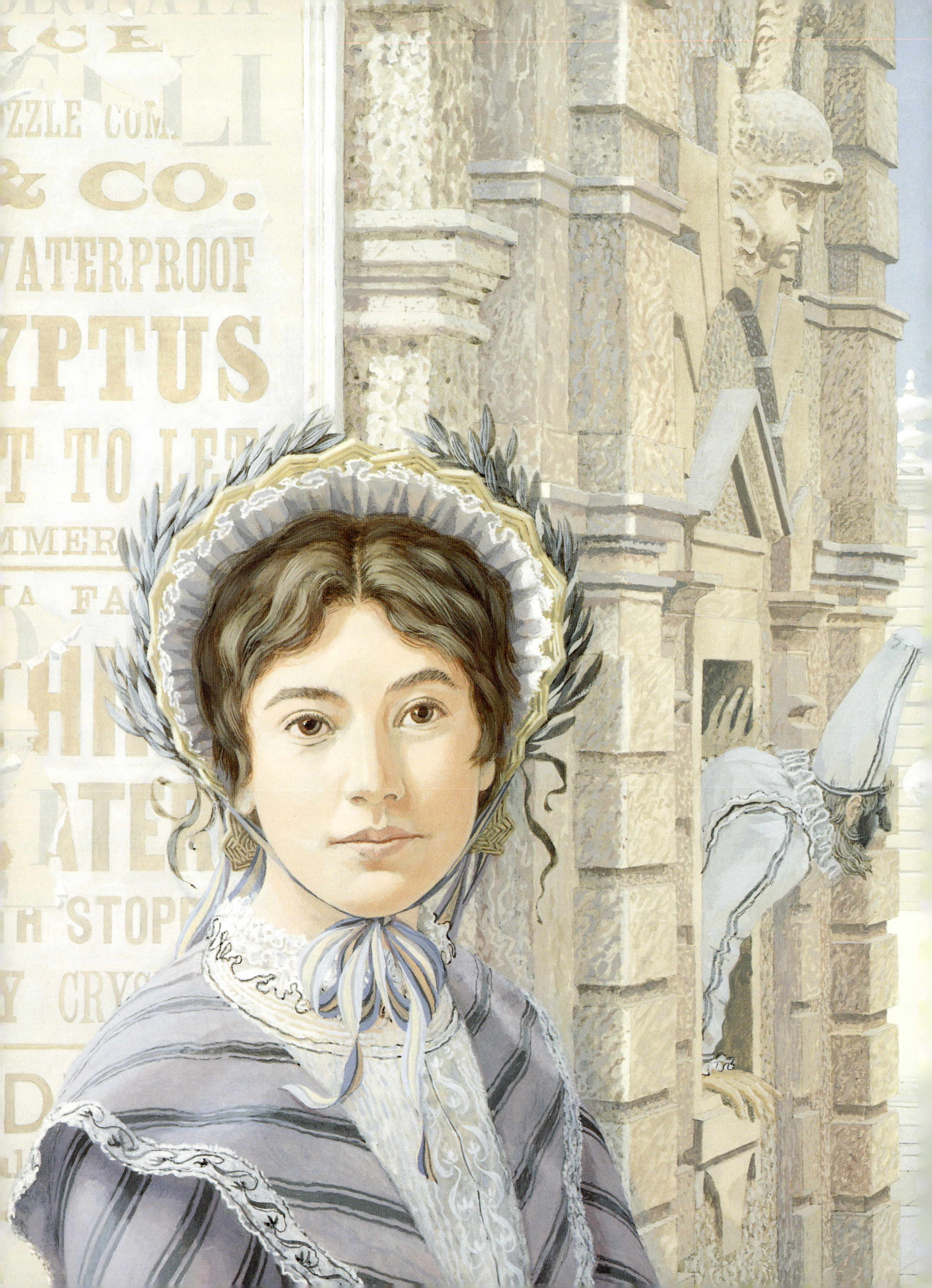
& CO.
WATERPROOF
TO LET

THREE

Theatrical Figures & Architecture

Among the senses that many modern painters have mislaid must be included the architectonic sense. The construction accompanying the human figure whether alone or in a group, the episodes of life and historical drama were a great concern for the painters of old, who applied themselves with a loving and severe spirit, studying and perfecting the laws of perspective.

GIORGIO DE CHIRICO

IN 1976 LANCE WRIGHT saw my first Oxford Gallery solo show and wrote a fully illustrated article in the March 1977 issue of the *Architectural Review*, of which he was the editor. He deftly picks out the love of Italy and its architecture and also the theatrical use of figures with architecture. He comments on 'Shirley Smith's power to observe and to capture precisely those warring elements of vitality and timelessness in the Italian scene which have always impressed the English visitor to Italy – and which the English visitor in his turn converts from a Classical experience into a Romantic memory'. He continues: 'This mood is consistently theatrical. All the items which appear figure unashamedly as stage props, the human figures are all making stage gestures or (what amounts to much the same thing) posing for a photograph and they are clearly wearing stage costume. (This goes too for that admirable dolled-up cow. (Fig.61)) The theatrical allusion is perhaps a complement to the theatrical nature of the architectural fragments themselves, round which everything revolves. It crops up constantly. It can be seen, for instance, in the 'folding platforms and stairs' which hang suspended in the ether above the Castrum Doloris'. (Fig.48)

It was as a result of this article that Sir Frederick Gibberd bought *Fatal Allegations* for his collection (Fig.57). Through an artist's training and technique he or she seems to practice a special magic. A poem may mean much but, magically, it both scans and rhymes; polyphony has both interweaving horizontal voices and mysteriously vertical harmonies. In the same way, a painting can be made of a beautiful deployment of areas of colour on a plane but, at the same time, space and perspective are implied. Architecture and lettering are a delight to me seen in perspective from various angles, as they are so precise, unlike clouds or bushes. Another telling geometry I love is the projection of shadows.

OPPOSITE: Fig.60 *Alicia* (*detail*), acrylic on paper. 43 × 64cm. 1975 (*ptg.cat.36*). The lady is based on a youthful photograph of the artist's mother; the architecture is from Villa Contarini, Piazzola sul Brenta. Collection of Michael & Joanna Brown

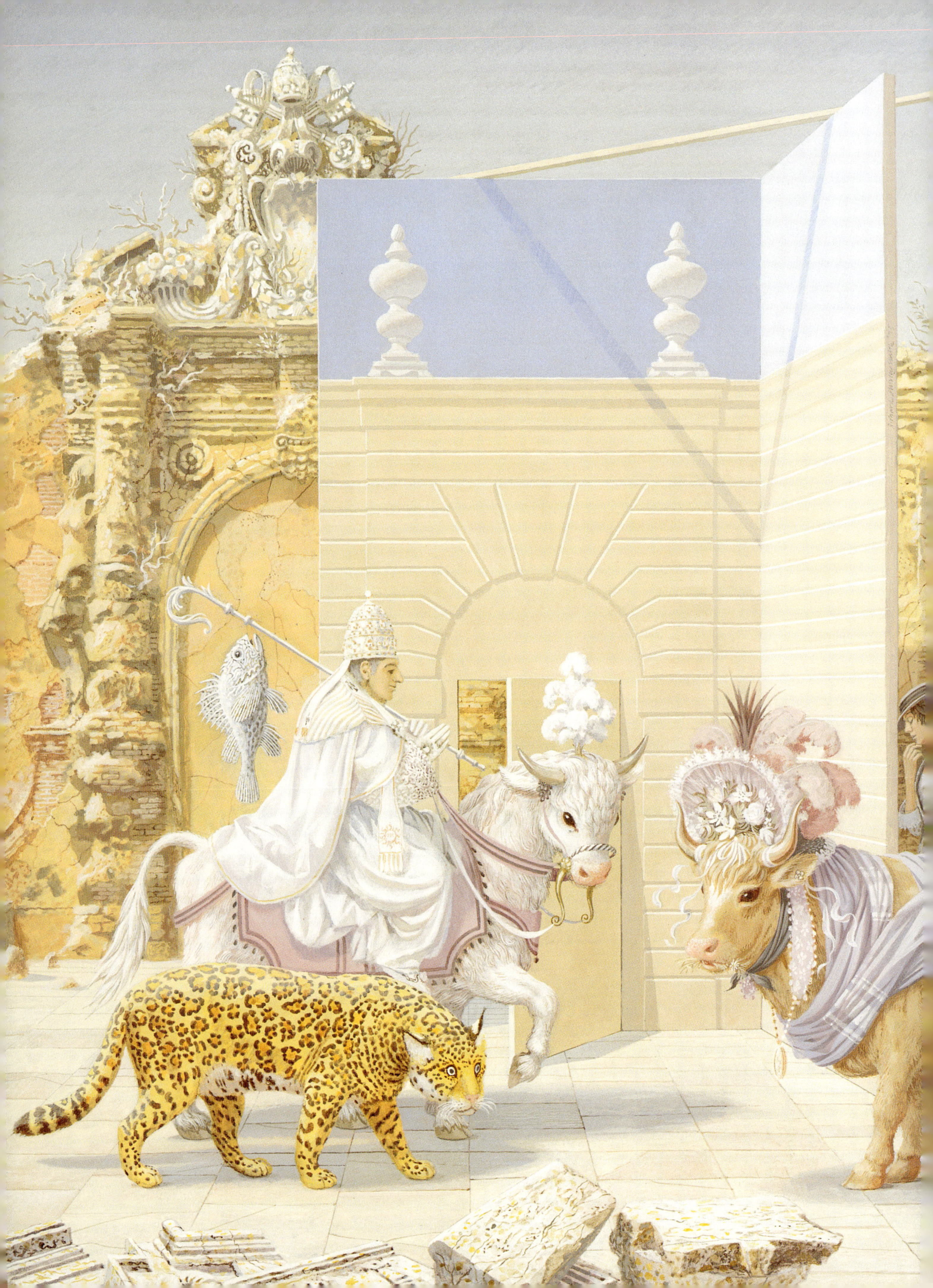

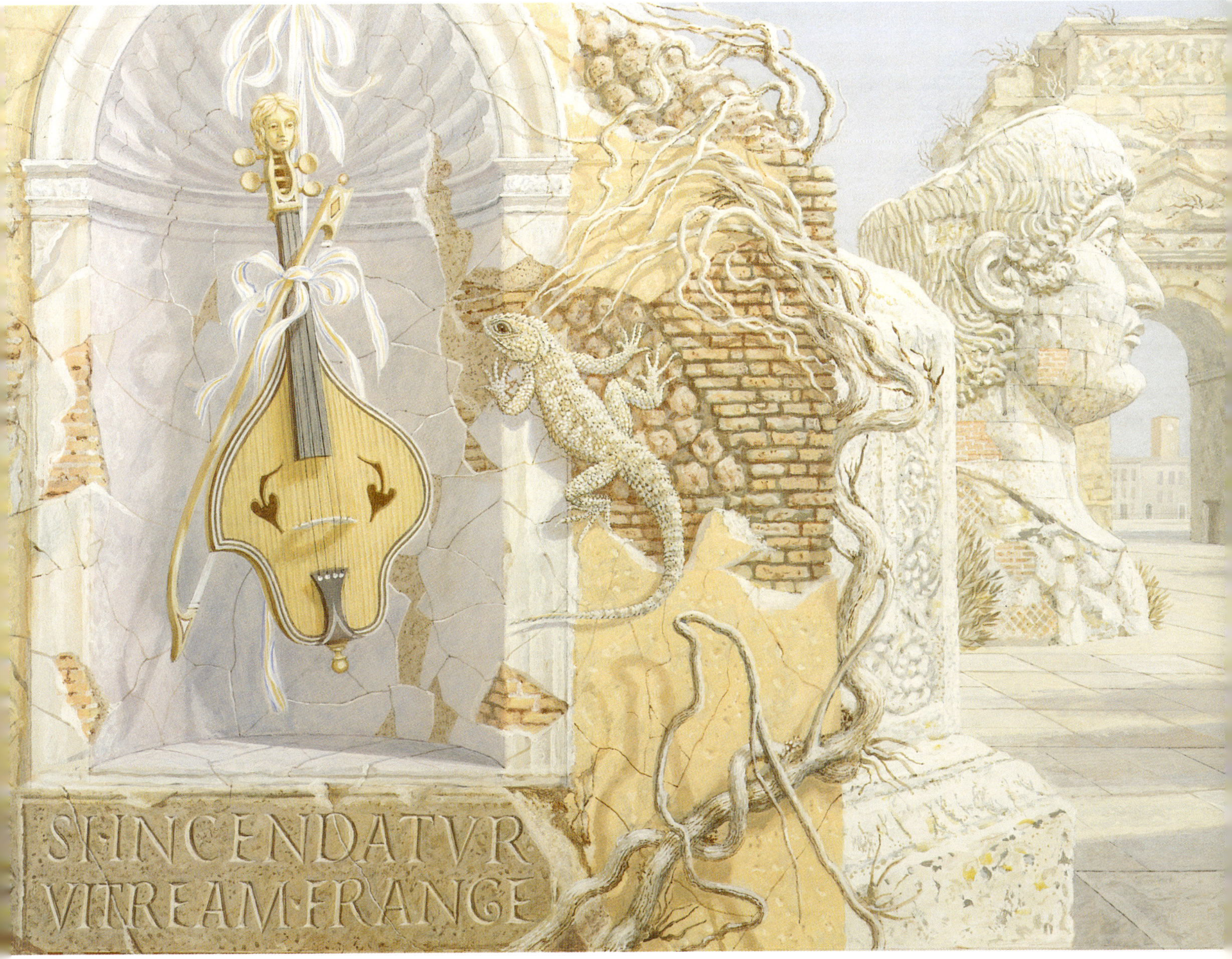

ABOVE: Fig.62 *Roman Extinguisher*, acrylic on paper. 36 × 49cm. 1977 (*ptg.cat.65*). This painting illustrates a silly joke: the obvious view of Rome, the colossal head not unlike Nero, the weird shaped fiddle and the inscription is all one needs to know. The Latin reads: 'In case of fire, break glass'. Collection of Pippa Walker

OPPOSITE: Fig.61 *Quo Vadis?,* acrylic on paper. 56 × 46cm. 1976 (*ptg.cat.56*). There is a slight reference both to the Renaissance court fête and to political cartoons like Gilray's. There is no particular point being made here. The decorative leopard pads alongside as the two tigers do in the Galleria of the Palazzo Farnese, Rome. It was St Peter who was asked: 'Where are you going?' (*quo vadis?*) when fleeing persecution in Rome. He graduated from fisherman to shepherd and here rides upon a, presumably, 'papal' bull. Collection of Alan J. Tyldesley

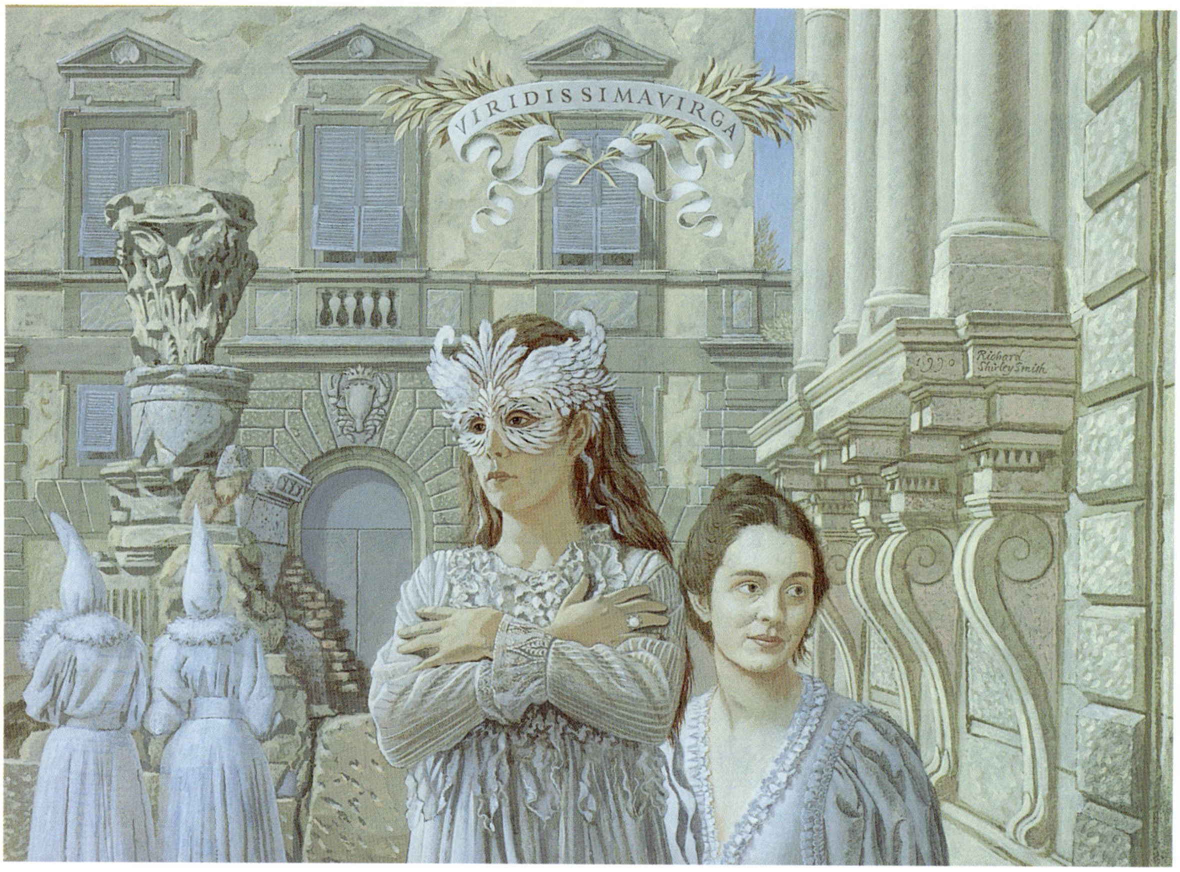
VIRIDISSIMAVIRGA
1990
Richard Shirley Smith

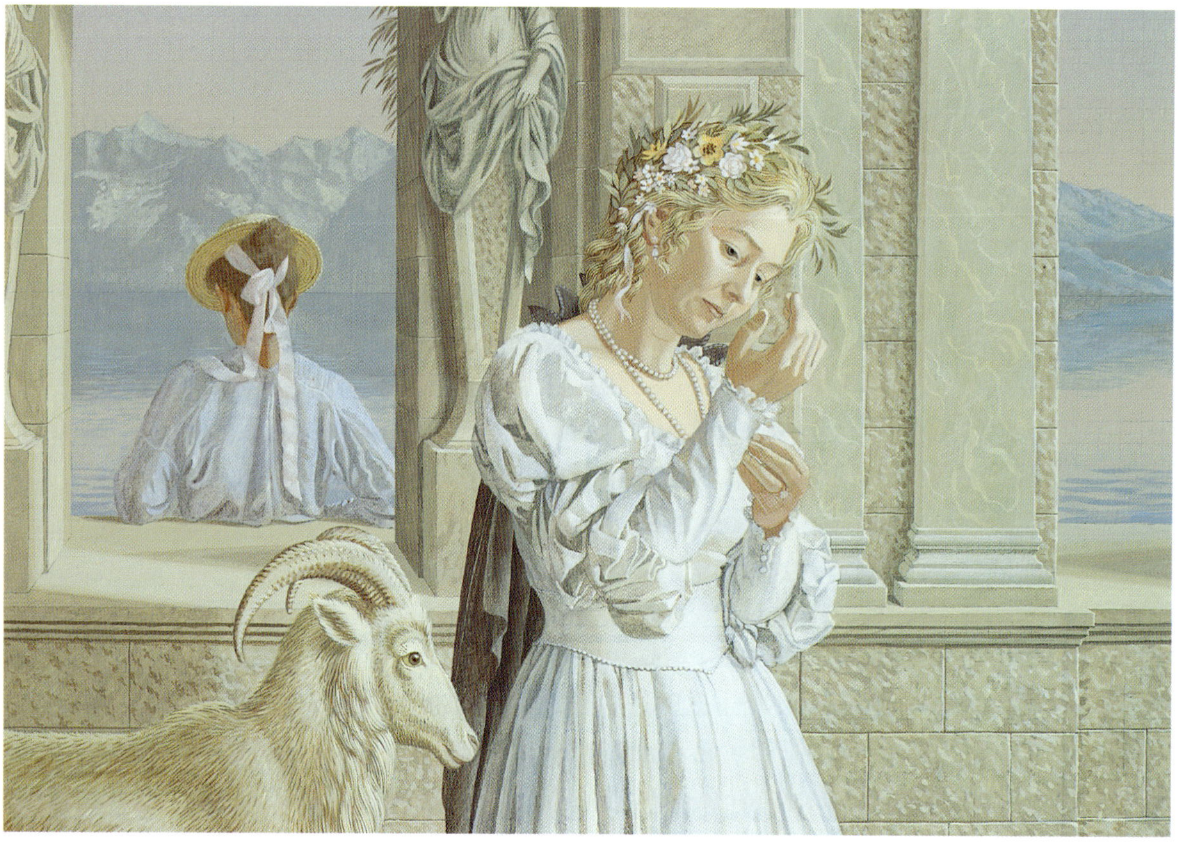

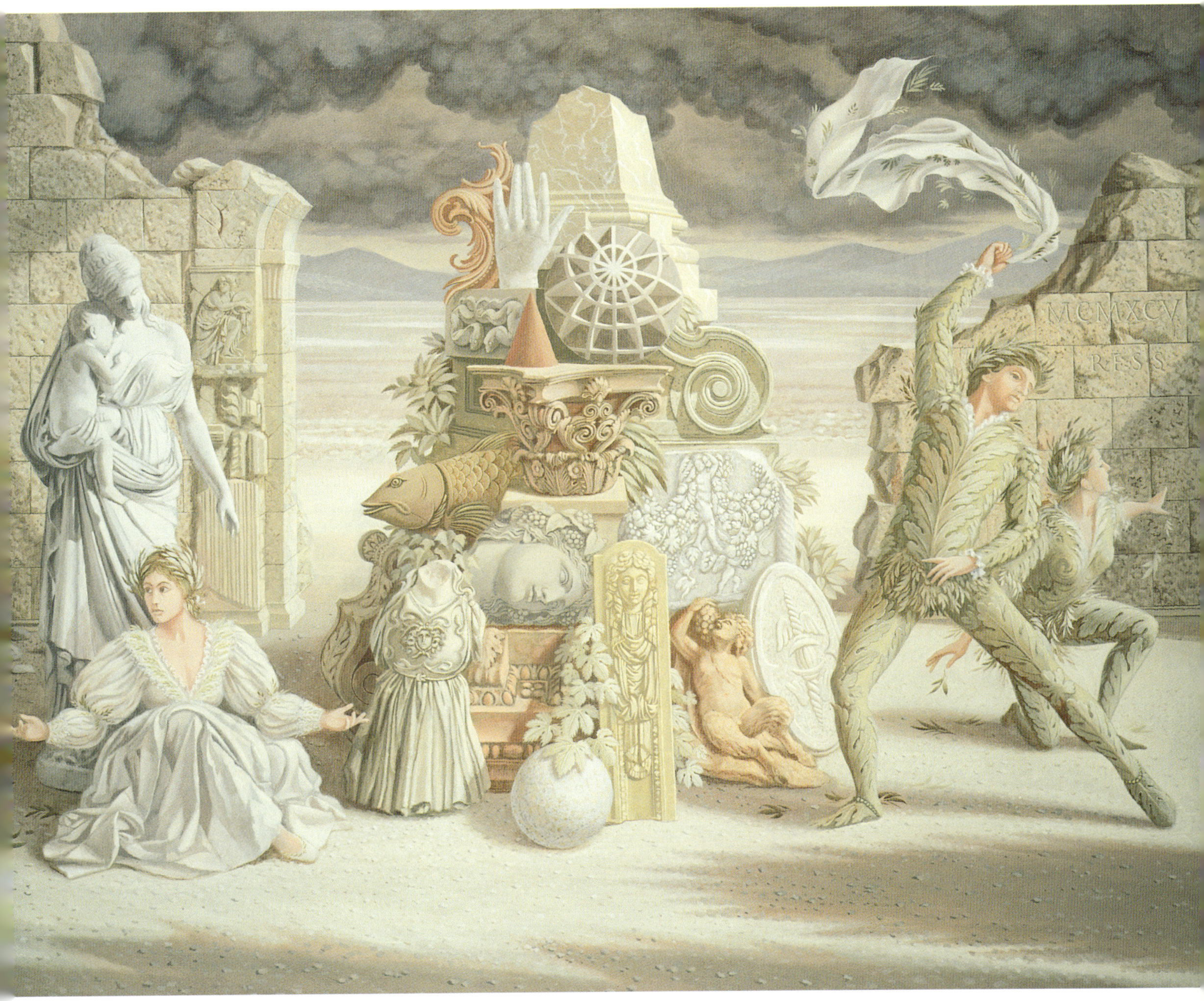

ABOVE: Fig.65 *Rehearsal, Trophy with Dancers*, acrylic on canvas. 95 × 127cm. 1995 (*ptg.cat.220*). This started as a half-scale study for a mural for the Regalian Project. The dancers were added later. Collection of Mike & Genna Eilers

OPPOSITE ABOVE: Fig.63 *Viridissima Virga*, 51 × 73cm. 1990 (*ptg.cat.187*). The setting is mostly Lucca. There is no story here, just characters rehearsing. Collection of Alison Brown

OPPOSITE BELOW: Fig.64 *Lady with Goat* (*detail*), acrylic on paper. 45 × 57cm. 1992 (*ptg.cat.203*). Rosemarie Timmis posed for this painting. Collection of Alison Brown

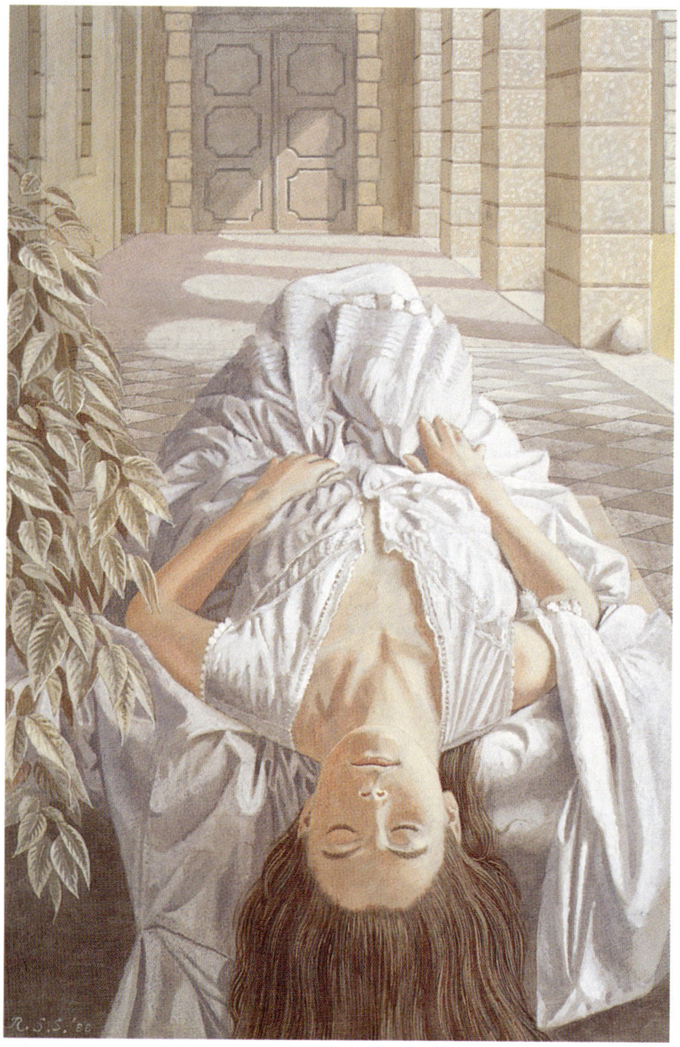

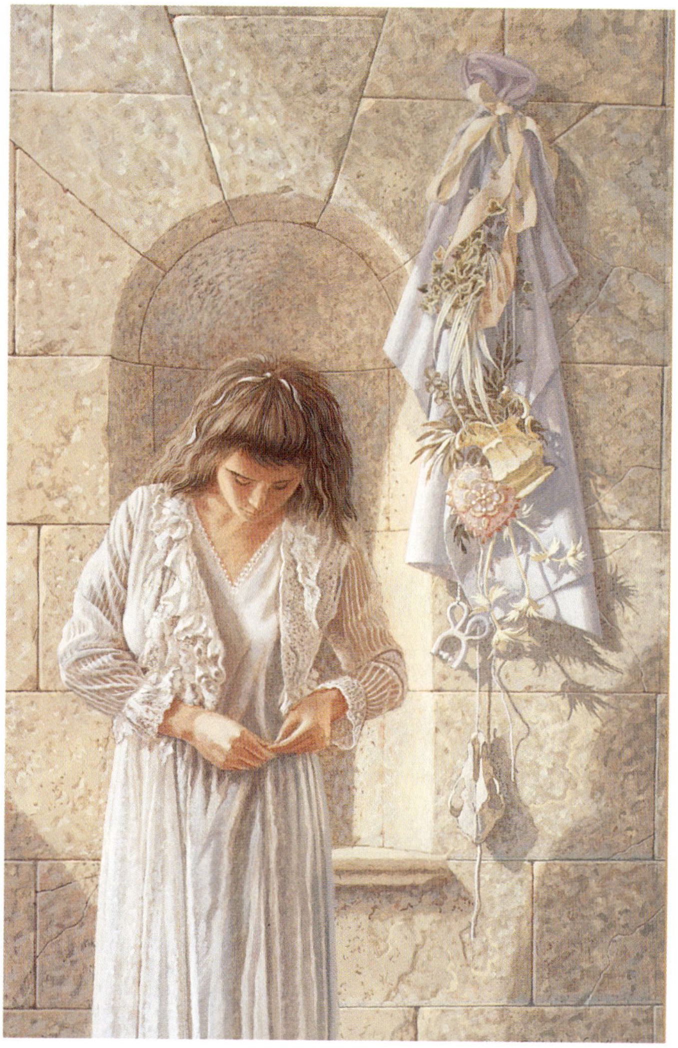

LEFT: Fig.66 *Katie Lying*, acrylic on paper. 51 × 34cm. 1988 (*ptg.cat.185*). The image of the lifeless young woman was a typical romantic idea appealing to such creative minds as Eugène Delacroix or Hector Berlioz. Berlioz particularly loved Shakespeare with his characters Ophelia and Juliet. Collection of Michael & Joanna Brown

RIGHT: Fig.67 *Katie Standing*, acrylic on paper. 52 × 35cm. c.1987 (*ptg.cat.186*). Collection of Michael & Joanna Brown

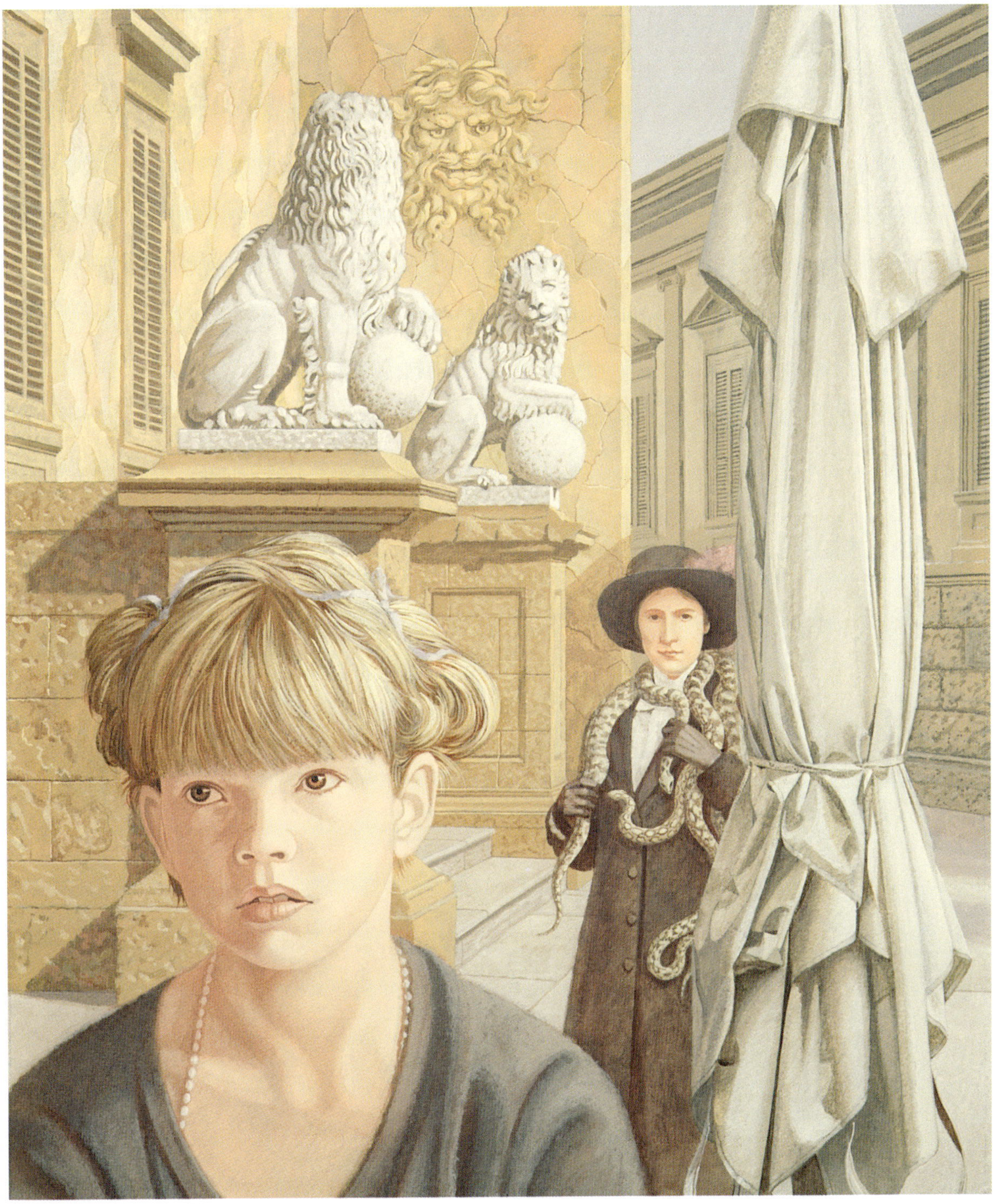

ABOVE: Fig.68 *Italian Snake Charmer*, acrylic on paper. 61 × 52cm. 1995 (*ptg.cat.227*). Collection of the artist

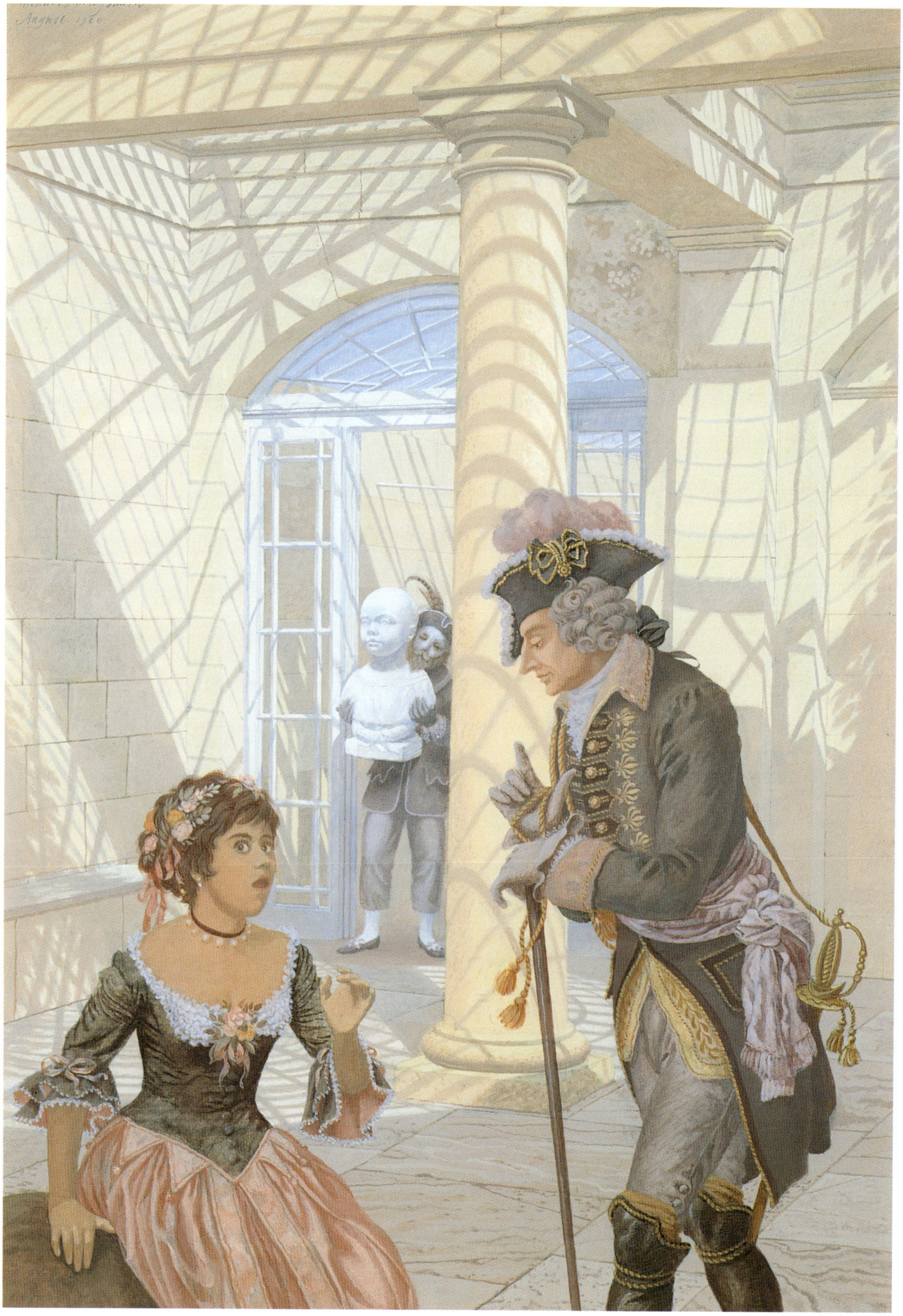

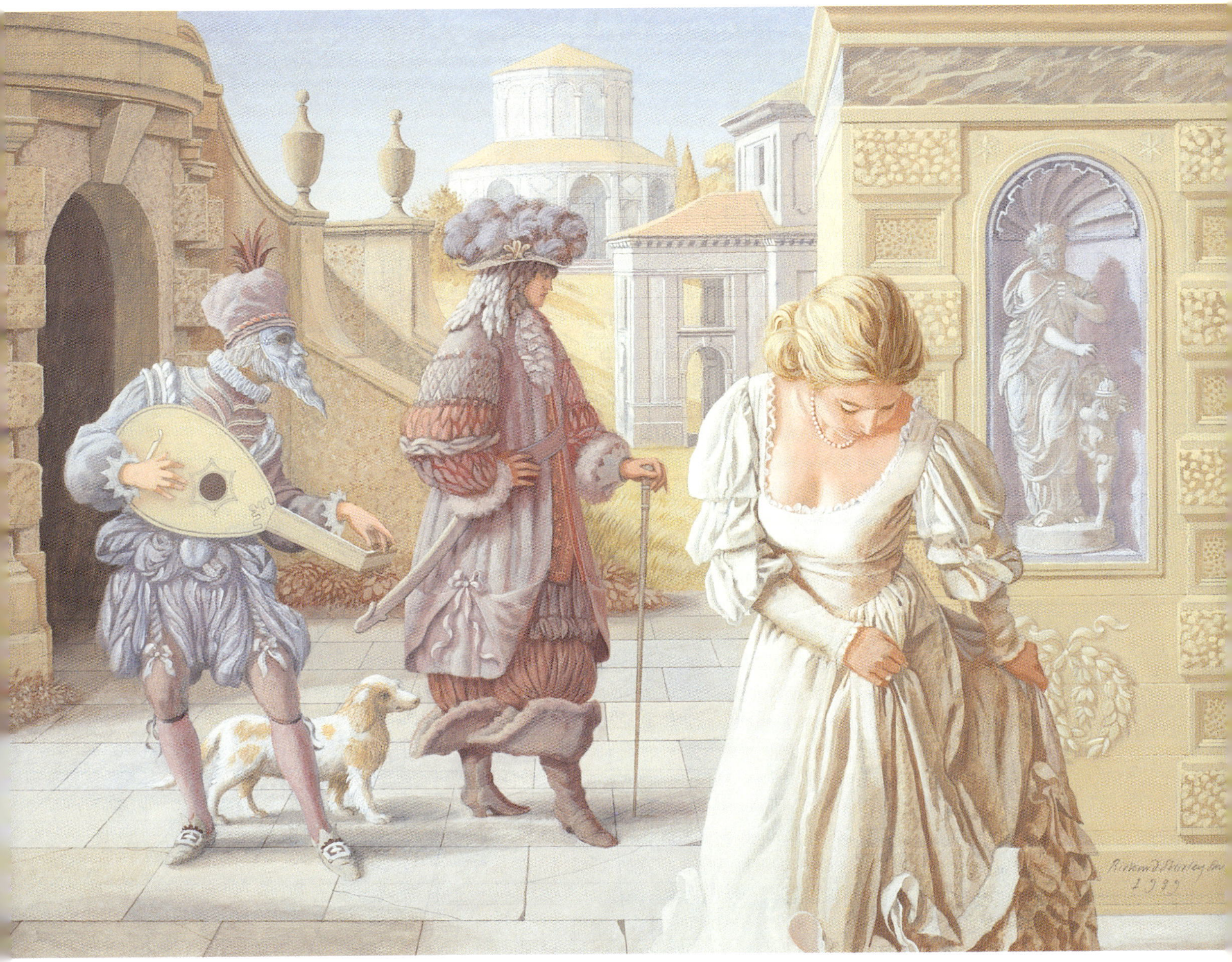

ABOVE: Fig.70 *The Suitor*, acrylic on paper. 48 × 60cm. 1989-95 (*ptg.cat.225*). Actors rehearsing with chapels from Sacro Monte d'Orta in the background. My interest in history, styles of costume and architecture has obviously helped me in my mural decorations and illustrations. The historical figures make sense in so far as they are part of theatrical situations. Collection of Mike & Genna Eilers

OPPOSITE: Fig.69 *The Visitor*, acrylic on paper. 56 × 41cm. 1980 (*ptg.cat.88*). These are figures on a stage. The set was studied at some conservatories at Alton Towers, where shadows were being projected onto classical architecture. Private collection

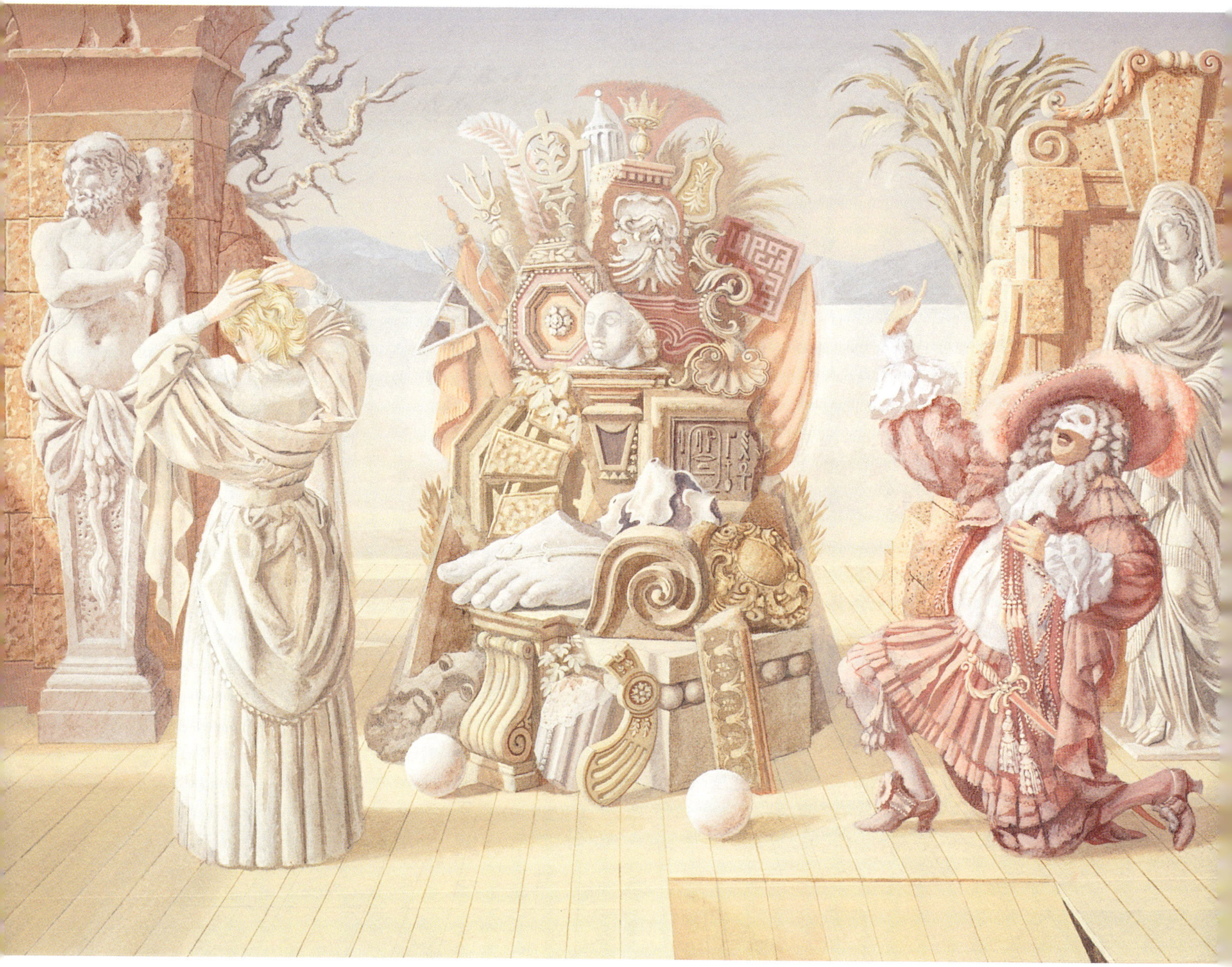

ABOVE: Fig.71 *Suitor & Regalian Trophy*, acrylic on paper. 50 × 75cm. 1997 (*ptg.cat.252*). The painting started life as a quarter-scale study for a mural. Theatrical figures were later added. Collection of A. B. Ward

OPPOSITE ABOVE: Fig.72 *The Emperor (detail)*, acrylic on paper. 43 × 51cm. 1975 (*ptg.cat.37*). The bull's head sculpture was observed in Verona. Private collection

OPPOSITE BELOW: Fig.73 *Lucy in Straw Hat*, acrylic on board. 46 × 39cm. 1997 (*ptg.cat.251*). The doors in raking sunlight were studied in Florence. Collection of the artist

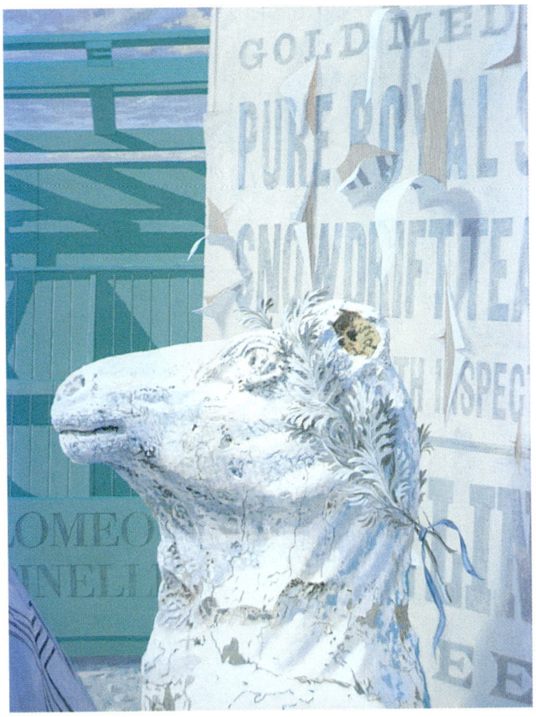
GOLD MED
PURE ROYAL
SNOWDRIFT TEA

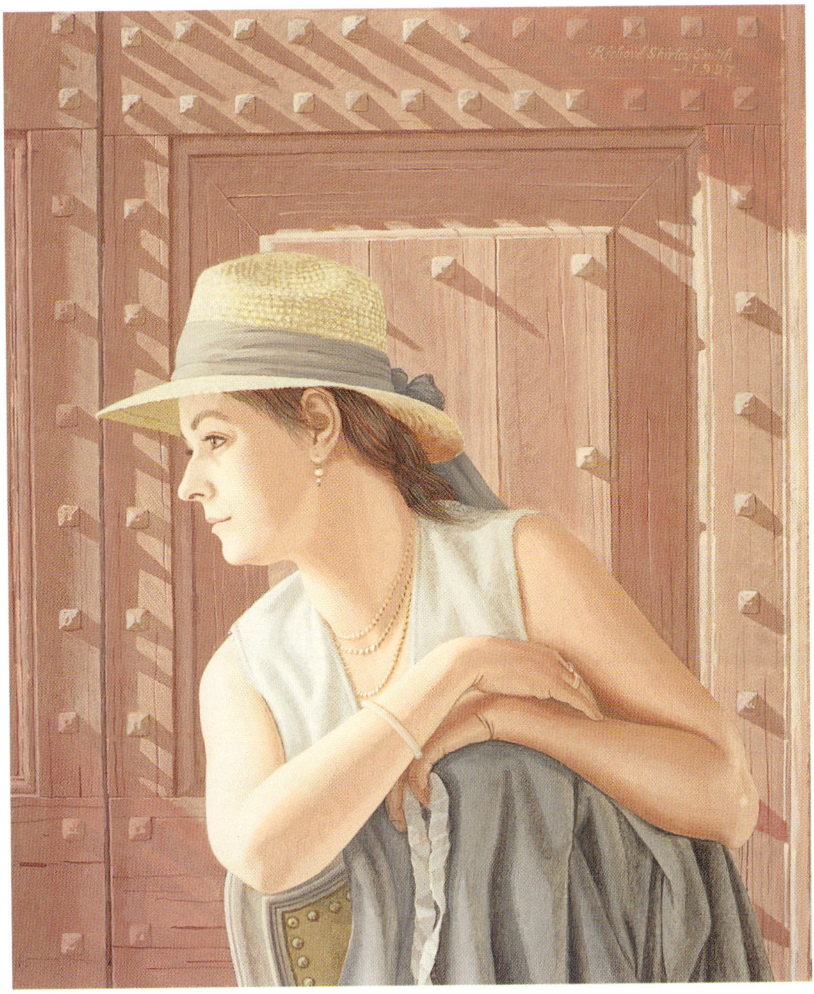

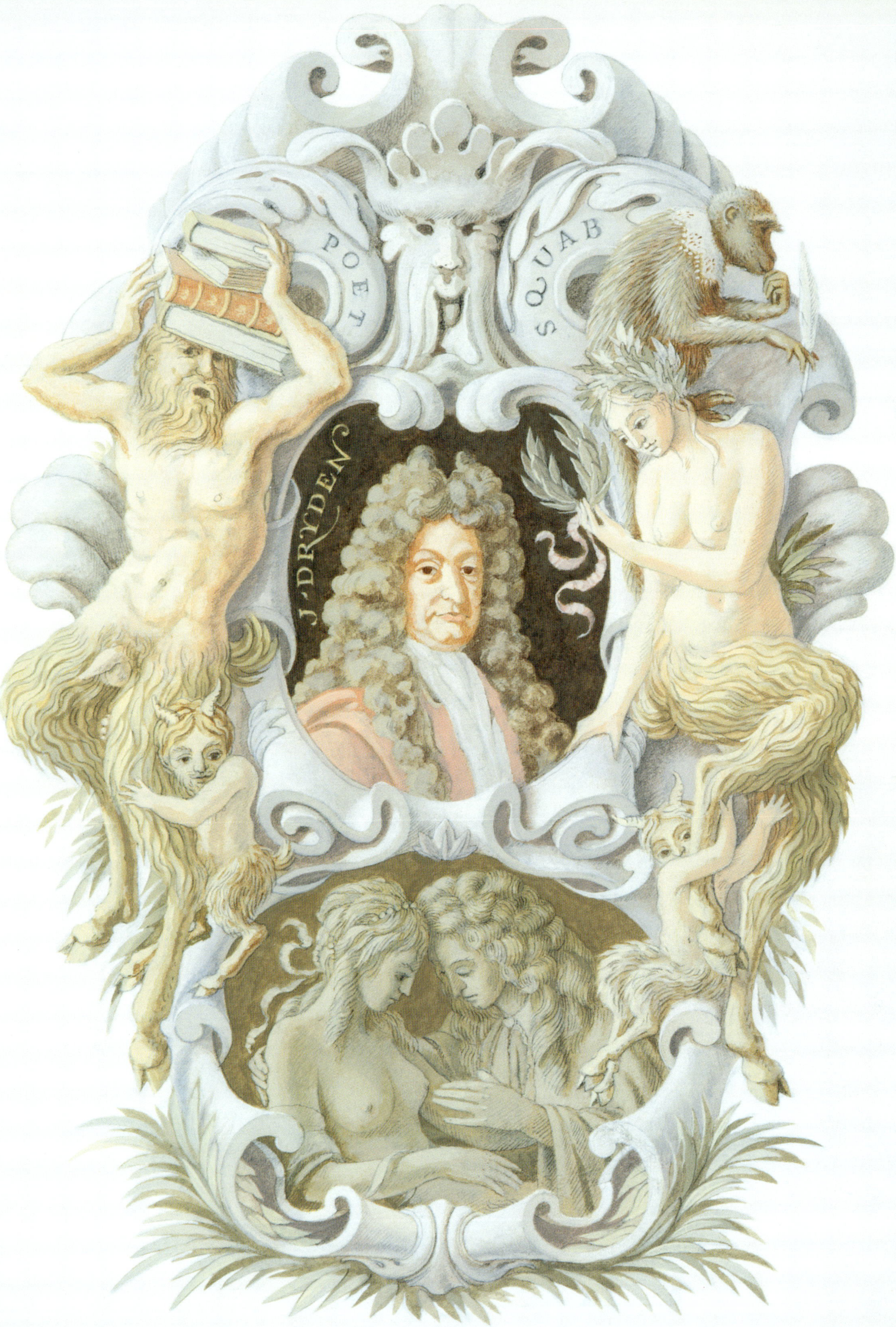
POET
SQUAB
J. DRYDEN

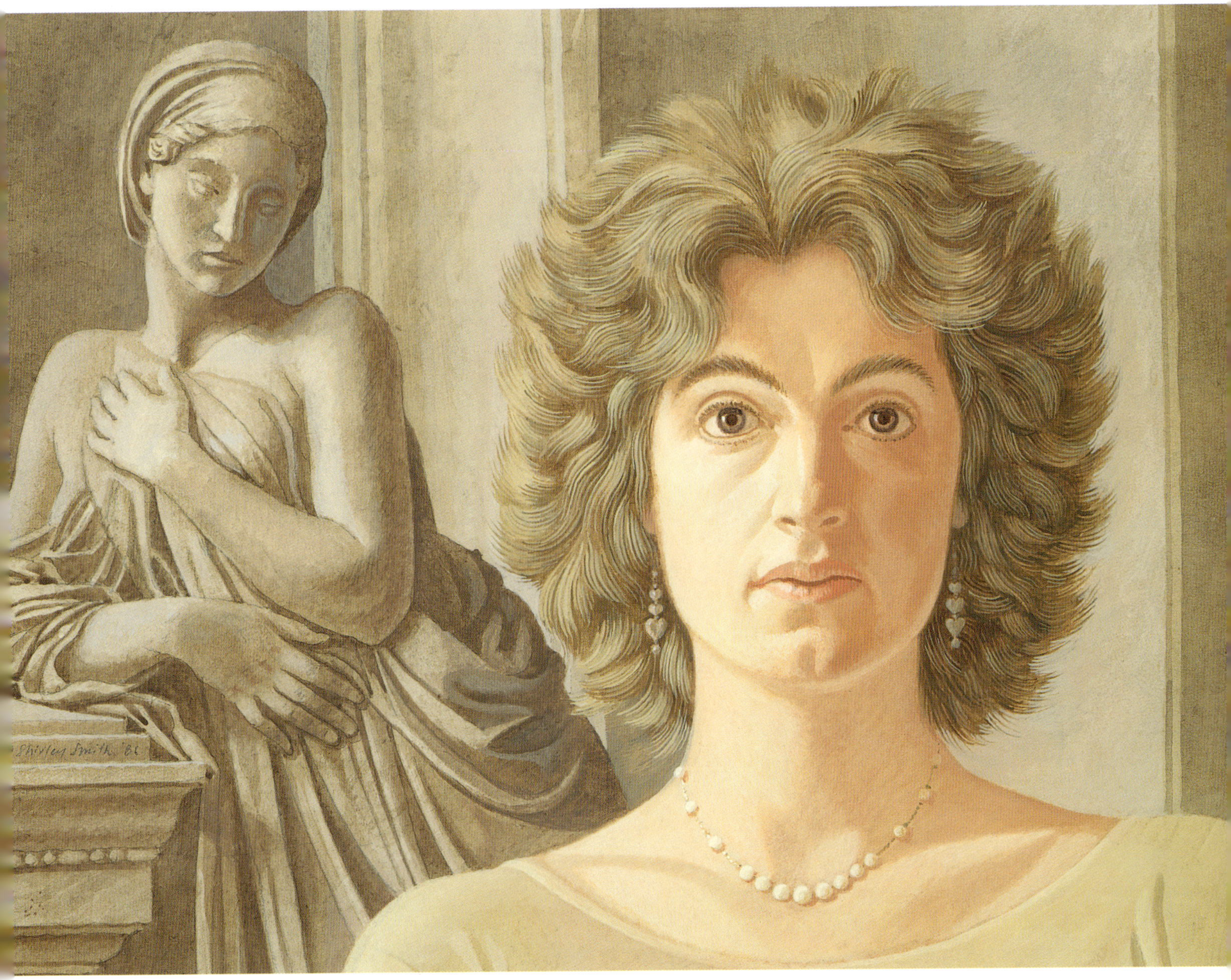

ABOVE: Fig.75 *Portrait of a Lady,* acrylic on paper. 25 × 35cm. 1986 (*ptg.cat.152*). This is not painted as a portrait but more a composition with a lady and a draped figure from a monumental sculpture. Barley Roscoe kindly posed for this painting. Collection of Peter & Lorna Drew

LEFT: Fig.74 *A Satire on John Dryden,* from *Perfect & Imperfect Enjoyments* (Rochester's Poems), acrylic on paper. 40 × 28cm. 1992 (*ptg.cat.196*). The Earl of Rochester turned against Dryden, who he described as 'Poet Squab'. The female satyr has withdrawn Dryden's laurels and may bestow them on Lord Rochester's monkey who has taken up the quill. I love to explore the decorative possibilities of the baroque cartouche. The Folio Society. Private collection

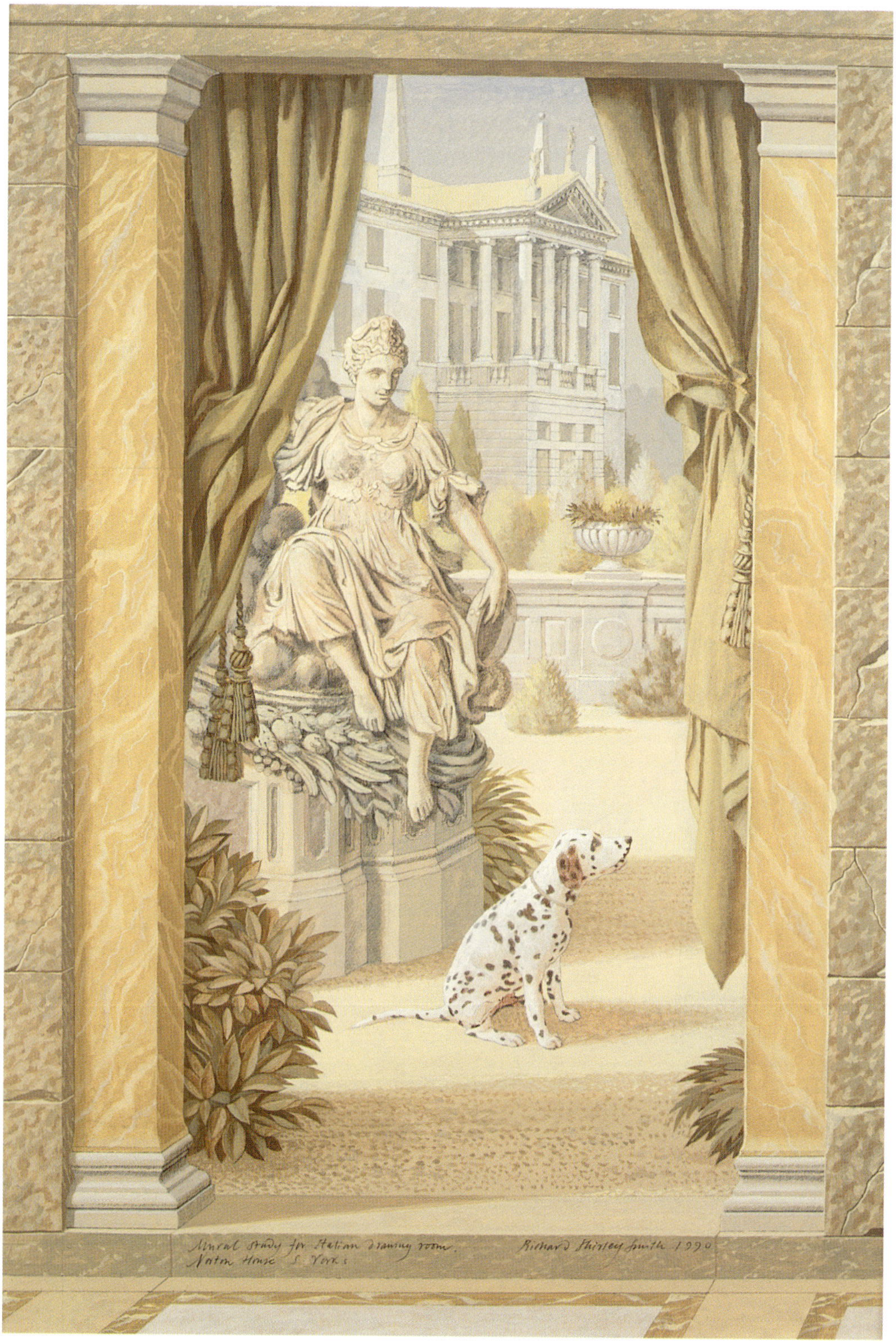

ABOVE: Fig.76 *Cartoon with Venetian Villa & Dalmatian,* acrylic on paper. 58 × 41cm. 1990-92 (*ptg.cat.181*). A cartoon for an Italian drawing-room near Doncaster. The Palladian villa was seen from the Brenta Waterway on the Veneto and the sculpture is to be seen sitting on the corner of Michelangelo's tomb in Florence. Collection of Charles Empson

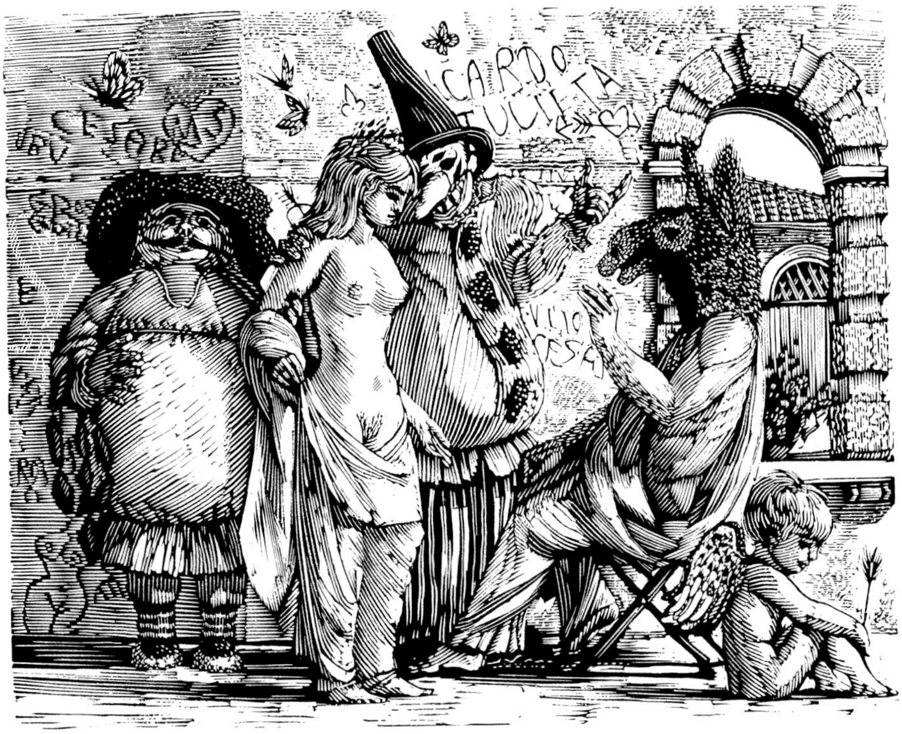

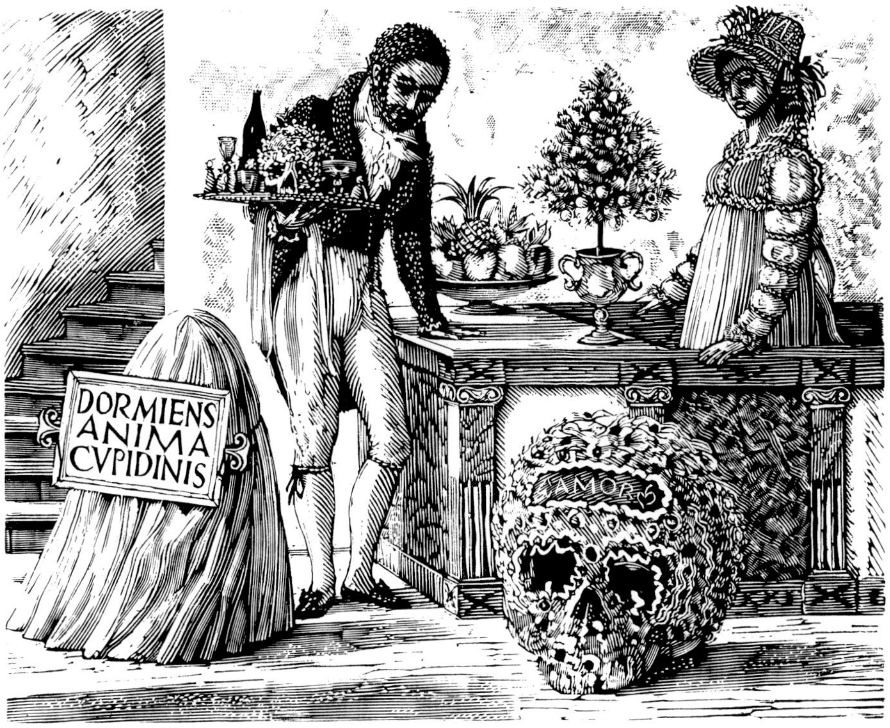

Fig.77 and 78 *Summer* and *Winter* from *Cupid's Progress* or *The Four Seasons,* for *The Periodical,* Oxford University Press, wood engravings. 1970 (*eng.cat.162 & 164*). I include these as they encapsulate so many of my interests: figures with architecture, letter forms in pictures, and the *Commedia dell'Arte*. There is also the symbolism of the 'Sleeping soul of Cupid' and the Mexican skull of love, as well as reference to Venetian Villas. The rusticated, arched window was seen at Villa Cordellina near Vicenza.

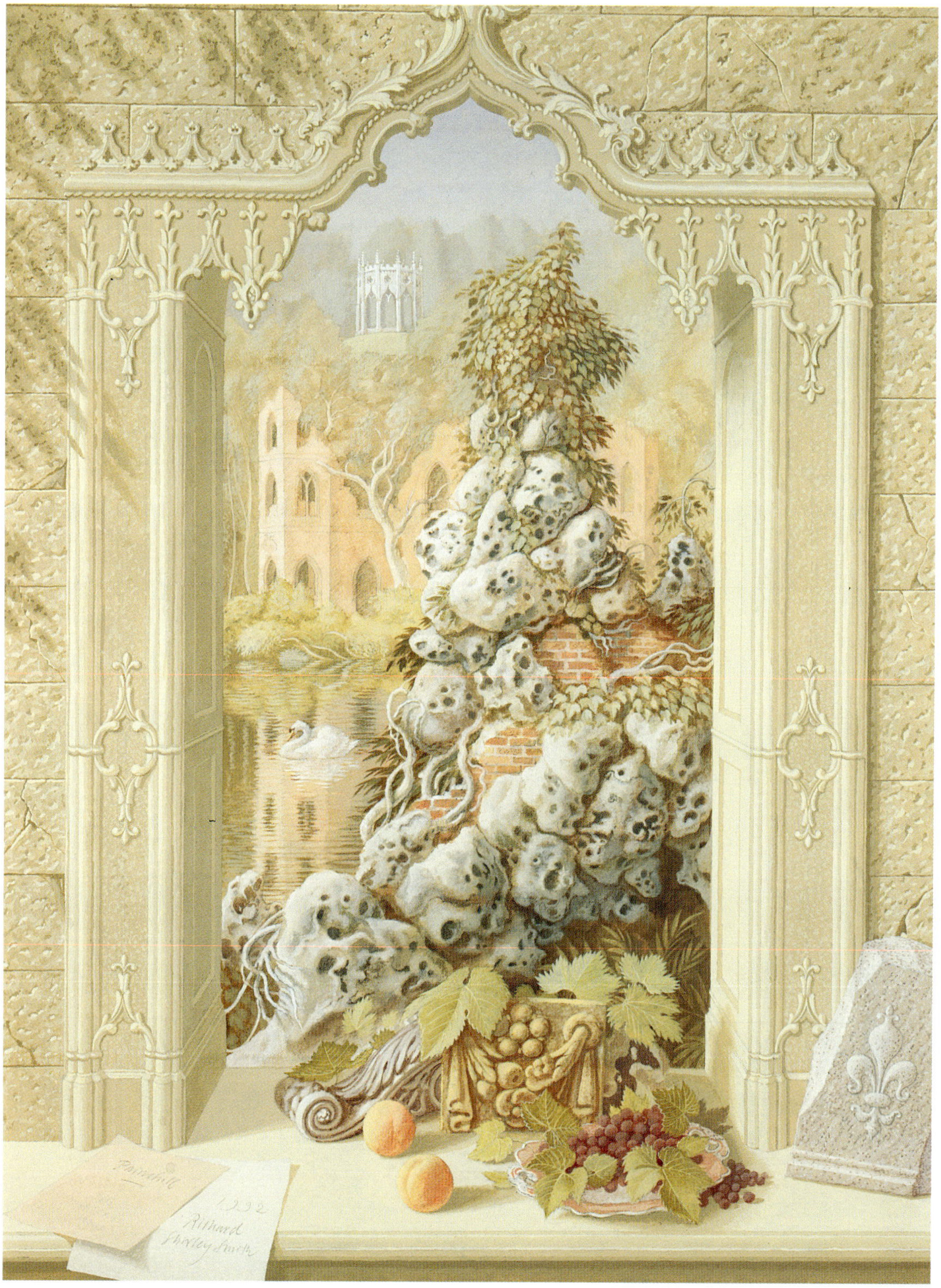

Fig.79 *Painshill, Large version,* acrylic on paper, 63 × 48cm. 1992 (*ptg.cat.207*). Charles Hamilton, being a younger son, did not have a great house to go with his magnificent romantic garden round the lake. This 'capriccio' shows the distant gothick belvedere, the convent built as a romantic ruin (as Shakespeare had put it, 'Bare ruin'd choirs, where late the sweet birds sang') and the remains of the grotto in the foreground. The fleur-de-lys is part of the Hamilton arms and there were family connections between Charles Hamilton, William Beckford's daughter the Duchess of Hamilton and Sir William and Lady Hamilton (see Fig.80). Wyliman Collection

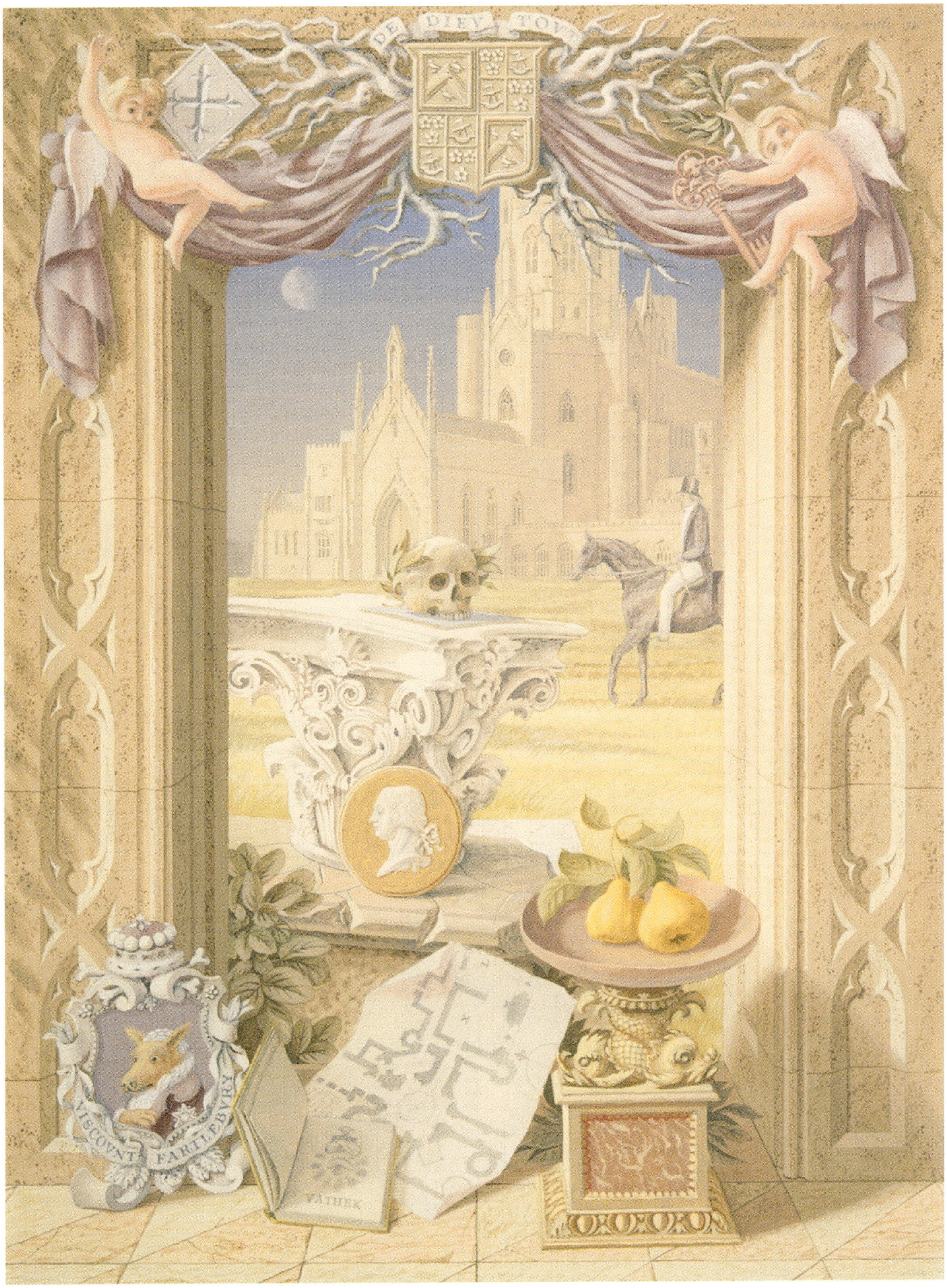

ABOVE: Fig.80 *Fonthill Abbey, Large version*, acrylic on paper. 63 × 48cm. 1992 (*ptg.cat.206*). This is almost a 'Three ages of William Beckford'. The relief medal shows the boy who had had music lessons from Mozart. This leans against a capital from Beckford's father's Palladian house, Fonthill Splendens, which the son demolished in order to build his Gothic Revival Fonthill Abbey. We see William Beckford on his horse in the early nineteenth century, and a fictitious portrait of his dog, Viscount Fartleberry, who was the only member of the aristocracy allowed on his land; the other exceptions seem to have been Lord Nelson and Lady Hamilton who were ceremoniously welcomed in 1800. Collection of Sir John & Lady Sykes

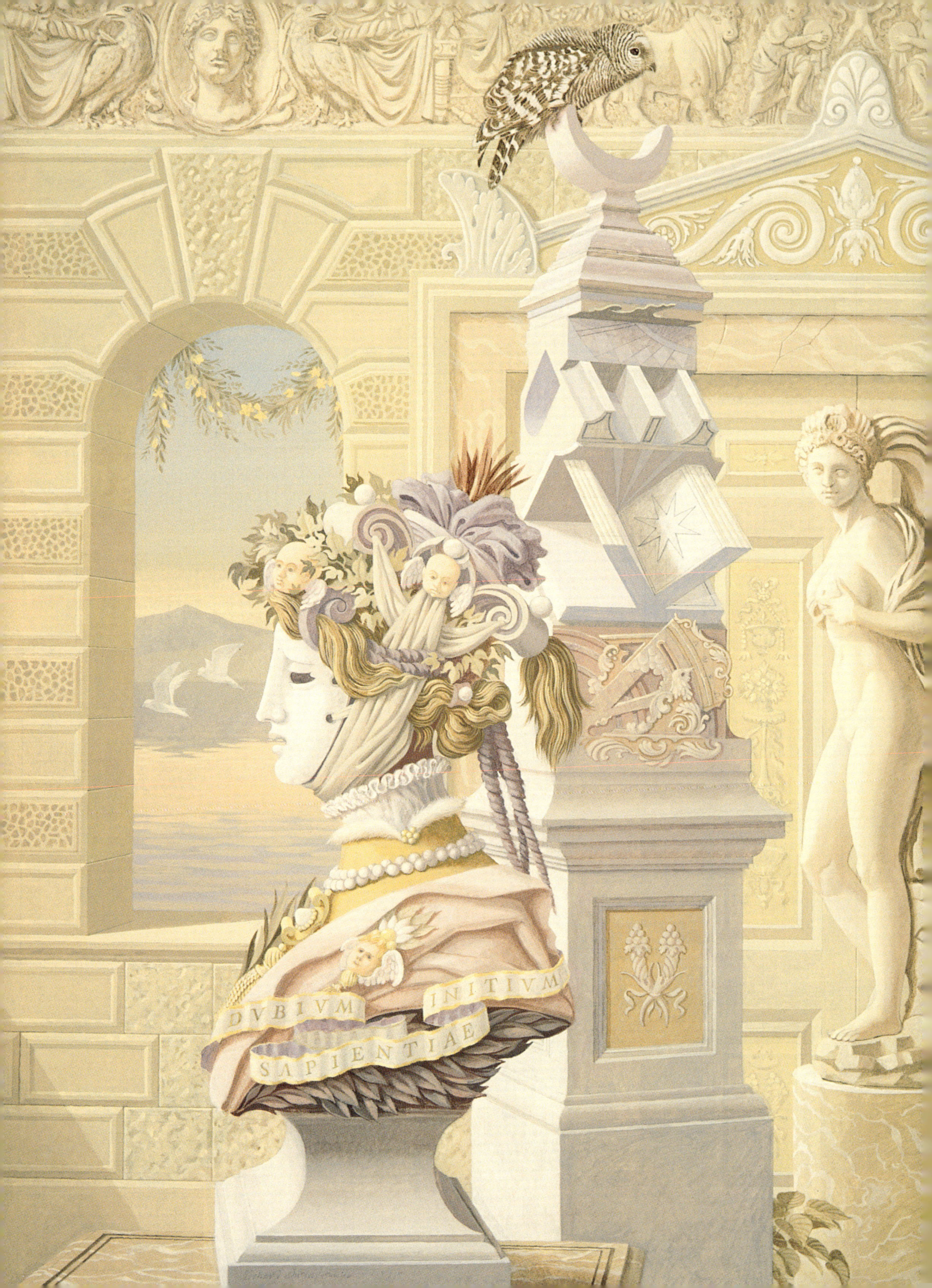
DVBIVM INITIVM
SAPIENTIAE

FOUR

Surrealist Influence

The effect of furniture placed in deserted countryside in the midst of infinite Nature is also very profound: like an armchair, a divan and chairs grouped together on a Greek plain.

GIORGIO DE CHIRICO

SURREALISM HAS ALWAYS SEEMED to me enormously creative and exciting, as it brings art into the Freudian era. André Breton wanted to liberate the workings of the subconscious from the calculations of the rational frame of mind by drawing attention to dreams, coincidences, Freudian slips, and games of chance such as folding ink blots or 'heads, bodies & legs'. The Surrealists were inspired by forerunners: Bosch, Arcimboldo, Rabelais, de Sade, Goya, Blake, Fuseli and Moreau. The results were fascinating and various: de Chirico's unforgettable Metaphysical paintings, Magritte's puns and jokes, Man Ray's fantastic objects, Max Ernst's montages of engravings, and Dali's hugely imaginative compositions from the nineteen-twenties and thirties. Breton, the leader of Surrealism, might have thought that Dali's painterly texture and modelling were a bit too rational, and that he was too grasping, but Dali, being by then a household name, was able to respond '*Surréalism c'est moi*'. I don't believe this marvellous tradition should be swept out of fashion because artists have thought up new styles, and I feel at liberty to make variations of my own on these fascinating themes and ideas.

When I make a painting to please myself, I intuitively select what I most desire to go in the composition, only discovering afterwards what my subconscious might have been trying to say. Blake would hold that, for instance, water can be a symbol for drowning, drinking and/or purifying and not necessarily have just one meaning.

In a letter of 1882 to Thomas Butts, William Blake ends an untitled poem:

> . . . May God us keep
> From single vision and Newton's sleep.

I at once think of Blake's magnificent 1795 image of Newton and his downward-looking, material measuring, unconcerned with visions or symbols.

OPPOSITE Fig 81. *Dubium Initium Sapientiae*, acrylic on paper. 73 × 56cm. 1992 (*ptg.cat.208*)
'Doubt is the beginning of wisdom' is an interesting variation upon 'The beginning of wisdom is the fear of God', which is a prominent latin inscription in Borromini's Roman Baroque church of S Ivo della Sapienza. The elaborate masked head was inspired by the droll 'Masquerade Headdress' engravings of René Boyvin. Behind this we have what Surrealists might have seen as a complicated '*jamais vu*' or 'Found Object': its purpose mysterious, maybe astrological? The background is a *trompe-l'oeil* wall of a large Eaton Square dining-room. I here elaborated the fifth-scale working cartoon after the full-scale decoration job was completed. Collection of Richard Blackford

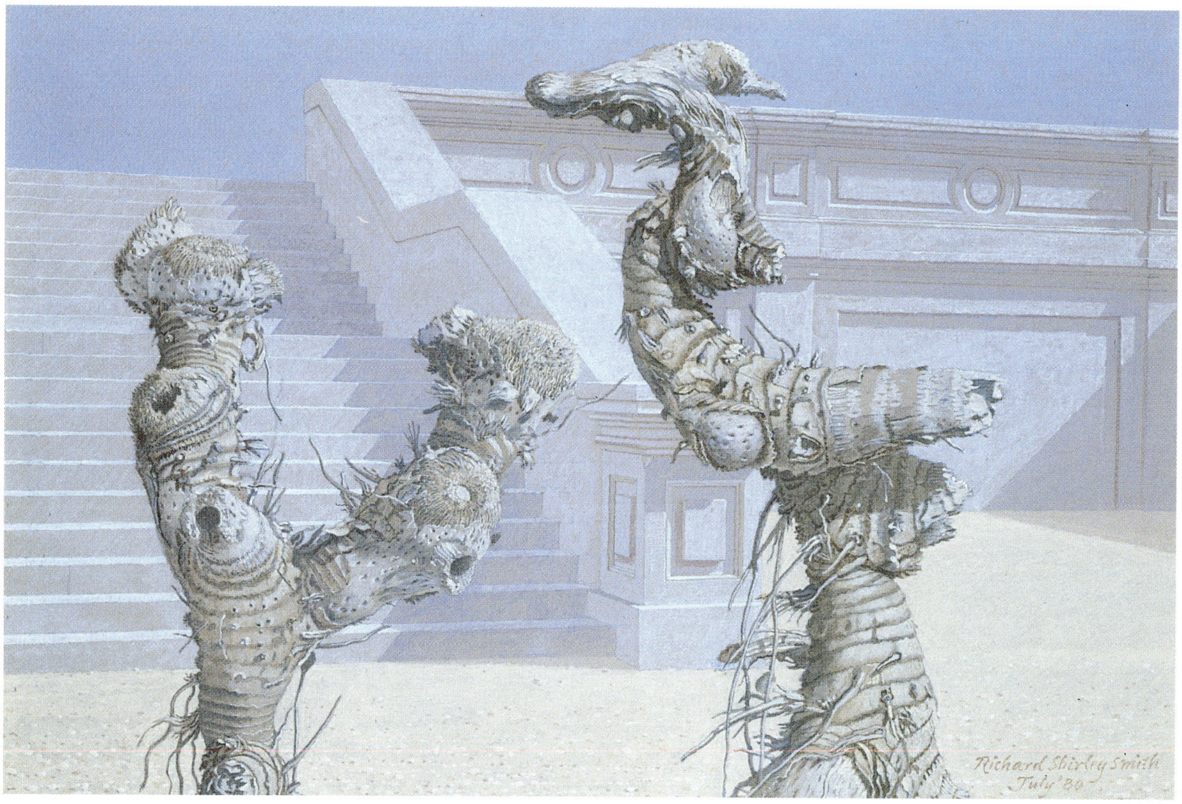
Richard Shirley Smith
July '89

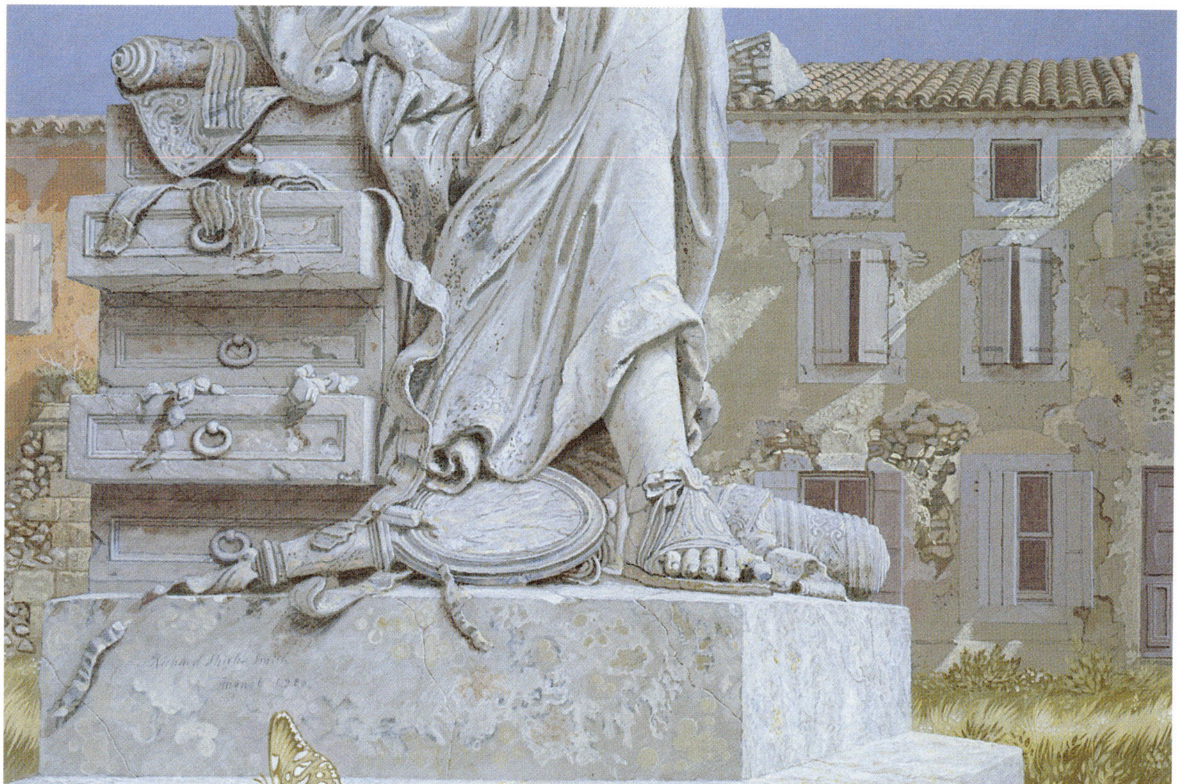

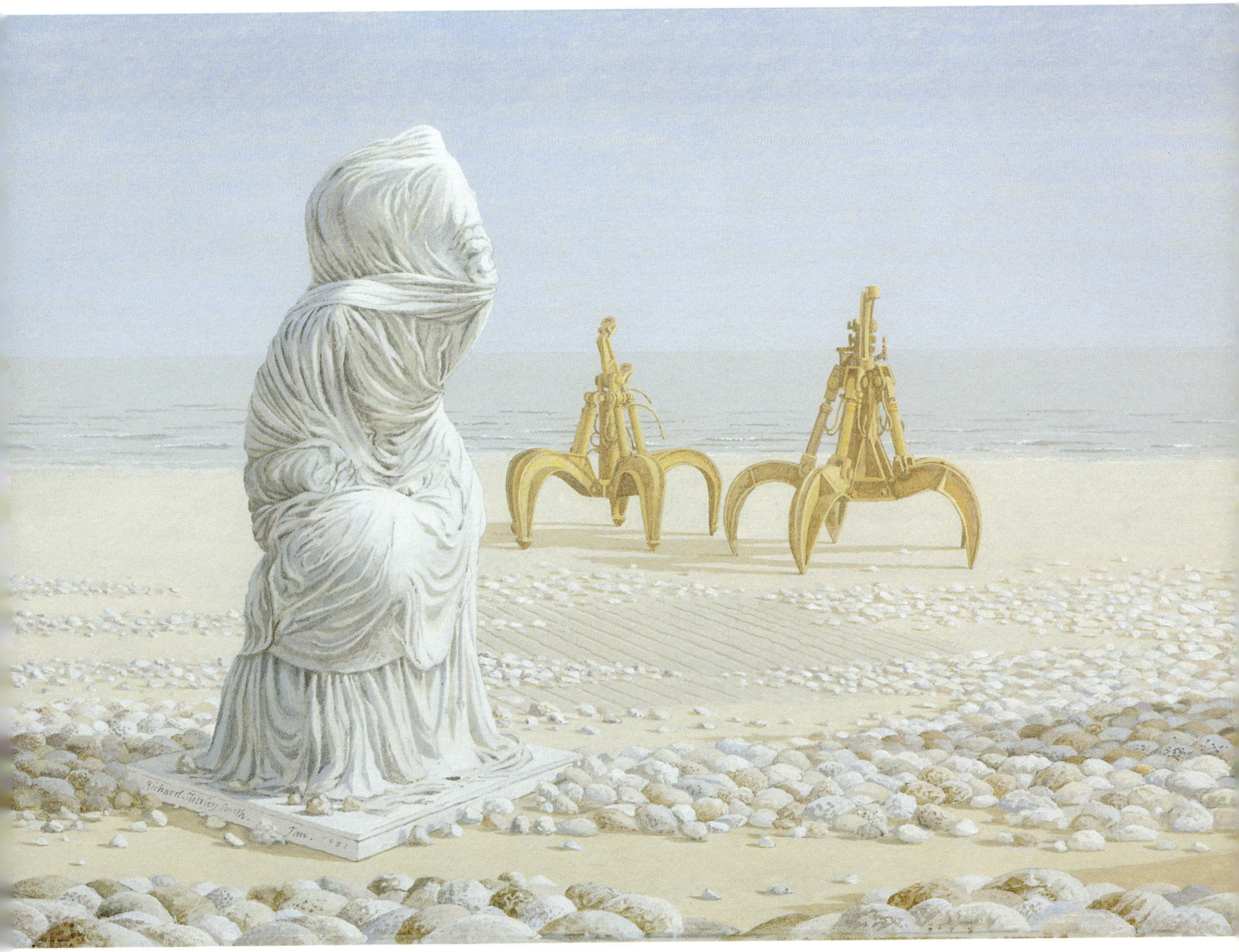

ABOVE: Fig.84 *Grabs II,* acrylic on paper. 1980-1 (*ptg.cat.84*)
While driving along the Belgian coast in the company of Joy Finzi, Michael Mitchell and Leo Wyatt to an engraving exhibition, I observed these crablike grabs on the beach. The subconscious and dreams are, of course, the stock in trade of the Surrealists. The impeded escape is an all too familiar nightmare. Private collection

OPPOSITE ABOVE: Fig.82 *Radical Graduates,* acrylic on paper. 36 × 53cm. 1980 (*ptg.cat.85*)
René Magritte used to provide his paintings with most improbable titles. *Gradus* and *Radix* are the Latin words for 'step' and 'root', so there may be a little method in the madness of my title. Is there some Max Ernst inspiration in these vegetable monsters? Private collection

OPPOSITE BELOW: Fig.83 *Vanity,* acrylic on paper. 36 × 51cm. 1980 (*ptg.cat.86*)
Here we have some symbols of vanity: ribbons, hand-mirror and butterfly. An open chest of drawers carved out of solid stone brings Magritte to my mind. The sculpture was observed at Versailles. Collection of Mike & Genna Eilers

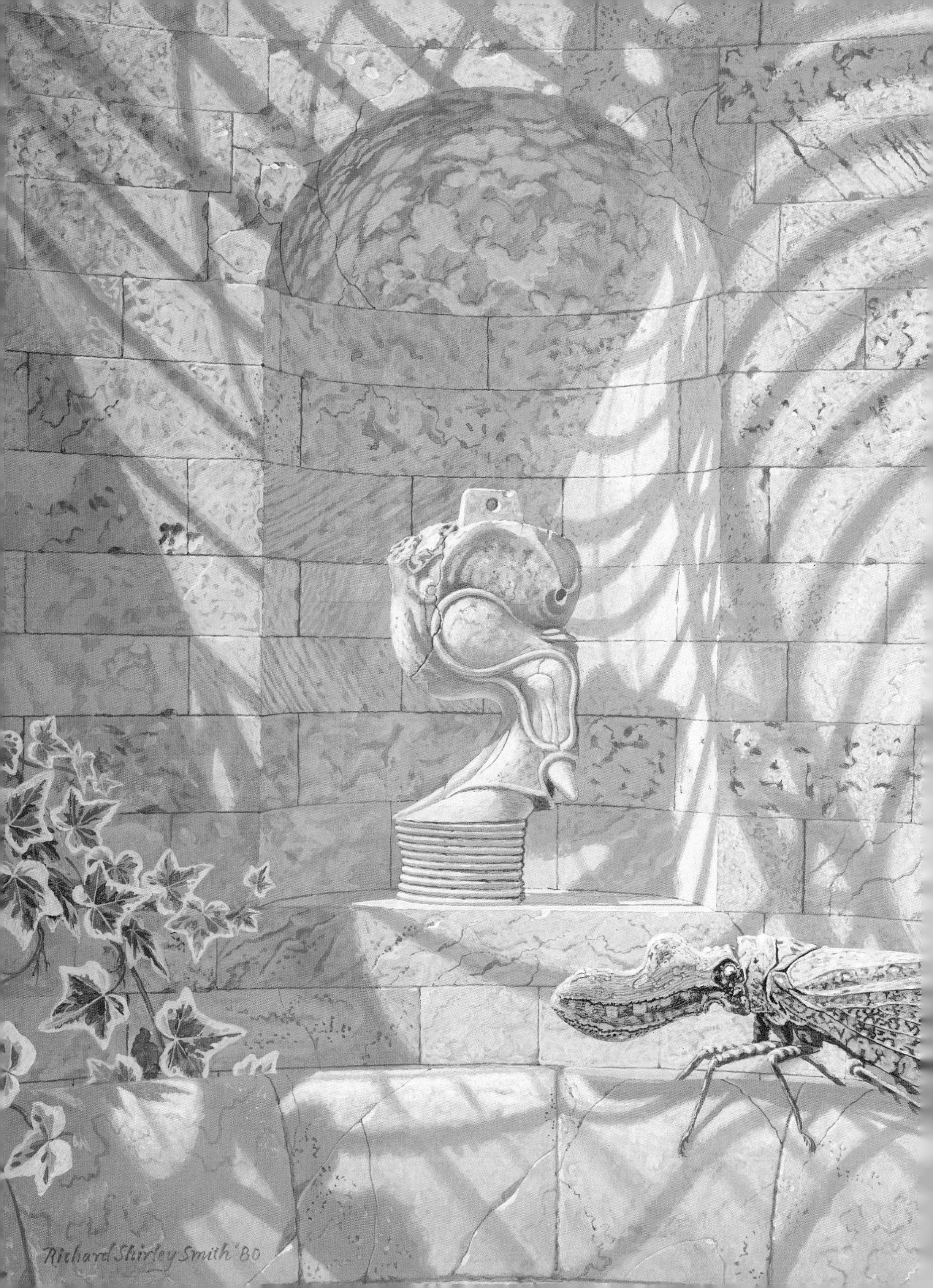
Richard Shirley Smith '80

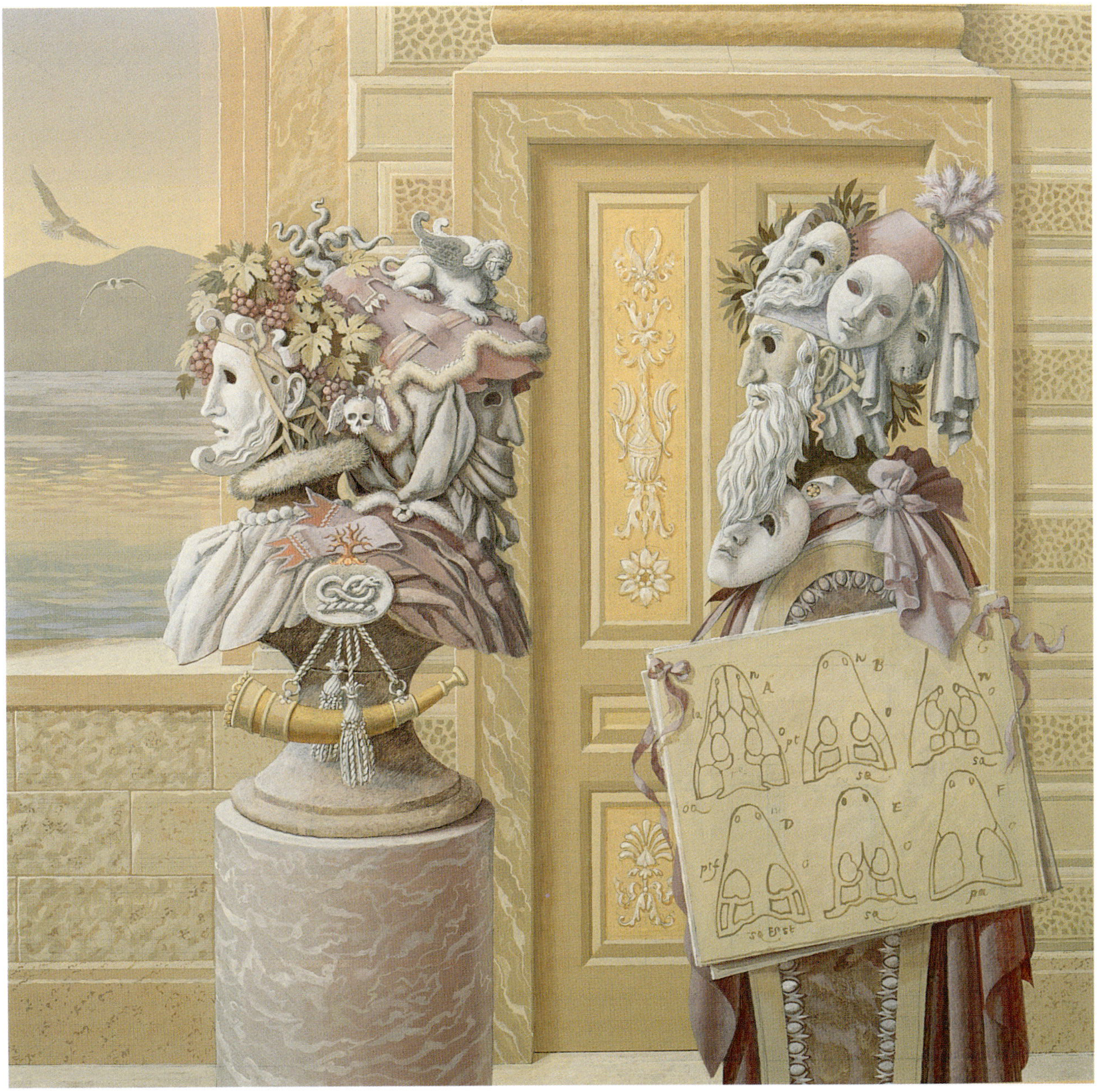

ABOVE: Fig.86 *Masked Figures, Hommage à René Boyvin (detail)*, acrylic on paper. 67 × 55cm. 1992 (*ptg.cat.204*) These are painted variations upon much admired engravings of masked heads. The placard seems to illustrate various types of reptile skulls, and the background started life as a cartoon for a dining-room mural in Eaton Square. Wyliman Collection

OPPOSITE: Fig.85 *Crocodile Cicada (detail)*, acrylic on paper. 53 × 38cm. 1980 (*ptg.cat.89*). The crocodile cicada is a genuine insect, and the central object is an Egyptian chair-leg. The shadows were studied in a conservatory at Alton Towers. Collection of Alan J. Tyldesley

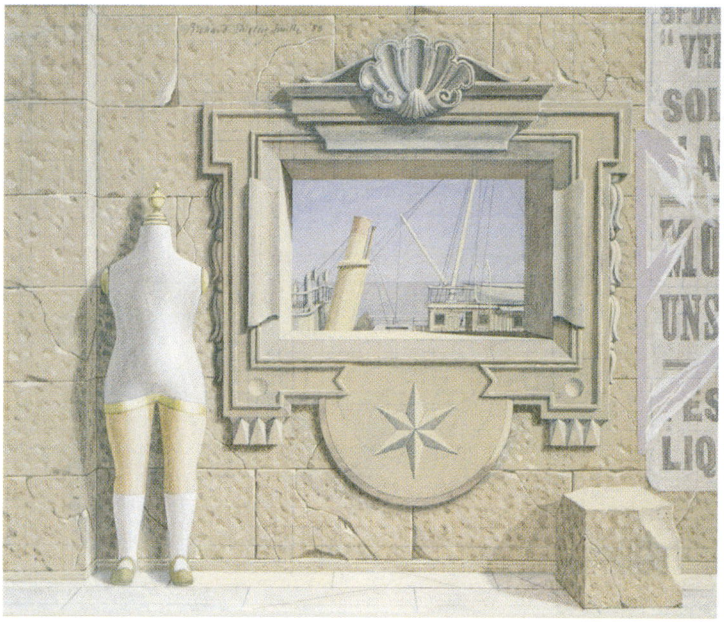

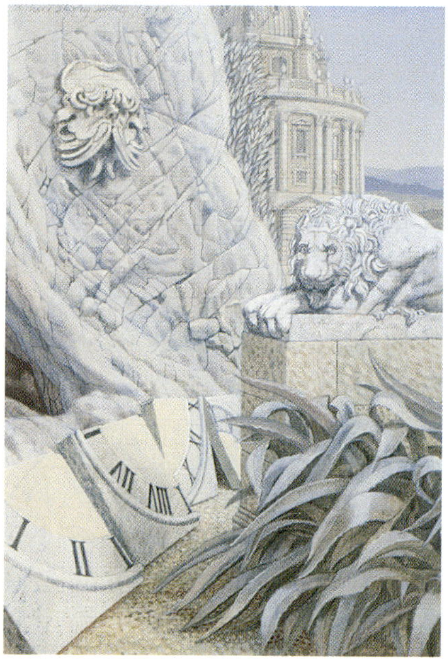

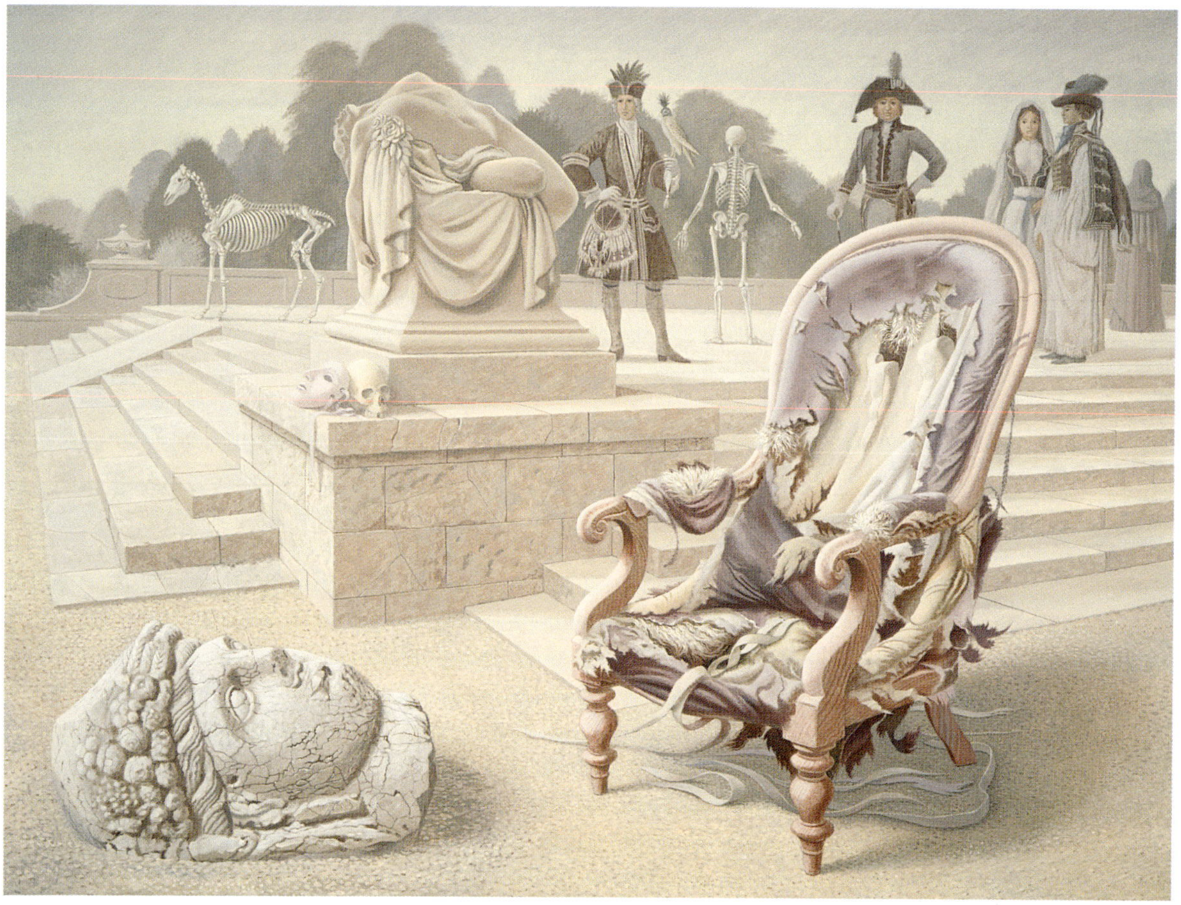

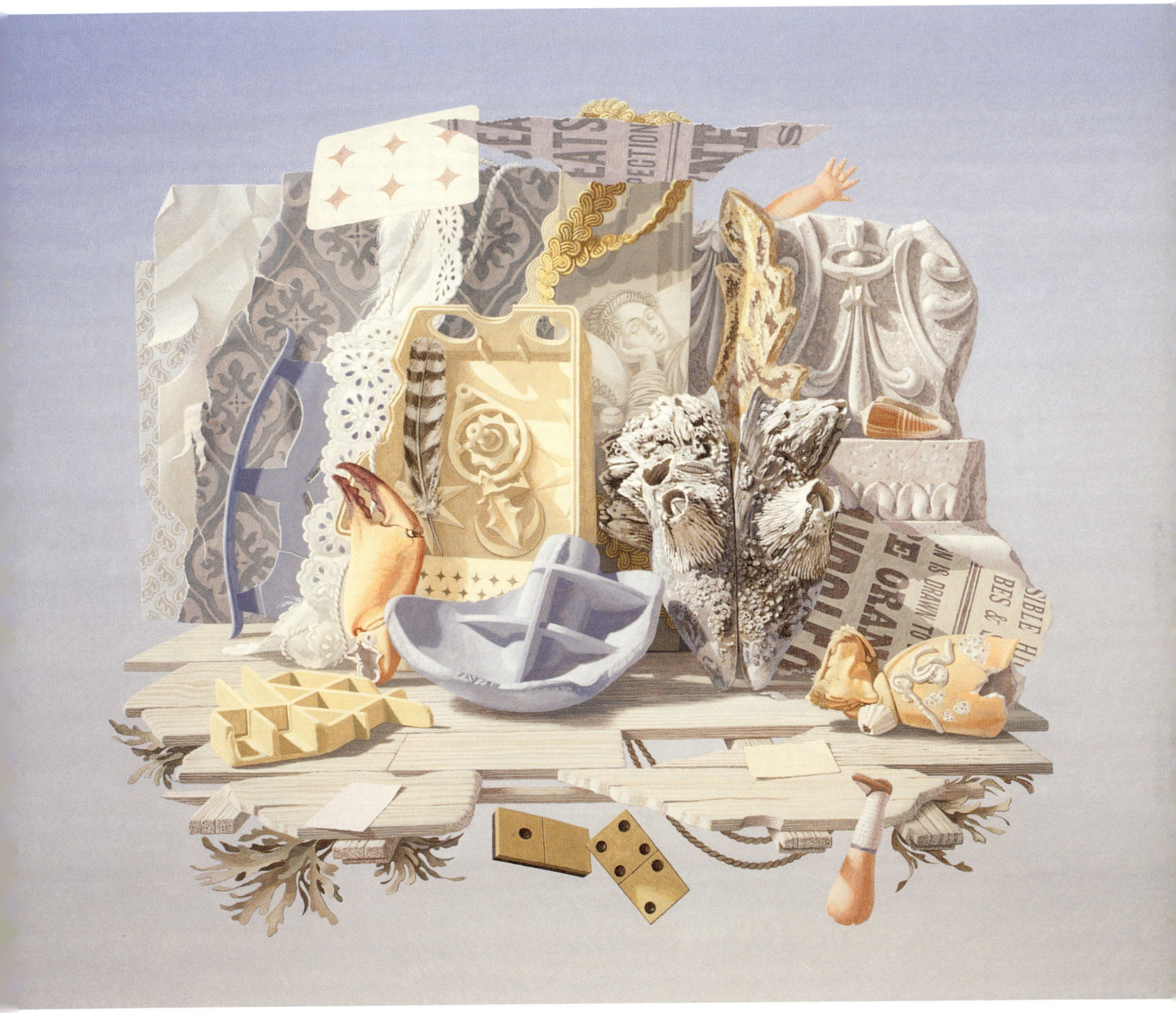

ABOVE: Fig.90 *Sea Change*, acrylic on board. 99 × 121cm. 1998 (*ptg.cat.263*). In the end, the painting seems to suggest that, while material things appear so solid, we are only one silly accident away from extinction and nothingness. Collection of the artist

OPPOSITE TOP LEFT: Fig.87 *Marine Window*, acrylic on paper. 33 × 40cm. 1988 (*ptg.cat.168*). Collection of Alan J. Tyldesley

OPPOSITE TOP RIGHT: Fig.88 *Fragmented Time*, acrylic on paper. 38 × 28cm. 1988 (*ptg.cat.169*). A friend sent me a photo of these sections of a clock face, which he saw on holiday and thought must have escaped from one of my paintings! Collection of Charles Empson

OPPOSITE BELOW: Fig.89 *Ancien Régime*, acrylic on canvas. 99 × 135cm. 1995 (*ptg.cat.228*). There is no story. Collection of the artist

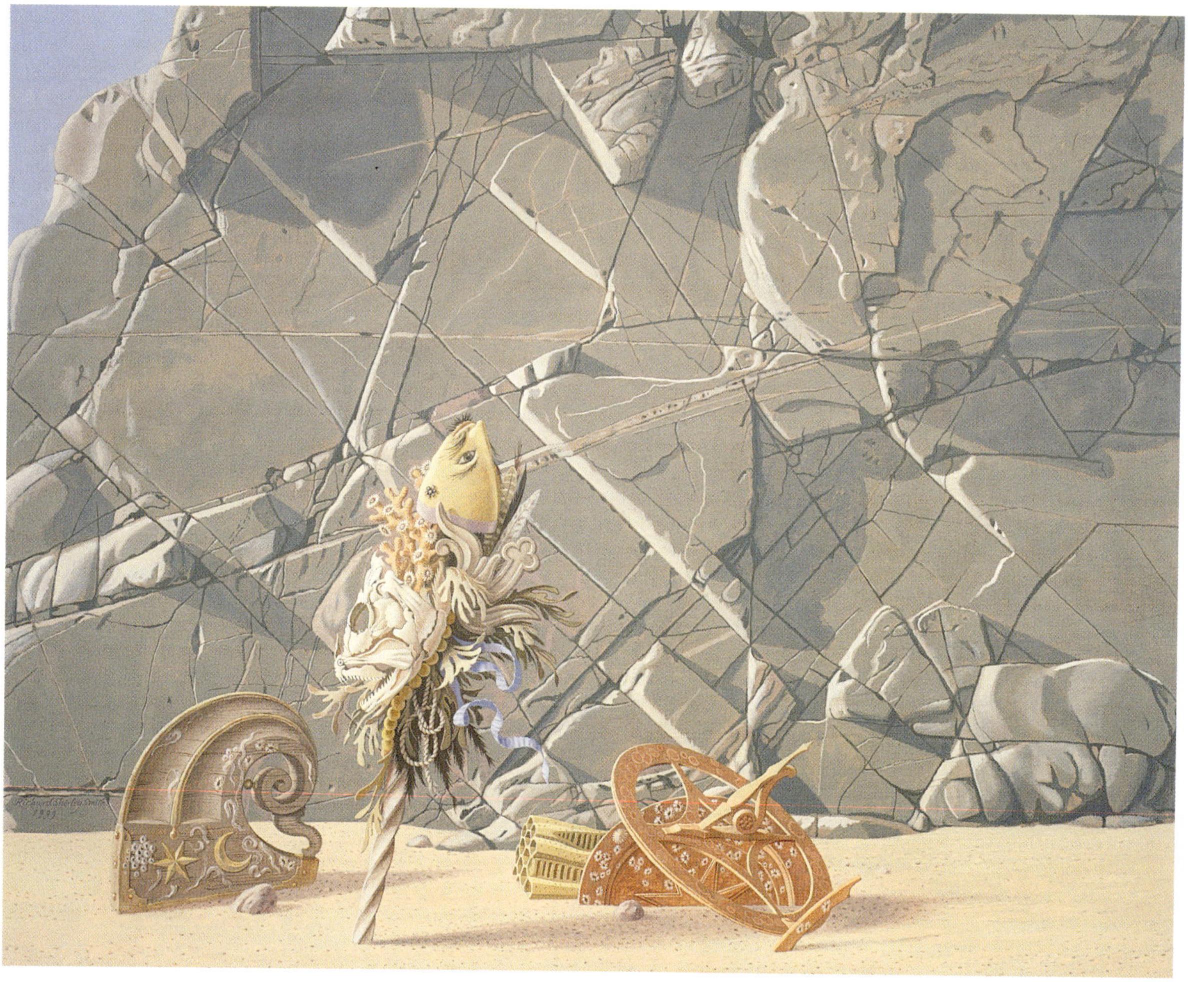

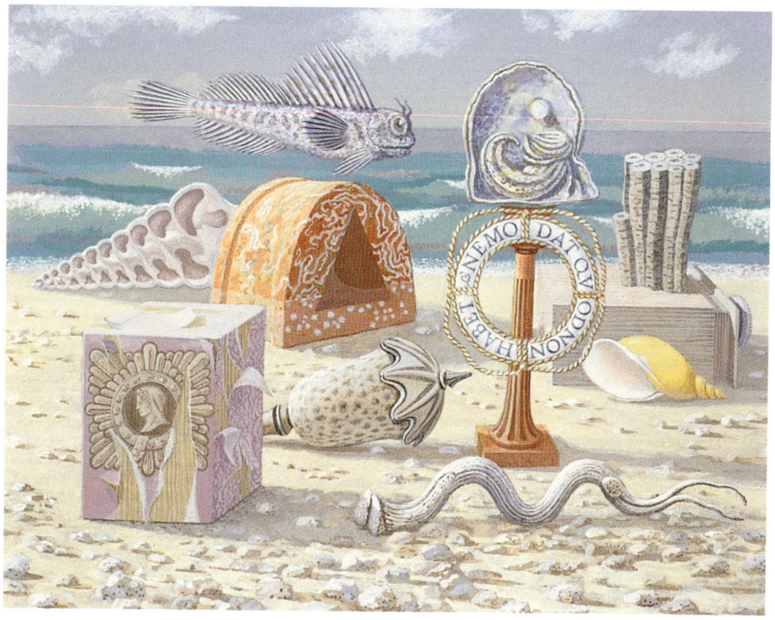

ABOVE: Fig.91 *Rock Face,* acrylic on canvas. 97 × 121cm. 1999 (*ptg.cat.280*). The rock formation was observed in Pembrokeshire. Collection of the artist

OPPOSITE: Fig.93 *Rock Face* (*detail*)

BELOW: Fig.92 *Victorian Beach*, acrylic on paper. 25 × 31cm. 1976 (*ptg.cat.58*). This design started as a montage of Victorian engravings. The latin inscription, 'No one gives what they haven't got', is very true, especially when applied to artists and art. Collection of Janet Boulton

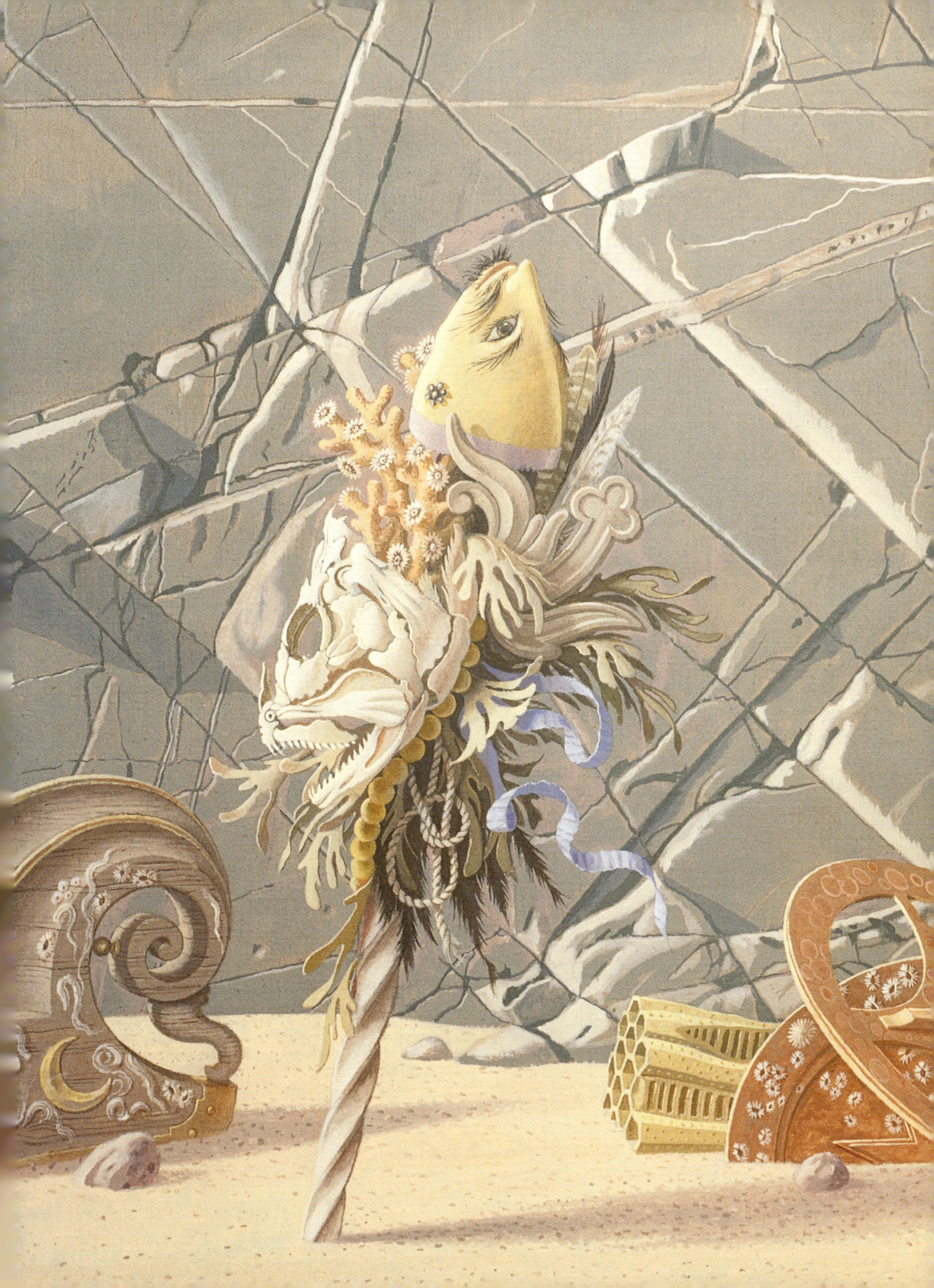

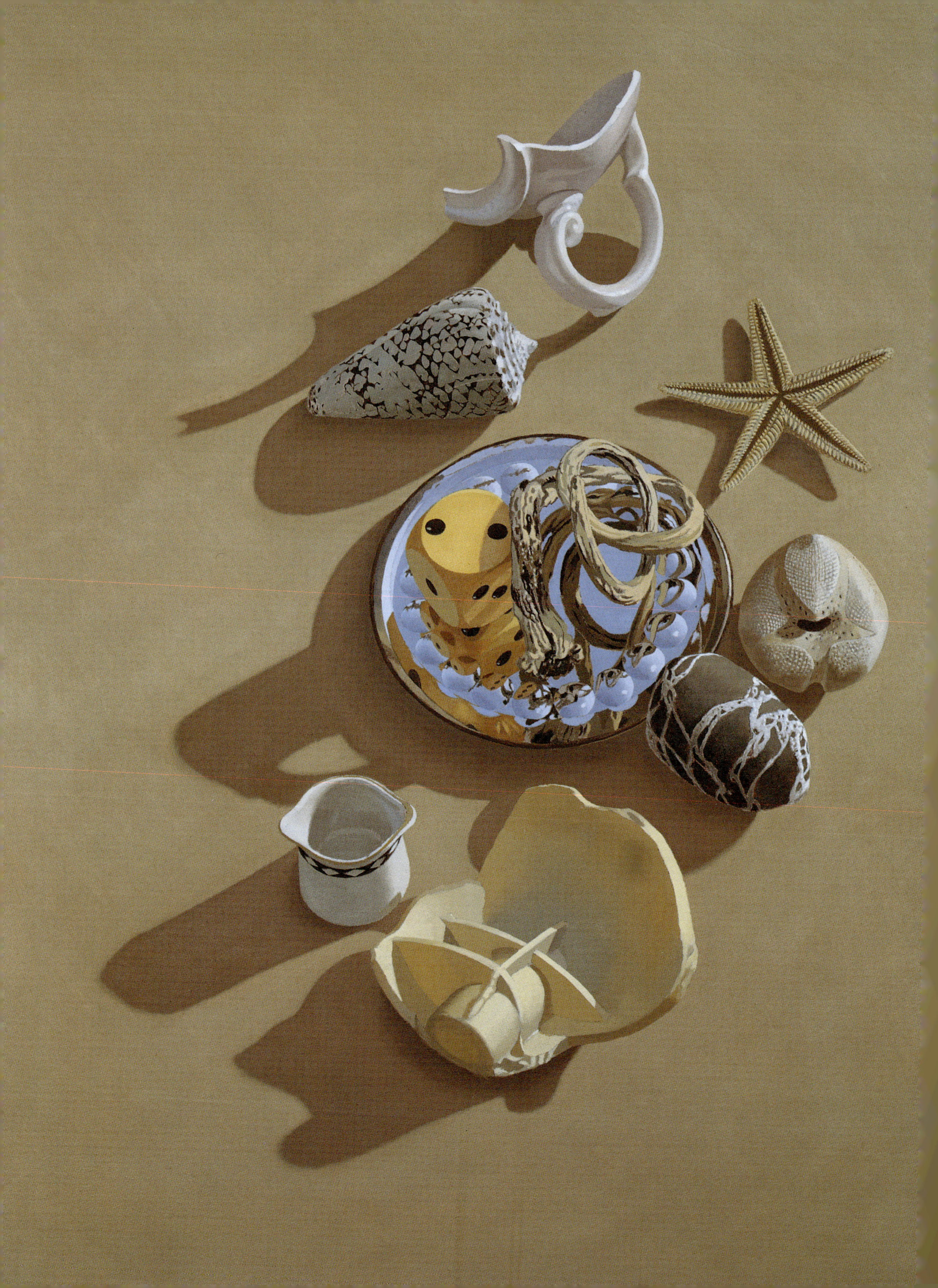

FIVE

Objects on the Sand

If a neglected object of this kind were forcibly isolated that is divested of its environment or even ironically combined with completely unrelated things, it would reassert its dignity in the new context and stand there, incomprehensible, weird, mysterious.

MASSIMO CARRA

The tide coming in will remove to another location or hide forever this chance coming together of these things in this place. But of course this is all illusion and so the artist may do the sea's work to make objects reappear in another controlled reality elsewhere.

BRIAN DUNCE

THE SEA ABRADES AND erodes shells, bones and branches down to their basic structures. These simple but subtle results have a beauty that inspired Henry Moore's sculpture. The tide presents us with all these items bleached and washed on the smooth yellow sand upon which the sun throws shadows telling us yet more about their forms.

Beach-combing is a good source of the puzzling '*jamais vu*' or 'found object' beloved of the Surrealists. In the background of the painting *Angels & Skull* (Fig.97), there is a clump of bits of wood and canvas bolted and wired together of which the original purpose is far from clear.

Then there are the strange metamorphoses that happen under the sea: large shells festooned with sea weed, embroidered with small white star-shaped shells, and inhabited, maybe, by an asymmetrical hermit crab. Shakespeare has the last word on this subject:

Full fathom five thy father lies;
Of his bones are coral made:
Those are pearls that were his eyes:
Nothing of him that doth fade,
But doth suffer a sea change
Into something rich and strange.

OPPOSITE: Fig.94 *Objects on Sand*, oil on canvas. 91 × 71cm. 1979 (*ptg.cat.73*). Collection of Mr & Mrs M. W. Elliott

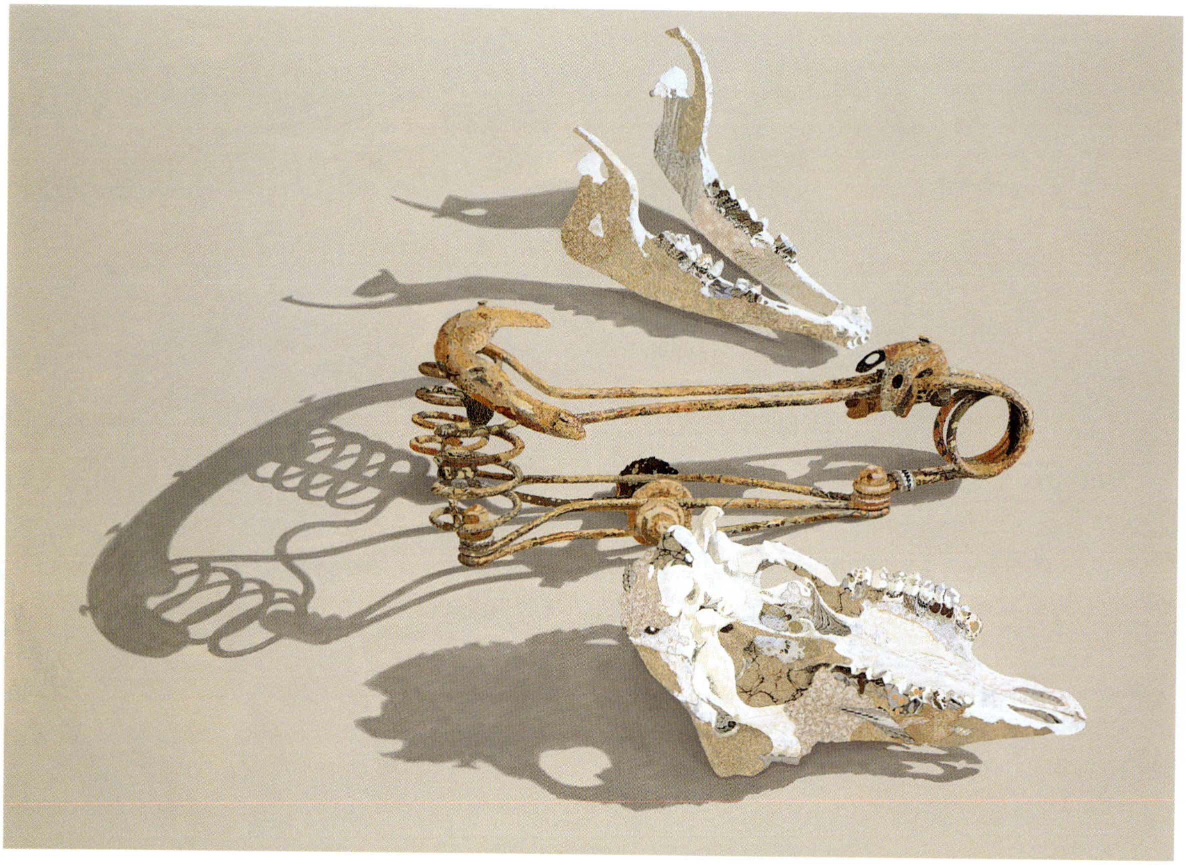

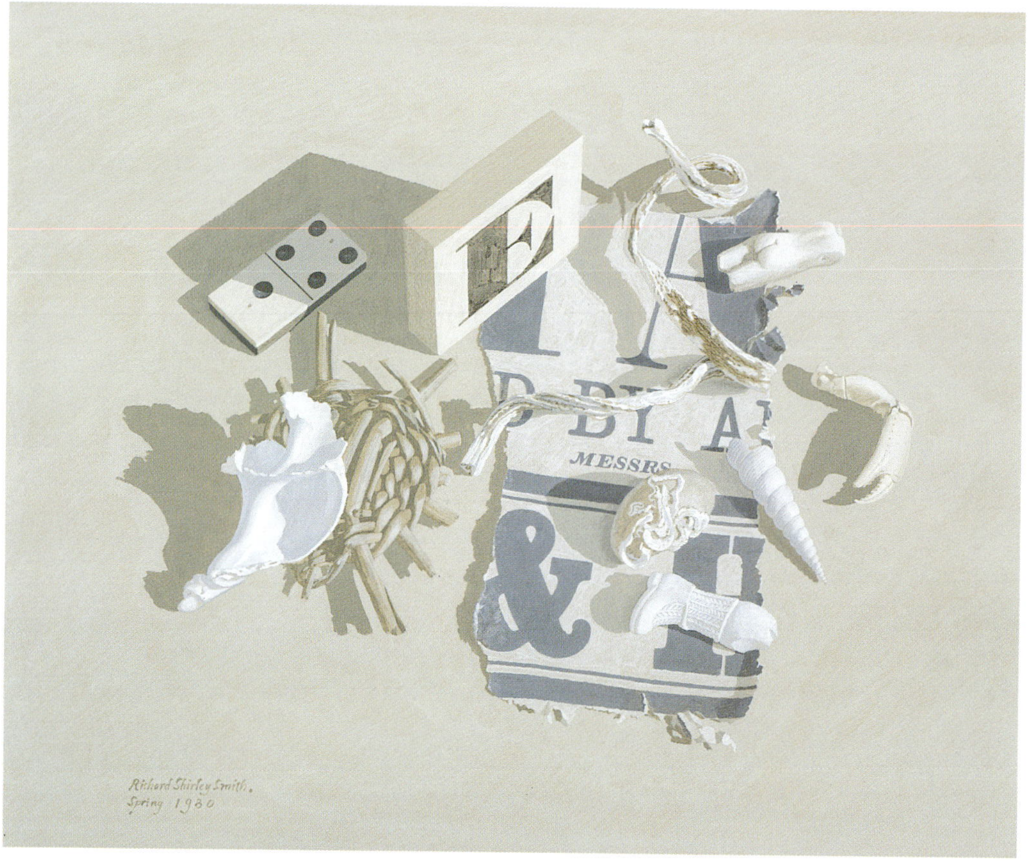

D BY A
MESSRS
&
Richard Shirley Smith.
Spring 1980

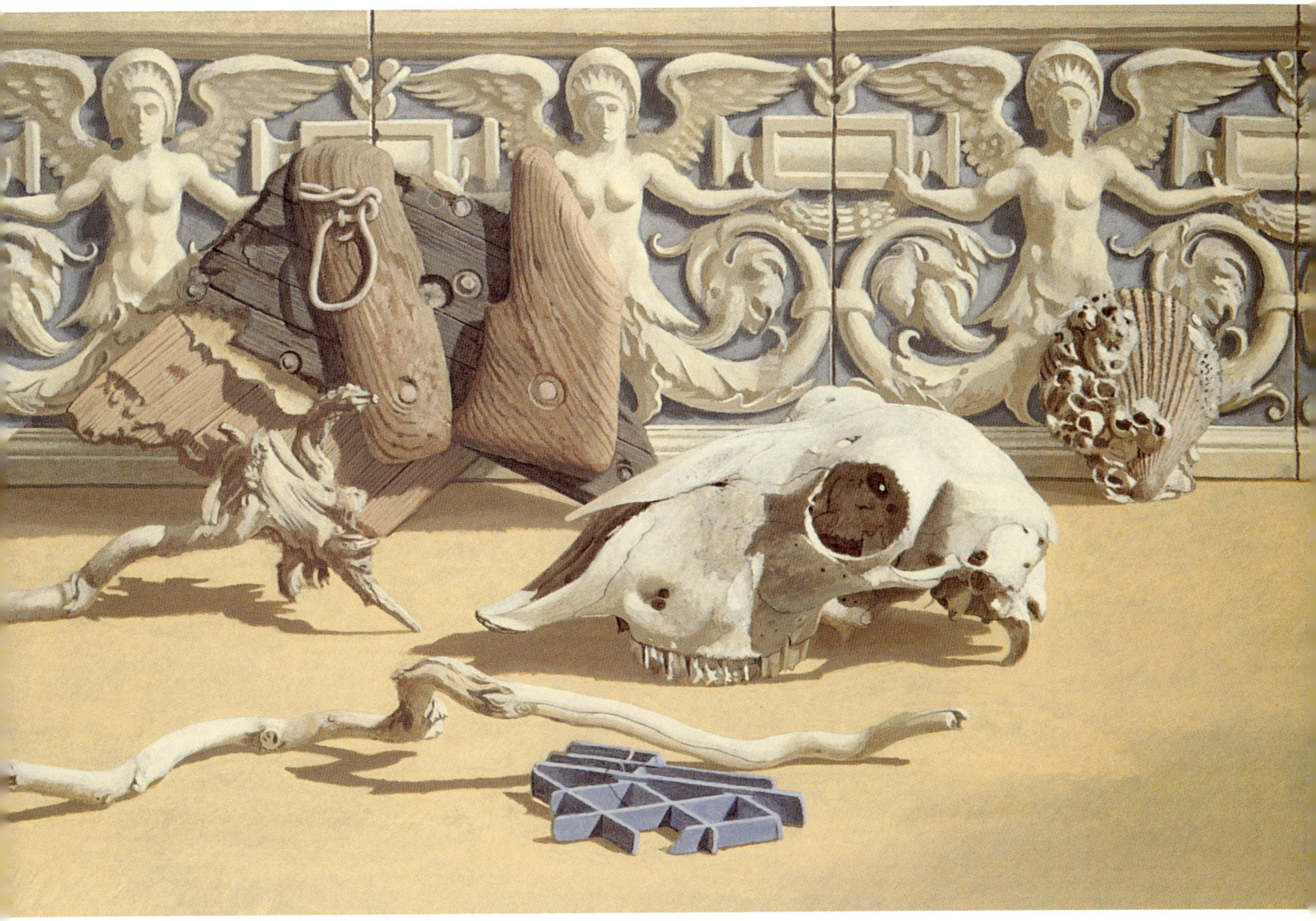

ABOVE: Fig.97 *Angels & Skull*, acrylic on board, *approx*. 36 × 48cm. 1995 (*ptg.cat.221*). Private collection

OPPOSITE ABOVE: Fig.95 *Skull & Saddle,* collage and acrylic. 71 × 102cm. 1976 (*ptg.cat.63*)
This must be one of the very last pictures of this period to have any use of collage. Is there a vague reference to Picasso's saddle and handle-bar assemblage (*Bull's Head,* bronze, 1943)? Collection of Richard & Frances Latcham

OPPOSITE BELOW: Fig.96 *Ampersand,* acrylic on paper. 51 × 62cm. 1980 (*ptg.cat.94*)
This painting could be said to be a duochrome: black, white and raw umber only. With objects being broken, moveable and throwing telling shadows, the artist has no excuse for not making a satisfactory composition. I have always loved these Victorian advertising typefaces such as Consort and Fat Face as here. Collection of Michael & Caroline Mitchell

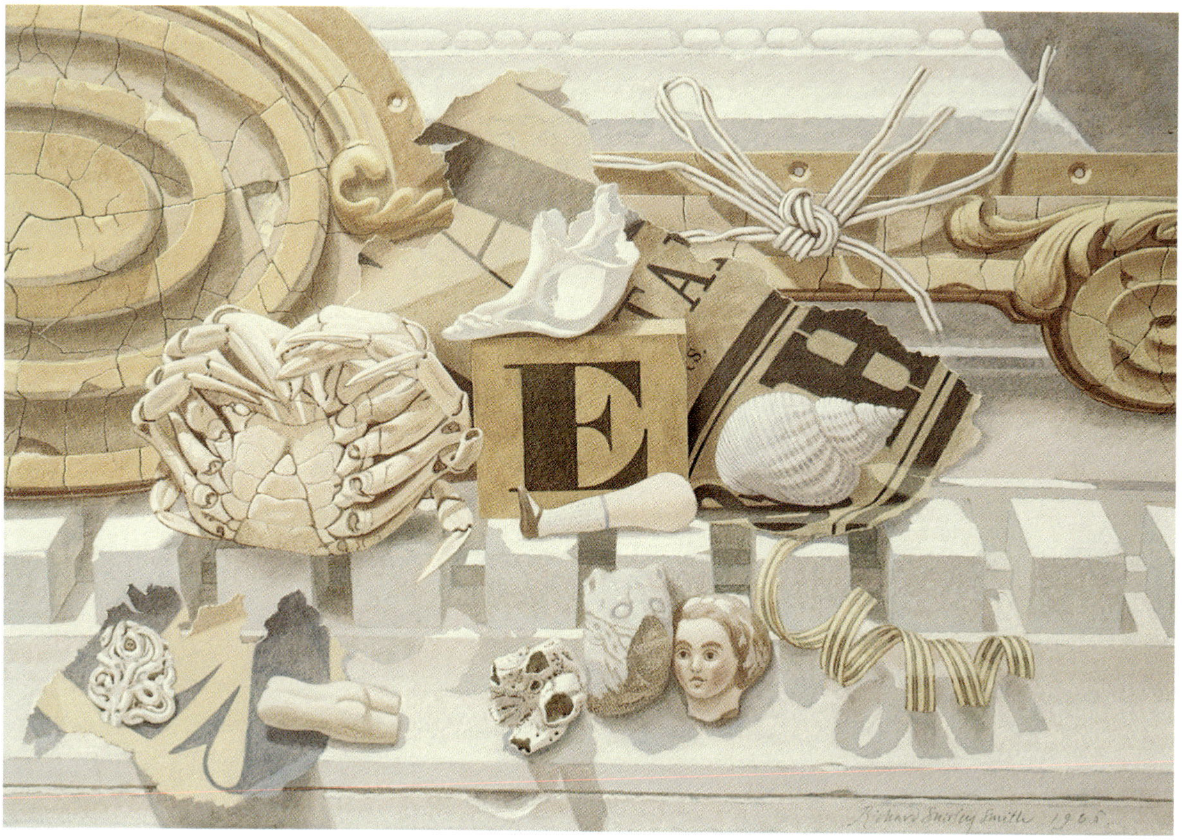
E
Richard Shirley Smith 1965.

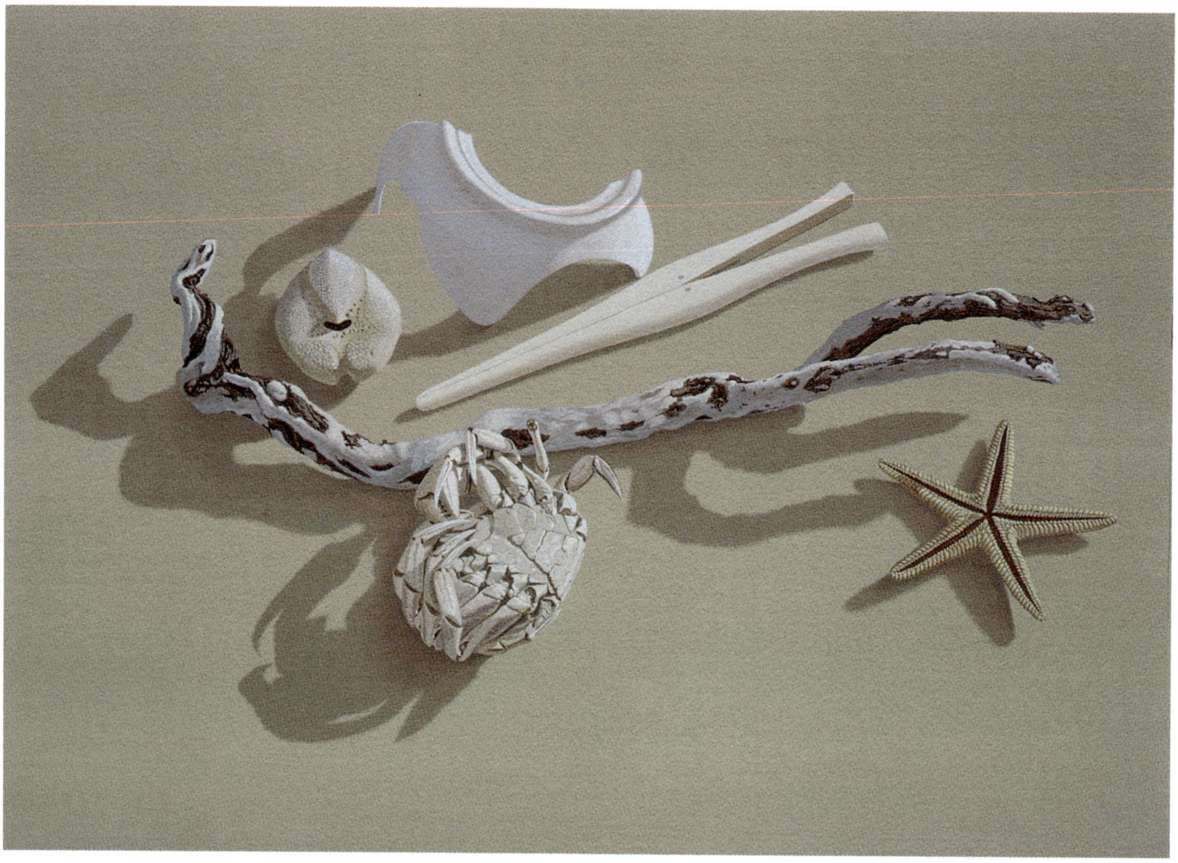

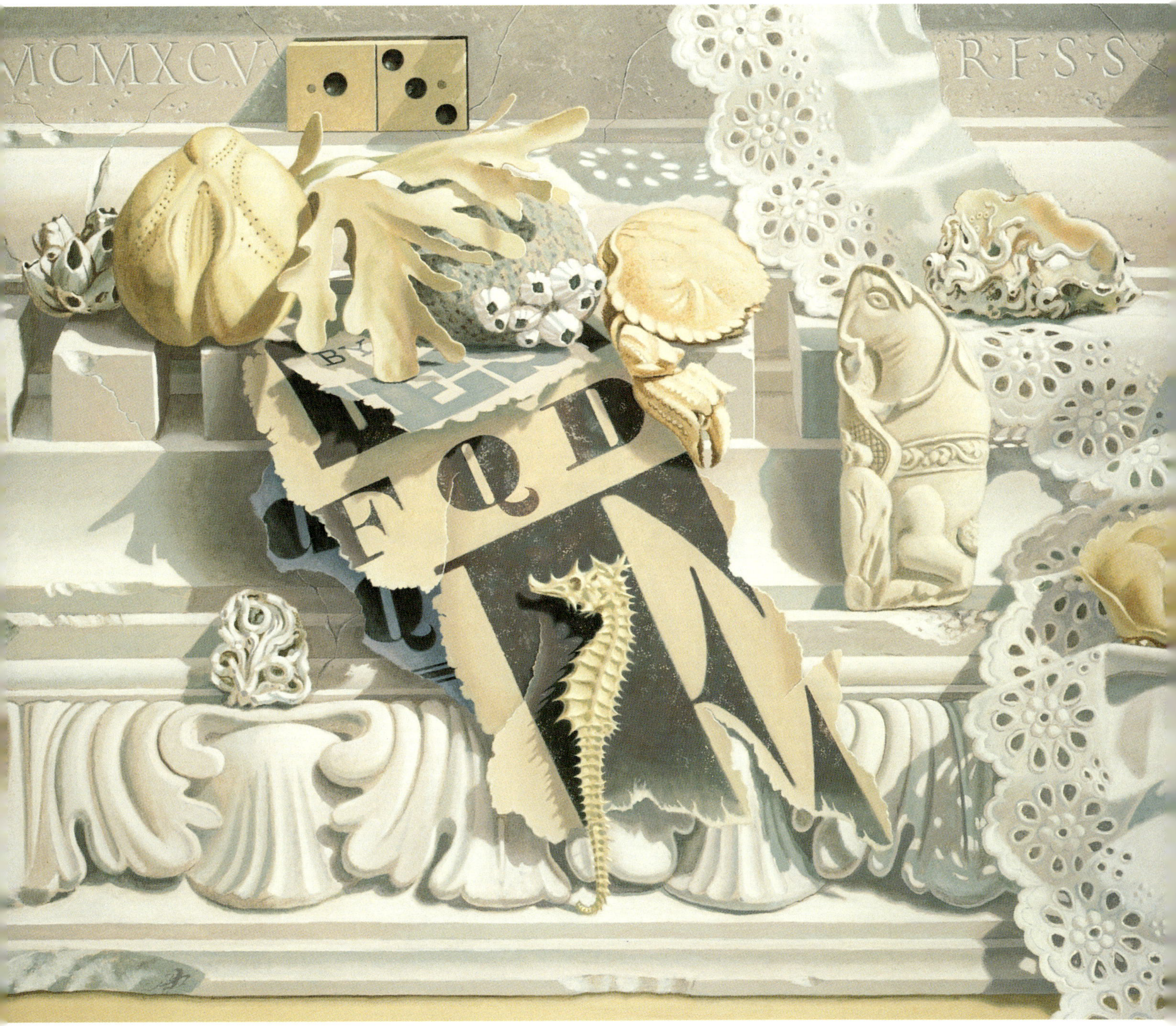

ABOVE: Fig.100 *Sea Horse & Domino*, acrylic on canvas. 96 × 121cm. finished 1995 (*ptg.cat.230*). While working on murals, I used to rescue, from skips, offcuts of elaborate cornices, which took the light well in still lifes. Collection of the artist

OPPOSITE ABOVE: Fig.98 *Crab & Volute*, acrylic on paper. 50 × 72cm. 1985-6 (*ptg.cat.148*). Private collection

OPPOSITE BELOW: Fig.99 *Glove Stretcher*, acrylic on paper. 46 × 71cm. 1980 (*ptg.cat.76*). Private collection

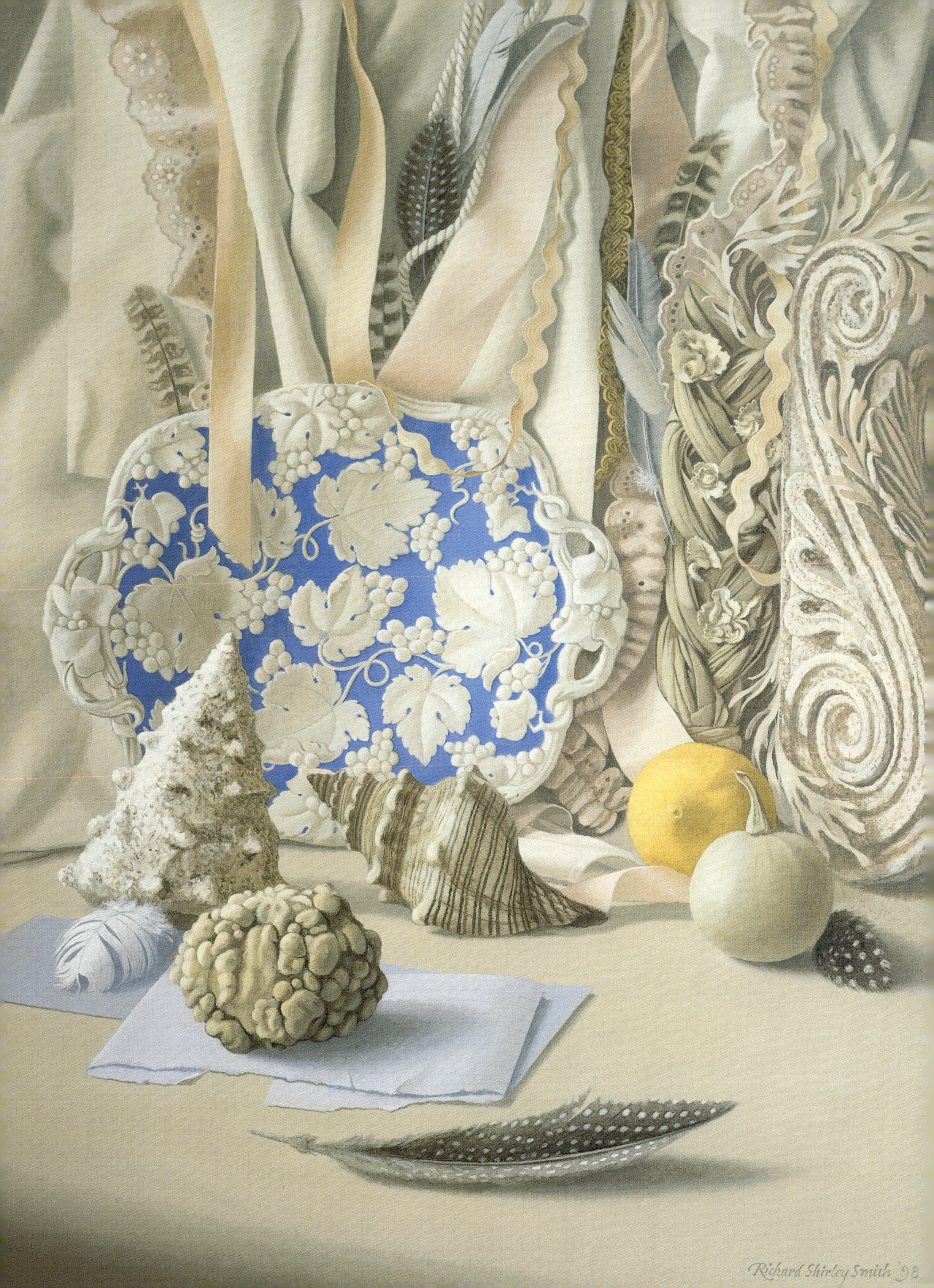
Richard Shirley Smith '98

SIX

Domestic Still Life

But we who know the signs of the Metaphysical Alphabet are aware of the joy and the solitude enclosed by a portico, the corner of a street or even in a room on the surface of a table, between the sides of a box.

GIORGIO DE CHIRICO

I lived in quiet screened unknown
Pondering upon some stick or stone
Or news of some rare book or bird
Latterly bought or seen or heard.

THOMAS HARDY

STILL LIFE HAS SELDOM been thought of as the most exciting and prestigious of the genres of painting but has certainly had its moments, as in seventeenth-century Holland and Spain and the liberating Cubist experiments of the early twentieth century. I have greatly admired the still-life specialists Chardin and Giorgio Morandi, who seem to have a great dignity that derives from their not attempting to do too much, but doing it beautifully. A portrait or landscape painter might complain that a sitter's features or the trees in a park might not be very well arranged, but the still-life artist has total control over his composition, selection, arrangement and lighting, and can even move things around as work progresses.

I very much enjoy the 'artefacts' in my still lifes (as distinct from natural creatures) for this reason. The artist essentially *makes* things in order that they then *convey* ideas to the mind, and I think I am therefore 'tuned in' to the enormous amount that all artefacts have to tell us about the technique, taste and sensibility of their makers, and the historical, geographical and stylistic circumstances of their manufacture. Things that are made *by* people who don't use their eyes *for* people who don't use their eyes quickly reach my dustbin. William Morris advised: 'Have nothing in your house that you do not know to be useful or believe to be beautiful'.

OPPOSITE: Fig.101 *Still Life with Blue Vine Plate,* acrylic on canvas. 94 × 71cm. 1998 (*ptg.cat.266*). As soon as I saw the plate, I wanted to describe it in paint, not only for its bright colour but its concavity combined with the relief vine pattern. Collection of Mr & Mrs John Poynton

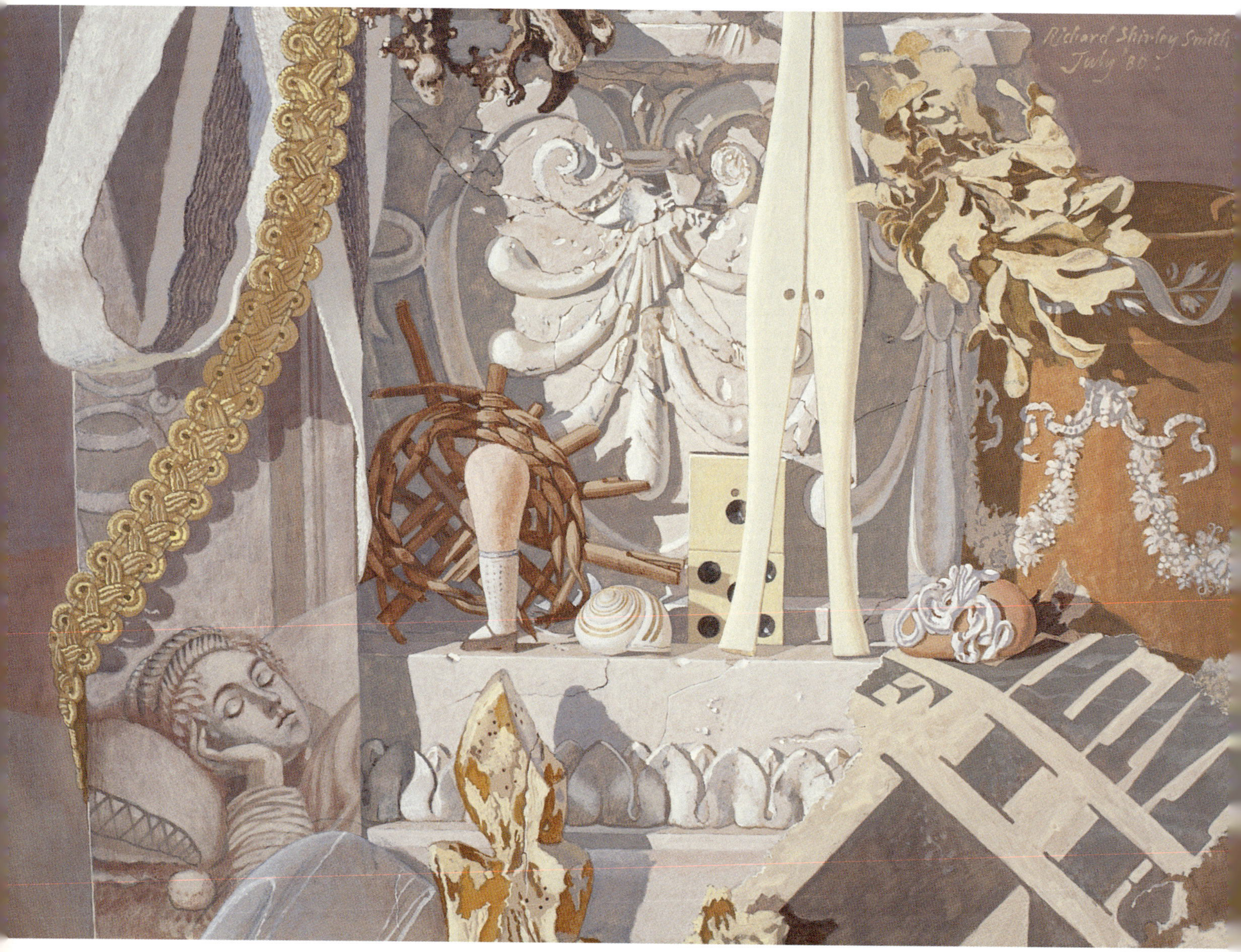

ABOVE: Fig.102 *Dream of St Ursula*, acrylic on paper. 36 × 51cm. 1980 (*ptg.cat.81*).
Collection of Rodney & Cornelia Hayes

OPPOSITE: Fig.103 *French Still Life with Pipe*, acrylic on paper. 36 × 24cm. 1980 (*ptg.cat.79*). This was observed while I was cleaning and repairing some overdoors in a château near Avignon. Collection of Anne Stevens

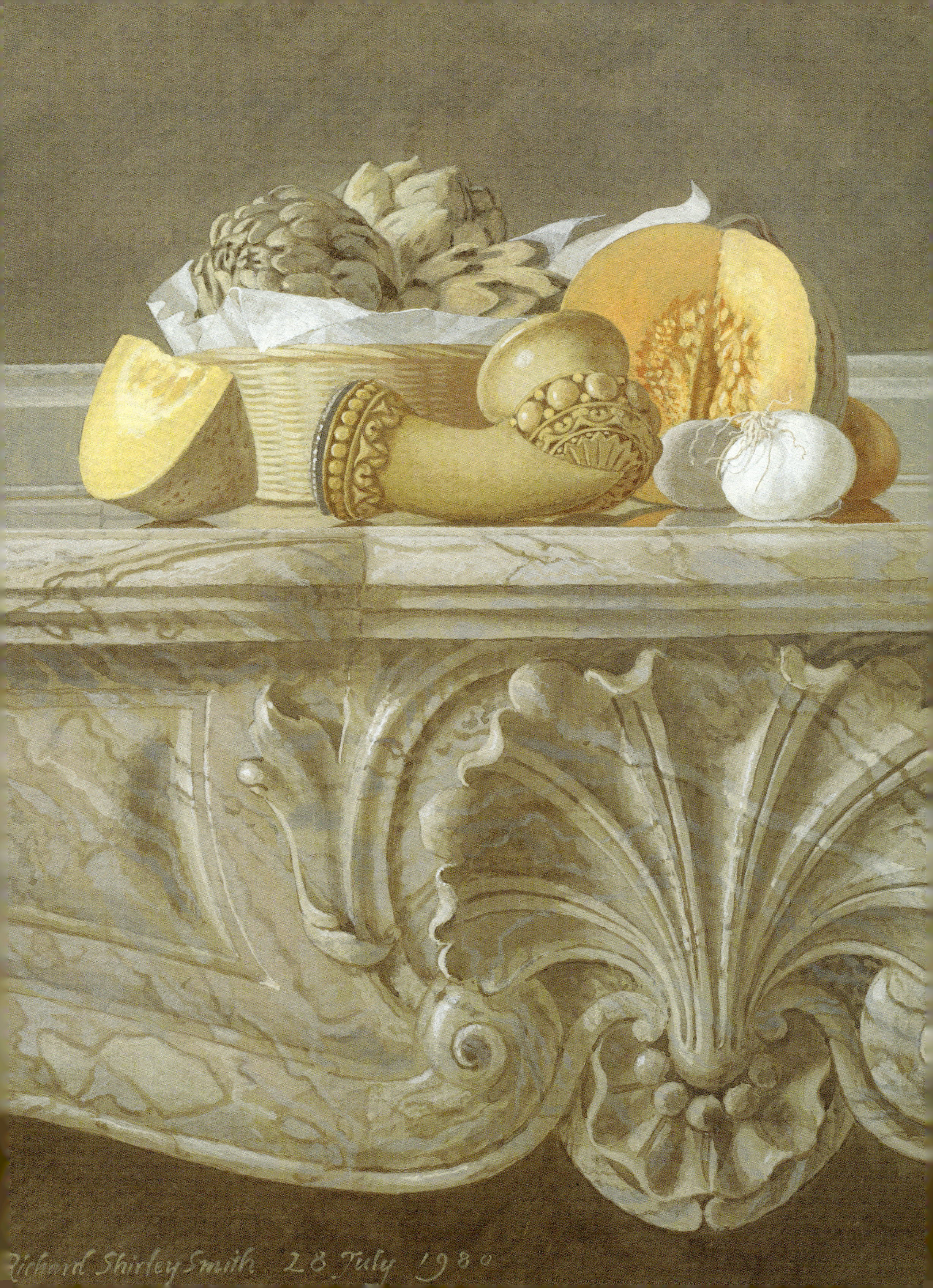
Richard Shirley Smith 28 July 1980

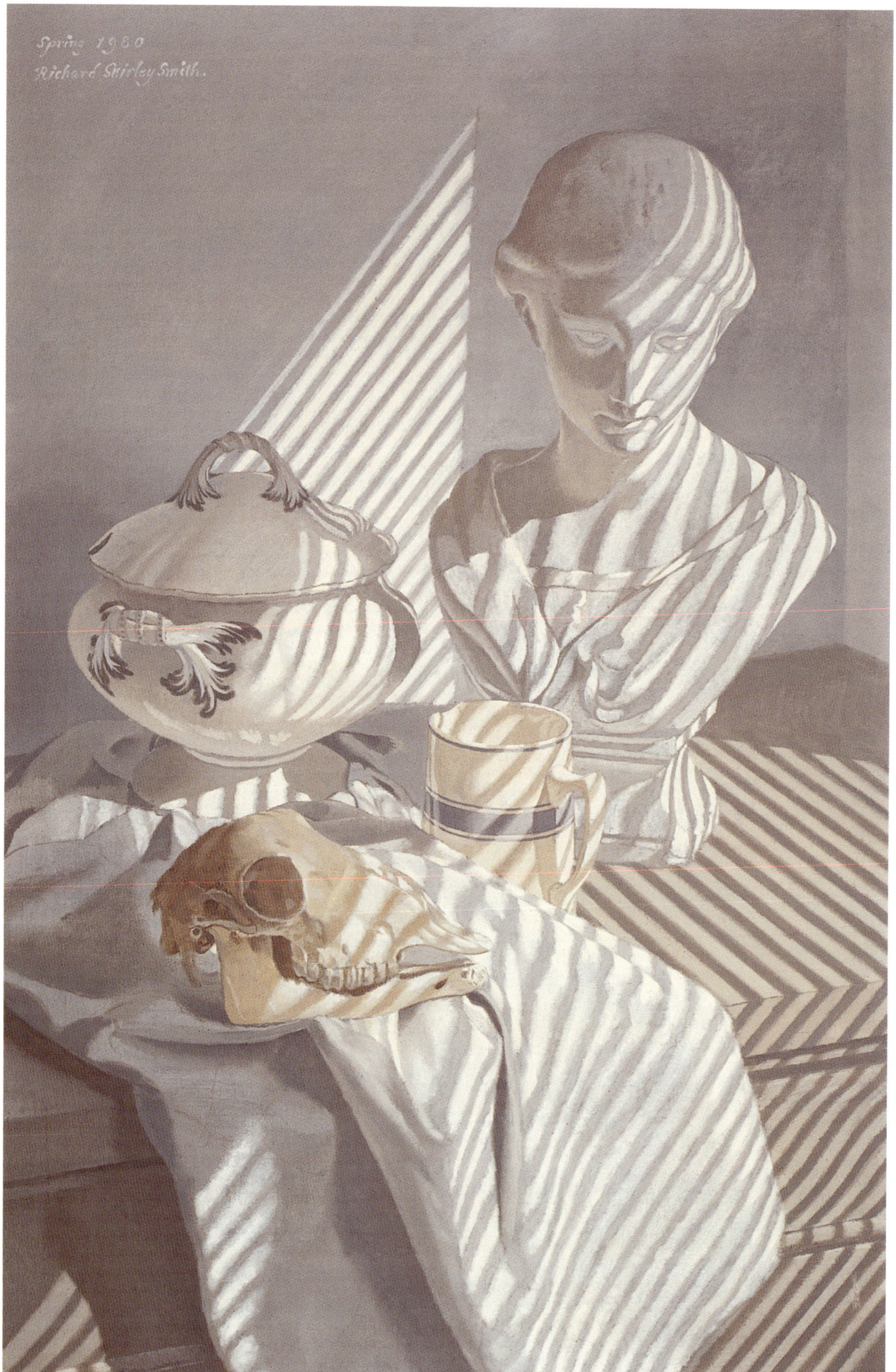
Spring 1980
Richard Shirley Smith.

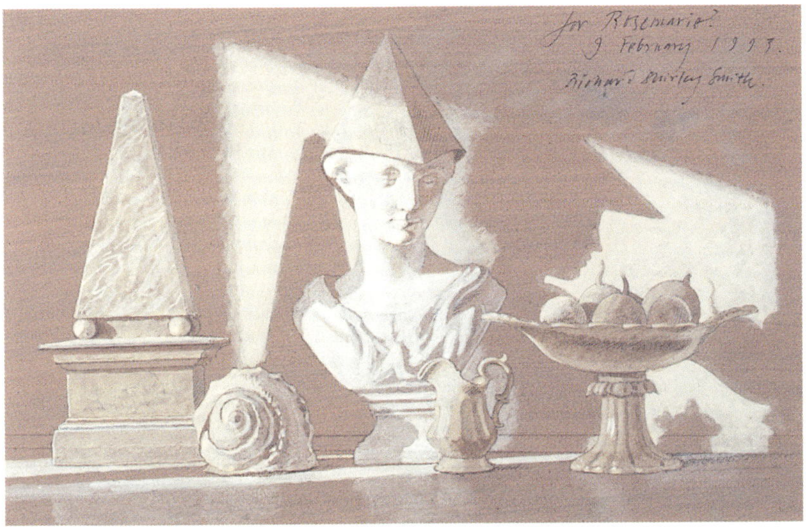

OPPOSITE: Fig.104 *Venetian Blinds & Bust*, oil on canvas. 76 × 51cm. 1980 (*ptg.cat.95*). These three still lifes are painted in white, black and raw umber only. Collection of Paula Boyland

ABOVE: Fig.105 *Paper Hat, Duochrome*, acrylic on paper. 17 × 27cm. 1993 (*ptg.cat.211*). Collection of Rosemarie Timmis

BELOW: Fig.106 *Decanter & Venetian Blinds*, oil on canvas. 71 × 91cm. 1980 (*ptg.cat.93*). Private collection

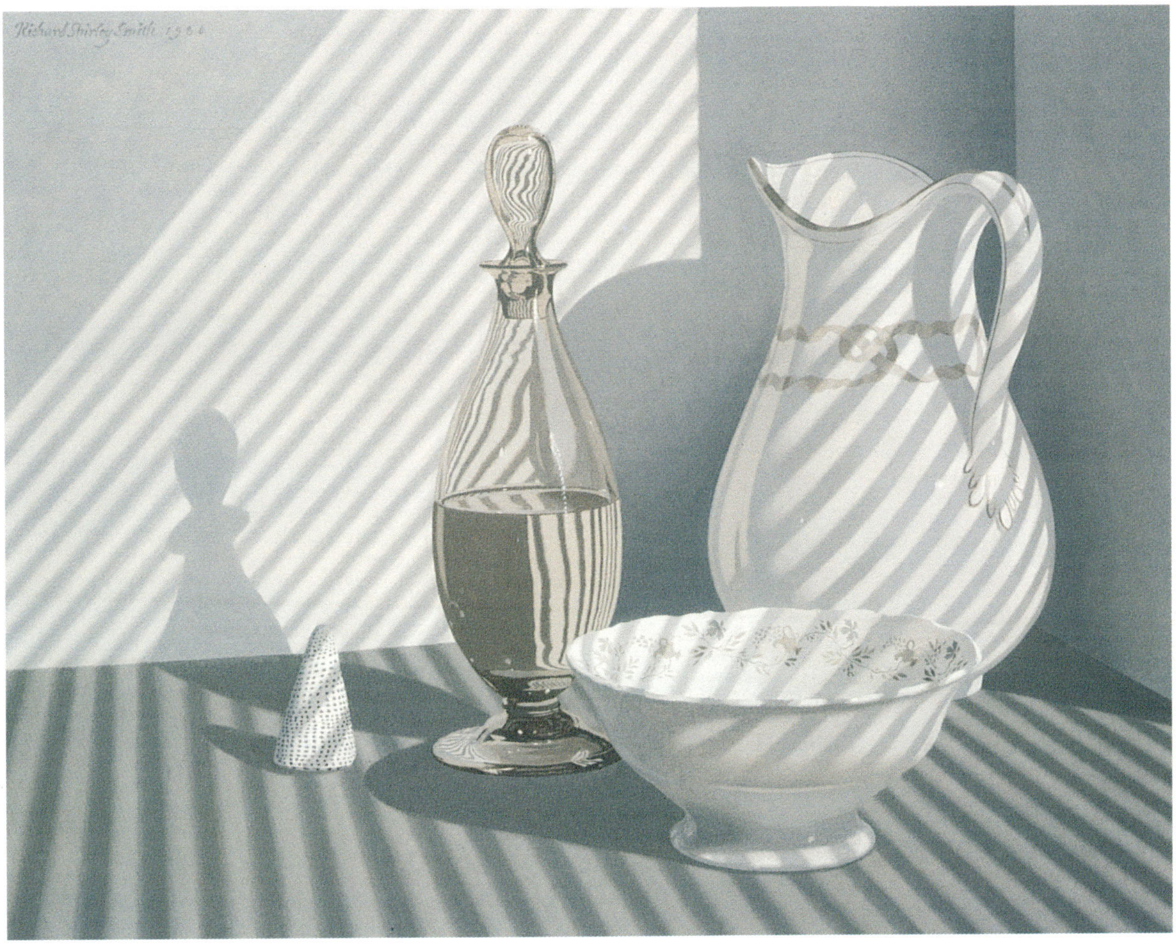

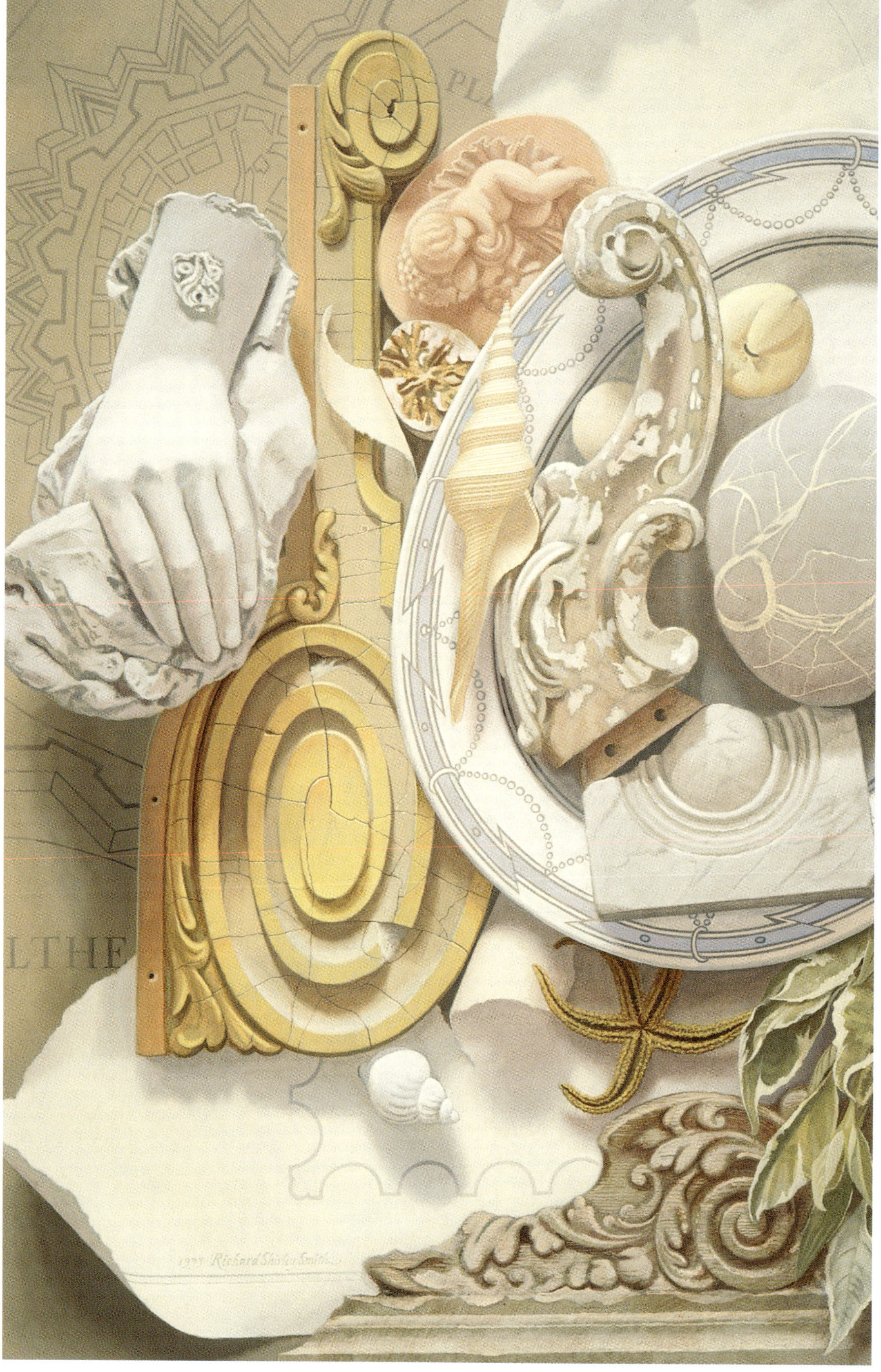
LTHE

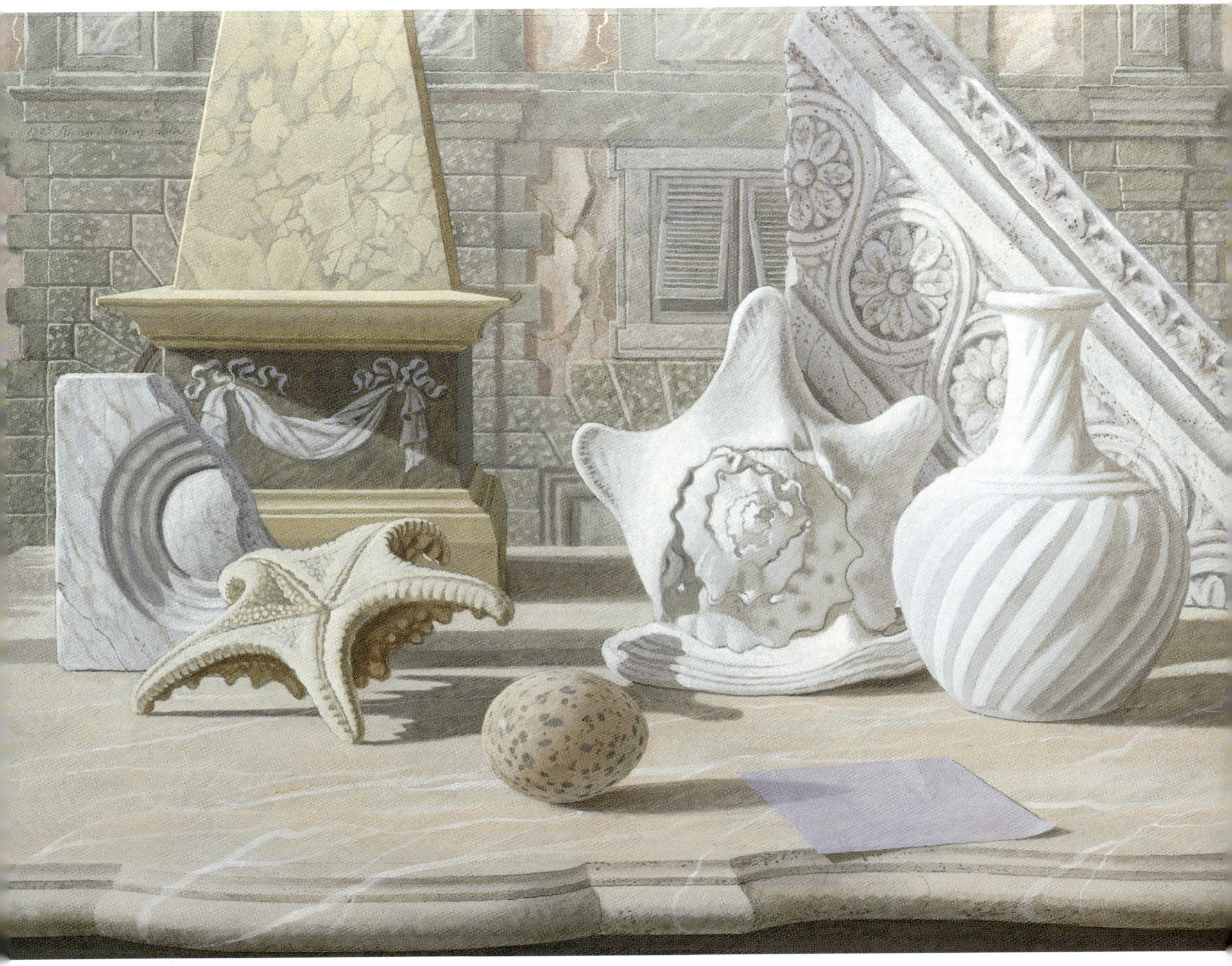

ABOVE: Fig.108 *Still Life at Lucca*, acrylic on paper. 52 × 73cm. 1989 (*ptg.cat.178*). This obelisk was made to my design by Sir Evelyn Shuckburgh while he was waiting for me to finish decorating his clavichord. The architectural study in the background was from Lucca. Collection of the artist

OPPOSITE: Fig.107 *Three Volutes*, acrylic on canvas. 78 × 117cm. 1993-5 (*ptg.cat.223*). Private collection

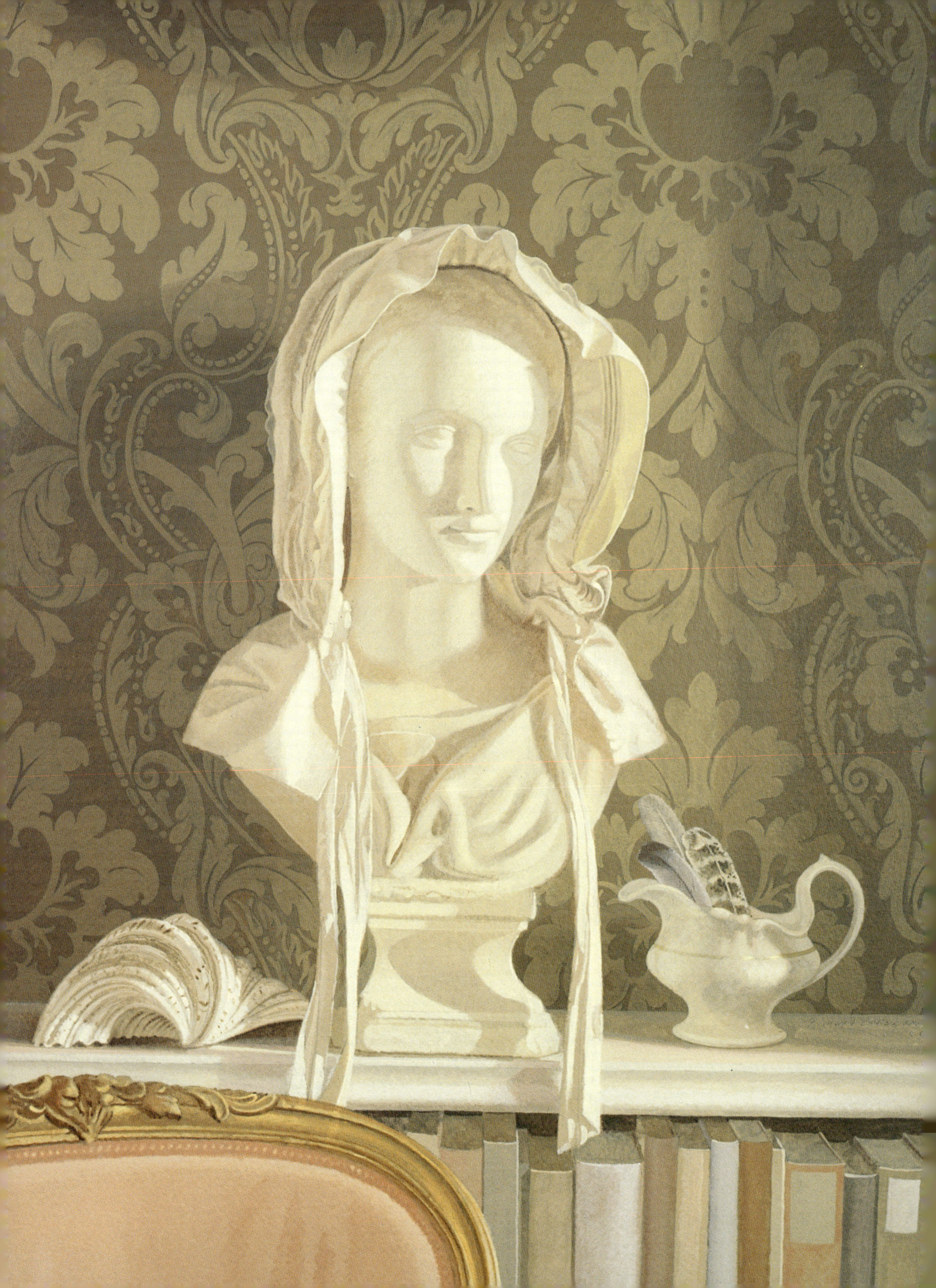

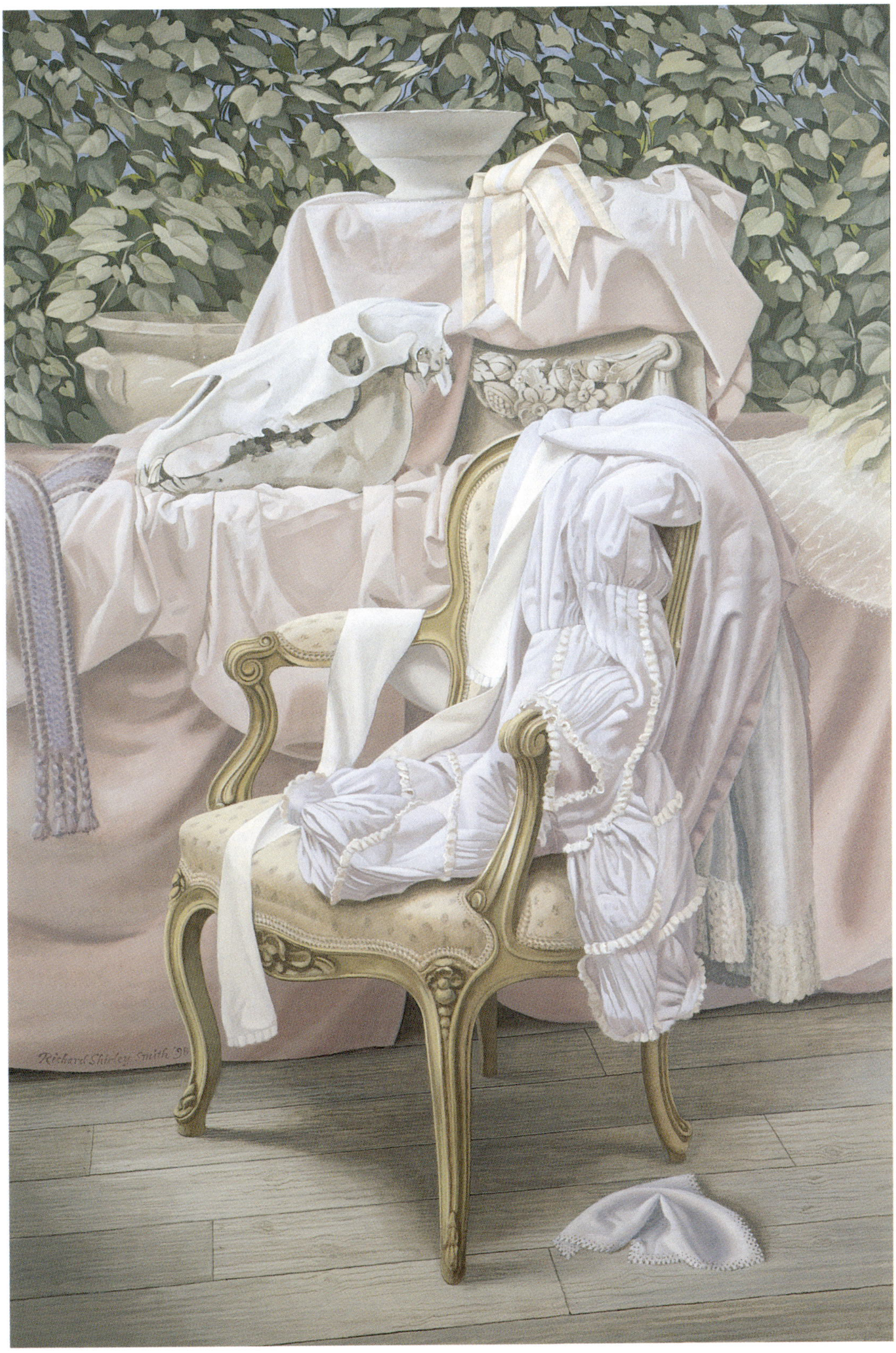

ABOVE: Fig.110 *Rococo Chair with Frock*, acrylic on canvas. 134 × 92cm. 1998 (*ptg.cat.264*). Collection of the artist

OPPOSITE: Fig.109 *Cast & Bonnet*, acrylic on paper. 96 × 72cm. 1995 (*ptg.cat.226*). Collection of John & Kathy Evans

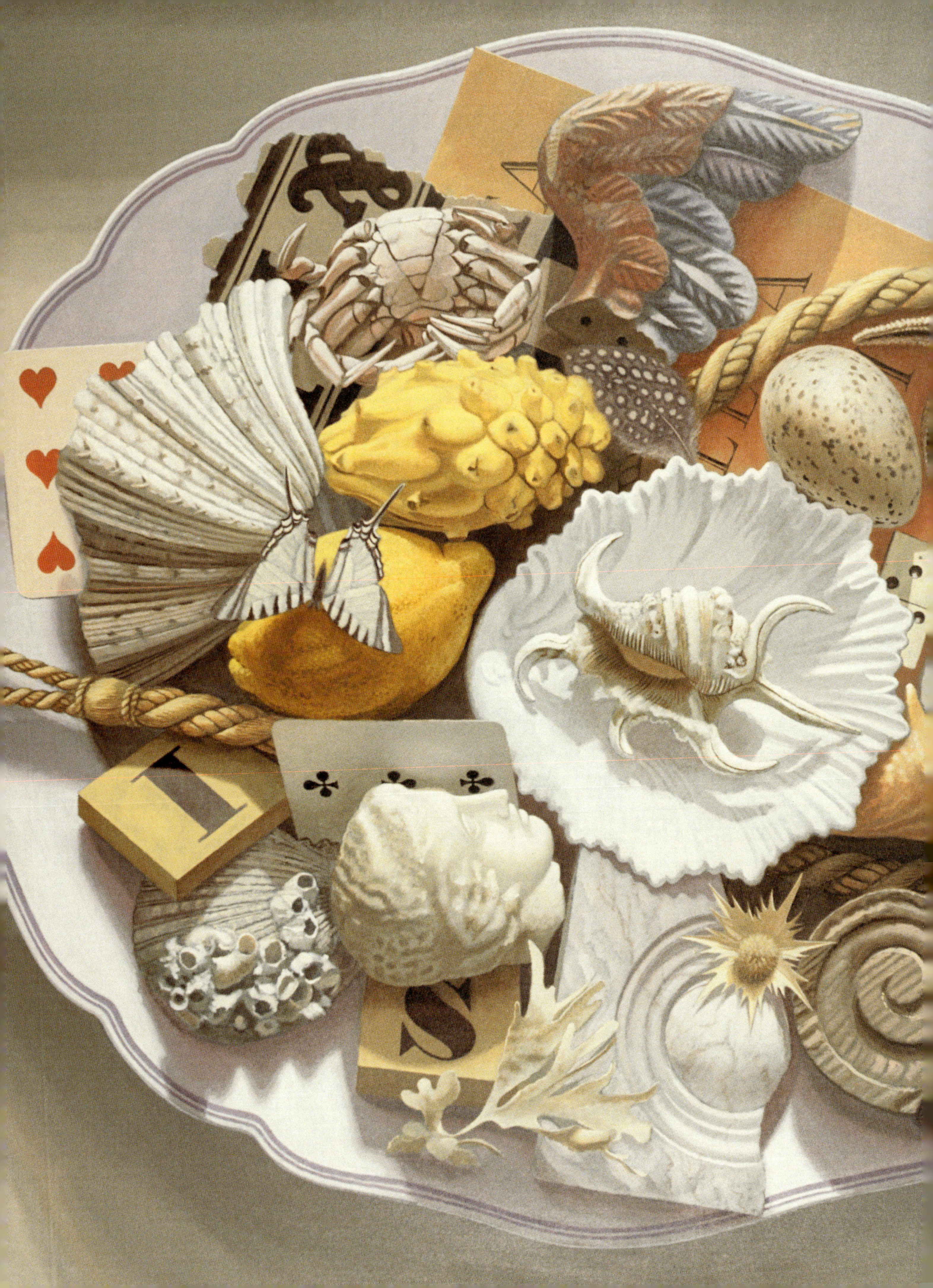

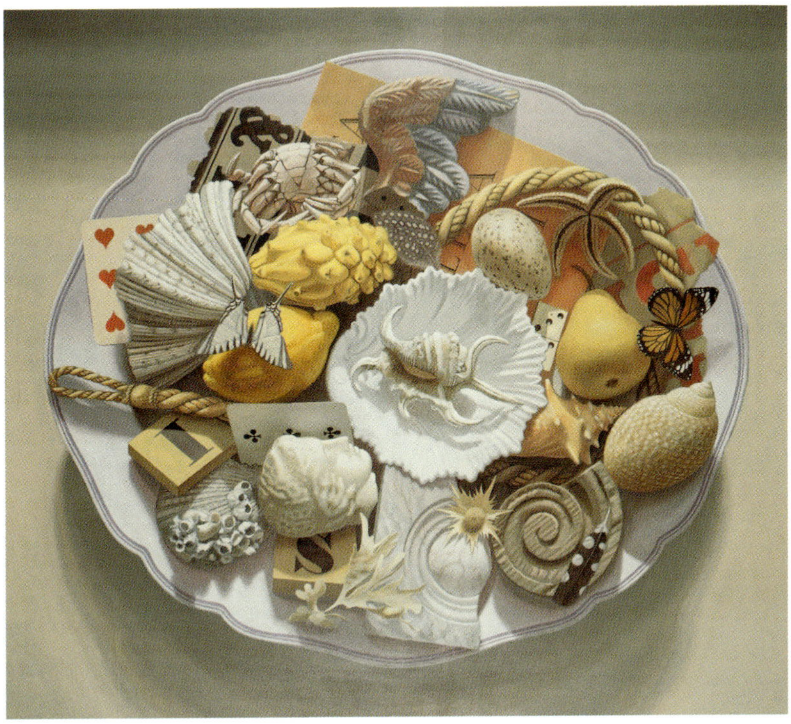

ABOVE: Fig.112 *Large Dish with Lemon*, acrylic on canvas. 130 × 151cm. 1993 (*ptg.cat.213*). A representational artist has two subjects: nature and other art. These decorative panels mix and compare the two: real feathers and carved feathers, spiral shells and ropes, spotted feathers and dominoes. Collection of Mr & Mrs Andrew Dalton

OPPOSITE: Fig.111 *Large Dish with Lemon* (*detail*)

BELOW: Fig.113 *Still Life on Book* (*detail*), acrylic on canvas. 59 × 90cm. 1989 (*ptg.cat.177*). Collection of Peter & Claire Bates

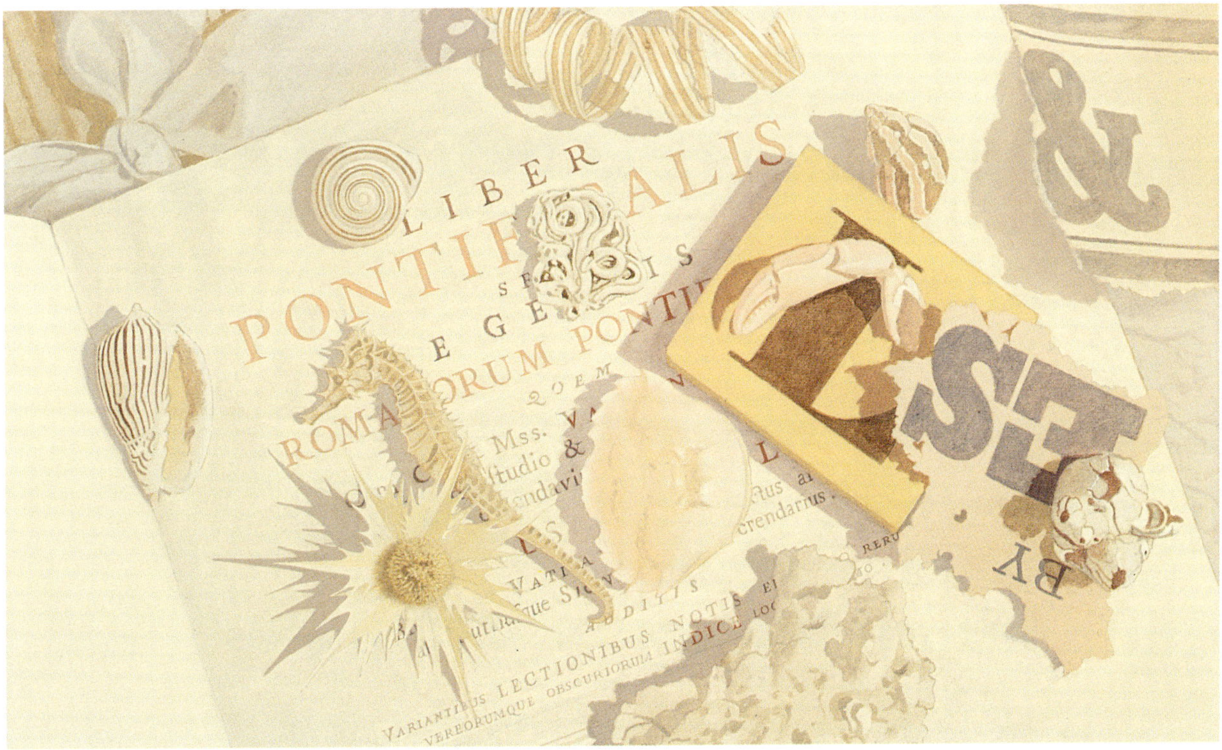

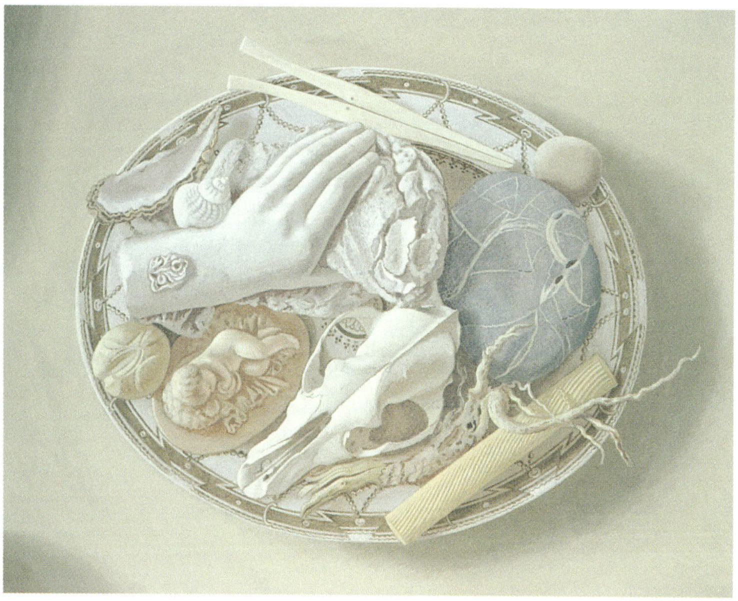

LEFT: Fig.114 *Dish Still Life with Hand*, acrylic on canvas, *approx*. 24 × 36cm. 1985 (*ptg.cat.147*). Private collection

BELOW: Fig.115 *Starfish & Doll's Arm* (*detail*), acrylic on paper. 41 × 30cm. 1997 (*ptg.cat.249*). Collection of the artist

OPPOSITE: Fig.116 *Still Life on Dish with George I Medal*, acrylic on canvas. 95 × 74cm. 1989 (*ptg.cat.179*). Collection of The Keepers and Governors of Harrow School (presented to the Old Speech Room Gallery by Charles Empson OH, 2001)

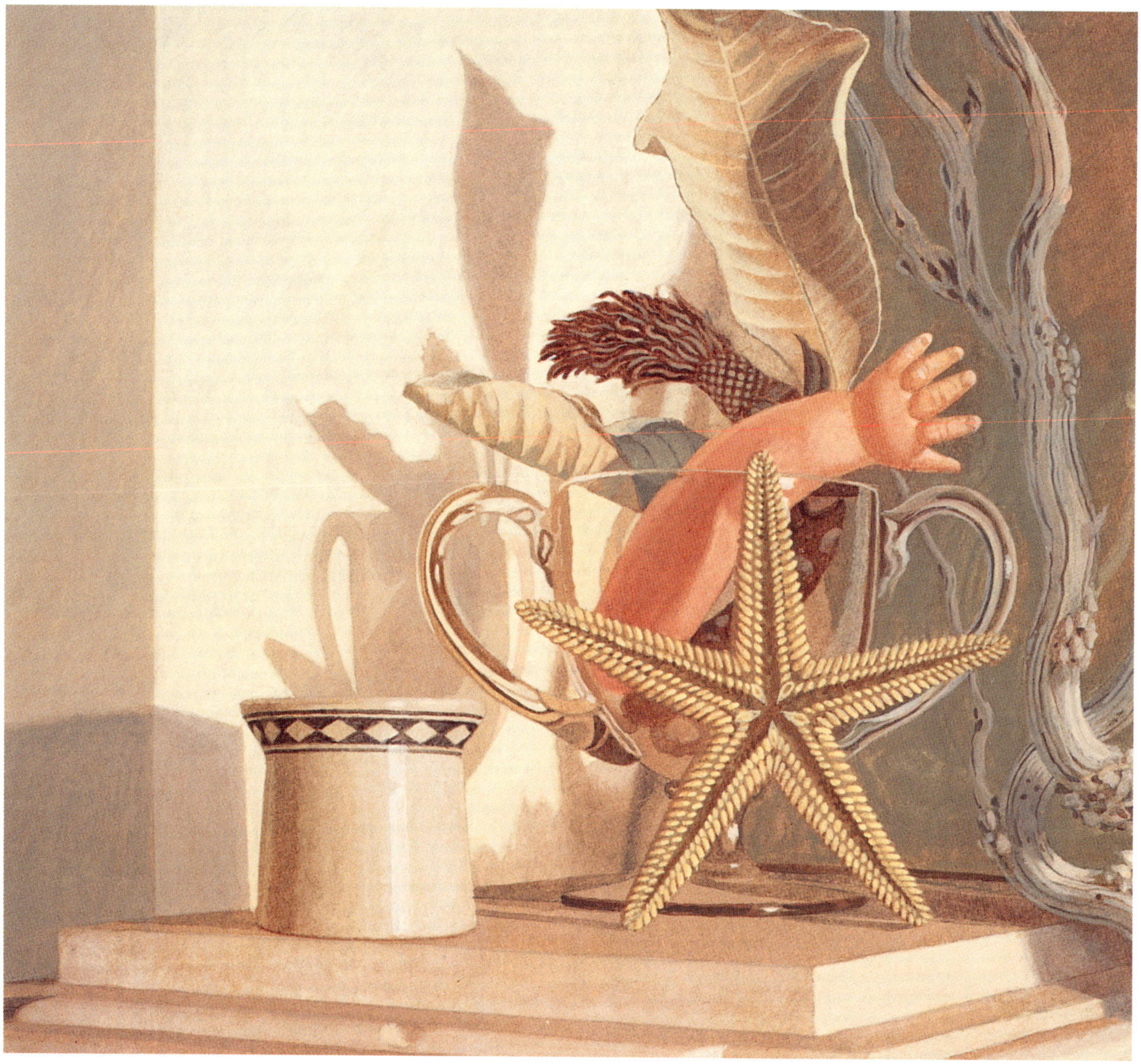

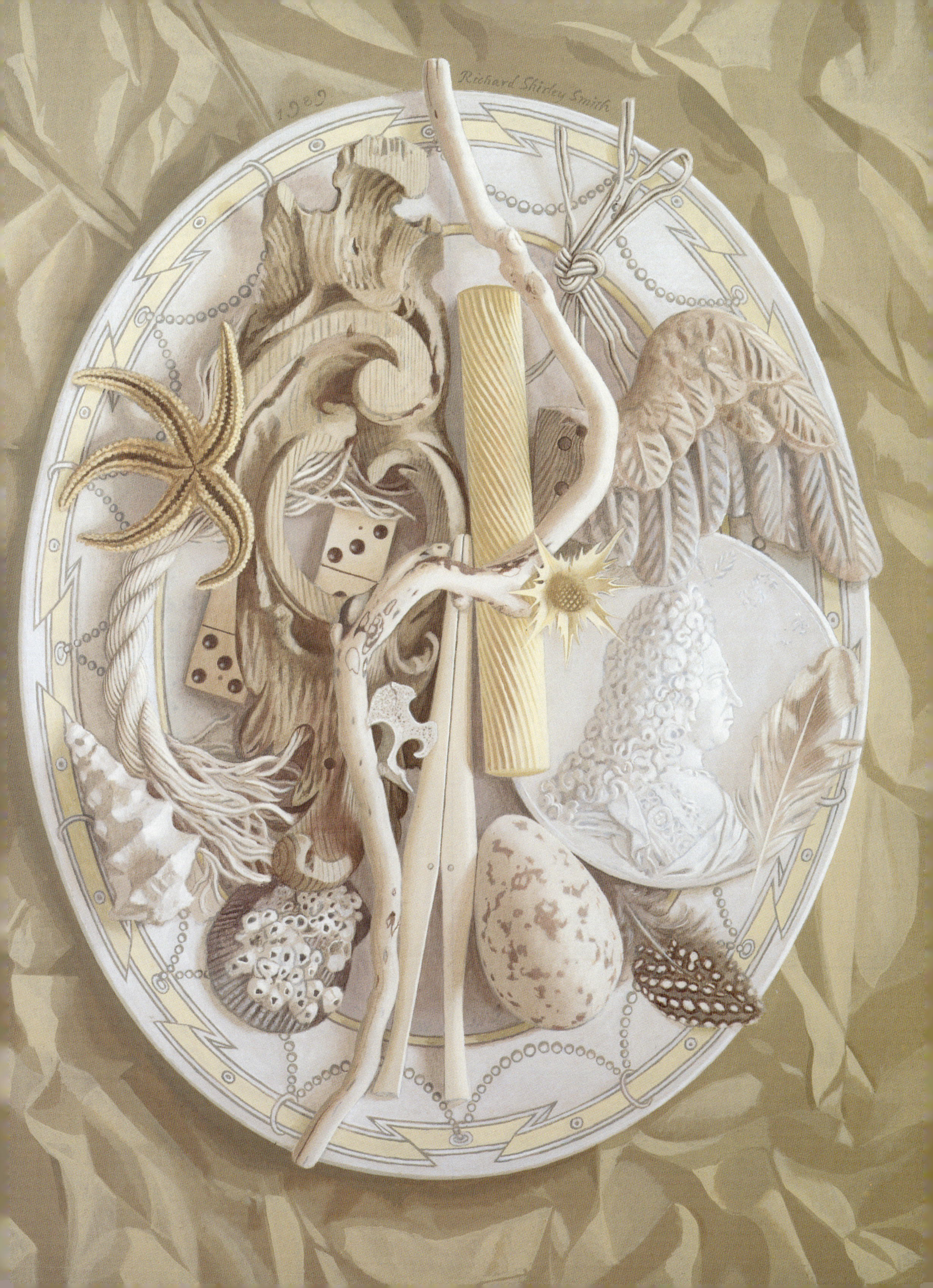
1989
Richard Shirley Smith

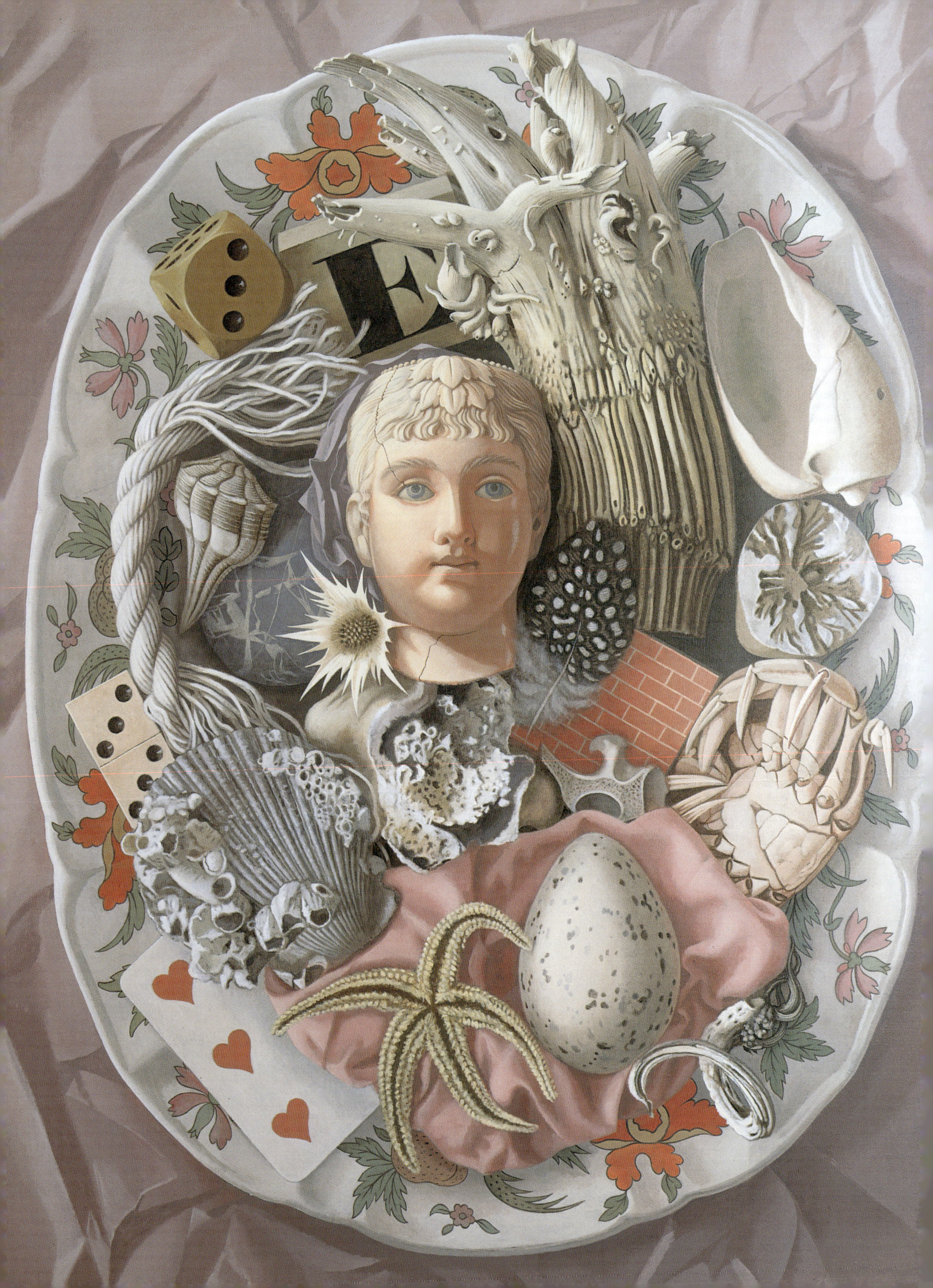
E

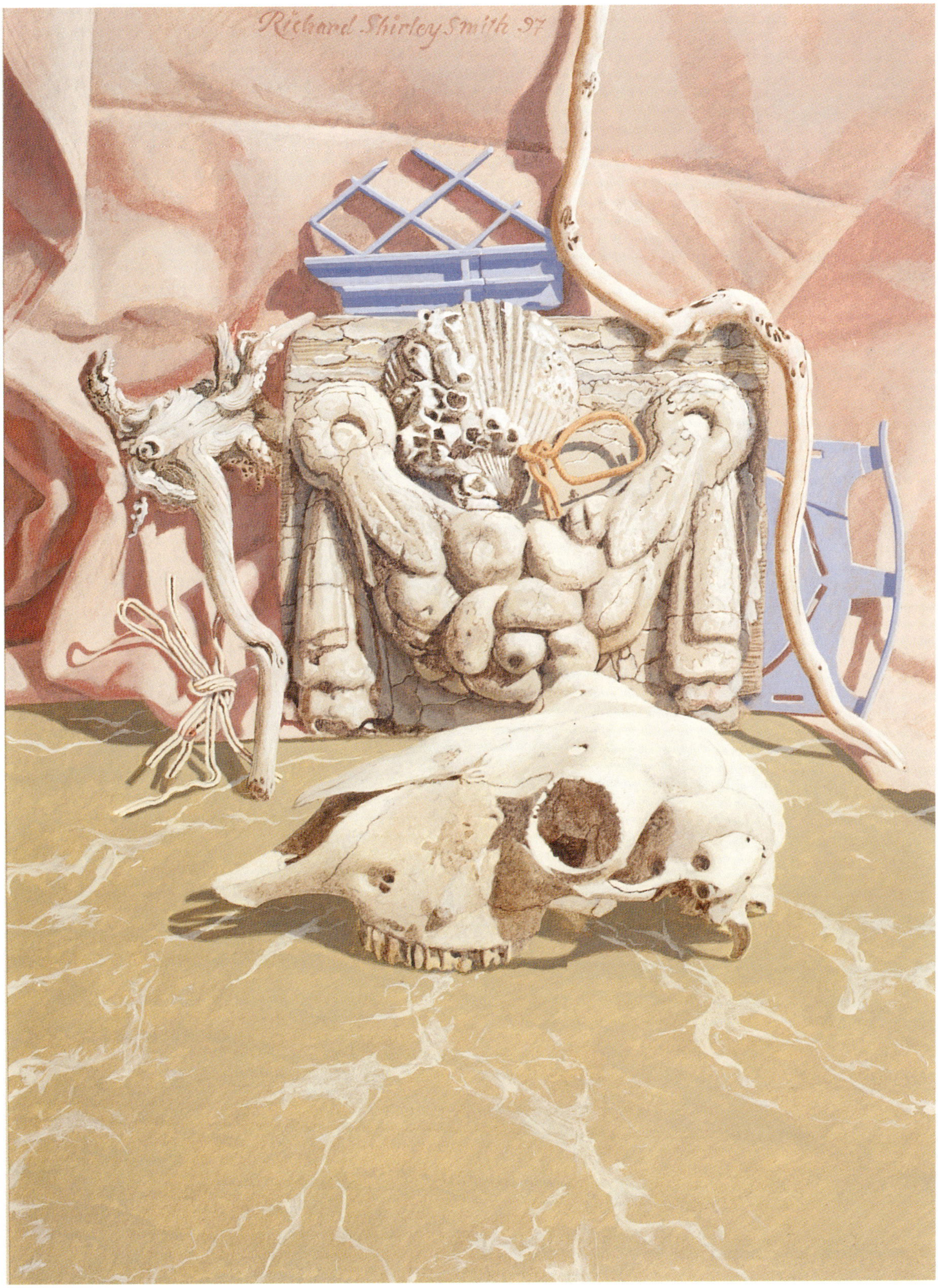

ABOVE: Fig.118 *Swag & Skull*, acrylic on paper. 42 × 32cm. 1997 (*ptg.cat.248*). Collection of the artist

OPPOSITE: Fig.117 *Large Dish with Doll's Head*, acrylic on canvas. 143 × 114cm. 1995 (*ptg.cat.231*). There are creatures here from sea, earth and sky. Collection of the artist

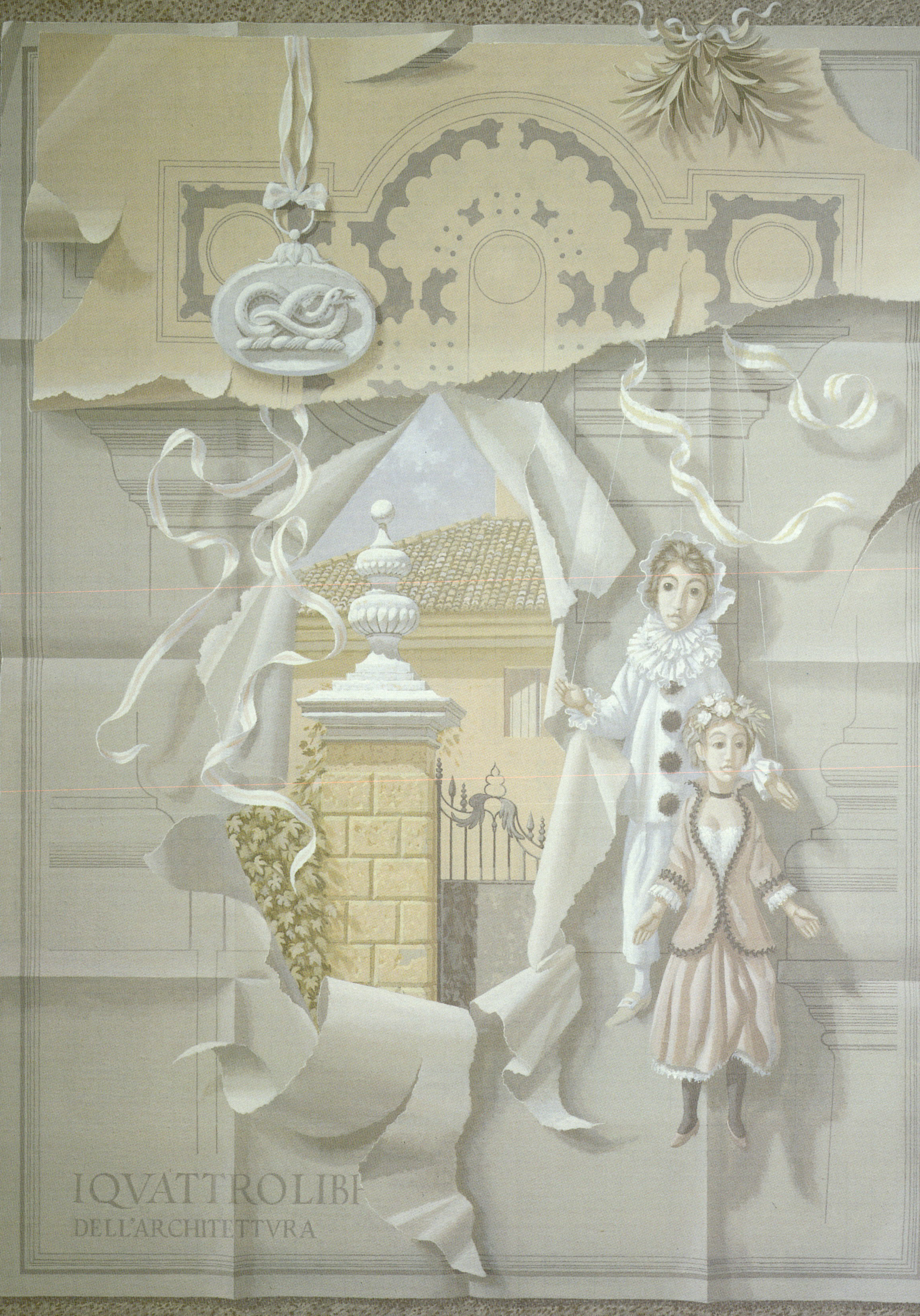
IQVATTRO LIBI
DELL'ARCHITETTVRA

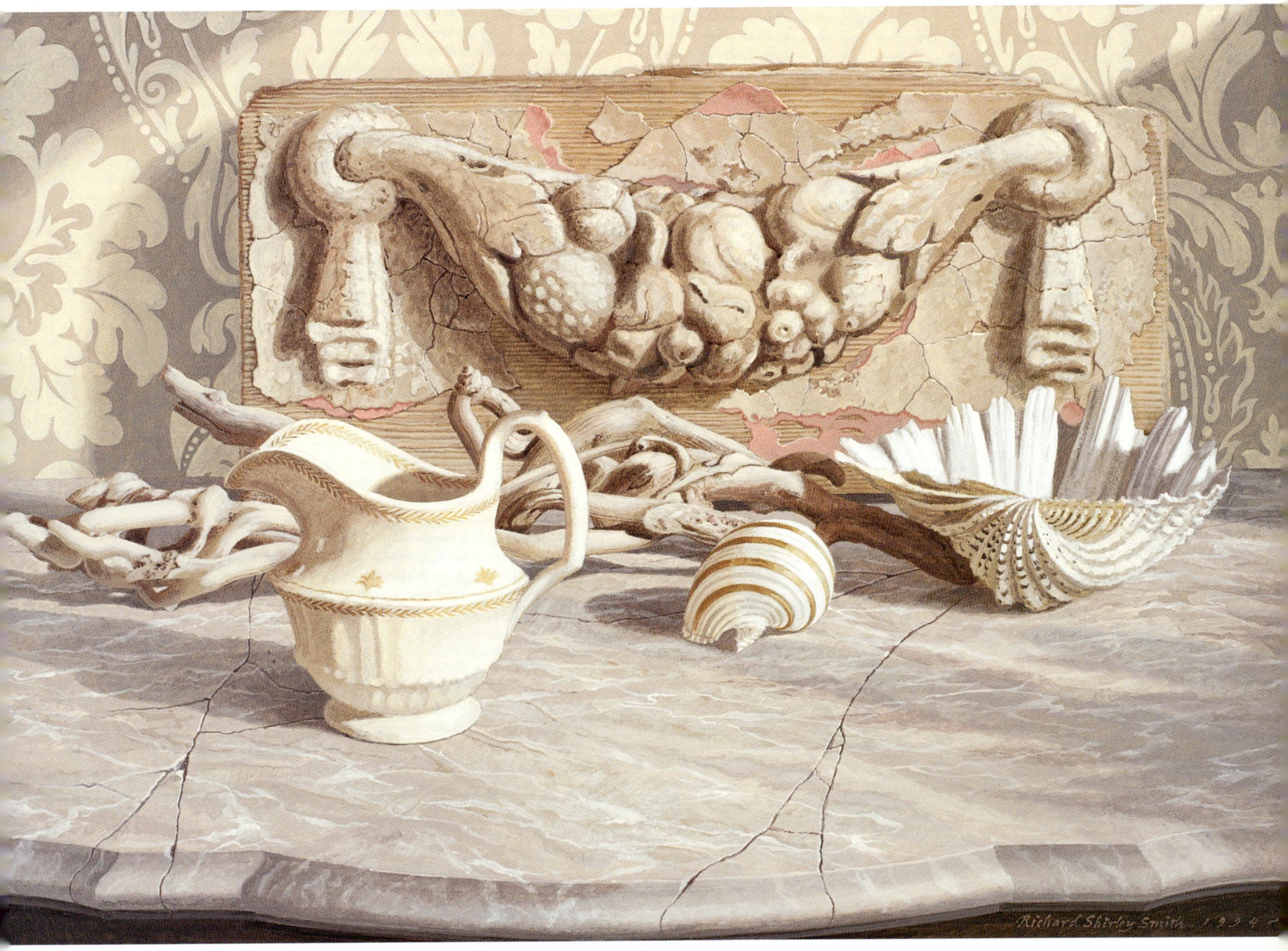

ABOVE: Fig.120 *Swag & Jug (first version)*, acrylic on board. 37 × 55cm. 1994 (*ptg.cat.218*). Collection of Anne Stevens

OPPOSITE: Fig.119 *Mural panel at 24 Bruton Street,* acrylic on board, *approx.* 183 × 147cm. 1983. The cartoon for this is (*ptg.cat.123*). I used the idea of torn paper decoratively in these five panels in order to show just as much of the architectural drawing as I wished and reveal beyond, in the background, exactly what I wanted. Still-life objects and plants have been added. So many of my interests are brought together here: the marionettes, the Venetian villa and the architectural drawing from Palladio's *I Quatro Libri*.

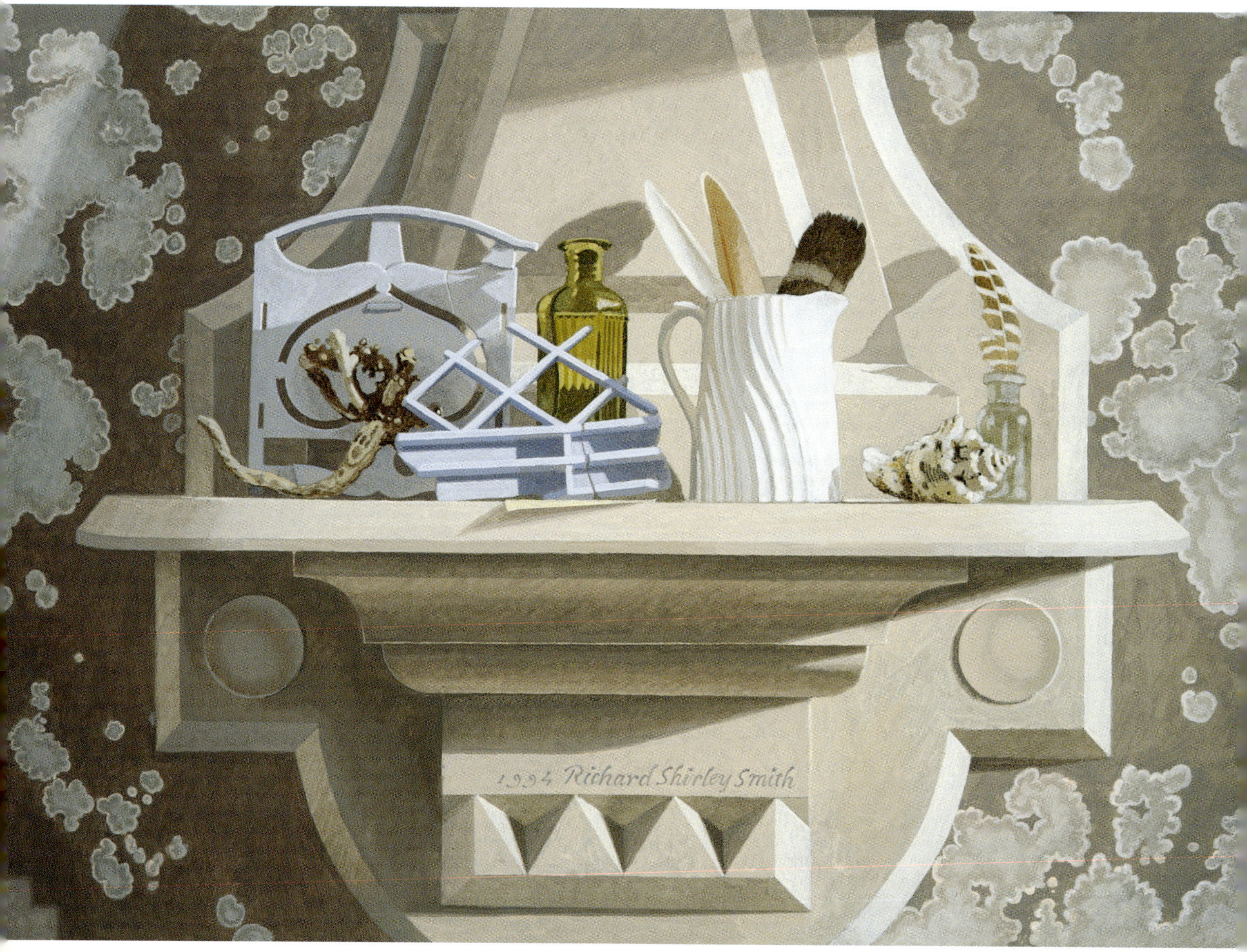

ABOVE: Fig.121 *Obelisk Shelf with Green Bottle*, acrylic on board. 35 × 50cm. 1994 (*ptg.cat.217*). This was observed in very low Christmas sunlight. Collection of the artist

OPPOSITE: Fig.122 *Obelisk Shelf & Tasso Medal*, acrylic on board. 55 × 60cm. 1995 (*ptg.cat.229*). I designed the obelisk shelf on graph paper and it was made in wood by my son, Leo. The plaster cast is of a medal of Torquato Tasso the sixteenth-century humanist writer. I made a squeeze of the background inscription of the first century AD, when in Rome in 1961. Ambrosius, a freed man of the Emperor, commemorates Nice, his wife of forty-five years. Collection of Mr & Mrs John Poynton

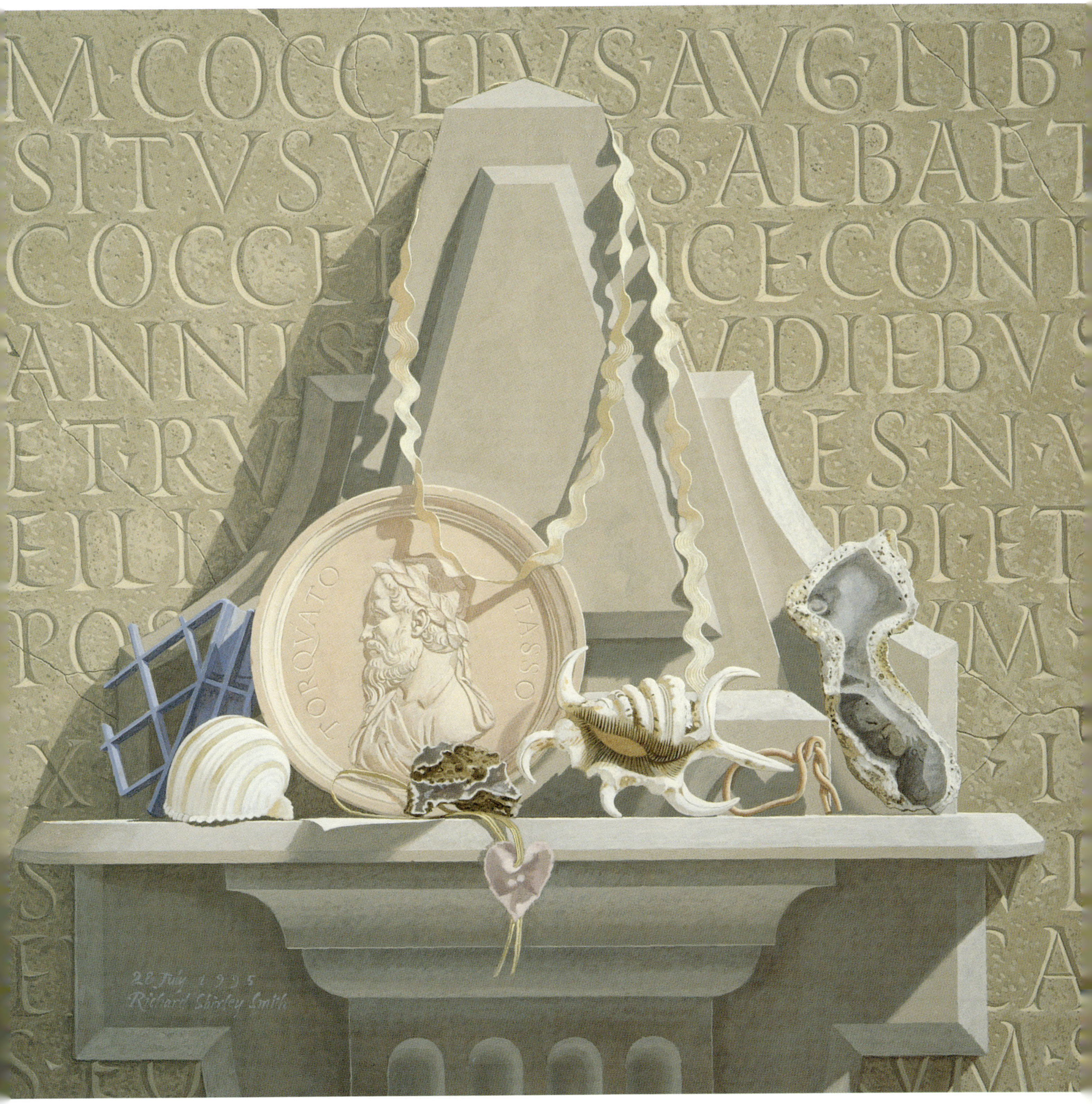
M·COCCEIVS·AVG·LIB·
TORQVATO TASSO
28 July 1995
Richard Shirley Smith

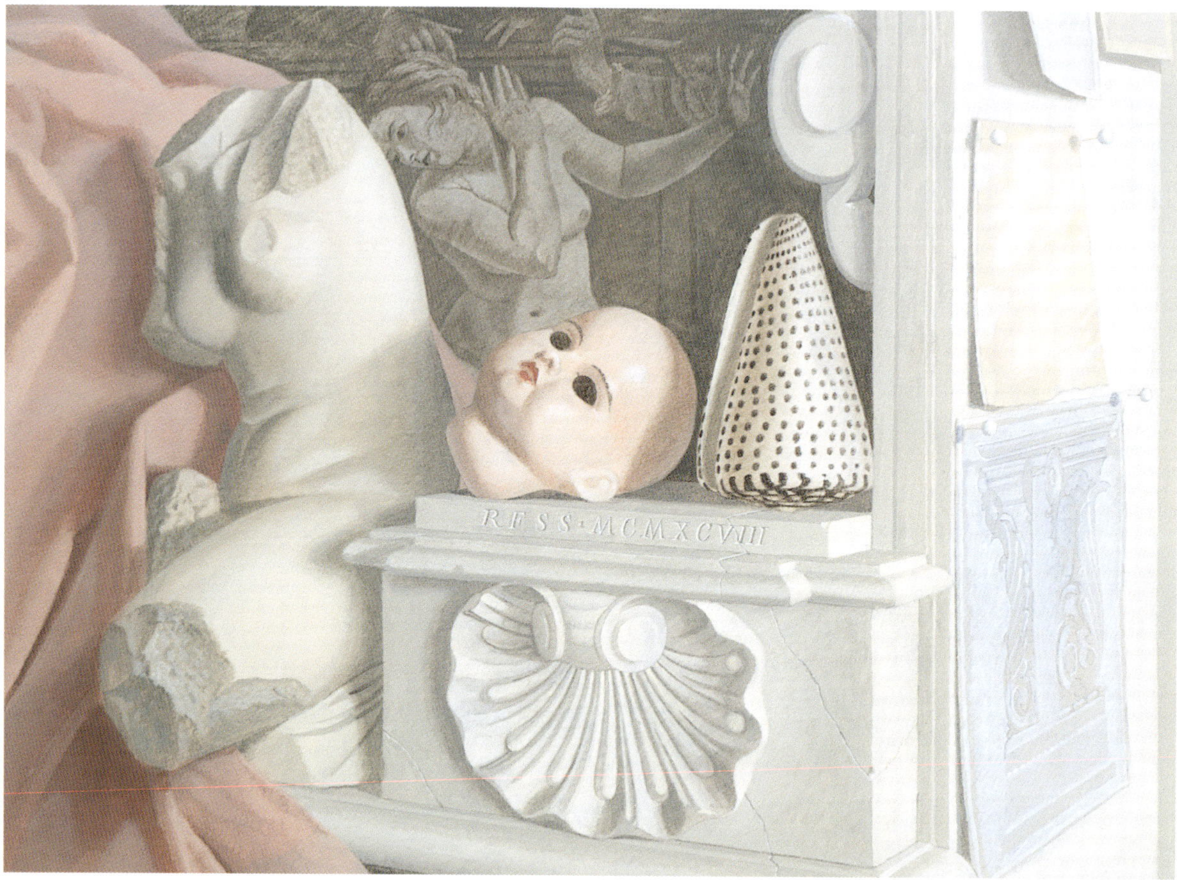
RESS·MCMXCVIII

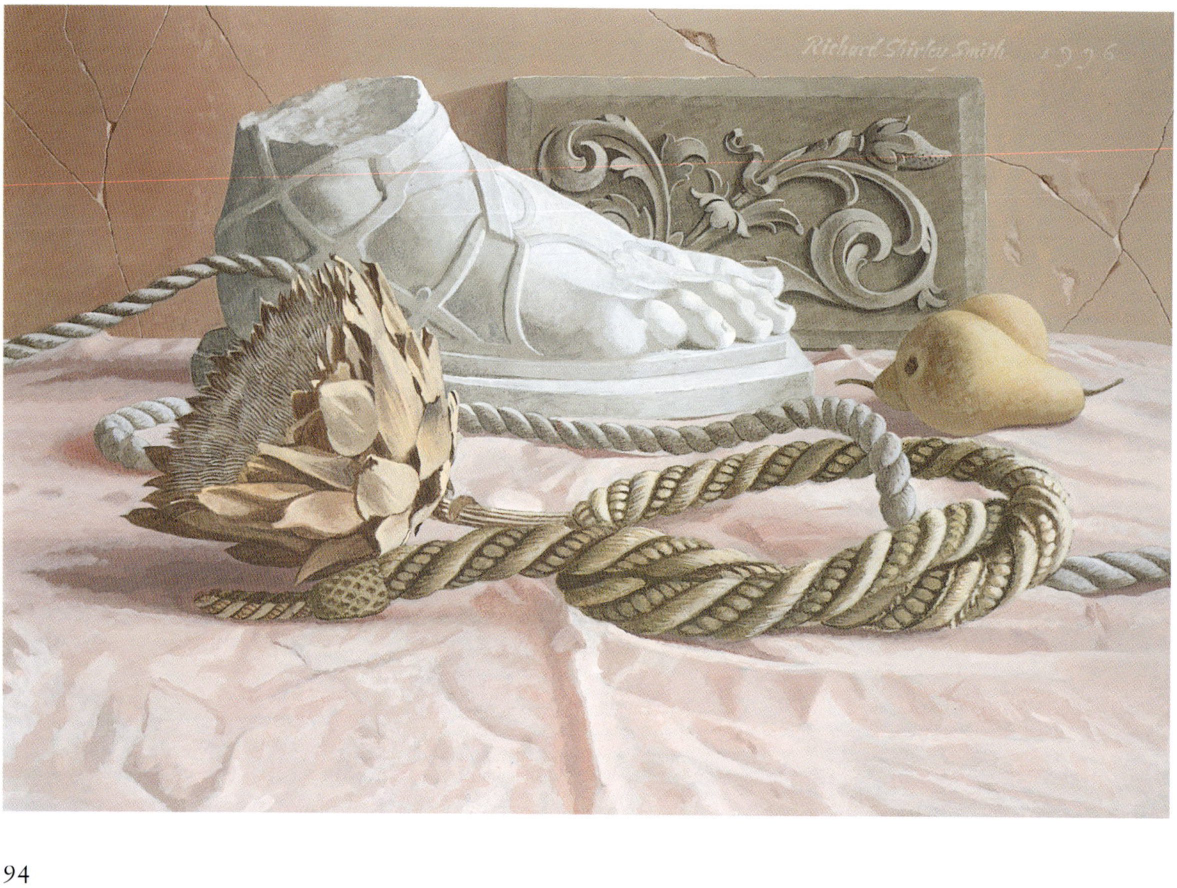
Richard Shirley Smith 1996

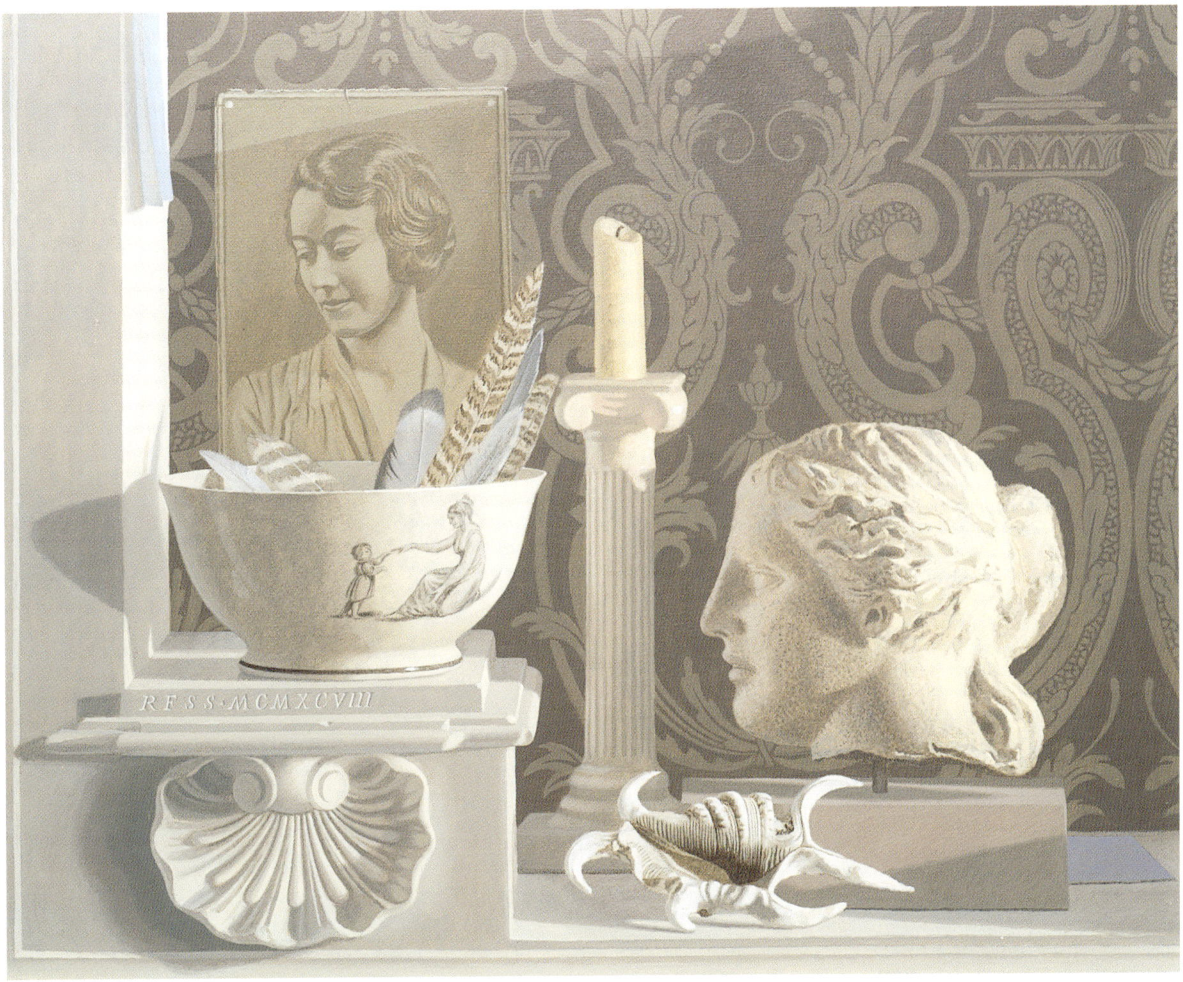

ABOVE: Fig.125 *Venus, Candle & Bowl,* acrylic on canvas. 61 × 76cm. 1998 (*ptg.cat.267*).
One of William Blake's important tenets was 'Innocence must be followed by experience', or 'Teach these souls to fly'. This might have been a better title for this painting, I afterwards thought, as the bowl and its decoration are very much in Blake's style. It is also full of wing feathers. The photograph is of my mother in the 1920s.
Collection of Ben & Jan Hoogewerf

OPPOSITE ABOVE: Fig.123 *Doll's Head & Spotted Shell,* acrylic on paper. 42 × 58cm. 1998 (*ptg.cat.268*).
This still life was first inspired by low evening sun lighting up objects in the studio. One can see in the background part of a photograph of *Susanna and the Elders* by Artemesia Gentileschi (1593–1652). Collection of the artist

OPPOSITE BELOW: Fig.124 *Foot & Artichoke,* acrylic on board. 34 × 51cm. 1996 (*ptg.cat.244*).
The foot is really a cast of the right foot of the Apollo Belvedere in the Vatican. It has been cast so that it seems to be a fragment. The painting originated from studies for *Still Life with Marble Foot,* now in the Ashmolean Museum (see Fig.153). Private collection

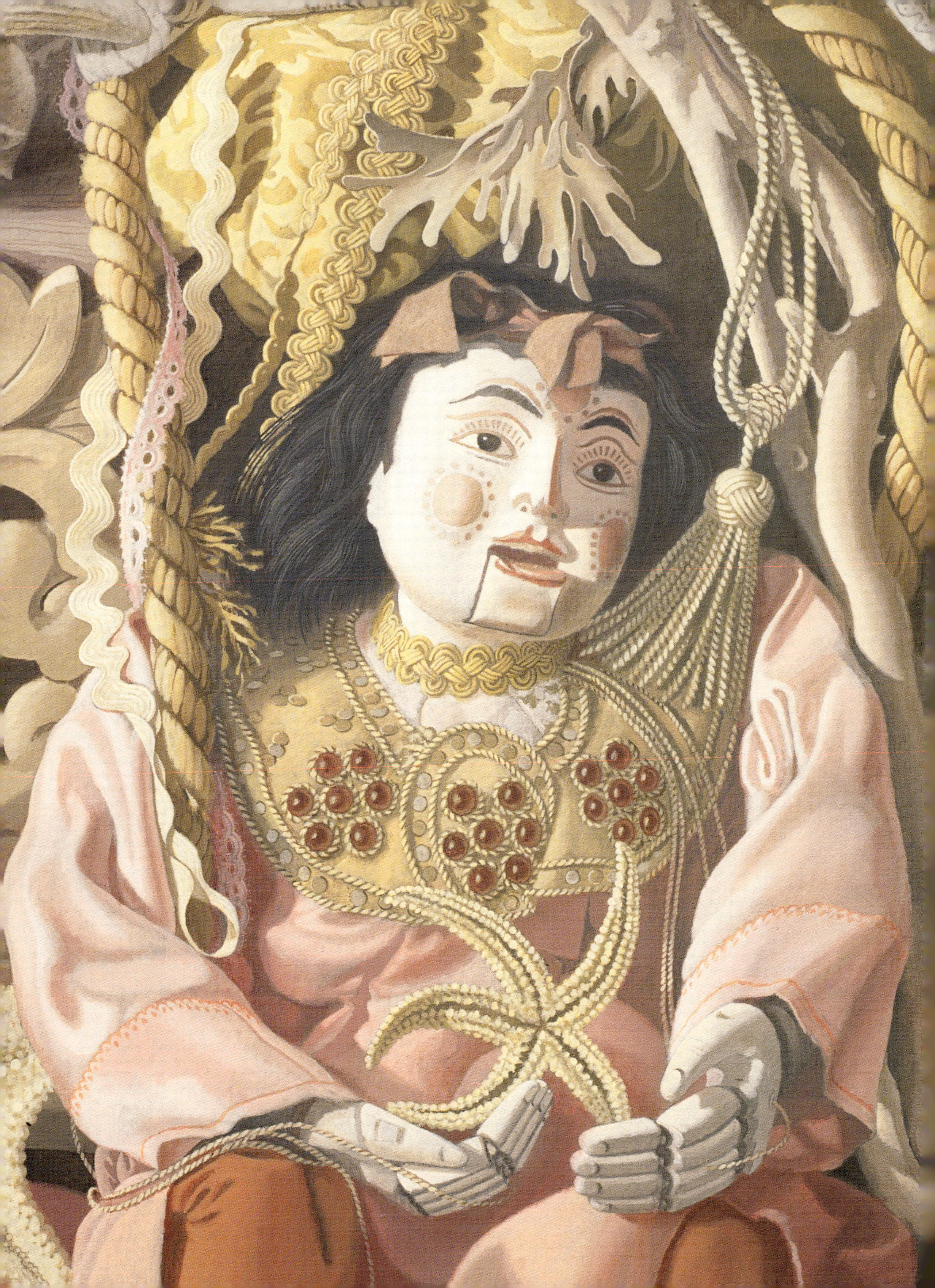

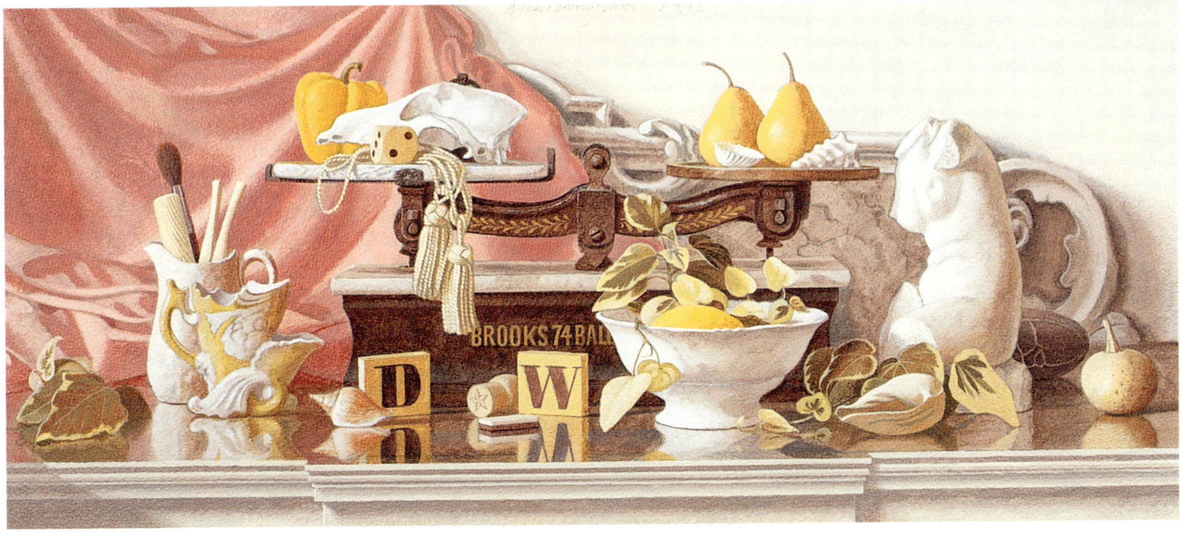

ABOVE: Fig.127 *Scales & Pears* (small version), acrylic on paper. 30 × 66cm. 1992 (*ptg.cat.210*). Jeremy Maas asked me to design a card for the *World of Drawings and Watercolours* fair at The Park Lane Hotel, Piccadilly. On the front of these scales is painted: CROOKS, 74 BALLS POND ROAD. At first the organisers thought of retaining this for fun but later feared that customers might get 'the wrong idea'. Collection of Justin & Tracy Shirley-Smith

BELOW: Fig.128 *Burmese Marionette,* acrylic on canvas. 76 × 110cm. 1999 (*eng.cat.278*). Collection of the artist

OPPOSITE: Fig.126 *Burmese Marionette* (*detail*)

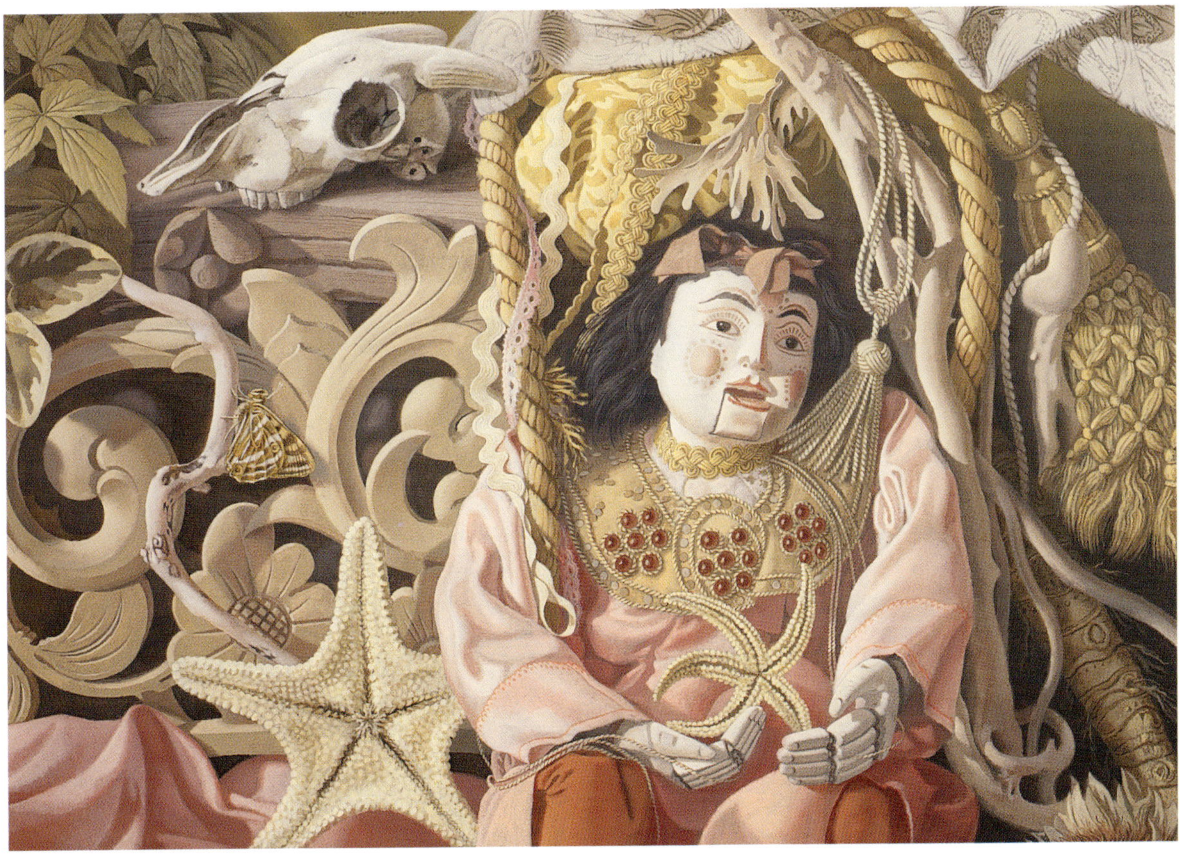

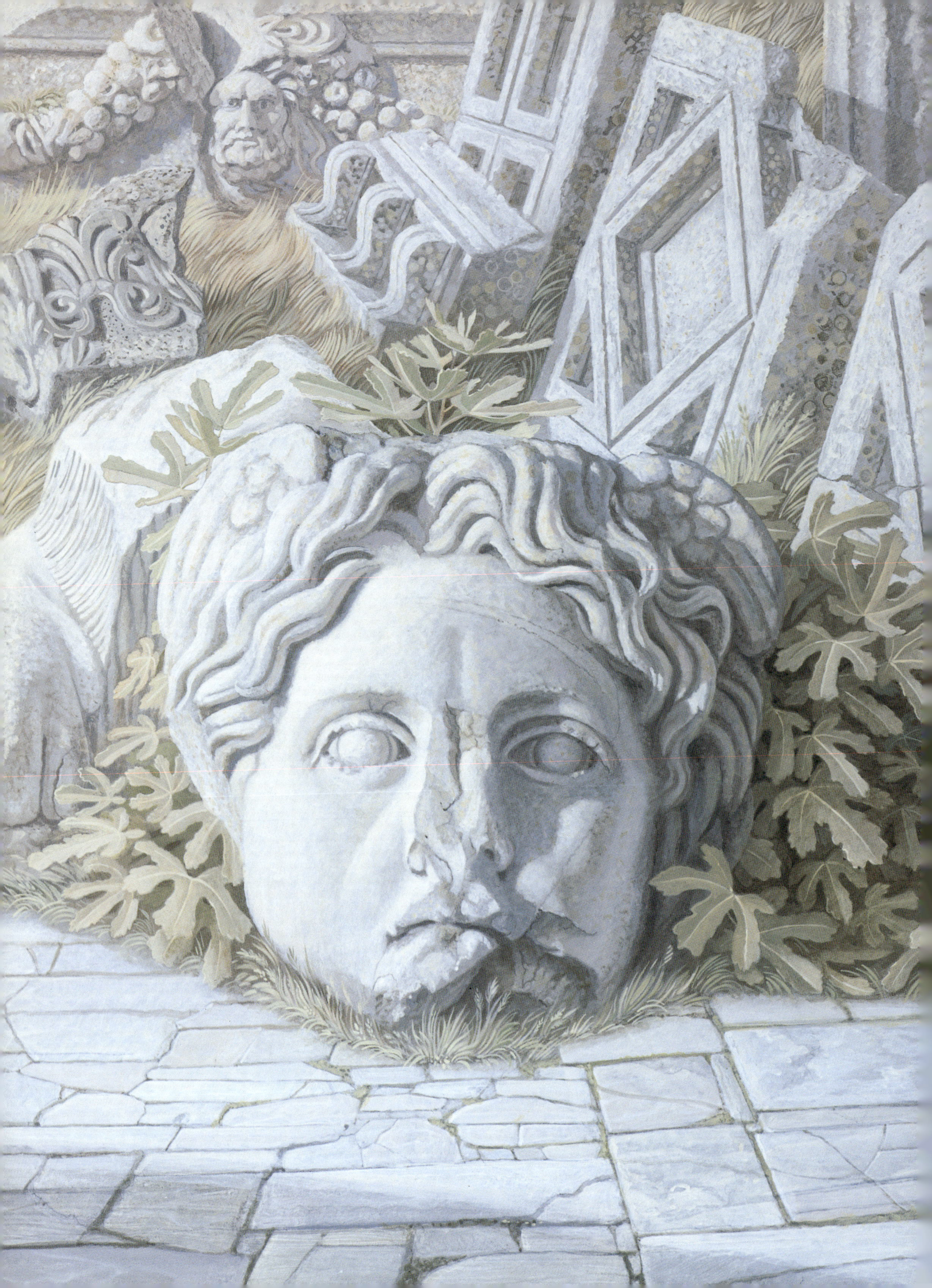

SEVEN
Classical Fragments

I have made a heap of all that I can find.

NENNIUS, HISTORIA BRITTONUM

There's a fascination frantic
In a ruin that's romantic.

W. S. GILBERT, THE MIKADO

EVER SINCE I CAN REMEMBER, I have been fascinated by ancient civilisations and traces of art history reaching back into obscurity. Soon after my return from Rome in 1961, where I had looked at much Roman architecture and sculpture, my eye was caught by the great beauty, in various press photos, of sculptures being unearthed at Aphrodisias, Western Turkey. I was at long last able to see and study these in 1997 with Jane Andrews, who is skilled at organising such expeditions. The most wonderful ruins and sculptures are to be found in such places, rather than in continuously inhabited and built-over cities. These ancient sites of Asia Minor had been weakened by conquest or silting of harbours and often finally extinguished by great earthquakes. Later excavations have left substantial fragments scattered among acanthus, fig and bay leaves, which is for me a perfect image of mutability. To the south of Ephesus we studied three fabulous sites. Priene is the most spectacular of any of the Ionian cities, on a great sloping shelf backed by a towering wall of rock and overlooking the now silted plane. The abandoned streets and houses are evocative and haunting. At Miletus we were confronted by a colossal theatre, formidable to ascend on a hot day. From the top we looked across the ruins of this greatest of the Ionian cities, famous for its scholars and colonies; from here ships sailed all over the ancient world. Didyma, in contrast, is one gigantic ruined temple, started in 300 BC, and continued for five hundred years. I found it impossible to imagine how the combination of that scale, ornamentation and perfection could be achieved in marble at that date. The temple was never quite finished.

OPPOSITE: Fig.129 *Shattered Head with Classical Fragments* (*detail*), acrylic on board. 55 × 64cm. 1998 (*ptg.cat.269*). Collection of the artist

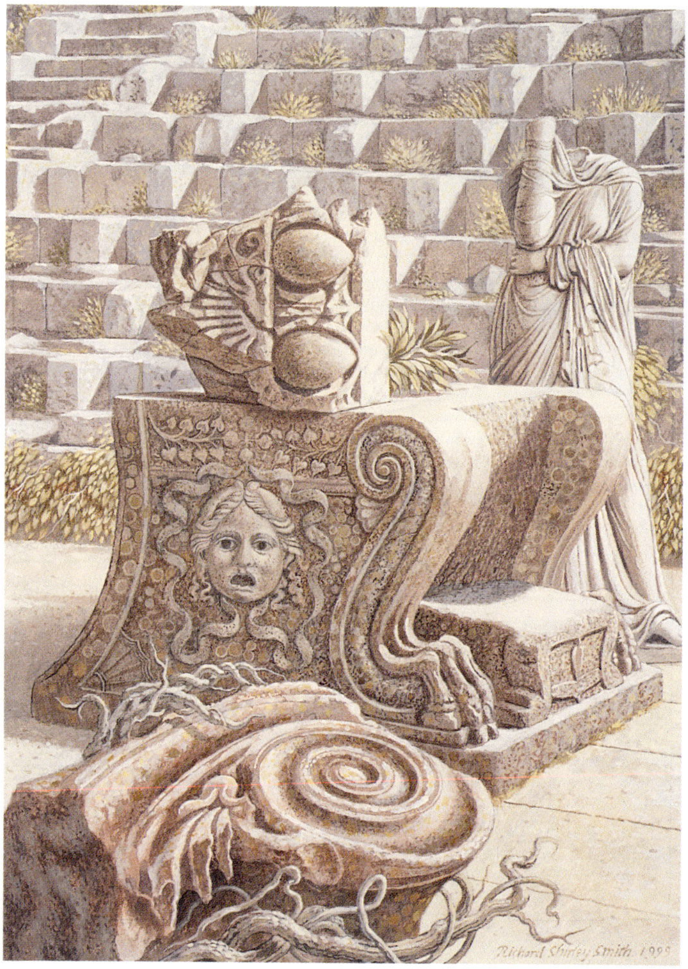

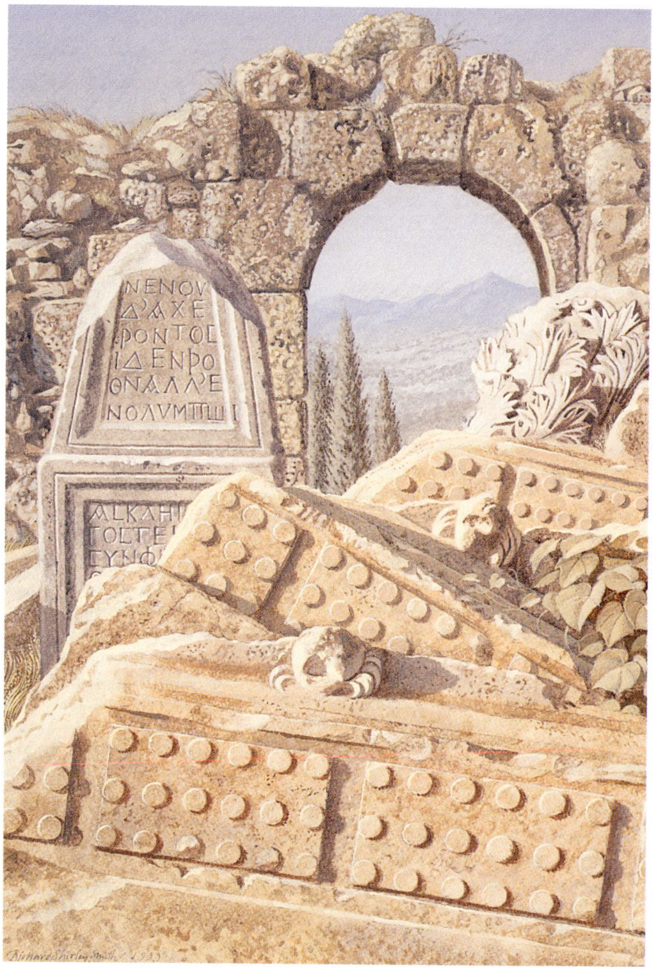

ABOVE LEFT: Fig.130 *Giant Egg & Dart Fragment,* acrylic on paper. 47 × 35cm. 1999 (*ptg.cat.274*).
The inspiration and the background for this painting was the Hellenistic Theatre among the impressive excavations of Priene, W. Turkey. Collection of Roger W. Moss & Gail C. Winkler

ABOVE RIGHT: Fig.131 *Obelisk, Arch & Fragments,* acrylic on paper. 49 × 34cm. 1999 (*ptg.cat.270*).
All these elements were at the fabulous excavation at Aphrodisias, W. Turkey. They have been recomposed in the tradition of the Italian *capriccio*. Private collection

OPPOSITE: Fig.132 *Empty Tombs,* acrylic on paper. 50 × 35cm. 1999 (*ptg.cat.272*).
The first sight of the necropolis at Hierapolis, tilted and shattered by earthquake and robbery, is astonishing. It is a magnificent embodiment of death and destruction. The mausoleum in this image has been violently shaken and the sarcophagus on top crumpled like a cardboard carton. Collection of Roger W. Moss & Gail C. Winkler

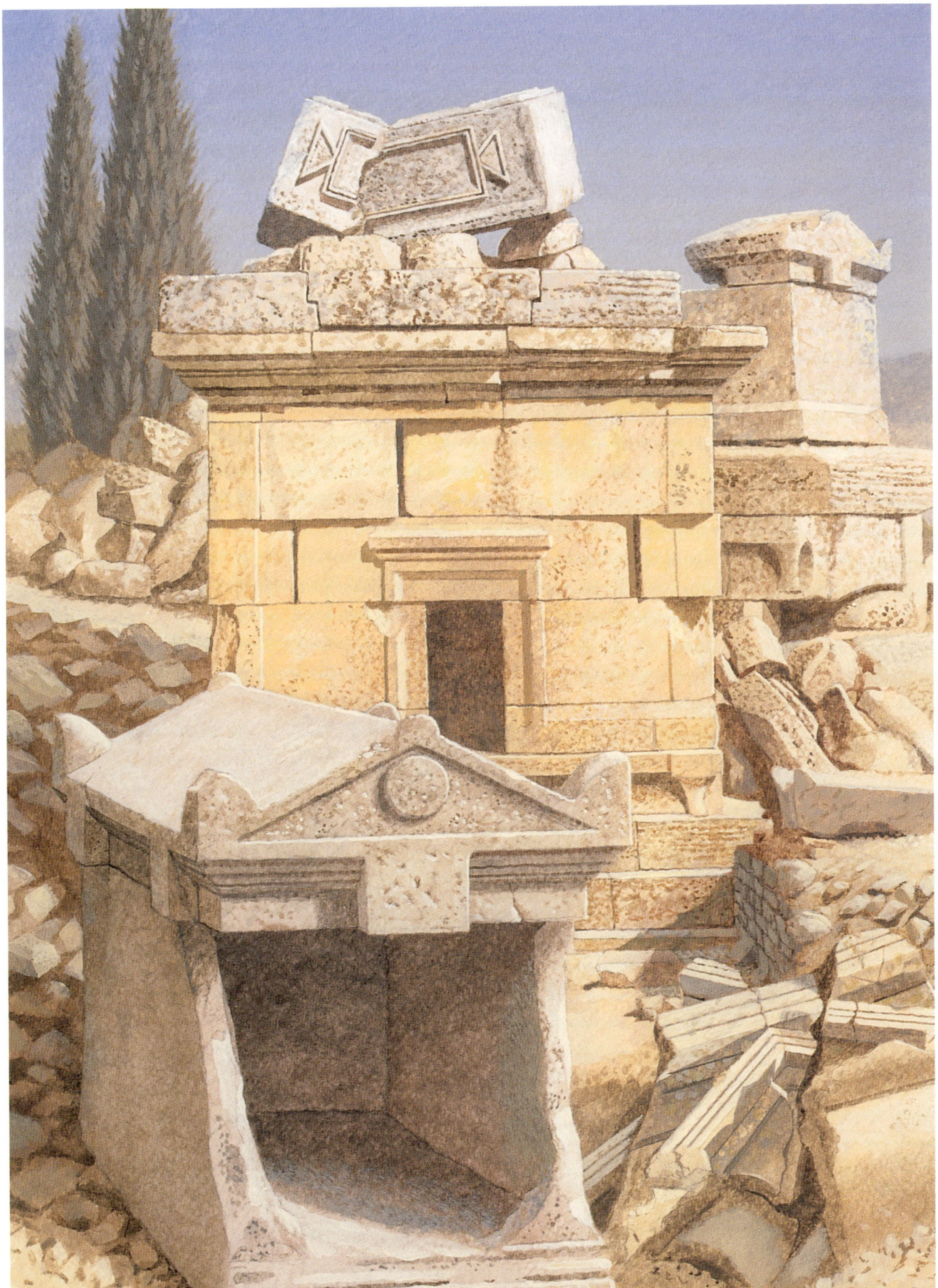
Richard Shirley Smith 1999

BELOW: Fig.133 *Shattered Head with Classical Fragments*, acrylic on board. 55 × 64cm. 1998 (*ptg.cat.*269).
These marble sculptures were studied at Aphrodisias, a spectacular and extensive excavation high above the Meander Valley with lovely views. There is a marble quarry near the city, which resulted in a sculpture school of Aphrodisias in antiquity. Collection of the artist

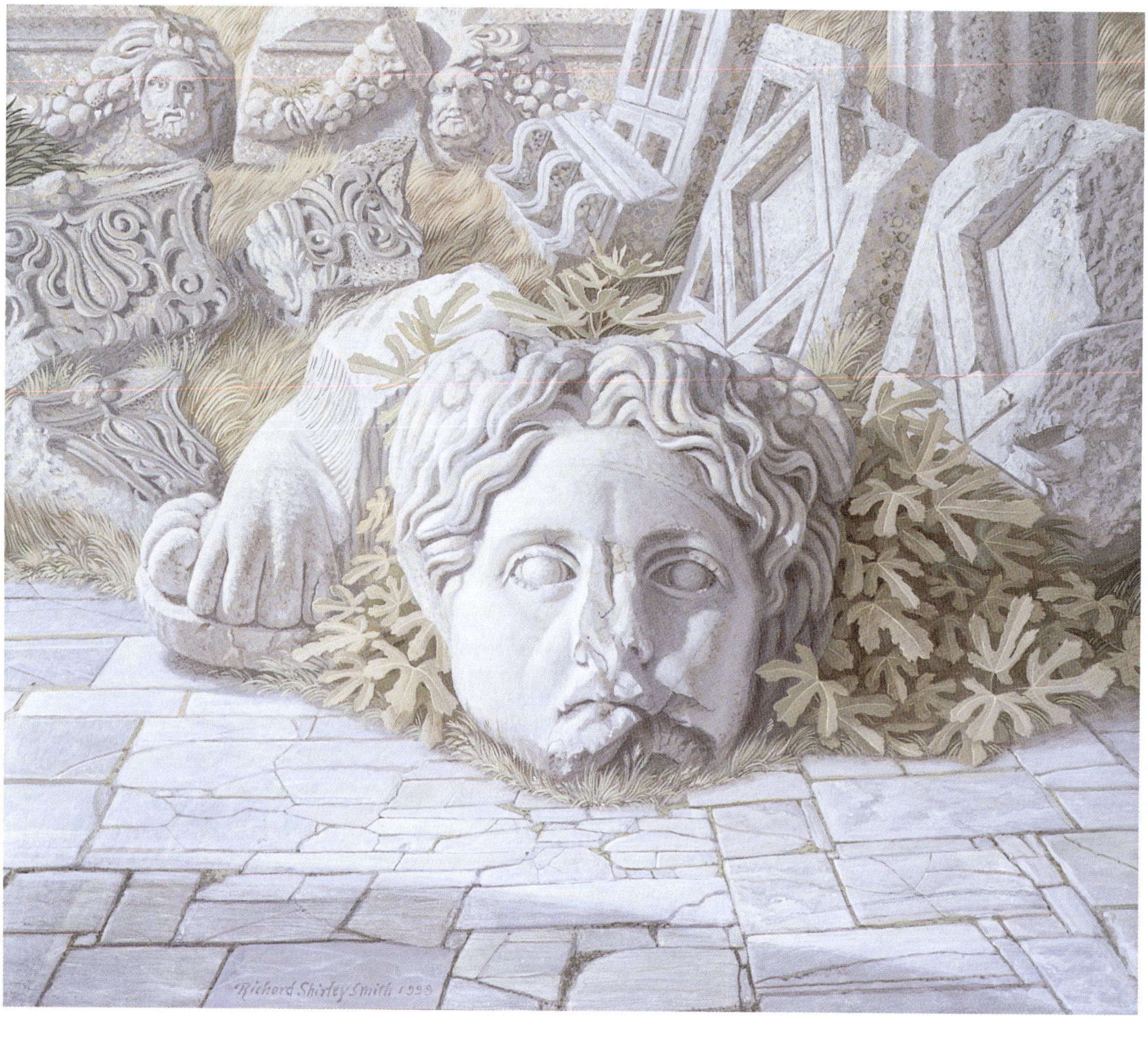

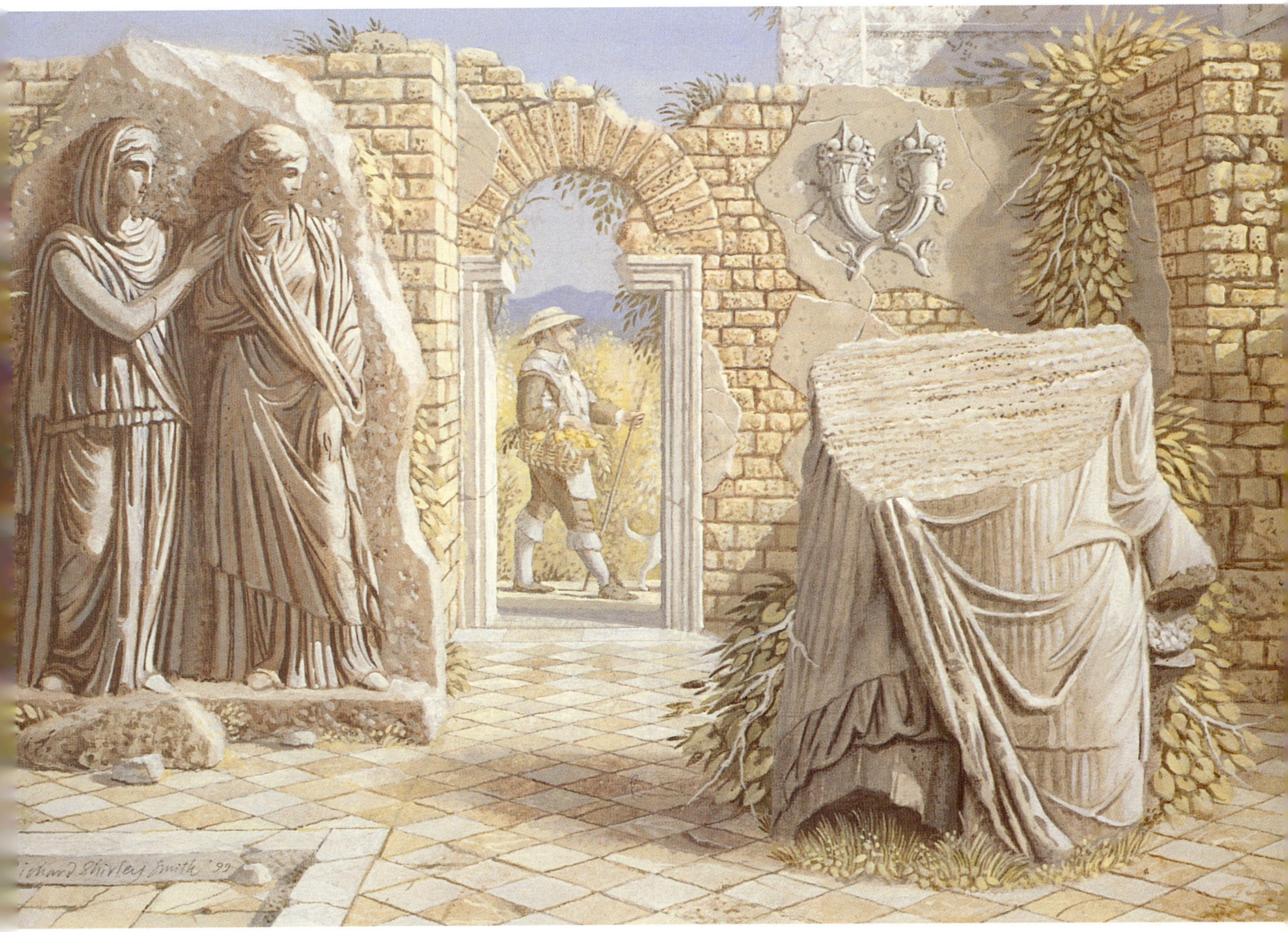

ABOVE: Fig.134 *Matrons & Torso Fragment*, acrylic on paper. 30 × 46cm. 1999 (*ptg.cat.271*). All these sculptures were observed at Aphrodisias, West Turkey. The farmer and his dog head for market oblivious to the artefacts of previous millennia. Collection of the artist

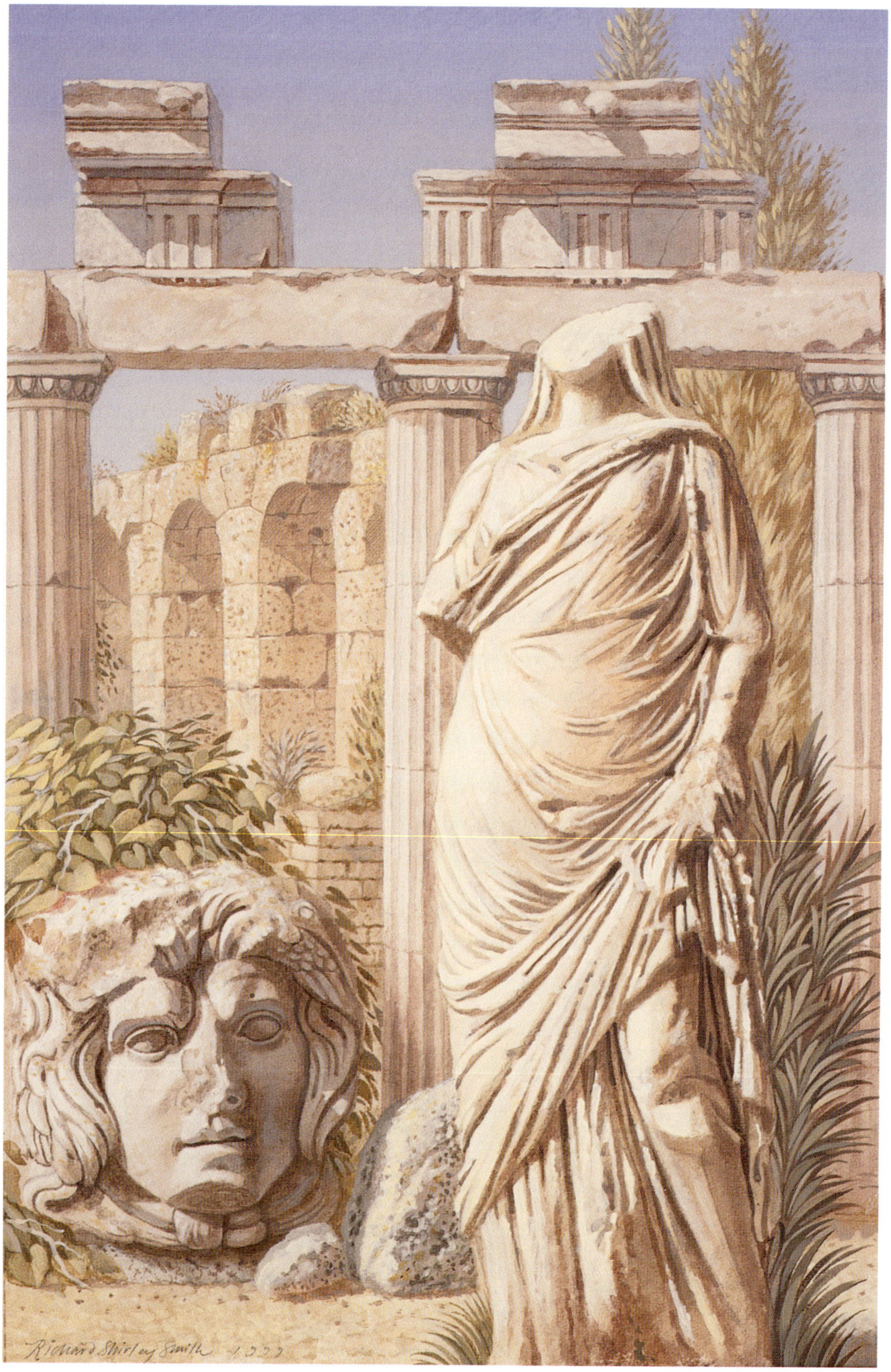

ABOVE: Fig.135 *Aphrodisias*, acrylic on paper, 46 × 31cm. 1999 (*ptg.cat.273*). Everything here was observed at Aphrodisias but rearranged in the tradition of the *capriccio* or *vedute da fantasia*. Collection of the artist

OPPOSITE: Fig.136 *Lady at Theatre*, acrylic on board. 100 × 69cm. 1999 (*ptg.cat.275*). Much of the background was studied at the theatre at Miletus in Asia Minor. Collection of the artist

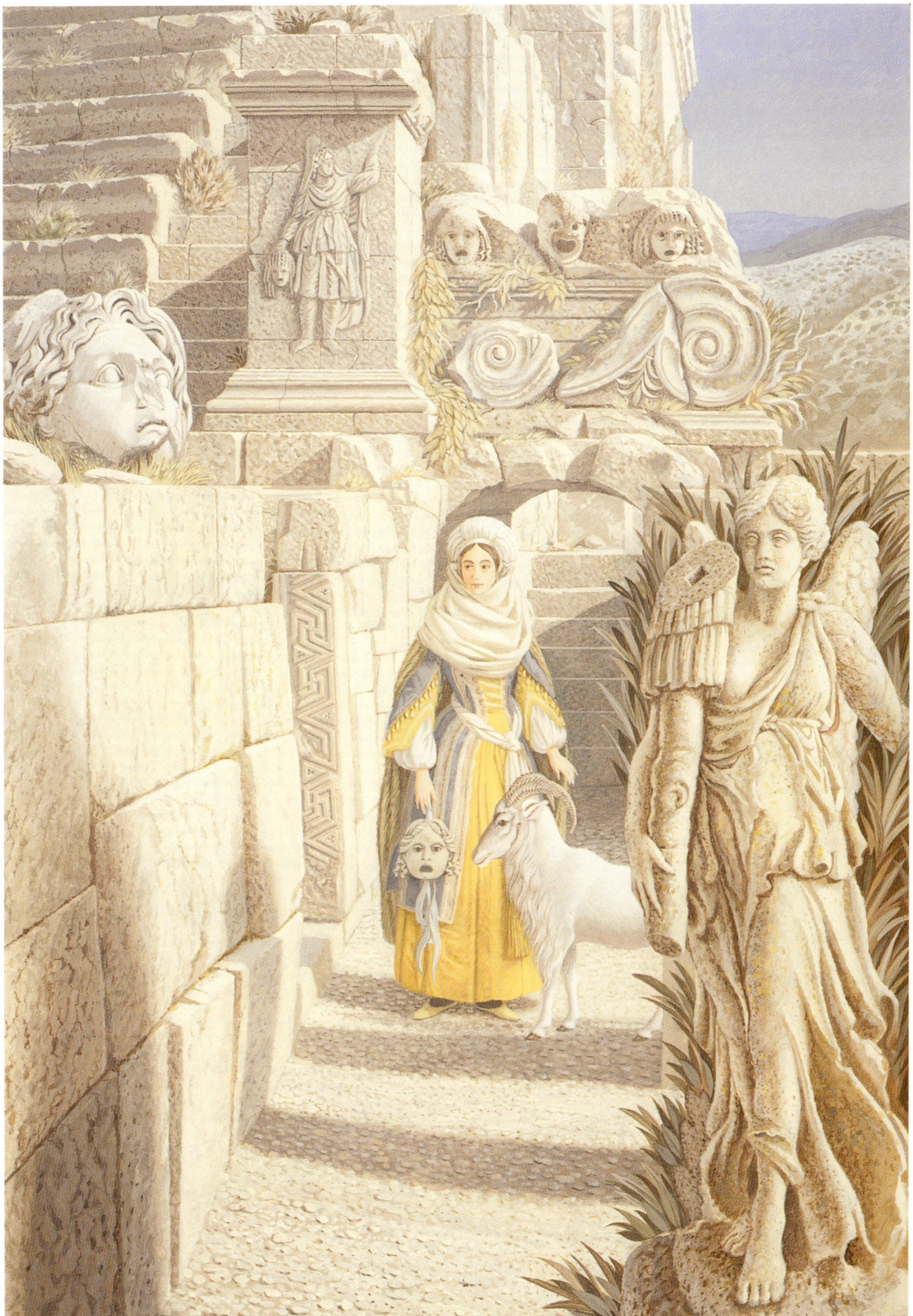

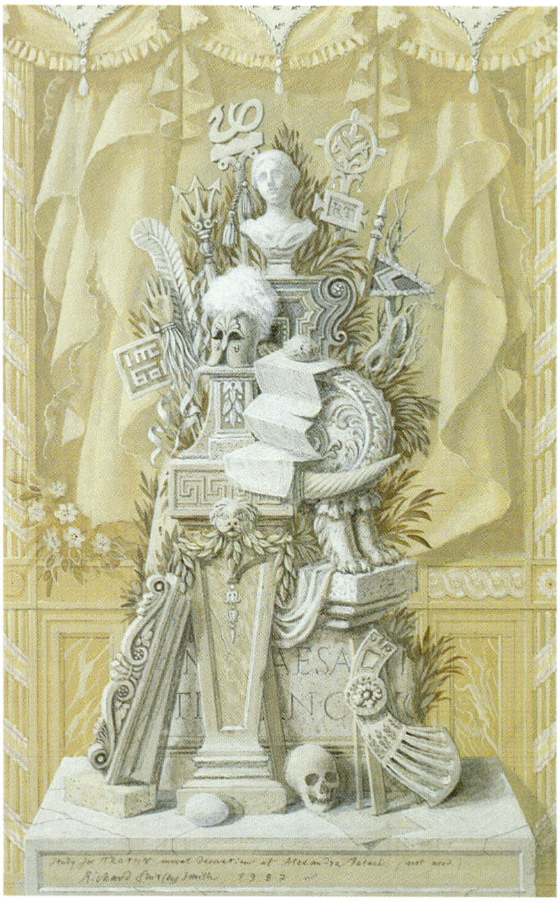

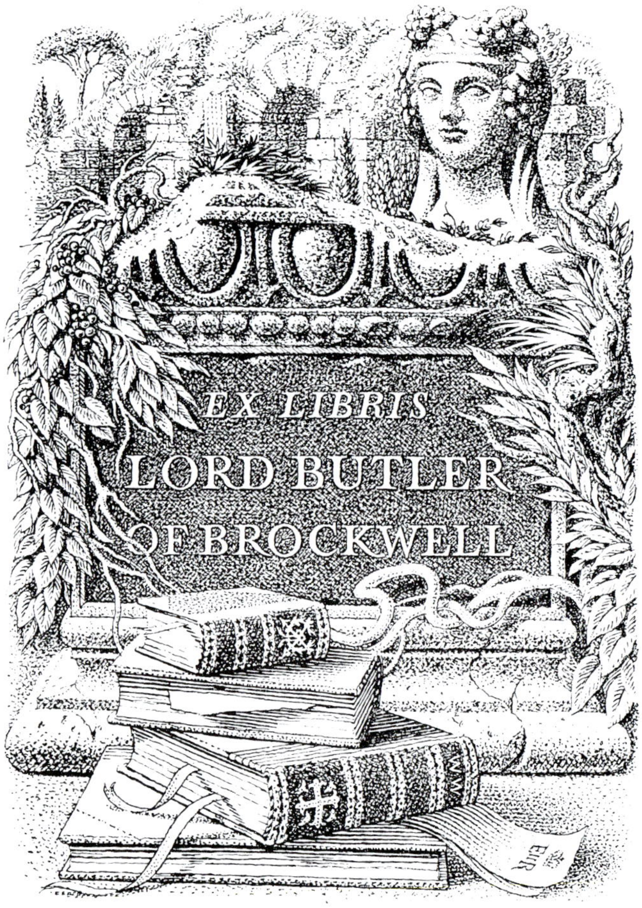

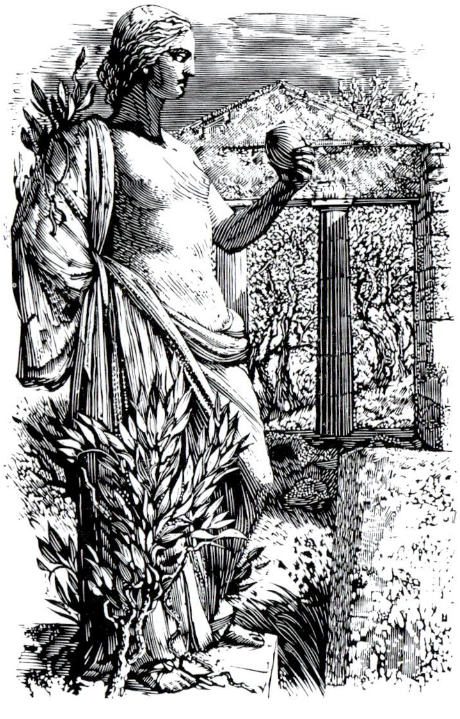

ABOVE LEFT: Fig.137 *Trophy, Helmet & Skull (detail)*, acrylic on paper. 60 × 31cm. 1987 (*ptg.cat.165*). Wyliman Collection

ABOVE RIGHT: Fig.138 Bookplate for Lord Butler of Brockwell, line drawing, 2000. While the background reflects his studies of the classics, the emblems on the books and papers record his considerable contribution at Harrow School and his work as Master of University College, Oxford, and as Cabinet Secretary

LEFT: Fig.139 *Aphrodite in Greek Temple* from *The Poems of Percy Bysshe Shelley*, wood engraving. 1971 (*eng.cat.191*). Limited Editions Club of New York

OPPOSITE: Fig.140 *Trophy, Wheel & Bonnet*, acrylic on paper. 53 × 38cm. 1985-7 (*ptg.cat.145*).
These two trophies were studies for a mural in Alexandra Palace. The building in the background was inspired by Wendel Dieterlin's fantastic book *Architectura* of 1598. Collection of Anne Stevens

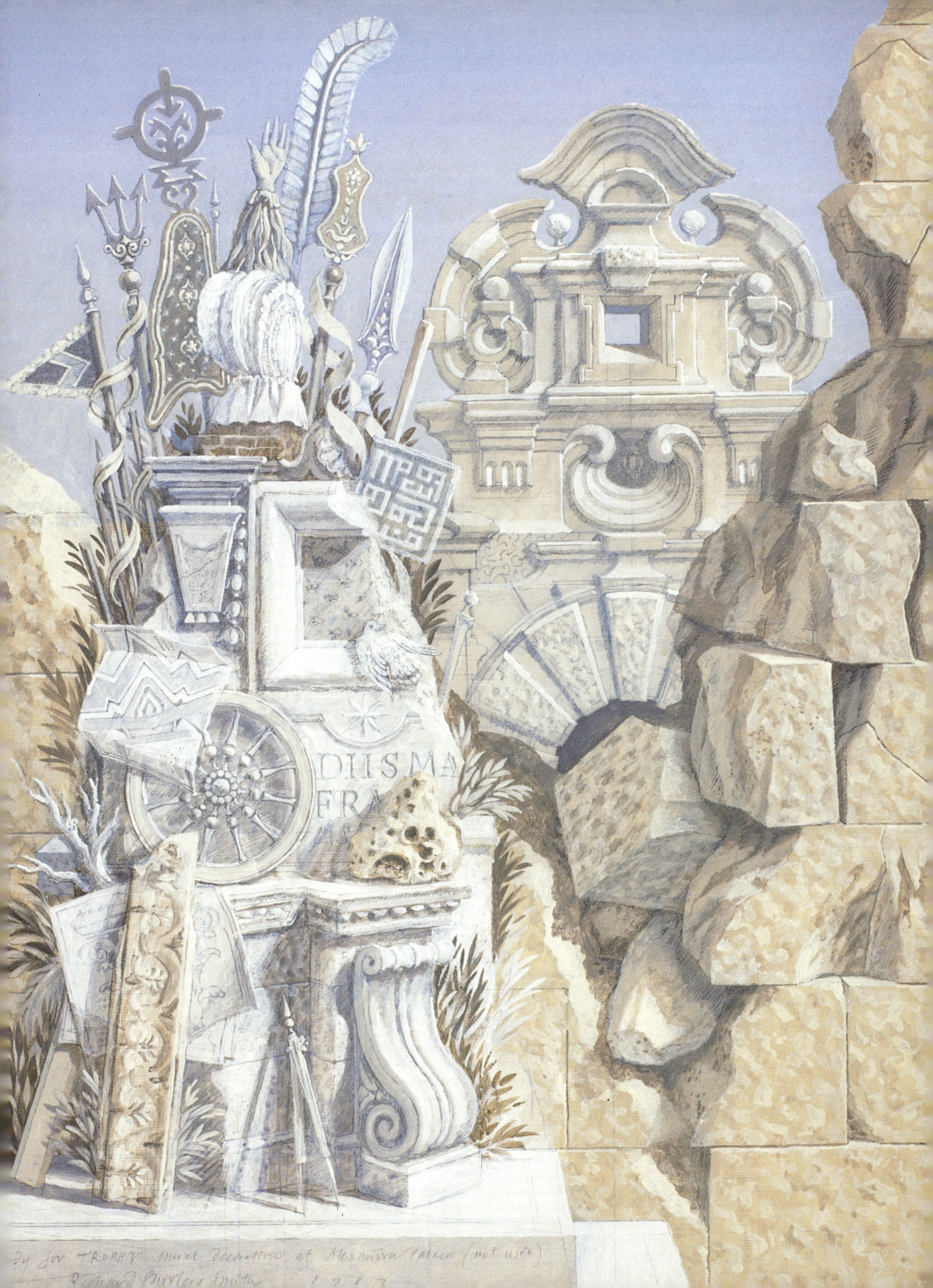
DIIS MA
FRA
for TROPHY Mural Decoration at Alexandra Palace (not used)
Richard Shirley Smith

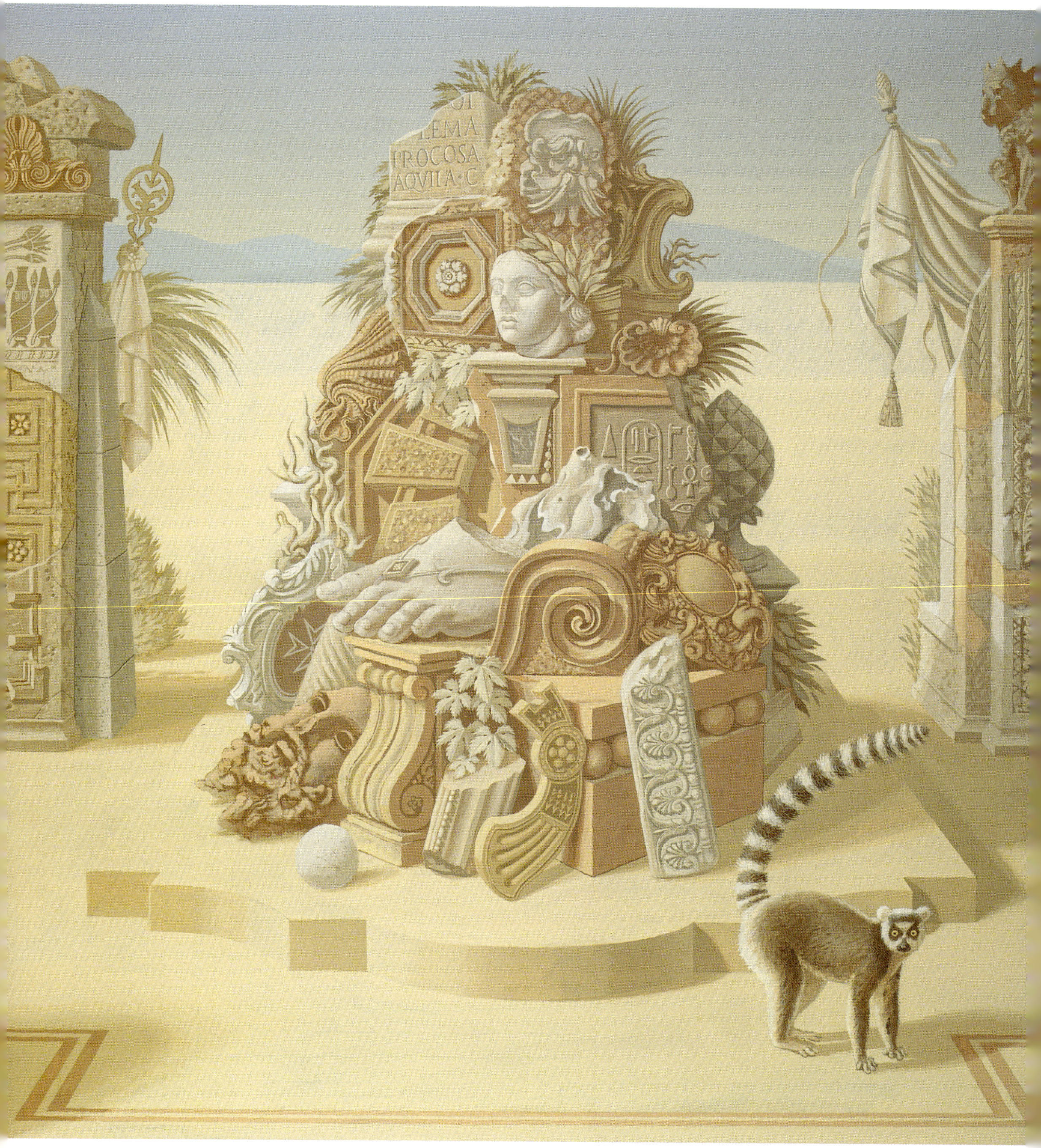
LEMA
PROCOSA
AQVIIA·C

VARIOUS ESSAYS

OPPOSITE: Fig.141 *Regalian Cartoon with Racoon*, acrylic on canvas. 92 × 88cm. 1992 (*ptg.cat.202*). Collection of Alison Brown

An Account of a Friendship with David Jones

Richard Shirley Smith

from *David Jones, Ten Letters*. Agenda Editions 1996

DAVID JONES (1895–1974) is one of the finest British artists of the twentieth century. When at sixteen I first met him, I only vaguely realised that after surviving the inferno of the First World War he had become a Roman Catholic, soon afterwards moving to Ditchling to work with Eric Gill, the stone-carver, engraver and typographer; that he had engraved cycles of illustrations on wood and copper for various limited editions in the twenties; and that from 1928 to 1932 he had painted an outstanding series of watercolours. As a schoolboy I was more aware of his poetry: *The Anathemata* had only recently been published and his earlier and less demanding poem *In Parenthesis* of 1937 had, I knew, won the Hawthornden Prize. I became fascinated by the still lifes on which he was working, of stemmed glasses with flowers, his *Calix* pictures, set up in the window of his room, and subsequently, in 1954, was intrigued by his major exhibition at the Tate Gallery.

My first sight of David Jones must have been about 1951, when I was at Harrow School. Walking up the hill, he modestly stepped off the pavement to convenience a bunch of hatted and tailed Harrovians. He wore a voluminous, ancient overcoat. Later, he told me of his indignation when his tailor said he would repair it 'just this once more'.

At that time he lived at Northwick Lodge, a porticoed, grey brick, Victorian mansion, his room at the back overlooking much of distant London beyond the steep garden and nearby trees, which are to be seen in many of his drawings. The house suited him reasonably well, even if it was run by an elderly, ex-Harrow master who used sometimes to sleepwalk his way downstairs and refill the salt-cellars.

Audrey Malan, the wife of my housemaster, introduced me to Jones as he lived almost next door. Soon afterwards I made the mistake of calling on him one morning about 11.30. He kindly explained to me, while making his bed, that as he worked at night until 3 o'clock he preferred visits at tea-time. He, however, did not always realise how unusual these hours could be. Some years later Louis Bonnerot, a distinguished and courteous Frenchman, was planning to visit him the following day. The professor found himself woken by a phone call in the middle of the night and asked if he wouldn't mind bringing a supply of cigarettes with him. No sooner had he got back to sleep than the telephone rang again – would he make sure he got cork tips.

I recall going to see him another day with a school friend who thought that, because of Jones's evocative drawings of large cats in the zoo, he would enjoy our taking a lively Burmese cat with us. This was not a success as it knocked things over while exploring the clutter of his room; gently we were advised not to bring it again.

David Jones was kind enough to sponsor my application to enter the Slade School; while I am certain I have justified the place I was offered, I believe I would not have been accepted without his sponsorship. I then did my National Service in Germany before starting at the Slade, where Juliet Wood and I met. We visited Jones together on many occasions and thus the friendship developed. He said that Juliet was an artist to her very finger-tips. One evening, some years before it was published, he read aloud the whole of his poem *The Dream of Private Clitus*, but it was usually only when it was time to catch the last bus that he would drag out bulging folios of watercolours and prints in an attempt to delay our departure.

His great seriousness and fits of exasperation were always spiced with irresistible humour, as in his story of the sudden disappearance of a tube of paint, which, after a whole day of exhausting search, he discovered stuck to the underside of a paintbox upon the bed where he worked.

The fact that we happened to be Catholics helped us understand him. He was, for instance, often refreshingly playful about his religious duties, for he did not like Christian teaching to be unnecessarily rigid. He described how once he went to a long-overdue confession by taxi, as he was nervous away from home and liked to keep open his lines of retreat. The priest solemnly pointed out that if he had had an accident on the way there, he might well have gone to perdition. Jones replied that no one relished a long theological discussion more than he but, if it were all the same to the priest, he would prefer to postpone it – particularly as he had a taxi ticking away outside.

Although not liking to venture out much, he could sometimes be tempted by a Nuptial Mass, so, to our delight, he attended our wedding in September 1960. There he made friends who visited him while we were abroad studying in Italy.

Looking through his letters now they seem affectionate and very encouraging: responding to postcards of places or objects that we knew he would like, informative about his own work and richly ornamented with historical, Classical or Christian allusions and texts.

On our return I made simple frames for his last two great paintings *Tristan & Essyllt* and *The Greeting to Mary*; in thanks for doing this he gave us a print of his *Everyman* engraving of 1929, which has proved such an inspiration to me.

When Northwick Lodge closed, Jones moved to a small guest-house, Monksdene, at the foot of Harrow Hill, consisting of two suburban houses joined by passages. These were decorated with flocked wallpaper, aquariums and curly wrought-iron, an effect he wryly likened to a Moroccan brothel. His room favoured writing rather than painting as it was long and dark with a window at one end giving onto an orchard, soon after his arrival transformed into a car park.

I took him by car one afternoon to Cullen's, where he bought grapefruit, biscuits and eggs, by then almost his staple diet. On our way back we stopped at Northwick Lodge. Only the front doorstep remained at the edge of a crater, from which the house seemed to have been wrenched like a great tooth from the clay of the hillside. This suggested to me another upheaval being hotly debated at the time, which concerned Jones a great deal more profoundly: the abandonment of the traditional Latin liturgy to which so much of his written work refers.

Our feelings as to what an artist should be must have been deeply affected by meeting this extraordinary painter and poet at such an impressionable age. Jones's logical, commonsense ideas about how to express his learned and subtle visions seemed as normal to us as his total lack of material success, even though, at that period, he was so admired and frequently visited by his most discerning and established contemporaries.

We continued with letters and contacts until 1964 when our second child was born. Then our lives became more and more desperately busy until we moved to Wiltshire, where I ran the art department at Marlborough College.

For Christmas, in 1971, I sent him a print of my favourite amongst forty-two engravings I had made for Shelley's poems, illustrating lines from *Adonais*, his lament for the death of Keats:

> . . . faded violets, white and pied and blue;
> And a light spear topped with a cypress cone,
> Round whose rude shaft dark ivy-tresses grew . . .

In the very substantial obituary in *The Times* of 29 October 1974, E. C. Hodgkin presents all David Jones's achievements yet, seeming to find something missing, adds 'David Jones was a singularly dignified, gentle and warm spirit, amused and amusing'.

Marlborough 1995.

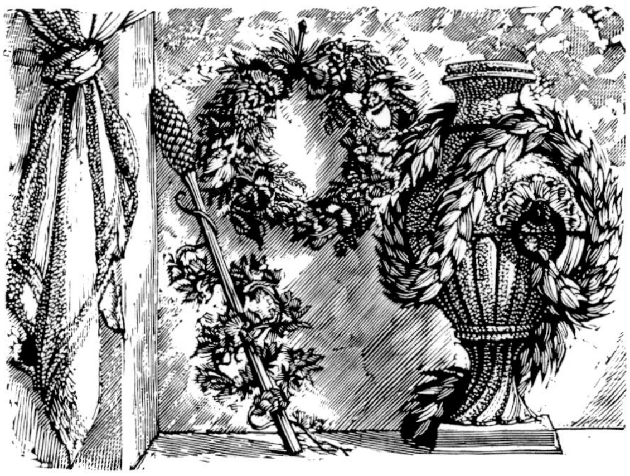

Fig.142 *Wreathed Urn, Cone Spear & Curtain* from *The Poems of Percy Bysshe Shelley*, wood engraving. 1971 (*eng.cat.182*). Limited Editions Club of New York

Two Notes about a Painted Clavichord

Sir Evelyn Shuckburgh who constructed it and Richard Shirley Smith who decorated it. From the *Antique Collector*, August 1982

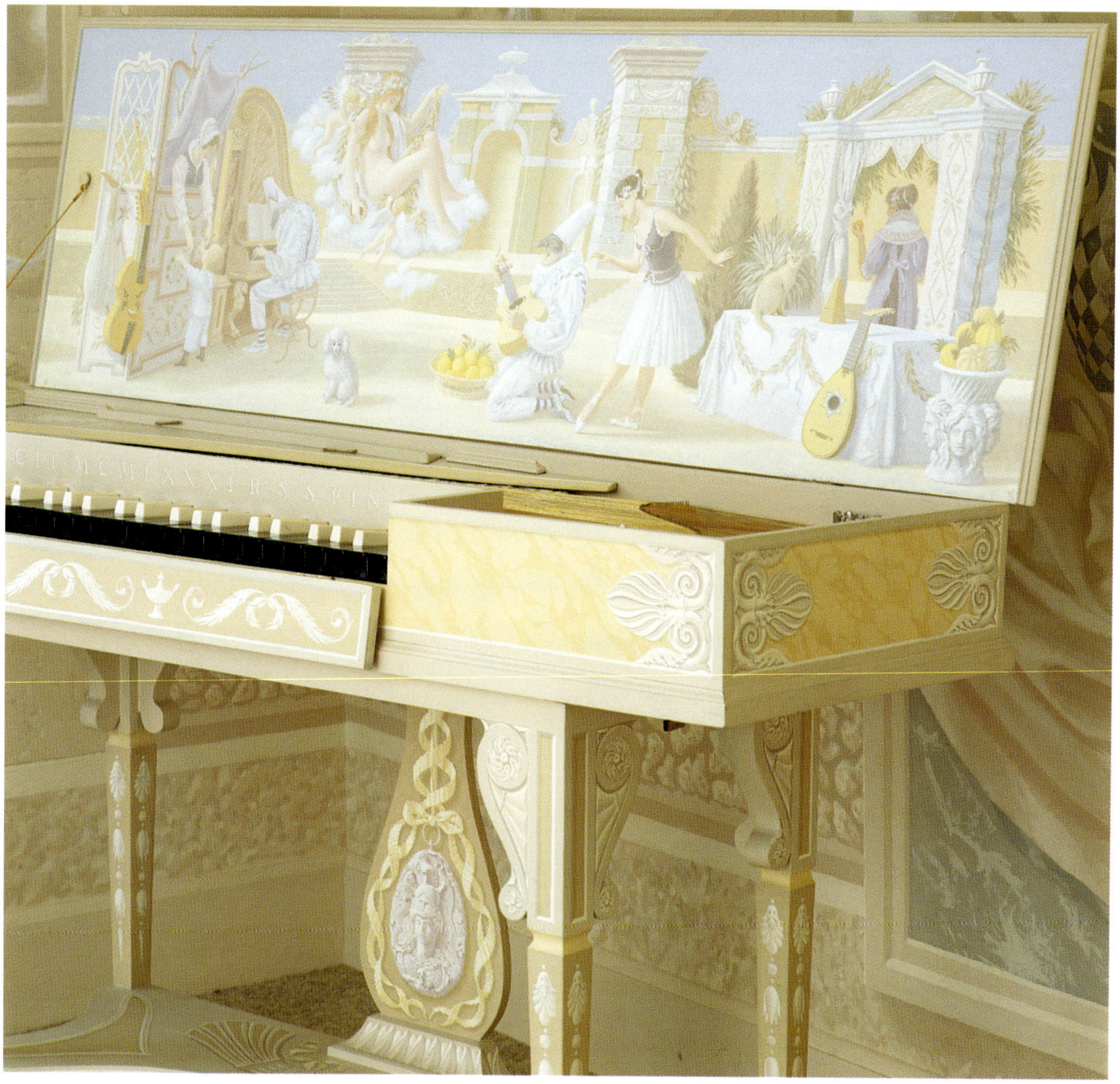

IN NOVEMBER 1973, Thomas Goff, who for many years had been making harpsichords and clavichords in his house in Pont Street, London, and had become a recognised pioneer in the revival of interest in old instruments of music, wrote and asked me whether I would like to help him, once a week, building his instruments. His lifelong partner, James Cobby, had just retired and he was looking for an apprentice. My own experience in instrument making had been limited till then to constructing a harpsichord from a Hubbard kit. So I accepted Tom's offer with alacrity and for the next two years, until the time of his death, I spent practically every Tuesday in his workshop assisting him with his clavichords and making one for myself under his instruction.

Most of Tom's clavichords were veneered, either in walnut or in rosewood, and he attached the same importance to the beauty of their outward appearance as to their musical quality, designing and cutting elaborate brass hinges and making the best use of the figuration of the veneer. However, sometimes they were painted. About thirty-five years previously, before the War, he had made an unusual clavichord of which he was very proud and on which he used sometimes to play after lunch while I was working with him. It was decorated all over by Rex Whistler, and the inside of the lid contained an enchanting Whistler painting of gods and goddesses disporting themselves in an idyllic scene. There is a colour photograph of it on the cover of a volume of keyboard music by Herbert Howells. The day after Tom's death in 1975 this instrument was stolen from his house and has not been seen again.

It occured to me that, since I can make clavichords in exact conformity with Tom's instructions and using his very templates, I might attempt to compensate for the loss of that instrument by finding an artist of today who would decorate a new one in the same sort of spirit. I consulted various people but it was Rex's brother, Laurence Whistler, the glass engraver, who suggested that Richard Shirley Smith was the man to do it.

Tom Goff's clavichords usually stood on absolutely plain stands consisting of inch-square legs and side pieces. Richard, with an eye to the decorative use he could make of it, designed the more elaborate stand on which this instrument is set. He also designed the brass hinges. While it is in no sense a copy, I think this clavichord can be regarded as a worthy successor to the lost Goff/Whistler, and one can only hope that one day it may be possible to set them side by side for comparison in tone and beauty.

Evelyn Shuckburgh

A clavichord is a keyboard instrument, used from the fourteenth century to the early nineteenth century, which although too quiet for any but solo use, offers a little emphasis and vibrato lacking in the harpsichord. The strings are not plucked or tapped as in a harpsichord or piano respectively, but are set in motion by a 'tangent' rising from below, which both determines the pitch and divides off a length of vibrating string from the damping felt for as long as the key is kept depressed. In Germany clavichord and harpsichord types existed side by side for at least four centuries until the advent of the pianoforte.

It cannot be said that my choice of early nineteenth-century Neo-Classical style was very fitting to a clavichord, as this was the age of Beethoven and the piano. The truth is that, at the time, I was much influenced by the rich decorative imagination of Piranesi, expressed so strongly in the magnificent 1978 exhibition at the Hayward Gallery.

The long oil-painted panel inside the lid shows an Italianate *Commedia dell'Arte* scene with animals,

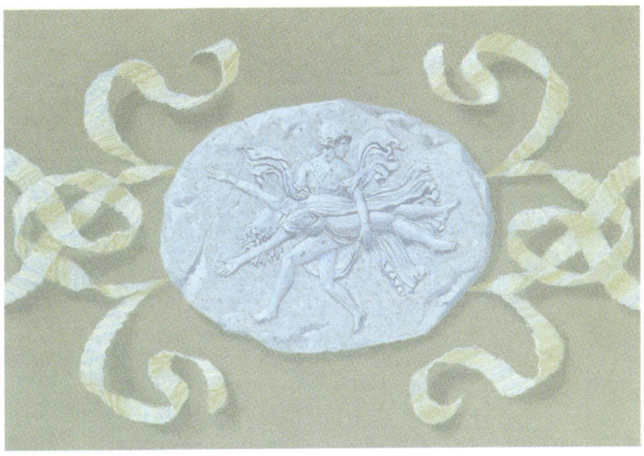

ABOVE: Fig.144 (*detail*) the outside of the lid

OPPOSITE: Fig.143 *Painted Clavichord*, oil on wood. 1981 (*ptg.cat.75*). Collection of Rex & Ruth Muffett

market stalls and various musical instruments including a giraffe piano, baryton and lute. The *Commedia dell'Arte* troupes specialised in extemporisation, acrobatics, music and dancing, and so it is not surprising that they should receive a visit from Terpsichore – identified by her lyre – Muse of the Dance and one of the nine daughters of Zeus. The two Pulcinelle react rather differently to her inspiration.

While I was studying in Rome in 1961, I particularly admired some very lively stucco relief ceiling decorations in a subterranean basilica near the Porta Maggiore, and as Sir Evelyn Shuckburgh was Ambassador in Rome some years later, I thought it appropriate to use this motif on the outside of the lid. The subject is said to be one of the Dioscuri or sons of Zeus, running off with a daughter of Leucippus.

The white keys are made of ivory and the black are faced with ebony and arcaded on the front edge. The inscription above the keyboard is painted in *trompe-l'oeil* 'v' cut and is in the traditional form of the initials of the maker and painter and the date:

E.S.FECIT MCMLXXXI R.S.S. PINXIT

Richard Shirley Smith

The Painter as Wood Engraver

Richard Shirley Smith in his studio in Blewbury

Linda Saunders: from *The Green Book*, Autumn 1985

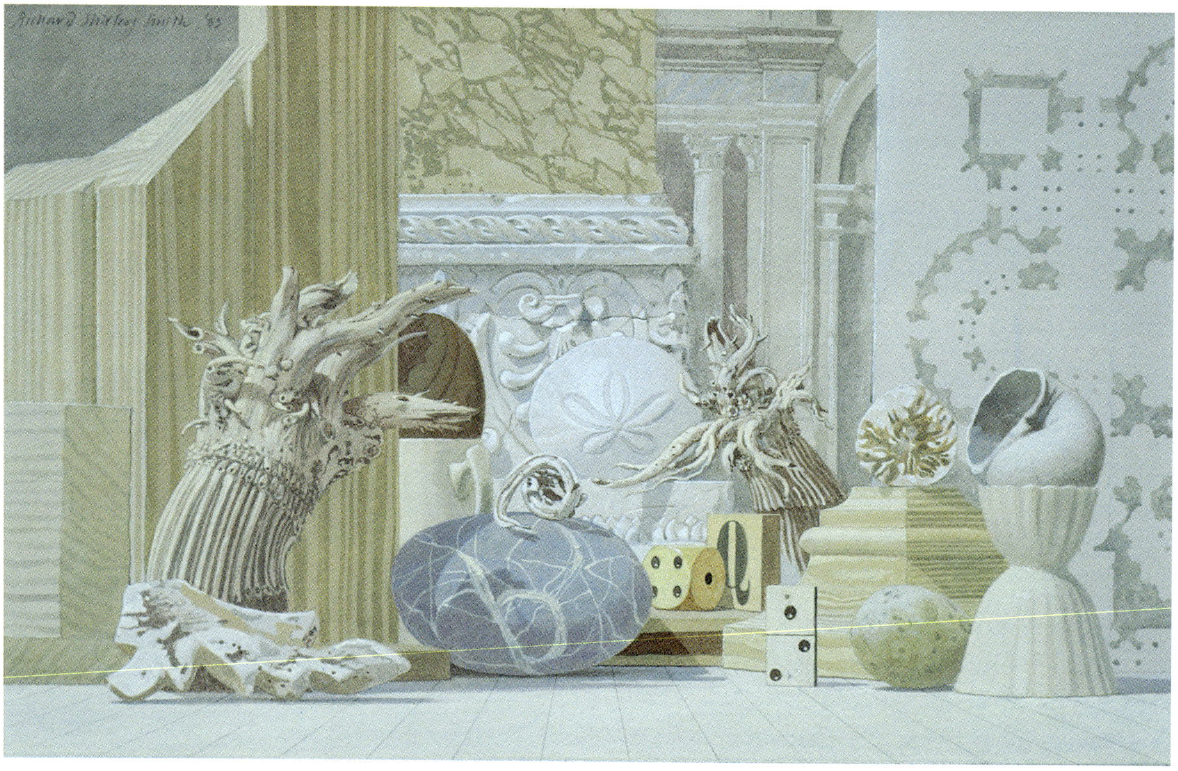

MANY OF US ARE still in the nursery, suggests Richard Shirley Smith: 'artists go on playing, other people grow up and become bank managers'. Certainly there is an unworldliness, a sense of excitement and relish about this artist. In his work there is a strong element of play, of masks and theatre, of the roguish characters of the *Commedia dell'Arte*, but it is of a mature and elaborate kind, layered, suggestive, knowingly surreal.

He is talking in his own 'nursery', or studio. Most articulately this is his room, an extension of his avid and fun-loving mind, very orderly but prolific. Efficient work surfaces, well-stocked bookshelves (bibliophiles might well drool like infants), engraving tools and stereo equipment share the highly organised space with a weird and wonderful collection of *objets trouvés* and ephemera. The room combines the functional and the fabulous, academe with fairground baroque, and has been composed by an extremely idiosyncractic eye.

Images in Richard Shirley Smith's pictures are often juxtaposed in disturbing and baffling relationships. In his studio, objects intrigue in the same way. The child in the interviewer needs to know, 'What's this? And this?' and conversation is diverted into an explanation of the use of an ivory glove stretcher, or a glass Italian picnic flask with a spout that allows family and friends to drink from a fine jet of wine without slobbering the only container. 'But be careful, some of those things' – the sea horse, the wavy shells? – 'are fragile'. Gently chastised, the interviewer reluctantly takes up the biro.

Like other artists who have been fine engravers, Shirley Smith is versatile and energetic: his abilities

ABOVE: Fig.145 *Stage Set Still Life*, acrylic on paper. 33 × 53cm. 1983 (*ptg.cat.130*). Collection of Catherine Bates

cover roughly the same area as those of an earlier generation – Eric Ravilious, Rex Whistler, Edward Bawden. He delights in large painted canvases, great rooms to decorate with murals, *tromps l'oeil* of incredible detail on a grand scale, pillars, obelisks, drapery falling in rich folds, Palladian vistas, overgrown ruins. His settings are observed with meticulous attention to historical and architectural detail; they may be peopled by a masque of characters from myth or street theatre; realism is teased by fantasy. Technical virtuosity carries over into photography too, and he works from slides for precise information and perspectives; then he may add incongruous elements, deliberate anachronisms, or contorted natural forms – the extraordinary roots of giant hogweed, perhaps, which are here in his room and, stood on end, have pleated skirts and a many-horned jester's cap. 'Everything comes from somewhere', and he can usually show you where. 'Now where is it?' – riffling through a tome – 'Ah, but isn't *that* marvellous!'

What, for him, connects these different media? Decoration: whether it is a book to be decorated or a wall, the only difference is that of scale. In whatever medium, there is the same loving description of forms and elegance of design. However, he does value wood engraving for attributes peculiar to its small scale: 'A whole life's work can be posted in an airmail envelope'. Behind this practical view, one might read an awareness of mutability, spiking his love of the monumental, of magnificent buildings and romantic decay. Nor is he afraid of large themes and subjects in his engravings, which have a rare mastery of depth and perspective; the small scale is a challenge to the fineness of his marks and to his power of condensing imagery.

He shares all wood engravers' love of the medium's special qualities: the crispness of line, the tonal possibilities. In an account of his association with David Jones, an early mentor, he quotes from one of Jones's letters: 'Yes, in wood engravings, in general the most satisfactory kind are those where the blacks and the whites and the greys are so "organized" or managed as to give this unity. In one way old Bewick has never been surpassed in knowing how to get the best advantage out of the greys and whites very subtly set off against very small areas of solid black'. In Shirley Smith's own best work there is a marvellous tonal interplay and the areas of white, too, are managed with great subtlety, often giving a sculptural roundness to flesh (he is very good at women's bodies),

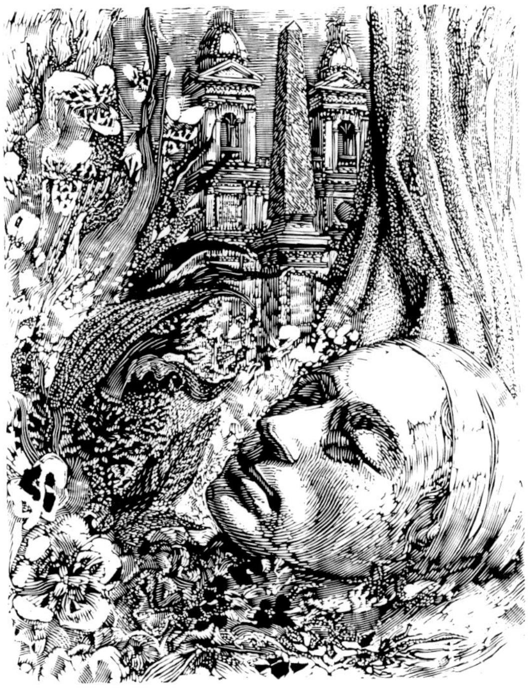

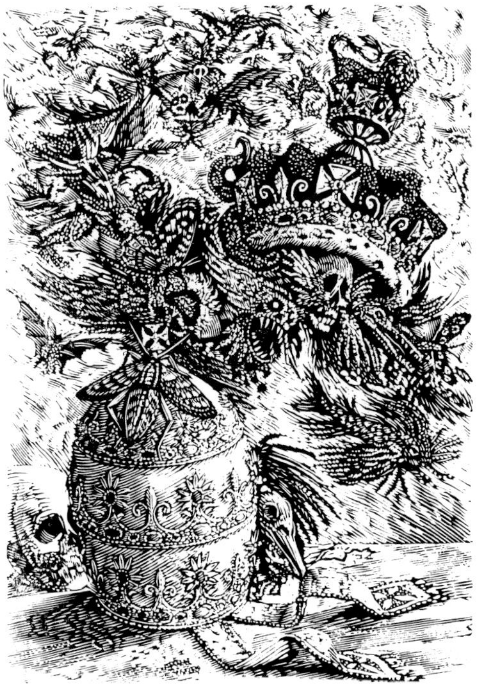

Fig.146 & fig.147 *Adonais* and *The Triumph of Life*, from *The Poems of Percy Bysshe Shelley*, wood engraving. 1971 (*eng.cat.167* & *188*). Limited Editions Club of New York

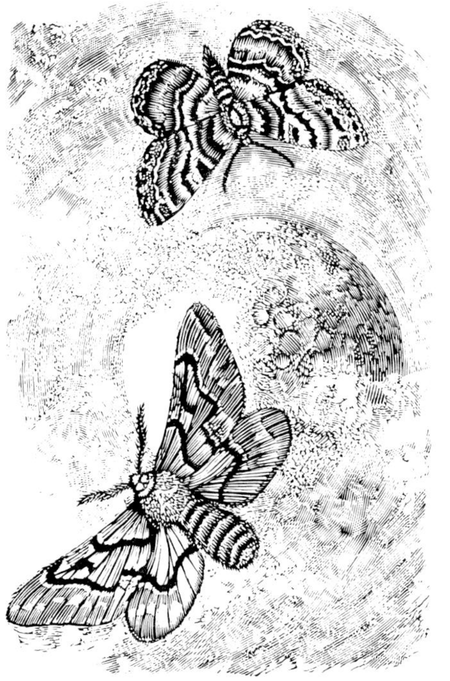

Fig.148 *Moths & Moon*, from *The Poems of Percy Bysshe Shelley*, wood engraving. 1971 (*eng.cat.192*). Limited Editions Club of New York

or a lyrical 'pied beauty' to, for example, the flowers and foliage which dissolve round the head of Keats in *Adonais*. (Fig.146).

Wood engraving is an exacting business, asking a particular integrity. 'I like an engraving to be faithful to the piece of wood', Shirley Smith explains. At the same time he wants it to be true to the sensual qualities of different subjects: water, stone, feathers, fur, even the carapace of a beetle . . . . He believes in making as great a variety of marks as possible, aiming for an exquisite sensitivity, not just to textures and planes, but to the original quick movements of brush and pen. This worked-for immediacy can be seen in *Adonais* where the engraver preserves the delicate dabs of the brush. The technical paradox fascinates. The ephemeral, random-seeming touch preserved with all the engraver's slow patience and skill is perhaps most evident in his 'finger-print' clouds (*Moths & Moon*), as Laurence Whistler calls them.

Shirley Smith explains that he begins with paint, using very thin watercolour to make a precise statement of tone on the block before engraving. At this stage it looks like a miniature painting. Then 'I stop being an artist and become an ant'. He 'crawls' over the surface very very slowly. The idea of a quick result is anathema: you must think of the most complicated, intricate way of doing things, anything that will slow you down. This is sheer craft, that of the nineteenth-century journeyman engravers, which aims at carrying out absolutely faithfully every-thing that has been proposed in paint. 'Ideally', says the artist, 'the first pull should be *it*, though this is seldom the case'. Clearly he finds every part of the process satisfying to his rigorous mind, but the exciting moment comes when, having wiped the paint from the block, leaving (anxiously) only the engraved wood, the ink is rolled across for the first time. After perhaps weeks of work, 'it all jumps to life'.

His most imaginative illustration work has been in response to poetry, very notably his magical engravings for Stephen Spender's edition of *The Poems of Percy Bysshe Shelley* (Limited Editions Club of New York, 1971, and reprinted by The Heritage Press, 1974). Ozymandias's 'vast and trunkless legs' suffer a stony degeneration that marvellously figures the hubristuc disease they symbolise; Endymion bathes swooningly in moonlight. Such subjects seem irrisistible to the gothic/romantic bent of his sensibility. And the hectic vision of *The Triumph of Life* with its 'ever-moving wings', 'ghastly shadows' and air 'peopled with dim forms, as when there hovers a flock of vampire bats' must have found more than an echo in his life. Shirley Smith was working on the engravings at a time when, through his first wife's nervous breakdown, he lost home, family and his Roman Catholic faith. The resulting engravings are a deeply felt response to the poetry itself.

Quite different in feeling, more formal but richly associative and finely engraved, are his bookplates. They are greatly admired by afficionados and experts such as Brian North Lee, whose own plate is a scene of profusely overgrown, crumbling masonry, 'a beautiful blending of classical with romantic', as North Lee puts it. In the *Ex Libris* Shirley Smith combines mythological and heraldic elements (another area of expertise) with symbols appropriate to the owner's interests and personality.

Talking of the themes which run through his work, the artist feels a sense of history is the most pervasive. He loves to 'slide back and forth in time', and clearly, to distort temporal perspectives. He plays an elaborate hide-and-seek among half-drawn

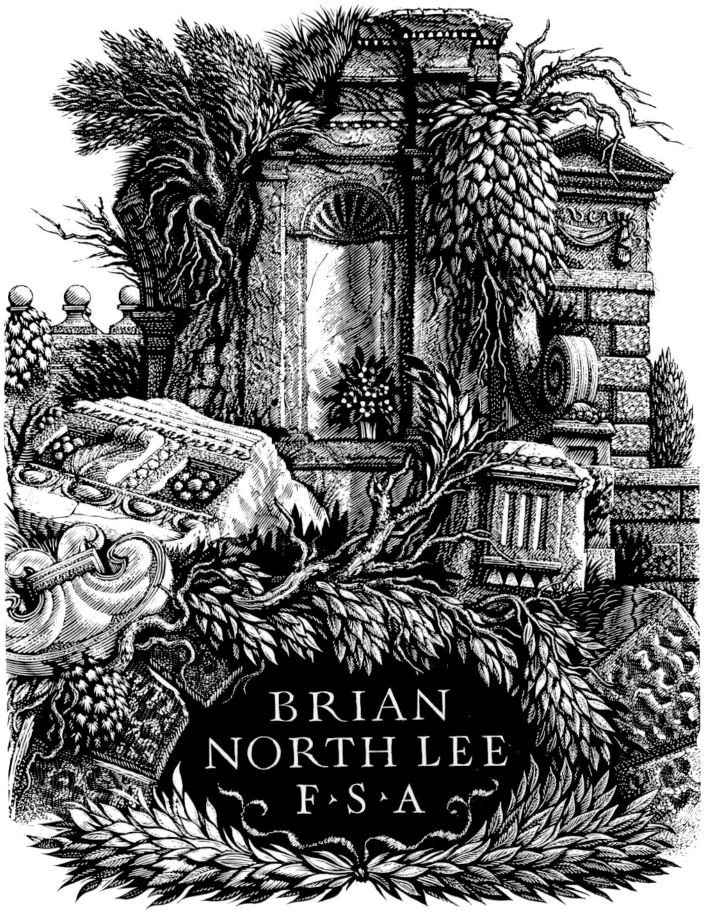

Fig.149 Bookplate for *Brian North Lee*, wood engraving. 1984 (*eng.cat.259*)
Fig.150 *Triumph of Death*, from *Messer Pietro Mio*, wood engraving. 1985 (*eng.cat.279*)

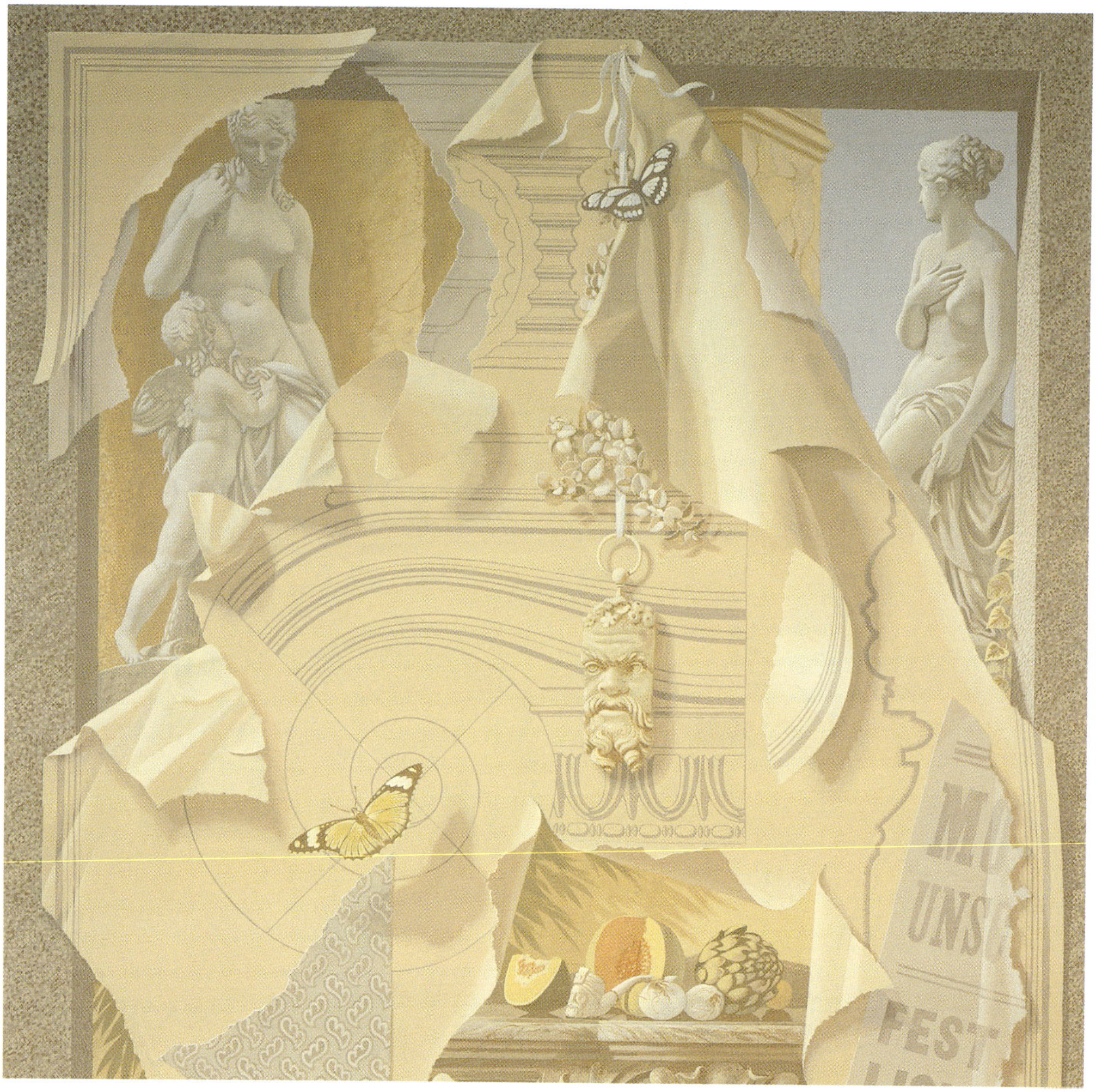

Fig.151 Detail from a mural decoration for the Landseer Property Corporation Ltd. at 24 Bruton Street, London, 1984

curtains, other times and places, realities and unrealities. We all become players on a metaphysical stage, subject to the pranks of Pulcinella, and to the unmasker, death. Against the flickering shadows and hurtling movement of *The Triumph of Life*, one can set the frightening immobility of *The Triumph of Death* from *The Love Letters between Lucrezia Borgia and Pietro Bembo* (translated by Hugh Shankland, Libanus Press, Marlborough, 1985). In this *memento mori* black sands run through the hour-glass and skulls grin among symbols of the lovers' lives and fortunes. The large areas of wood cut away expose this 'bare board' to a merciless light, which casts, under the table, a forbidding shadow (see Fig.150).

Images of transience, whether of the brief lives of moths or the slower histories of stone, abound. But there is also a sense of what endures, of timeless presence and of regeneration. As he engraves, Richard listens to music – without which 'ant wouldn't be prepared to move at all'. Bewick whistled, but he didn't have records, let alone a hi-fi. Richard demonstrates the quality of his stereophonic system with a soaring soprano passage from Monteverdi's *Vespers*. 'Now *there's* a voice straight from the seventeenth century!' It seems completely appropriate to this artist, and to the present moment.

Review of the Fiftieth Birthday Retrospective at the Ashmolean Museum

Simon Brett: from the *Society of Wood Engravers Journal*, 1986

IT WAS TO BE expected that each work in a selective retrospective exhibition would be a choice example of its kind and that in Richard Shirley Smith's case that would mean startling or surreal content mediated through a very refined taste, an ordered encrustation of detail and the most fastidious craftsmanship. Given such standards of craftsmanship it was to be expected that the exhibition would be beautifully and meticulously presented. But even given such high expectations, the exhibition is a surprise and a revelation. It glows on the walls. The assembled whole is so much greater than even a considerable familiarity with individual parts over the years had led me to expect.

Those who know Richard Shirley Smith chiefly as an engraver will be impressed by the amount of painting, elaborate collage and, from recent years, mural work. The murals are represented by large preliminary studies, things of great beauty in themselves. Those who know his work at all will know the very private world it inhabits, where, amid pitted Italianate ruins, decorative foliage and the broken fragments of antiquity, Victoriana and a travelling players' props basket, characters from the *Commedia dell'Arte* pose and creep and peer: beribboned doll-like girls and hunch-backed clowns in masks. What would be downright sinister in all this is made the stranger by the clean, bright light, sometimes the extreme pallor, in which it is presented. Reality it is not. The beautifully crafted, strongly decorative vein makes it entirely appropriate that the murals for the wealthy (or for the Landseer Property Corporation who have sponsored the fine catalogue) should have been commissioned.

But, if you were about to conclude that, in the light of such things as living in the twentieth century for example, this work sounds too much like Decorators' Fancy, this is where the exhibition springs its surprise. Accumulated, the sheer consistency of invention and polished execution builds its own seriousness, vindicating the cheek of having a retrospective at so young an age as fifty! In my judgement, Richard is at his best and most personal in the magnificent series of collages – his use of the medium is unique – and in the engravings, which, at Oxford, occupied a gallery to themselves. They are outside the main streams of twentieth-century engraving, as is the rest of his work, a magnificent and personal output. Decorative knowledge, private vision and, often, the stimulus of a text marry perfectly with a nervous, pecking, coruscating use of the wood, to produce whorls and textures that convey states of mind as powerfully as they describe the character of the objects.

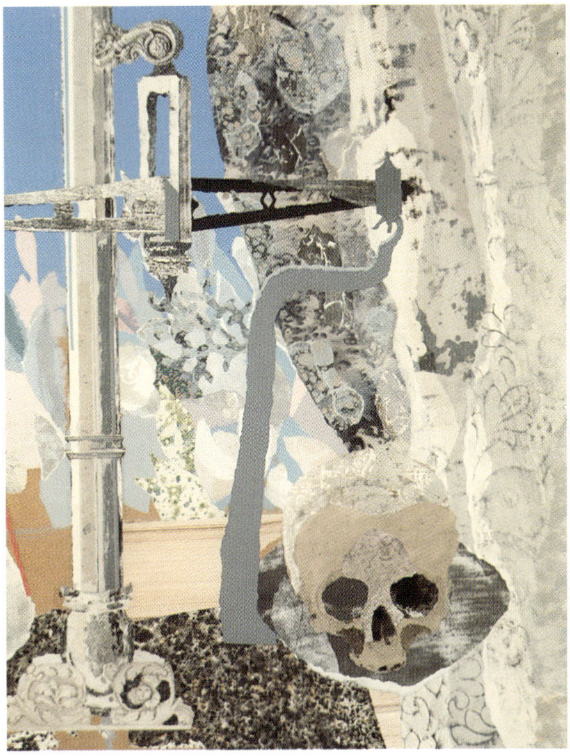

Fig.152 *Scales & Reliquary (detail)*, collage. 86 × 124cm. 1969 (*ptg.cat.15*). Private collection

There is no one who cuts so finely or with such an unerring sense of tone. Richard has been 'giving up engraving' for some years now; if he can continue to give it up to such effect until the time for the next retrospective, we shall all be the richer!

Still Life with Marble Foot

Acquired by the Ashmolean Museum in 1996

Ian Lowe: from *The Ashmolean*, Christmas 1997

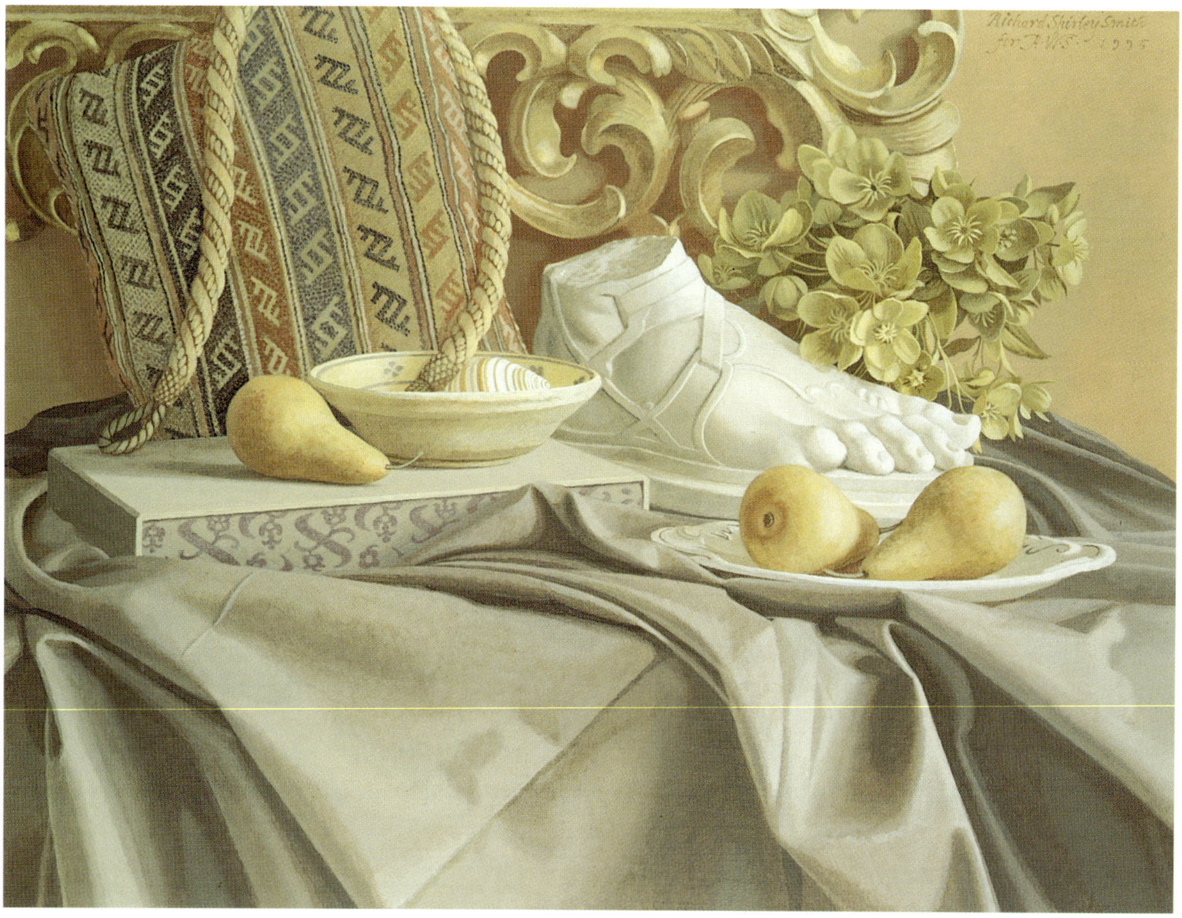

THE MUSEUM HAS RECENTLY been given by friends of Anne Stevens the painting, *Still Life with Marble Foot,* 1996, by Richard Shirley Smith. It has been handsomely framed by Julian Johnston, in consultation with the artist. Johnston hand-gilded the agreed moulding with white gold leaf, so that it looks like silver and complements the tones in the picture. The painting marks the association between the artist and collector, and is a tribute to Anne Stevens's nineteen years of devoted work in and for the Ashmolean Museum from 1976 to 1995. Her primary concern was the collection of twentieth-century British prints, her own interest inclining to wood engraving. It was because of her friendship with the artist that the retrospective exhibition to mark his fiftieth birthday was held in the Ashmolean in 1985. It, in turn, led to the Department acquiring a complete collection of Shirley Smith's wood engravings just at the moment when he had to lay aside his engraving tools. Among them was the bookplate that Anne Stevens had commissioned from him.

As varied technically as he is talented, Richard Shirley Smith was then engaged on a series of mural paintings while continuing to work on canvas and board. When a group of friends were invited to contribute to a fund to mark Anne Stevens's voluntary service to the Museum, it was on the understanding that the proceeds were to be at her disposal for making an acquisition for the Department of Western Art. One or two people felt that she should have the pleasure of enjoying the results of the contributions in her lifetime, but she readily accepted the terms of the gift and decided to spend it all on commissioning a painting from Richard Shirley Smith to add to the representation of his work in the Ashmolean. No choice could have been more suitable for either of them.

In *Still Life with Marble Foot*, might there be a courteous bow to, almost an echo of, Eliot Hodgkin in the three conference pears? The hellebore, on the right of the composition, is the native *foetidus*, which still grows in the wild as well as in gardens, a suitable attribute for Anne Stevens as botanist and gardener. The cast of the sandalled foot seems to hark back to the time when the artist was studying in the Antique Room at the Slade School, or to the period immediately afterwards when he was in Rome (1960–62). The cast is a recent acquisition made by John McGill from a first-century AD Roman copy of the Greek statue of the *Apollo Belvedere* in the Vatican. It is of the right foot and is made not out of plaster but a mixture of marble which glitters slightly. The artist bought it from Belinda Canosa's exhibition last year, 'The Commissioned Brush', in which he took part.

'What about the cushion? What is the book on which dish and pears rest?' These questions on the elements were answered by the artist (29 November 1996):

> The cushion is from Iran. The book, *The Little Flowers of St Francis of Assisi*, Limited Editions Club of New York, 1930. The mirror is nineteenth-century Italian, the carved gilt wood frame behind the cushion, picked up by my father during the last war. The cloth was given to me by Rosemarie Timmis who used it as the background for her portrait of the Sultan of Oman: it came from there. But none of the subjects have any intentional symbolism other than how they look.

That last sentence is a sufficient and accurate description of the way in which Richard Shirley Smith paints his still lifes. He uses the materials which lie to hand in his studio house. If asked, he may include an object, a plant, fruit, even a theme, but those who have been privileged to visit him at home know how completely his surroundings, his furniture, books, fabrics, objects – *trouvés* and collected – show his eye, judgement and taste. His environment perfectly reflects his subjects and vice versa: clarity, elegance, neatness, subtlety of colour, restraint. There is to be found harmony in the unexpected and, occasionally, the seemingly inharmonious, surprising juxtapositions which have suggested the word 'surreal' to describe his work. All is individual and personal. The subjects are combined with

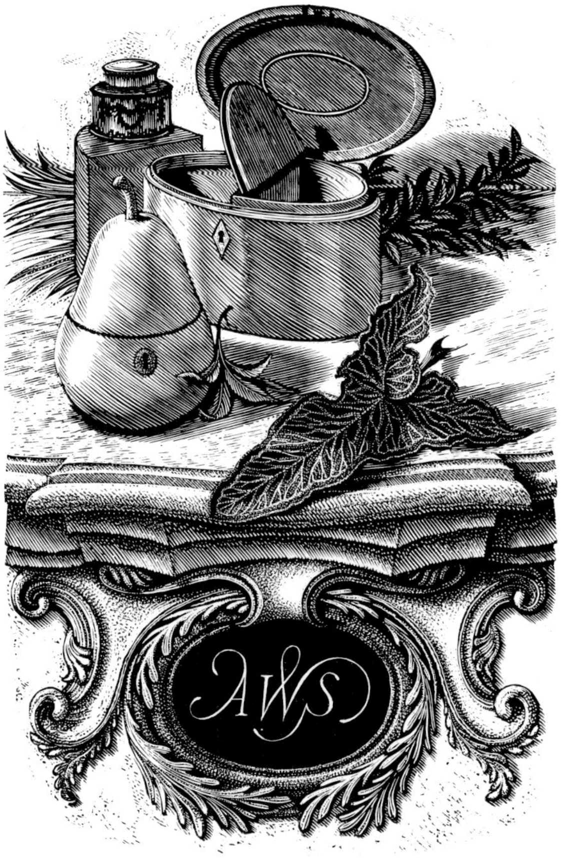

ABOVE: Fig.154 *Bookplate for Anne Stevens*, MBE
wood engraving. 1983 *(eng.cat.255)*

OPPOSITE: Fig.153 *Still Life with Marble Foot*, acrylic.
45 × 59cm. 1996 (*ptg.cat.247*). Ashmolean Museum, Oxford

what Anne Stevens has described as 'his vivid imagination and quizzical sense of humour'. To know and like Richard Shirley Smith's paintings is to be in sympathy with the nature of their creator, to feel an intimacy, a quietness, and a confident belief in his abilities. These qualities Anne Stevens has shared since their first encounter at Blewbury in 1979, and nothing could more fittingly celebrate their association than *Still Life with Marble Foot*.

Archaeological Fragments

Acquired by the Old Speech Room Gallery, Harrow School, in 1996

Carolyn Leder: from *Recent Acquisitions*, 1996

RICHARD SHIRLEY SMITH has characteristically drawn on a variety of sources for this virtuoso display of painterly technique whose subject complements the school's collection of antiquities. Writing about the picture for this catalogue, the artist comments:

'The initial inspiration came from a visit to the Archaeological Museum in Florence *c.*1984. Just inside the entrance was a collection of architectural fragments piled up with decorative effect and also sections of mouldings set in plaster. They were all very reminiscent of the Piranesi engravings that illustrate his polemical works. The magnificent Piranesi exhibition at the Hayward Gallery in 1978 had a great influence on me. Clearly a most powerful and fertile imagination had been at work. I had photographed Roman fragments while restoring some eighteenth-century murals near Avignon and also sculptures of shells and sea serpents on the Neptune Fountain in the Piazza della Signoria in Florence. I was able to draw upon some of this information for the foreground.

'One of the (Gibbs) Boycott Pavilions at Stowe in Buckinghamshire can be seen in the background. The superb glass engraver Sir Laurence Whistler, who has both inspired and encouraged my work, was visited while a schoolboy at Stowe by his elder brother Rex. The Pavilions may be familiar to us, as Rex Whistler, shortly after, depicted them in his mural in the Tate Gallery Restaurant.

'The sculptural form of the Roman Matron is in no way diminished by the ribbed wrappings or the wear on the marble. She is one of the wonderful antiquities to be seen in Turkey. On the wall behind there were clearly too many layers of posters pasted on and most of them seem to have been ripped away. I find that when this happens some unpredictable, lively and elegant torn effects often remain. I drew upon some of my photographs of these hoardings for the background of the painting.

'Why do I find fragmented and torn things more interesting than new and complete ones? How many paintings does one see of a brand new pair of shoes? A tramp's old dilapidated boot could tell me much more about the boot's construction and its human adventures. Also, broken pieces can be recomposed to exactly suit a painted composition. The Cubists used to fragment things in order to compose them freely and strongly within the picture area and of course to view them from different angles.

'In the rules of composition, in the creation of form by the fall of light and, I hope, in much else, I try to follow the teaching of my dear friend Maurice Percival who used to teach many of us at Harrow with so much character and good sense.'

The painting finds its counterpart in Shirley Smith's witty 'collage frame', of which he writes: 'I have boxes of wallpapers, marbled papers, well printed ephemera that come through the post – hence the crossed arrows, discarded print proofs etc., which I did use in the 70s for actual collage pictures. They come in very handy for decorating other objects or frames.' The collage includes elements as diverse as the coat of arms of Pope Leo X, excerpts from the score of Vivaldi's *Gloria*, fragments of Ordnance Survey maps of the Outer Hebrides and the Orkney Islands, and, most appropriately, the crest of Harrow School.

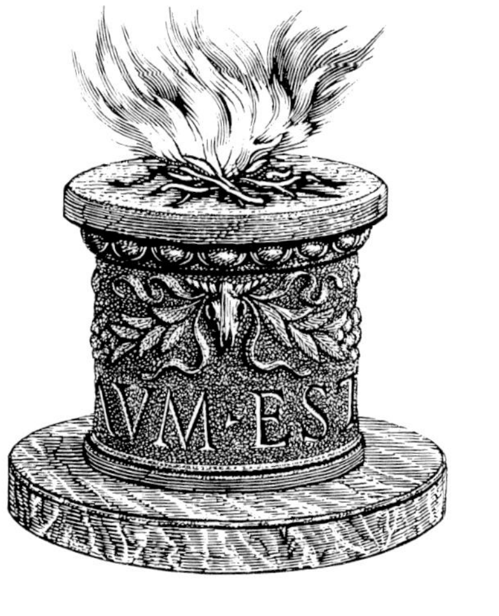

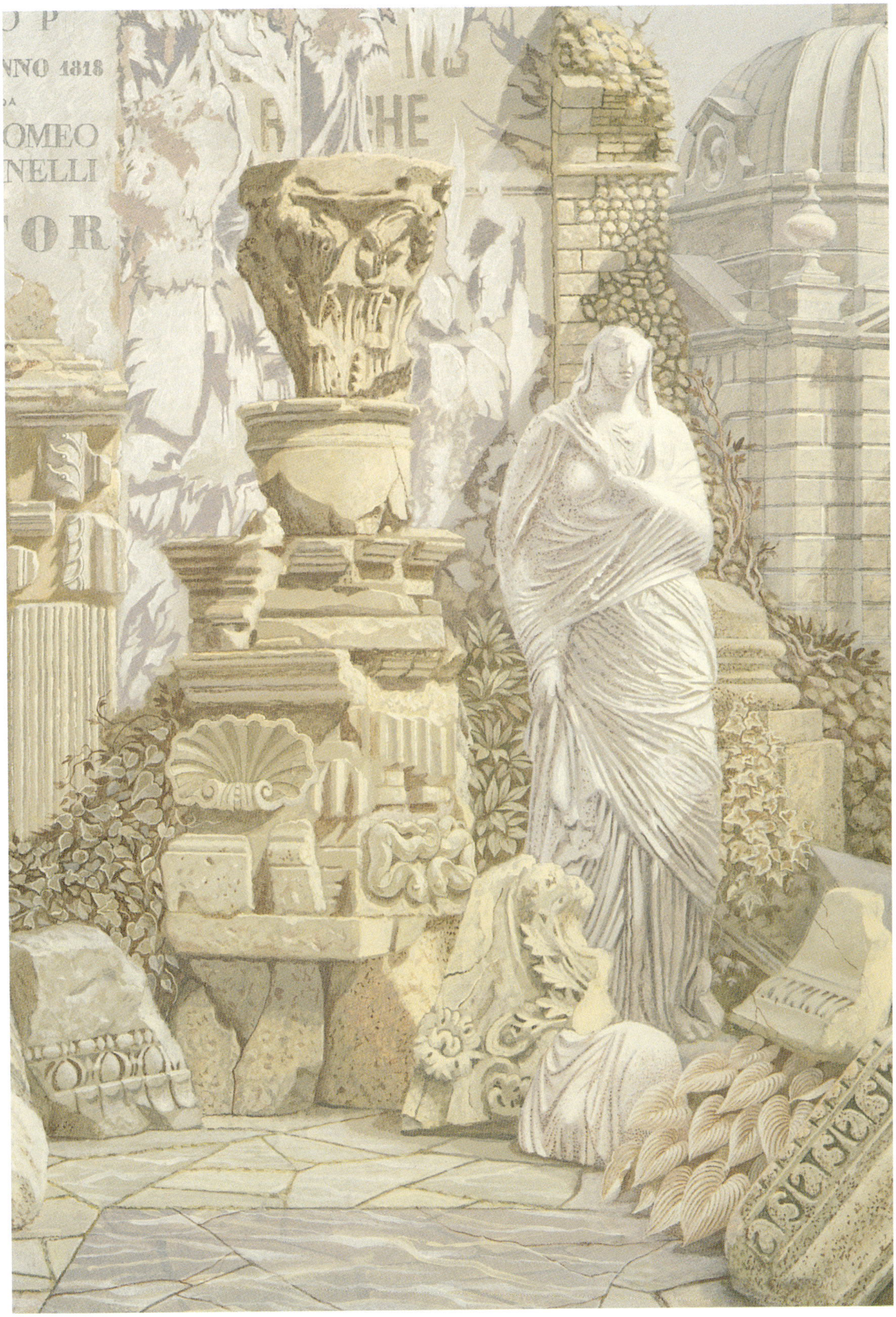

Fig.156 *Archaeological Fragments*, acrylic. 72 × 51cm. 1986 (*ptg.cat.154*). The Keepers & Governors of Harrow School

OPPOSITE: Fig.155 *Altar* from *Messer Pietro Mio*, Libanus Press, wood engraving. 1985 (*eng.cat.267*)

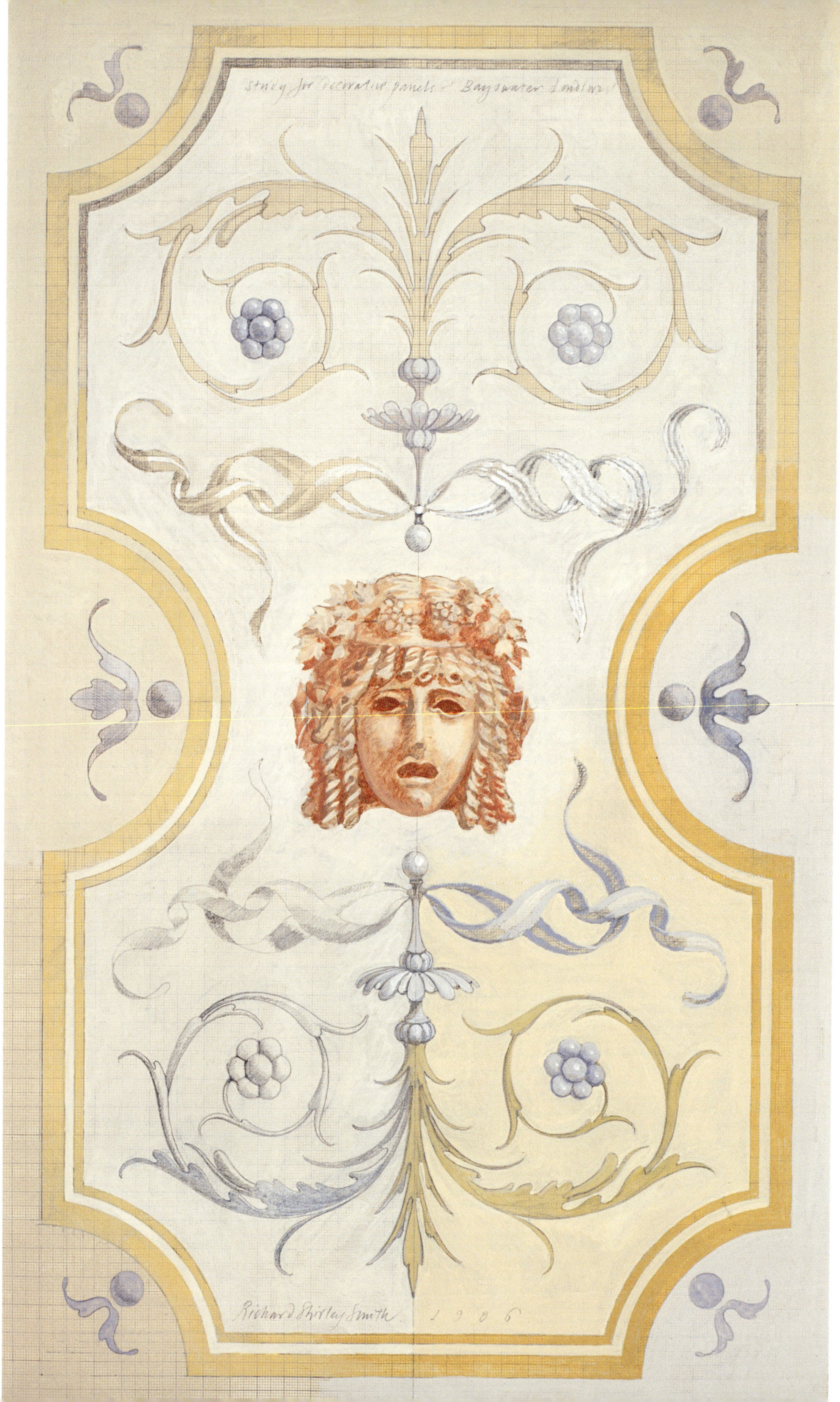
Study for decorative panels – Bayswater
Richard Shirley Smith 1986

Disasters of a Decorator

Richard Shirley Smith

I ONCE SHOWED SLIDES of my paintings of the misadventures of Pulcinella at an international conference on the *Commedia dell'Arte*. At the end, a student stood up and asked me if I liked disasters. He seemed quite satisfied when I replied that I did, as long as they didn't happen to me. Let me describe some that did. I mentioned in the Introduction that I did all the exciting and creative part of the murals in the peace and quiet of my studio. I set the designs out on graph paper, at usually 1:5 scale, and worked them out into small paintings. In this way I knew what I was able to do, the client could see what he or she would eventually get, and my assistants had accurate information to work from. As little time as possible was spent on the dirty, noisy site. The builders always overran the completion date, the clients couldn't wait to move in, and so we had to work along with the builders.

On one occasion my assistants and I arrived on site to find the floorboards had been taken up and the electricity was off owing to the hanging of a chandelier in the room below. Another time, needing to do some thoughtful painting, I arrived on site on a Sunday not knowing that someone had been detailed to drop hundreds of scaffolding poles three floors down a stairwell, landing a few feet away. These interiors were eventually so luxurious but the construction process seemed awfully chaotic: rare blue marble was mysteriously cracked while fitting gold taps, which in their turn would disappear over night.

I noticed that the painters and decorators never tired of pointing out to their apprentices that a plank has two ends, unlike something else that only had one. I was soon to find out why. An assistant was busy gold-leafing the cornice of a large reception room, where an antique cut-glass chandelier of exorbitant cost had been recently suspended. It was formed of hundreds of strings of glass pieces radiating and looping down. He told me afterwards that, while moving the scaffolding planks, one of them had got seriously entangled in the chandelier with a result not unlike a

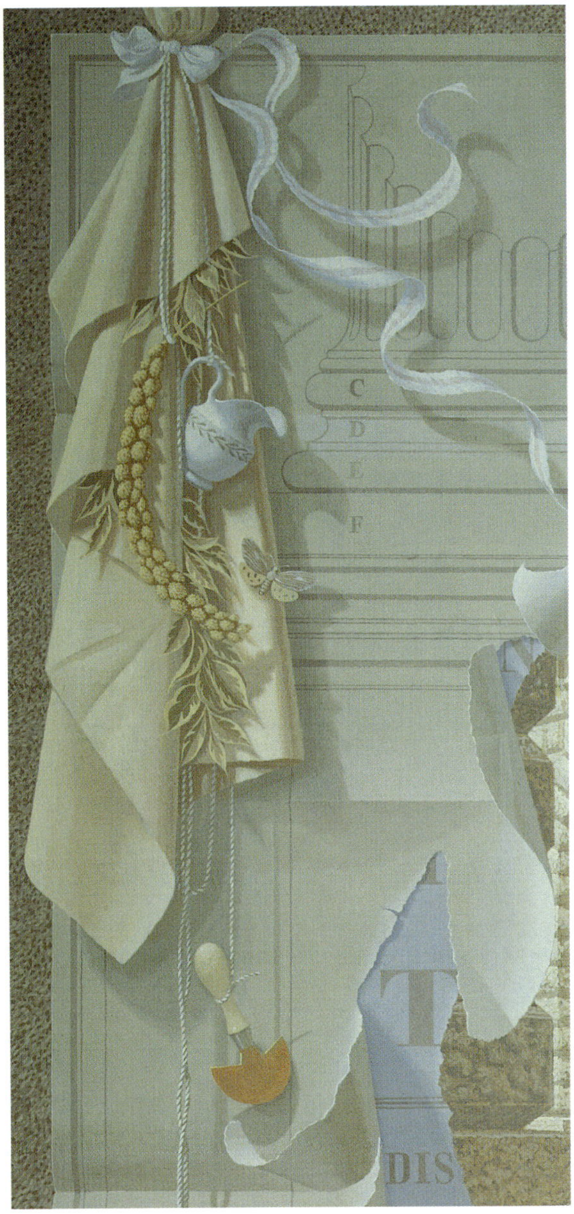

ABOVE: Fig.158 A detail from a mural decoration for the Landseer Property Corporation Ltd. at 24 Bruton Street, London, 1984

OPPOSITE: Fig.157 *Tragic Mask Study* (*same size*), acrylic on paper. 50 × 30cm. 1986 (*ptg.cat.156*).
This was for one of a number of decorative panels for built-in units in a Bayswater flat. Collection of the artist

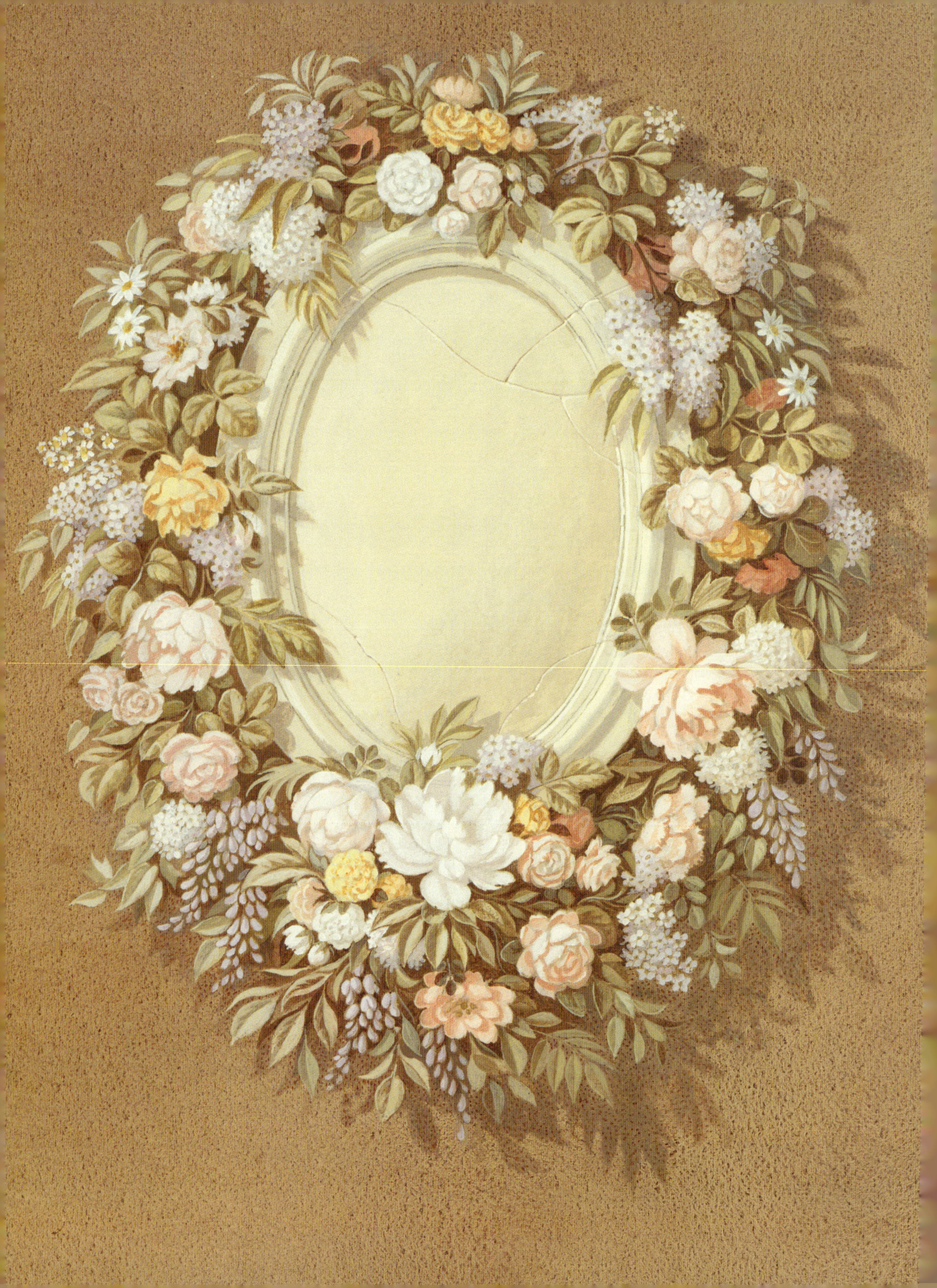

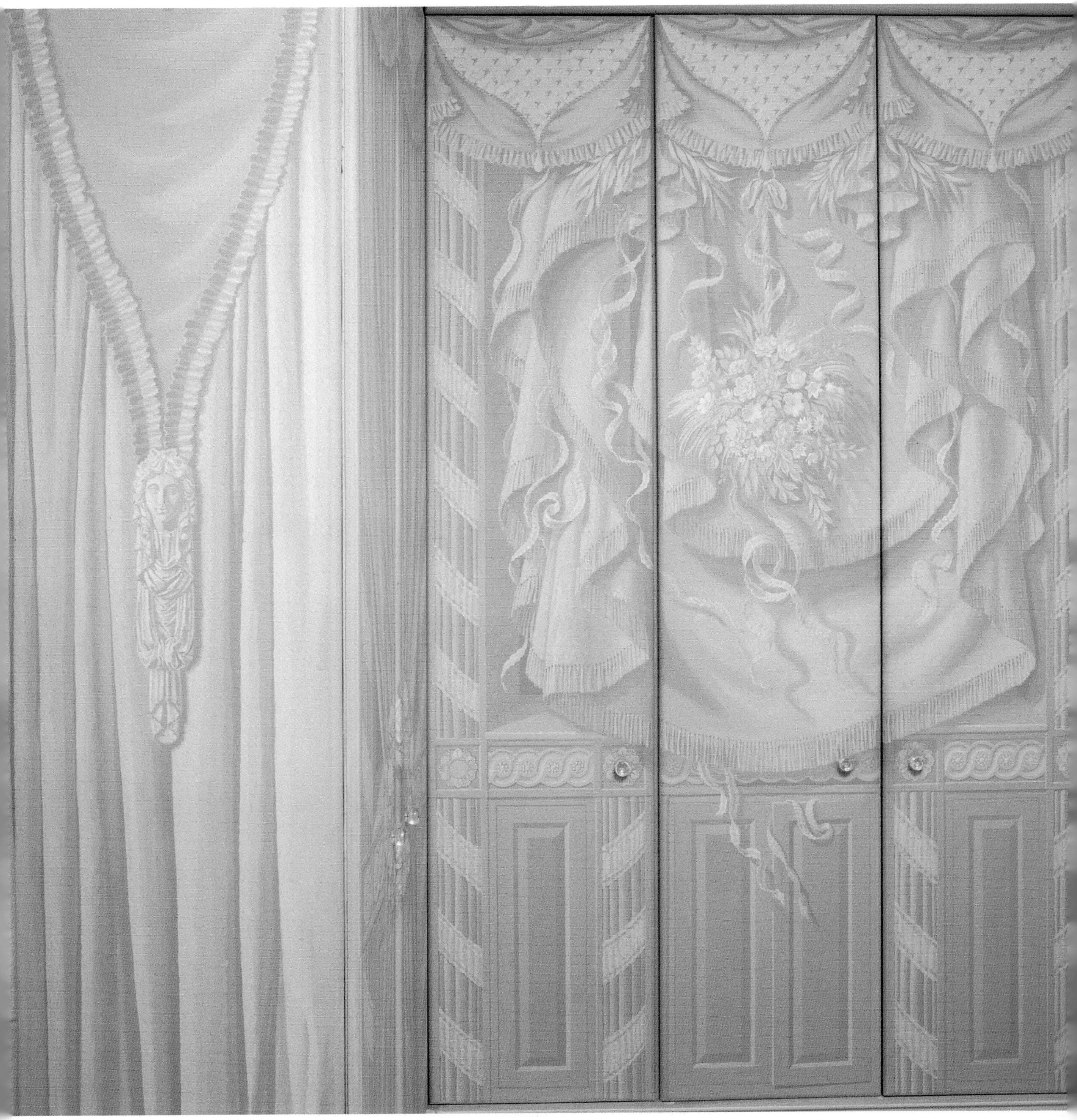

ABOVE: Fig.160 A dressing-room at Holland Villas Road, 1981. All the wardrobe doors are canvas-covered and painted in *trompe l'oeil*. Interior designer: Bill Bennette

OPPOSITE: Fig.159 *Cartouche of Flowers*, acrylic on paper, *approx.* 42 × 30cm. 1986 (*ptg.cat.151*). Private collection

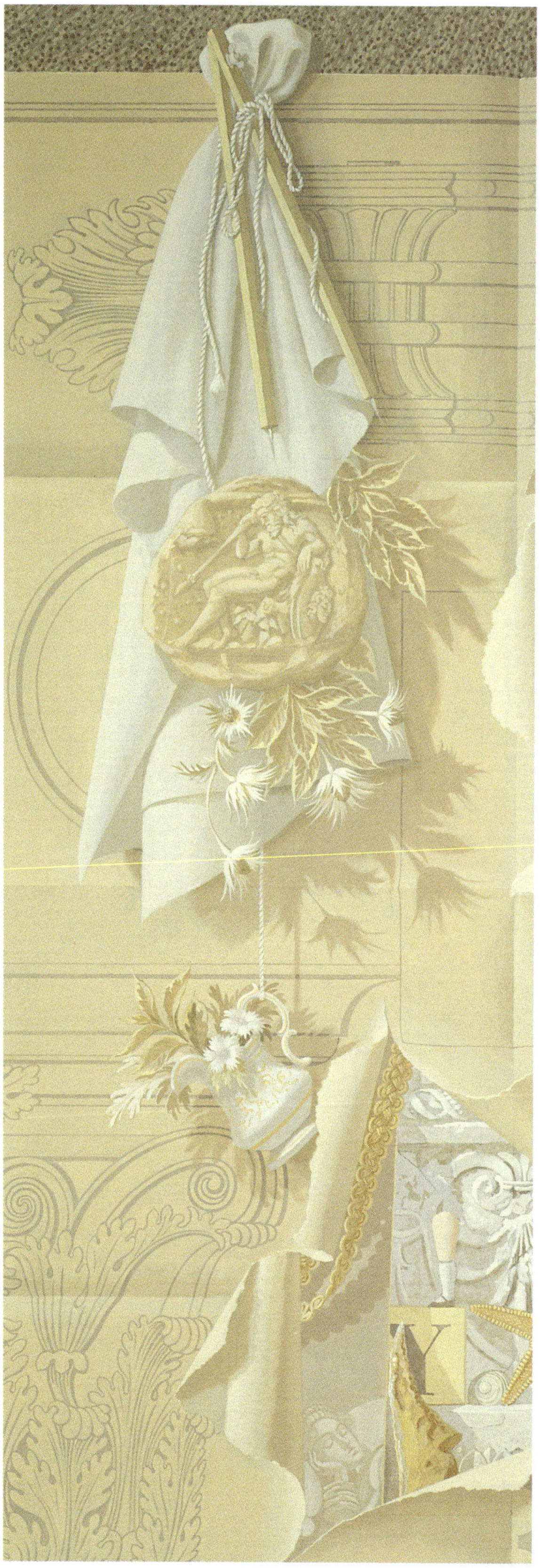

Fig.161 A detail from a mural for the Landseer Property Corporation Ltd. at 24 Bruton Street, London, 1984

Portuguese man of war with strings of beads hanging down. I asked what on earth he had done. He said that he locked the door and then by a miracle found, on the marble mantelpiece, a card of thick fuse wire. Luckily no one seemed to notice anything!

There was one site where a blue under-lit swimming pool had been constructed in a spectacular basement area. The wood-workers having completed all there was for them to do, after many months of work, went out for a celebratory liquid lunch. Not only did they return 'as tight as newts' but swam like newts too, as those who didn't fall into the pool were pushed in, including the foreman. If he had had any sense he would have locked them out. I even heard cries of 'where's Richard?' on the first floor where I was painting. I had to crawl under a large bed to escape. The pool was not improved by wood shavings, old boots and tea bags bobbing about, and there was no shortage of banana skins around – actual and proverbial.

Some of the builders found it amusing to raise false alarms of approaching traffic wardens. One unfortunate plumber, who had already received two parking tickets that week, shot out like greased lightning from a french window, forgetting that he was on the first floor! One notable exception to this noisy chaos was at Greys Court, where I was painting a summer-room for Lady Brunner. The only sounds to disturb our work here were the distant drone of a lawn mower and the jingle of sherry glasses at six o'clock. Another way of avoiding building noise and mess was to have the panels delivered to the studio and paint them there. This was partly possible at Dean Street, Bruton Street and Kensington Palace Gardens.

The only real disadvantage of acrylic is that mixtures get noticeably darker when they dry, therefore it is madness to try to mix colours to match existing paintwork, as at each attempt you would have to wait fifteen minutes to see the result (almost as boring as watching paint dry). At the start of painting a mural on site, we would make dozens of mixtures and keep them wet in plastic yogurt pots. These would last for months. There would be mixtures for stonework, marble, sky, ribbons and curtains in such a way that colour was consistent all round the room and that, with no mixing, it was simple for students and friends to help me. These mixtures were labelled and kept in cardboard cartons – always upright and always cool.

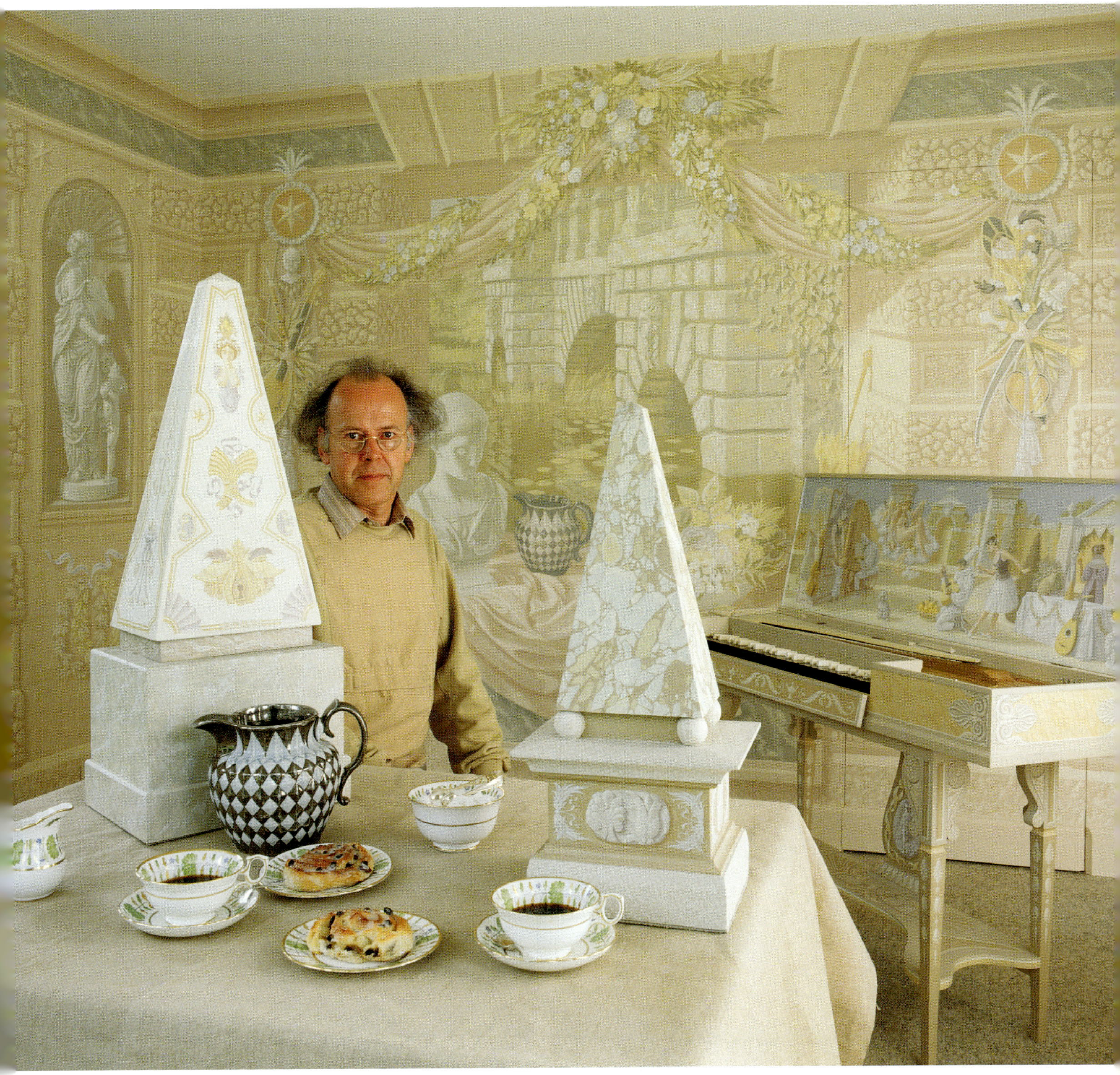

Fig.162 The artist in a private summer-room at Greys Court, decorated for Lady Brunner in 1985. This is clearly an 'all me own work' photograph. The painted clavichord from the collection of Rex Muffett was made by Sir Evelyn Shuckburgh, as were the obelisks, while he was waiting for me to finish decorating the clavichord in 1980. The obelisk on the left reflects 'Piranesi' inspiration following the 1978 Hayward Gallery Exhibition. The mural shows a Palladian bridge, of which there are three in England. Photograph: *Observer* magazine

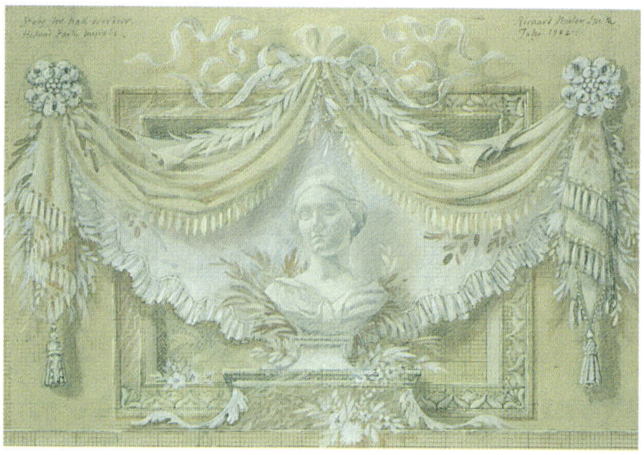

Fig.163 *Study for Overdoor*, Holland Villas Road, acrylic on paper. 29 × 42cm. 1982 (*ptg.cat.119*). Wyliman Collection

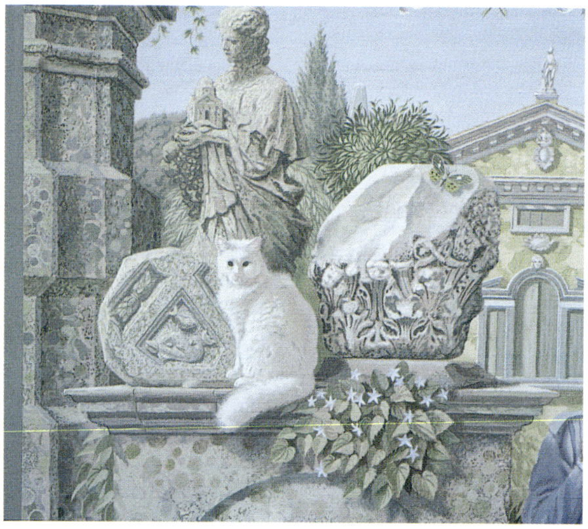

Fig.164 Detail from an overmantle painted for Anne Stevens in 1986. Our white cat, Mr Pitkin, was very friendly with visitors to the Blewbury Festival open studios exhibitions. On the first day we had six offers to buy the cat and none for paintings. Mr Pitkin spent the next day locked in the tool shed and sales were good. (*ptg.cat.150*)

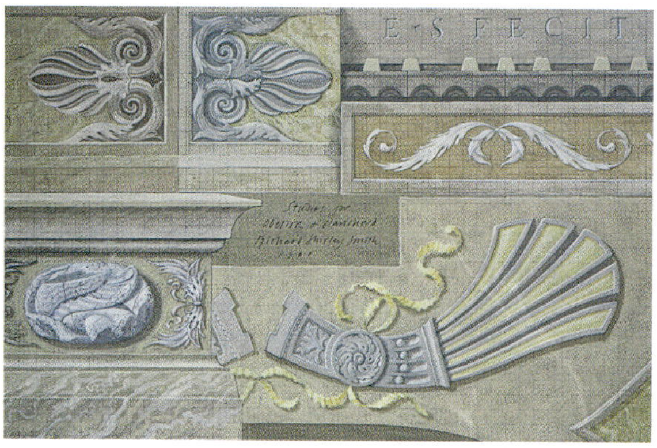

Fig.165 Study for *Clavichord & Obelisk*, acrylic on paper. 30 × 46cm. 1983 (*ptg.cat.132*). Private collection

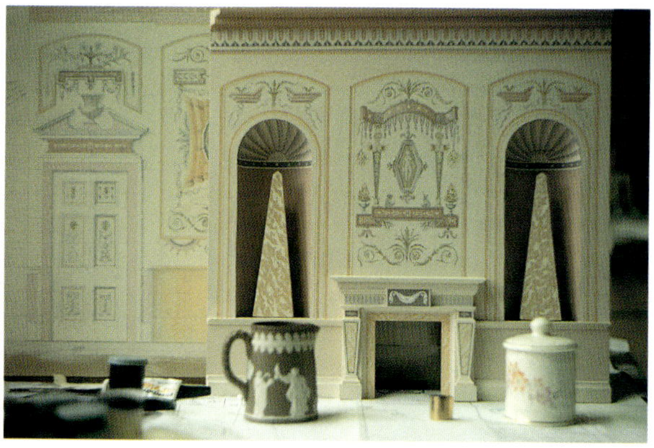

Fig.166 A wall and a full-scale cartoon for a mural in a 1:12 scale doll's house called Britannia House. Each room featured a different interior designer. The music room was designed by Bill Bennette, my mural being in the Pompeian style. 1987

I remember one disastrous occasion, returning from an Easter weekend to find that, as a result of a mindless clear-up, these cartons had been laid sideways on top of a very hot radiator for four days.

Likewise, children and animals were not always helpful. One little boy was in the habit of using my preparatory drawings as stepping stones in order not to dirty the marble floor with muddy gum-boots. On another occasion our efforts to paint an Italian drawing-room were bedevilled by two sprightly dalmatians, who barked like mad whenever they saw anyone's jaws moving. They took a lively interest in our painting sponges and, racing round the garden, were very unwilling to relinquish them.

There were other difficulties and embarrassments. I was working on a floor-to-ceiling *trompe-l'oeil* mural in a dining-room in Eaton Square. This was shortly before I realised that poor quality greying hair is best cut short. I was rather flattered when I found that all the builders, plumbers and carpenters addressed me as 'Professor'. Later, I discovered that this was only a shortened version of 'The Mad Professor', a nickname by which I was generally known on the six-floor building site.

I remember one little embarrassment, working in a warm, humorous, Jewish household. It was decided that a Greek bronze nude should be painted in a niche near the front door. I started working on a female nude but was soon voted down by the lady of the house and the interior designer, who both wanted a male athlete. Later I heard that the Rabbi had visited and observed

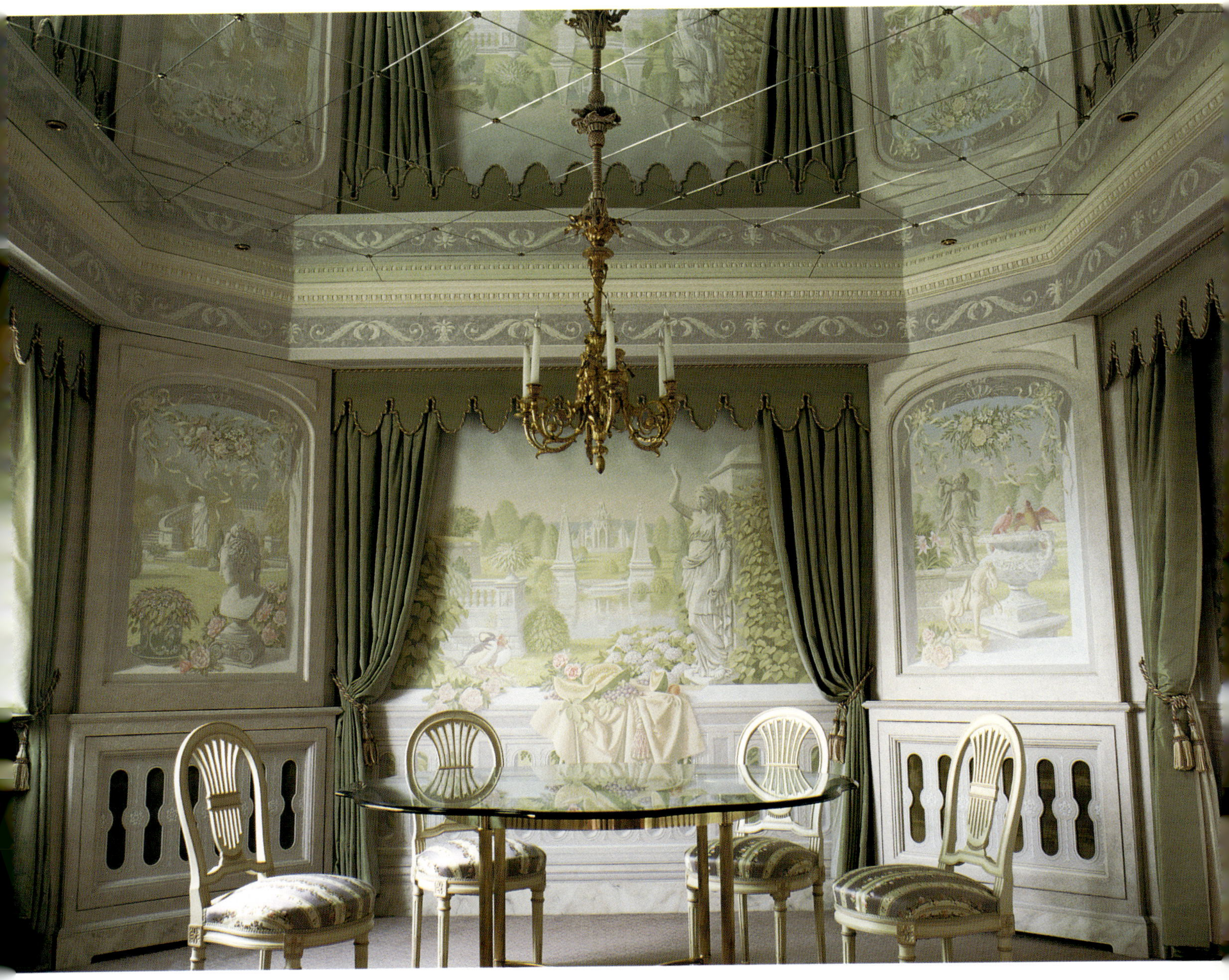

Fig.167 An octagonal dining-room in an apartment at Princes Gate, Knightsbridge. This room was designed by Bill Bennette in 1990. The ceiling was mirrored to give height and repetition, and the arched panels are cupboard doors

that it wasn't circumcised, as, being Greek, it wouldn't have been. A day or so later I was introduced to a robust gentleman in their drawing-room, who looked a bit puzzled, and then, hearing that I was the muralist, boomed out: 'Oh, so you're the penis painter!'

The most recent of my decorations was a Gothick architectural mural in the two-storey hall of a haunted house in Derbyshire. This house had recently been an old people's home and the present owner was a great practical joker. One wet and windy night with rattling casements, I noticed a very realistic hand, complete with lace cuff, protruding down the chimney with knuckles resting on the grate. This is more amusing to read about than it was to experience alone on the top floor at midnight. I wondered if the matron of the old people's home had finally been driven to carry out her threat to stuff one of the more annoying inmates up the chimney, or if the real ghost had finally 'shown its

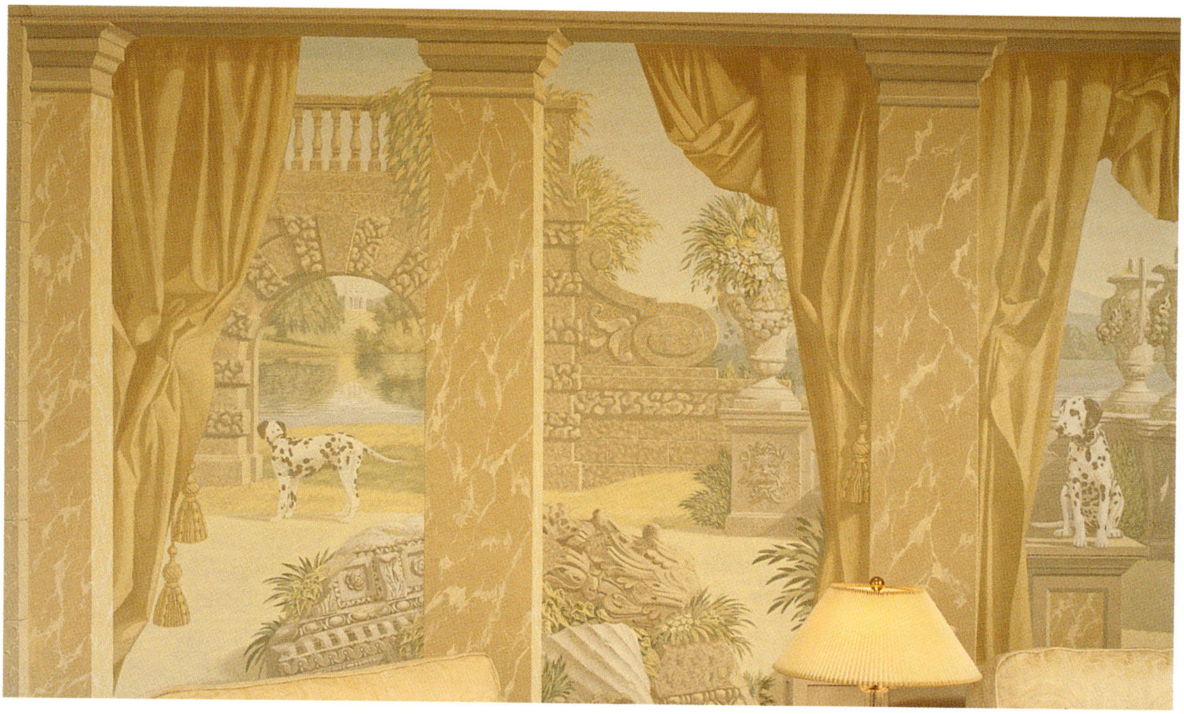

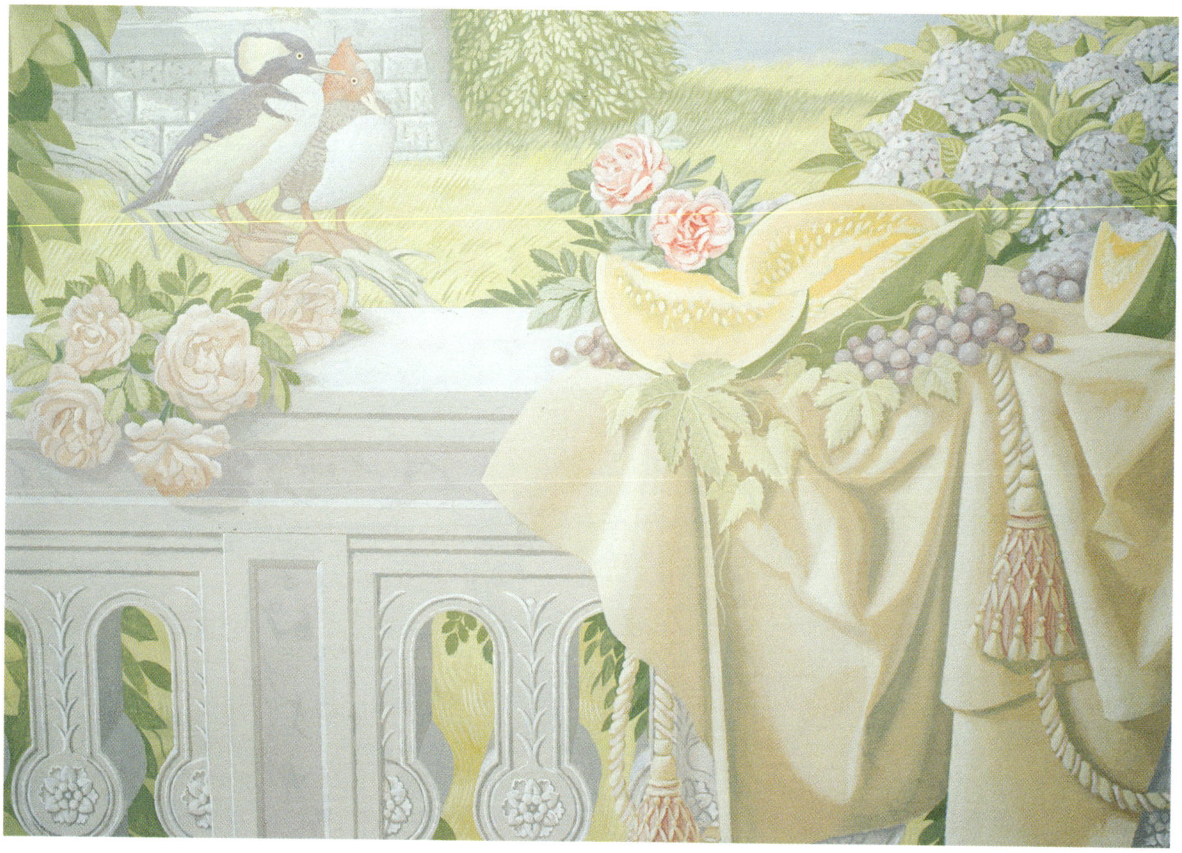

ABOVE: Fig. 168 Detail from a mural in an Italian drawing-room for Lord and Lady Kirkham, 1989. These are the Dalmatians that ran off with our painting sponges. The arch and volute were observed at Fonthill. Interior designer: John Evans

BELOW: Fig. 169 Detail from a mural in the octagonal dining-room at Princes Gate, 1990. I do not use strong tonal contrasts in my murals as I think they should be like well-behaved guests in the home – not clamouring for your attention all the time but, when concentrated upon, found to be full of interest.

hand' so to speak. I am glad to say that my assistant, an imaginative young lady, managed to smuggle a large, black, wind-up scuttling spider into the owner's four-poster bed. We discovered, after much questioning, that it had amply fulfilled our expectations. I was a bit nervous as to the attitude the real ghost might take to these disrespectful pranks. Somehow Malvolio's words spring to mind: 'You are idle shallow things; I am not of your element; you shall know more hereafter.'

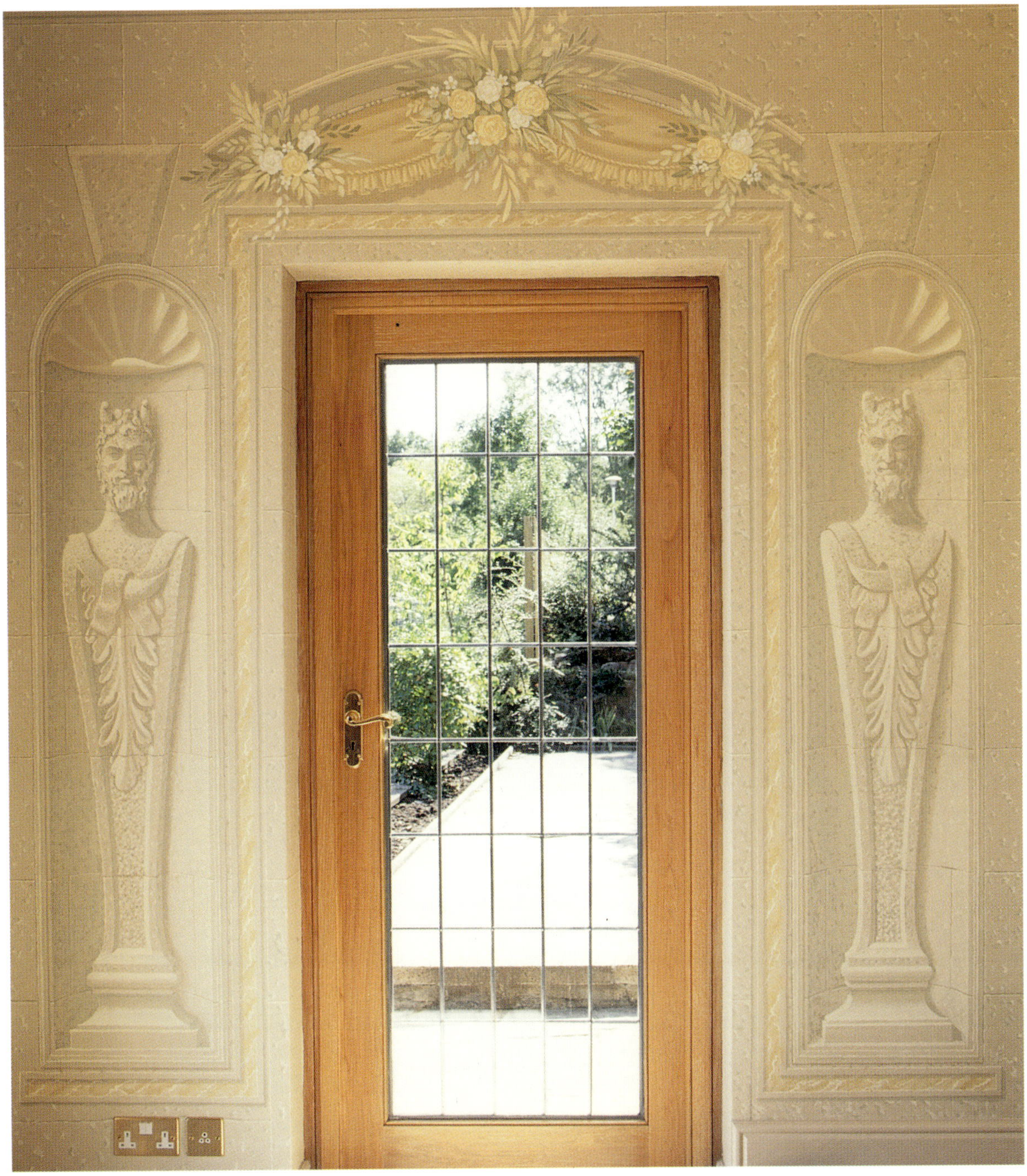

Fig.170. Another wall from the Italian drawing-room near Doncaster, 1989. The sculpted herms were studied at Mottisfont Abbey

MAIN EXHIBITIONS

Mount Gallery, Hampstead. One-man show of paintings, collages and engravings, 1963

Waterhouse Gallery, London W2. First one-man show of paintings, collages and engravings, 1971

Waterhouse Gallery, London W2. Second one-man show of collages and engravings, 1973

Oxford Gallery. First one-man show of collages, paintings and engravings, 1976

Durham University. One-man show of paintings, collages and illustrated books, 1977

Borough of Thamesdown Museum and Art Gallery, Swindon. 'Eight Figurative Painters', group exhibition, 1977

Oxford Gallery. Second one-man show of wood engravings and paintings, 1978

International Ex Libris Centre, Belgium. Group exhibition with Joan Hassall, Reynolds Stone and Leo Wyatt: wood engravings, 1978

Blewbury Festival One-man show of paintings and engravings featuring the Libanus Press, 1979

Kings Arms Yard, Dorchester. One-man show of paintings, montages and engravings, 1980

Oxford Gallery. Third one-man show of paintings, montages and engravings, 1980

Medici Gallery, London W1. Group exhibition with 'British Wood Engravers', 1980

Blewbury Festival. One-man show of paintings and engravings and the painted clavichord made by Sir Evelyn Shuckburgh, 1981

Katharine House Gallery, Marlborough. First one-man show mostly of mural studies, 1982

Borlase Gallery, Blewbury. One-man show of montages, studies for mural decorations, paintings and wood engravings, 1982

Katharine House Gallery, Marlborough. Second one-man show of mural studies, 1983

Harrow School. Group exhibition with Reynolds Stone, Leo Wyatt, Peter Reddick and George Tute: wood engravings, 1983

Eton College. One-man show of mural studies and wood engravings, 1984

Parkin Gallery, London W1. Group exhibition, 'The Artist as Illustrator': wood engravings, 1984

The Ashmolean Museum, McAlpine and Eldon Galleries, Oxford, and *RIBA Heinz Gallery*, 21 Portman Square, London W1. 'Richard Shirley Smith Fiftieth Birthday Retrospective Exhibition', 1985

Aldeburgh Festival of Music & the Arts. One-man show of wood engravings and mural cartoons, 1988

Galerie in der Muhle, Buxtehude, West Germany. Group exhibition, 'Six British Wood Engravers', 1990

Maas Gallery, London W1. One-man show of paintings and engravings, including paintings for the poems of Rochester, 1992

Katharine House Gallery, Marlborough Festival. 'The Wood Engravings of Richard Shirley Smith and Simon Brett', 1992

Maas Gallery, London W1. One-man show of paintings and engravings, including paintings for Ovid's *Metamorphoses*, 1995

Holburne Museum, Great Pulteney Street, Bath. One-man show of paintings, mural cartoons and limited edition books and engravings, 1996

Marlborough Festival. Open studio, 1996

Chris Beetles Limited, St James's, London. One-man show of paintings, drawings and wood engravings, 1999

OPPOSITE: Fig.171 *'Piranesi' Frieze* for Holland Villas Road (*same size cartoon*), acrylic on paper. 33 x 71cm. 1981 (*ptg.cat.114*). Collection of the artist

TROMPE-L'OEIL MURAL DECORATIONS

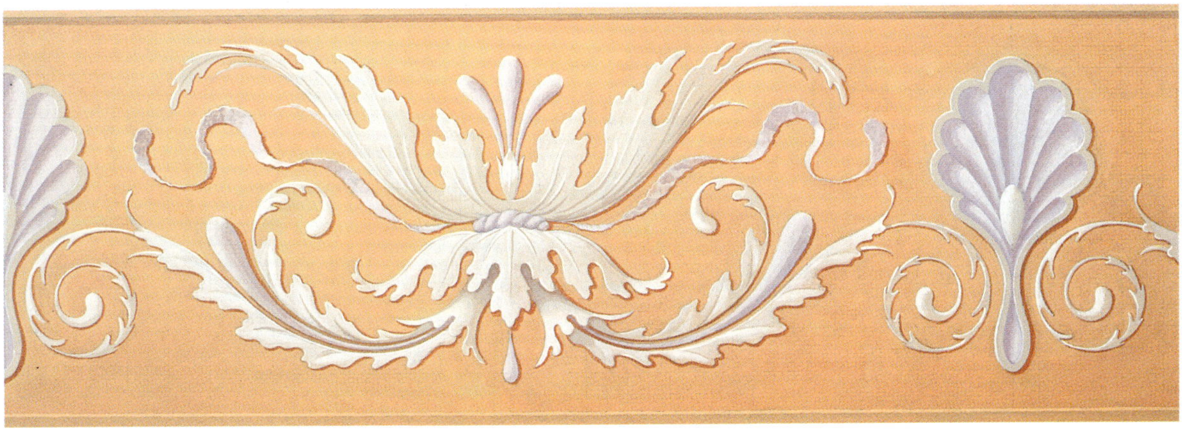

The Doric Villa, Regent's Park, London. Entrance hall with classical architecture, sculpture, flowers and water. 1976–1977

A private house in Holland Park, London. Entrance hall, doors, dressing-room and bathroom with figures, classical architecture, sculptures, curtains, niches and garlands. 1981–1982

A private house in Edgeware, London. Four decorative painted panels with sky and ribbons for dining-room. 1983

Landseer Property Corporation Ltd., 24 Bruton Street, London. Main hall, ten panels with classical architecture revealed through rents in architectural plans, decorated with still life, garlands and insects. 1983–1984

A private house at 20 Hill Street, London. Hall ceiling with perspective architecture, leaves and sky. 1984

A private apartment, Brompton, London. Dining-room for Bill Bennette with monochrome rustication and architecture. 1984

Greys Court, Oxfordshire. Garden-room with Palladian bridge, sculptures, flowers, fruit, decorative emblems and still life. 1985

Guardian Royal Exchange, Dean Street, London. Entrance hall with classical architecture. Commissioned by Frederick Gibberd, Coombes and Partners. 1986–1987

A private house, Fawley, Oxfordshire. Overdoors. 1986

A private house at Bampton, Oxfordshire. Overmantle (*Così fan tutte*). 1986

A Bayswater flat. Eight panels of archæological fragments. 1986

A private house in Heathgate, Hampstead. Hall mural of sculpture, figures and landscape. 1987

A private house in Eaton Square, Belgravia. Large dining-room with rustication, mountains and lakes. 1988

A private house at Doncaster, S. Yorks. Italian drawing-room with colonnades, gardens and sculpture. 1989

A private apartment in Princes Gate. Octagonal dining-room with gardens and exotic birds. 1990

Regalian Project, Kensington Palace Gardens. Entrance hall with trophies of architectural and sculpture fragments. 1991

A private house in Bonsall, Derbyshire. Two-storey entrance hall with gothic columns and ogee arches. 2000

MAIN ILLUSTRATED BOOKS

WOOD-ENGRAVED UNLESS OTHERWISE INDICATED

A Point of Departure, Joy Finzi, Golden Head Press, 1967 (engraved 1961)

Prospect, edited by Roger Bannister, Hutchinson (5 engravings of Rome), 1962

Of Flowers and a Village, Wilfrid Blunt, Hamish Hamilton, 1963 (line drawings)

The Gourmet's Garden, D. Bartrum, Faber & Faber, 1964

To Any Christian, A Benedictine of Stanbrook, Burns and Oates, 1964

The Darkening Green, E. Clarke, Faber & Faber, 1964

A Street in Suffolk, Adrian Bell, Faber & Faber, 1964 (monotype and line drawings)

A Fool in the Forest, Leonard Clark, Dobson, 1965 (monotypes)

Sir Roger de Coverly, Addison and Steele, The Folio Society, 1967

Memoirs of a London Doll, R. H. Horne, Andre Deutsch, 1967

The Prince and the Puppeteer, J. C. Bretherton, Compton Press, 1969 (lino-engraving)

Hero and Leander, David Burnett, published privately, 1975 (lino-engraving made in 1969)

The Periodical (Quarterly), Oxford University Press, 1970 (cover designs)

The Poems of Percy Bysshe Shelley, selected by Stephen Spender for the Limited Editions Club of New York, 1971

Letters to His Son, The Earl of Chesterfield, The Folio Society, 1973

The River Boy, Theresa Whistler, Oxford University Press, 1976 (line drawings)

The Closed Door, James Reeves, Gruffyground Press, 1977

Buzz Buzz, John Heath-Stubbs, Gruffyground Press, 1981

Selected Engravings of Richard Shirley Smith, 1960–77, introduction by Laurence Whistler, Cuckoo Hill Press, 1983

Vines, David Burnett, Rocket Press, 1984

Messer Pietro Mio, correspondence of Lucrezia Borgia and Pietro Bembo, translated by Hugh Shankland, Libanus Press, 1985

The Testament of Charlotte B, edited by M. Kociejowski, Libanus Press, 1988 (line drawings)

The Dramatic Monologues, Robert Browning, introduction by A. S. Byatt, The Folio Society, 1991 (line drawings)

Perfect & Imperfect Enjoyments: Poems by John Wilmot, Earl of Rochester, The Folio Society, 1992; this being their first signed and numbered limited edition publication, (The Folio Press) (8 paintings)

The Boke of Iford, Harold A. Peto, introduction by Robin Whalley, Libanus Press, 1993 (line drawings)

The Wood Engravings of Richard Shirley Smith, selected and introduced by Iain Bain, Silent Books, 1993

Metamorphoses, Ovid, translation and introduction by Mary M. Innes, The Folio Society, 1995 (8 paintings and line drawings)

Ten letters to two young artists working in Italy, Juliet Wood & Richard Shirley Smith, by David Jones, Agenda Editions, 1996. (The book designed with 27 engravings and photographs)

The Complete Plays, William Shakespeare, The Folio Society, 1997 (designs for slip cases and bindings for all 8 volumes)

Forbidden Fruit, selected tales in verse by Jean de la Fontaine, translated by Guido Waldman, The Harvill Press, 1998 (line drawings)

Eclogues, Virgil, introduction by Gilbert Highet, The Folio Society, 2000 (line drawings)

The Bookplates of Richard Shirley Smith, Brian North Lee, The Fleece Press, planned for 2002 (30 engraved plates and 30 line drawings)

Building Towers, Forming Gardens, Christopher Thacker, St Barnabas Press, planned for 2002 (5 paintings, 4 engravings)

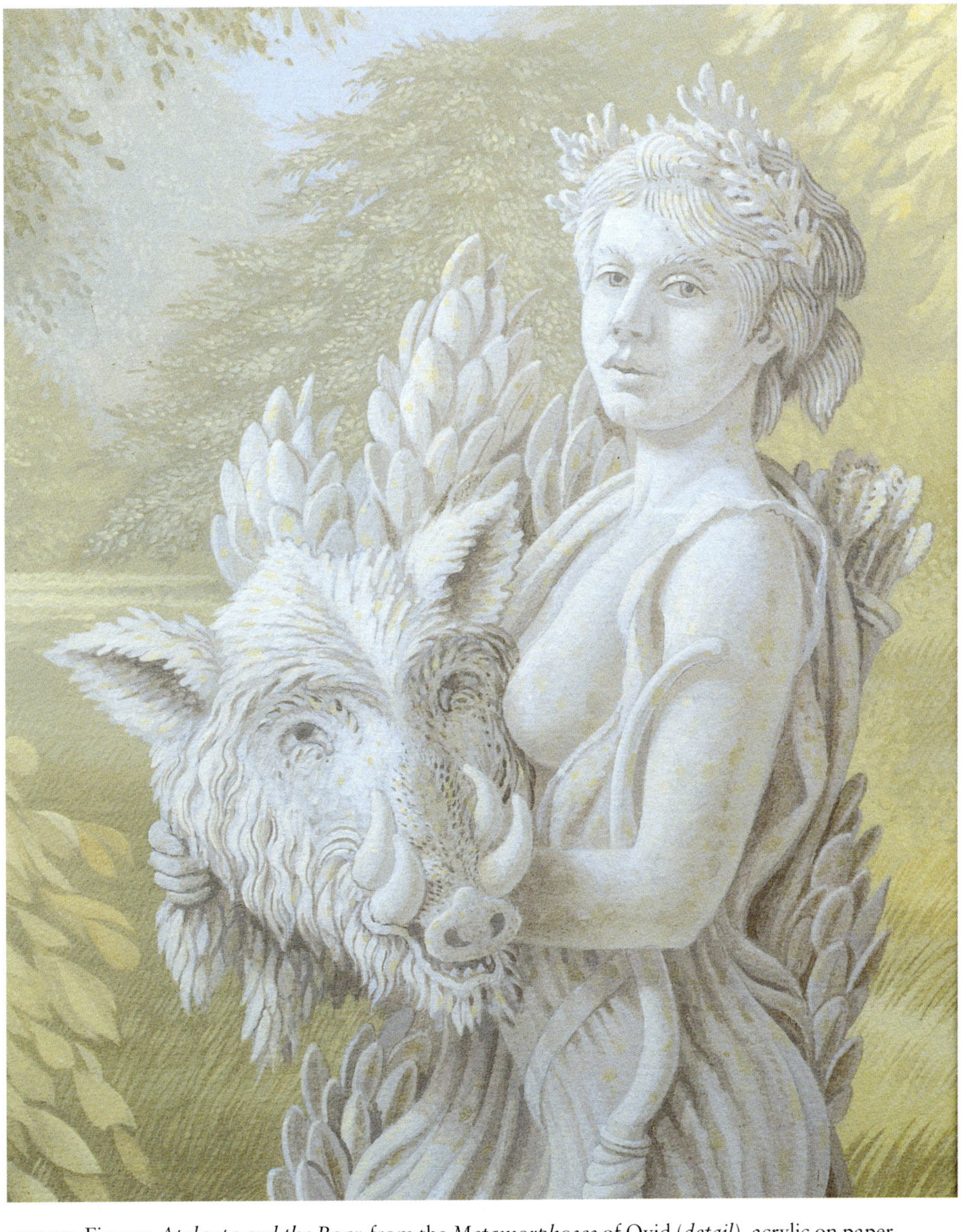

ABOVE: Fig.172 *Atalanta and the Boar*, from the *Metamorphoses* of Ovid (*detail*), acrylic on paper. 38×26cm. 1995 (*ptg.cat.236*). The Folio Society. Collection of Julian Jeffs

ILLUSTRATED PERIODICAL & NEWSPAPER ARTICLES

Waterhouse Gallery Exhibition, Marina Vaizey, *Financial Times,* 15 July 1971

Palladio's Venice brought to life, Simon Brett, *Times Educational Supplement,* January 1974

People into Buildings, the Editor, *Architectural Review,* Vol. CLXI, 1977

Bookplate Designs of Richard Shirley Smith, Brian North Lee, *The Private Library,* Vol.10, 1977

Wall to wall paintings, Lucy Hughes-Hallett, *Vogue,* 1 March 1979

An Eye for the Rich and Unreal, Diana Winsor, *Sunday Telegraph Magazine,* No.206, 7 September 1980

Unique painted clavichord, Antique Collector, August 1982

Richard Shirley Smith und seine Holzstich-Exlibris, Brian North Lee, *Österreichisches Jahrbuch für Ex Libris,* 1981–1982, Band 53

Profile of an Artist: Richard Shirley Smith, David Chambers, *The Bookplate Journal,* Vol.3 No.1, March 1985

Some New Works with Italian Inspiration, Elizabeth Williamson, *Daily Telegraph,* 3 September 1985

Richard Shirley Smith, The Ashmolean, No.8, Autumn 1985

My First Fifty Years, Country Life, 12 September 1985

Richard Shirley Smith, Megan Tressidder, *The World of Interiors,* October 1985

Renaissance Man, Isabelle Anscombe, *Observer,* 6 October 1985

The Painter as Wood Engraver, Linda Saunders, *The Green Book,* Vol.2 No.1, Autumn 1985

Richard Shirley Smith: Paintings, Collages and Murals, Henry Ford, in the *Fiftieth Birthday Retrospective Catalogue,* 1985

Richard Shirley Smith as a Wood Engraver, Brian North Lee, in the *Fiftieth Birthday Retrospective Catalogue,* 1985

The Enchantment of Decay and Melancholia, Sir Roy Strong, *Financial Times,* 21 November 1985

Review of Selected Engravings, Fine Print, No.4, October 1985

Exhibition of Work at the Ashmolean Museum, Oxford, Simon Brett. *Society of Wood Engravers Journal,* No.2, 1986

A Curious Art, Rachel Sylvester, *Telegraph Magazine,* 9 May 1992

A Perfectionist by Nature, Lindsay Fulcher, *The Lady,* 5–11, May 1992

Richard Shirley Smith, John Russell Taylor, Maas Gallery, *Catalogue,* 1992 exhibition

Rodney Armstrong Fund Plate, A. S. Arellanes (Ed.), *Bookplates in the News,* No. 89, July 1992, California USA

Text & Image, David Burnett, *Scottish Book Collector,* Vol. 3 No.6, August–September 1992

Introduction, Anne Stephens MBE, Maas Gallery, *Catalogue,* 1995 exhibition

Still Life with Marble Foot (new acquisition), Ian Lowe, *The Ashmolean,* No.33, Christmas 1998

Richard Shirley Smith, Carolyn Leder, recent acquisitions to Old Speech Room Gallery, Harrow School, 1998

Richard Shirley Smith: Classic Romantic Artist-Craftsman, David Wooton, Chris Beetles Ltd., *Catalogue,* 1999 exhibition

Richard Shirley Smith, Chris Beetles Ltd., Claire Andrews, *Multiples, Journal of the SWE,* Vol. 3 No.16, July 1999

From the Wood and Stone, Brian Dunce, *The David Jones Journal,* summer 1999

ILLUSTRATED SECTIONS IN REFERENCE BOOKS

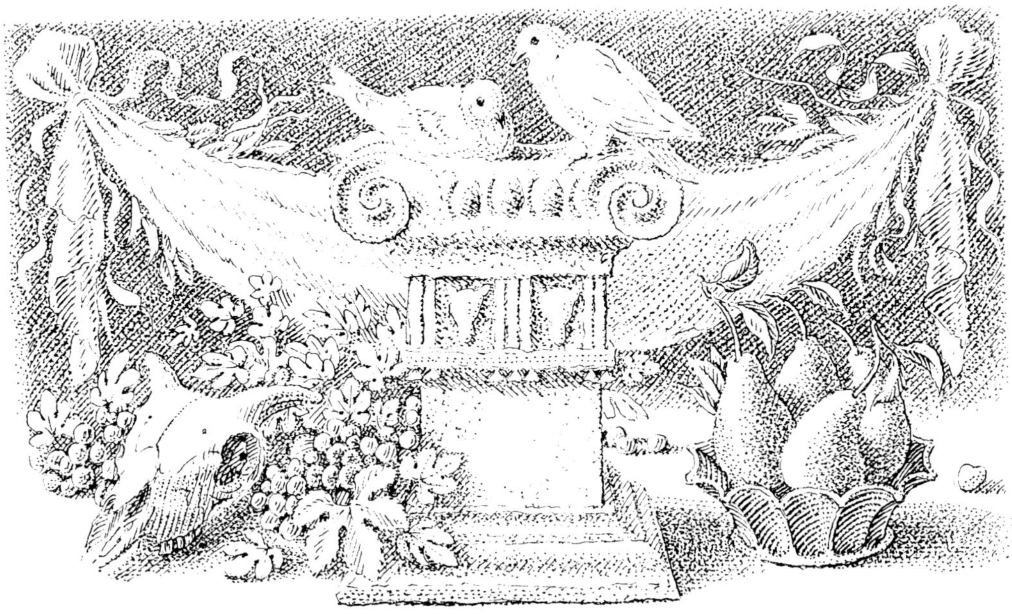

A History of British Wood Engraving, A. Garrett, Midas Books, 1978 (5 engravings)

British Bookplates, Brian North Lee, David and Charles, 1979 (1 engraving)

Dictionary of British Book Illustration (The Twentieth Century), Pepin and Michelthwaite, John Murray, 1980 (1 engraving)

Encyclopaedia (Bio-Bibliographical) of the Art of the Contemporary, Ex Libris, Vol. IV, Editorial Franciscana, Portugal, 1986 (17 engravings)

Engravers, A Handbook for the Nineties, Simon Brett for the Society of Wood Engravers, Silent Books, 1987 (8 engravings)

The Dictionary of 20th Century British Book Illustrators, Alan Horne, Antique Collectors Club, 1994 (2 engravings)

Painting Murals, Patricia Seligman, Macdonald Orbis, 1987 (3 colour plates)

Grand Illusions (contemporary interior murals), Caroline Cass, Phaidon, 1988 (6 colour pages)

Modern British Bookplates, W. E. and D. J. Butler, Silent Books, 1990 (frontispiece)

Wood Engraving & the Woodcut in Britain c.1890–1990, James Hamilton, Barrie & Jenkins (2 engravings)

The World of Exlibris, Exlibris and their owners, Belgrade, ed. Benôit Junod, 1995 (5 bookplates)

Folio 50. A Bibliography of the Folio Society, 1947–1996, The Folio Press, 1997 (1 painting, 2 drawings and 2 engravings)

The Folio Golden Treasury, Poems & wood engravings, selected by James Michie and Simon Brett, The Folio Society, 1997 (18 engravings)

Fig. 173 Chapter heading from *The Eclogues* of Virgil, ink on paper, 11 × 17cm.2000. The Folio Society

CHRONOLOGY

INCLUDING MAIN EXHIBITIONS, COMMISSIONS, PUBLICATIONS AND ARTICLES

1935 Born Hampstead

1941 Moved to Brimpton, near Newbury

First met Gerald and Joy Finzi who inspired his life's direction

1946–49 The Hall School, Hampstead

1949–54 Harrow School, much encouraged by Maurice Percival the art master

1952 First met David Jones and was greatly influenced

1954–56 National Service (Commission in Royal Artillery, British Army of the Rhine)

1955 First visit to Venice on local leave

1956–60 Studied drawing, painting and print-making at the Slade School of Fine Art with John Aldridge and Anthony Gross

1960 Married Juliet Wood

1960–61 Studied in and near Rome

1963 One-man show at the Mount Gallery, Hampstead. Paintings, collages and engravings

1963–66 Lived in Highgate, wood engraving for London publishers such as Faber & Faber and Oxford University Press, and lecturing part-time at St Albans and Watford Schools of Art on lithography, typography and illustration

1966–70 Head of Art Department, Marlborough College

1969 First photographic expedition to the villas of the Veneto

Commissioned by the Limited Editions Club of New York to illustrate *Poems of Percy Bysshe Shelley*, selected by Stephen Spender

1970 Second photographic expedition to the Veneto

1971 First one-man show at the Waterhouse Gallery, W2. Paintings, collages and engravings

Third photographic expedition to the Veneto

1971–72 Art master at Downe House School, Berkshire

1972–73 Lady Mary Dunn generously housed him for a year of painting at Stowell Park, Wiltshire,

1973 Married Bernardine Nielsen and moved to Wallingford

Second one-man show at the Waterhouse Gallery, W2. Collages and engravings

The Story of the Venetian Villas, an educational slide-strip. Visual Publications, 1973

1974–83 Part-time lecturer at Swindon School of Art on the History of Modern Art and Design

1977 One-man show at Durham University. Paintings, collages and illustrated books

1976–77 Mural decorations in The Doric Villa, Regent's Park, London: entrance hall with classical architecture, sculpture, flowers and water

1977 Moved to Blewbury, South Oxfordshire

People into Buildings, an article by the Editor in the *Architectural Review* vol. CLXI, 1977

Bookplate Designs, an article by Brian North Lee in *The Private Library* vol. 10, 1977

1978 Second one-man show at the Oxford Gallery, mostly wood engravings

Invited by Mark Severin to exhibit at the International Ex Libris Centre, Belgium, with Joan Hassall, Reynolds Stone and Leo Wyatt

1979 Restored eighteenth-century murals in a château near Avignon

1980 One-man show at Kings Arms Yard, Dorchester. Paintings, montages and engravings

An Eye for the Rich and Unreal, an article by Diana Winsor in the *Sunday Telegraph Magazine* no: 206, 7 September 1980

Third one-man show at the Oxford Gallery. Paintings, montages and engravings

Contributed to 'British Wood Engravers' at the Medici Gallery, London W1

1981 The decorated clavichord for Sir Evelyn Shuckburgh was exhibited at an open-house one-man show at the Blewbury Festival

1981–82 Murals in a private house in Holland Park, London. Entrance hall, doors, dressing-room and bathroom with figures, classical architecture, sculptures, curtains, niches and garlands

1982 First exhibition at the Katharine House Gallery, Marlborough, mostly mural studies

Unique Painted Clavichord, an article in *Antique Collector*, August 1982

1983–84 Mural decorations for the Landseer Property Corporation Limited, 24 Bruton Street, London. Main hall: ten panels with classical architecture revealed through rents in architectural plans decorated with still life, garlands and insects

1983 *R. S. S. und Seine Holzstich-Ex Libris*, an article by Brian North Lee in *Österreichisches Jahrbuch für Ex Libris etc.*: 1981–82 Band 53

Second exhibition at Katharine House Gallery, Marlborough, mostly mural studies

Selected Engravings 1960–77, introduced by Laurence Whistler and published by the Cuckoo Hill Press

1984 One-man show at Eton College, mural studies and engravings

Contributed to 'The Artist as Illustrator', Parkin Gallery, SW1

1985 Greys Court, Oxfordshire. Garden-room with Palladian bridge, sculptures, flowers, fruit, decorative emblems and still life

Messer Pietro Mio, the correspondence of Lucrezia Borgia and Pietro Bembo, translated by Hugh Shankland with 18 wood engravings, Libanus Press

Retrospective Exhibition at the Ashmolean Museum, Oxford and at the RIBA Heinz Gallery, Portman Square, London W1. The Ashmolean Museum acquired proofs of all the existing wood engravings for their Print Room

The Enchantment of Decay and Melancholia, Sir Roy Strong, *Financial Times*, 21 November 1985

The Painter as Wood Engraver, Linda Saunders, *The Green Book*, vol.2 no. 1, Autumn 1985

Elected to the Royal Society of Painter Printmakers

1986 Mural decoration for the Guardian Royal Exchange, Dean Street, London. Entrance hall with classical architecture. Commissioned by Frederick Gibberd, Coombes and Partners, 1986–1987

Overdoors, A Private House, Fawley, Oxfordshire

Overmantle (*Così fan tutte*), Bampton, Oxfordshire

Eight Panels for Bayswater flat: archaeological fragments

Moved to Kensington

1987 Hall mural, Heathgate, Hampstead (sculpture, figures & landscape)

1988 Large dining-room, Eaton Square, Belgravia (rustication, mountains and lakes)

Aldeburgh Festival of Music & the Arts. One-man show, wood engravings and mural cartoons

The Testament of Charlotte B, edited by M. Kociejowski, Libanus Press, 1988 (line drawings)

Move to Studio House, Marlborough

1989 Italian drawing-room, Doncaster, S.Yorkshire (colonnades, gardens and sculpture)

1990 Octagonal dining-room, Princes Gate, Knightsbridge (gardens, garlands and exotic birds)

Galerie in der Mühle, Buxtehude, West Germany. Group exibition, 'Six British Wood Engravers', 1990

1991 Entrance Hall, Regalian Project, Kensington Palace Gardens (decorative trophies)

The Dramatic Monologues, Robert Browning, introduction by A. S. Byatt, The Folio Society, 1991 (line drawings)

1992 *The Earl of Rochester's Poems*, The Folio Society, 1992. This being their first signed and numbered Limited Edition (8 paintings)

Maas Gallery, London W1. One-man show of paintings and engravings, including paintings for the Poems of Rochester, 1992

Katharine House Gallery, Marlborough Festival. 'The Wood Engravings of Richard Shirley Smith and Simon Brett', 1992

1993 *The Boke of Iford*, Harold A. Peto, introduction by Robin Whalley, Libanus Press, 1993 (line drawings)

The Wood Engravings of Richard Shirley Smith, selected and introduced by Iain Bain, Silent Books, 1993

1994 Invited to show slides of illustrations and paintings to graphic design students at the Royal College of Art

1995 *Metamorphoses*, Ovid, translation and introduction by Mary M. Innes, The Folio Society, 1995 (8 paintings and line drawings)

Maas Gallery, London W1. One-man show of paintings and engravings, including paintings for Ovid's *Metamorphoses*

1996 Holburne Museum, Great Pulteney Street, Bath. One-man show of paintings, mural cartoons and limited edition books and engravings

Marlborough Festival, Open Studio, 1996

Ten letters to two young artists working in Italy, Juliet Wood & Richard Shirley Smith, by David Jones, Agenda Editions, 1996 (the book designed with 27 engravings and photographs)

1997 Invited to show slides of Pulcinella paintings at an international conference on the *Commedia dell'Arte* at Wimbledon College of Art

Invited to show slides of The Folio Society 'Rochester' illustrations at an international conference on *The Poems of The Earl of Rochester* at Wadham College, Oxford

Paintings were acquired by the Ashmolean Museum and Harrow School

Still Life with Marble Foot (new acquisition), Ian Lowe, *The Ashmolean*, no.33, Christmas 1997

Richard Shirley Smith, Carolyn Leder, recent acquisitions to Old Speech Room Gallery, Harrow School, 1998

1998 *Forbidden Fruit, selected tales in verse by Jean de la Fontaine*, translated by Guido Waldman, The Harvill Press, 1998 (line drawings)

1999 Chris Beetles Ltd., St James's, London. One-man show of paintings, drawings and wood engravings

2000 *Eclogues*, Virgil, introduction by Gilbert Highet, The Folio Society (line drawings)

LIST OF FRAMED WORKS

This is the artist's list of framed and three-dimensional works including framed originals of illustrations and cartoons for murals. The list was compiled no earlier than 1995 and is therefore being continually added to and corrected. Owners' names have been omitted from this version of the list and dimensions are in centimetres – height before width. If a work is illustrated in the book, the catalogue number is in **bold**.

1. *Portrait of Juliet,* 1957, portrait, oil on canvas, 76 × 64
2. *Pyx & Chalice,* 1958, still life, collage on paper, 43 × 58
3. *Anticoli Corrado,* 1961, landscape, oil on canvas, 28 × 36
4. *Italian Farm Buildings*, 1961, landscape, oil on canvas, 30 × 24
5. *Mensa Florida*, 1963, still life, collage on board, 86 × 71
6. *Baths of Caracala*, 1965, still life, collage on board, *approx.* 122 × 90
7. *Puppet*, 1965, still life, collage on board, 78 × 110
8. *Black Altar*, 1966, still life, collage on paper, *approx.* 26 × 38
9. *Frog*, 1967, collage on board, *approx.* 90 × 122
10. *Egg & Skull,* 1968, still life, oil on board, 19 × 24
11. *Doll's Houses & Butterfly*, 1968, still life, collage on board, *approx.* 90 × 122
12. *Pyramid of Oranges*, 1968, still life, oil on canvas, 24 × 44
13. *Still Life with Death Mask*, 1968, still life, oil on canvas, 46 × 36
14. *Still Life with Cast*, 1969, still life, oil on canvas, *approx.* 26 × 20
15. *Scales & Reliquary*, 1969, still life, collage on board, 86 × 124
16. *Villa of Pan*, 1969, surrealist, oil on board, *approx.* 122 × 90
17. *Nude with Rocking Horse*, 1969, figure composition, oil on board, 30 × 36
18. *Jane with Rocking Horse*, 1969, portrait, oil on canvas, *approx.* 40 × 50
19. *Metamorphosis*, 1969, surrealist, collage on board, 92 × 122
20. *Keyboard & Flowers*, 1969, still life, collage on board, *approx.* 90 × 56
21. *Grasshopper*, 1969, collage on board, *approx.* 88 × 62
22. *Chameleon*, 1970, surrealist, collage on board, 81 × 108
23. *Giant Skull*, 1970, surrealist, collage on board, 83 × 123
24. *American Patchwork*, 1970, still life, collage on board, 84 × 84
25. *Study for Cyclops Villa*, 1970, surrealist, ink on paper, *approx.* 26 × 36
26. *Cyclops Villa*, 1970, surrealist, collage on board, 91 × 71
27. *Cubist Patchwork*, 1972, still life, collage on board, 71 × 71
28. *Euclid's Stables*, 1972, still life, collage on board, 86 × 122
29. *Effigy & Bonnet*, 1972, still life, collage on board, 86 × 120
30. *Pulcinella Visits Rome*, 1972, *Commedia dell'Arte*, collage on board, 97 × 122
31. *Palinurus Pontifex*, 1972, surrealist, collage on board, 122 × 91
32. *Lady at Venetian Villa*, 1973, figure composition, collage on board, 91 × 120
33. *Behind the Keys*, 1973, surrealist, collage on board, 86 × 124
34. *Demonstration*, 1973, surrealist, collage on board, 72 × 107
35. *Snake Charmer*, c.1975, figure composition, acrylic on paper, 46 × 56
36. *Alicia*, 1975, figure composition, acrylic on paper, 43 × 64
37. *Emperor*, 1975, figure composition, acrylic on paper, 43 × 51
38. *Cerberus*, 1975, figure composition, acrylic on paper, 43 × 38
39. *Castrum Doloris*, 1975, figure composition, collage on board, 91 × 122
40. *Clock Walk*, 1975, surrealist, collage on board, 122 × 91
41. *Pulcinella Bill Poster*, 1975, *Commedia dell'Arte*, acrylic on paper, 55 × 43
42. *Pulcinella Fishmonger*, 1975, *Commedia dell'Arte*, acrylic on paper, 60 × 45
43. *Pulcinella Engine Driver*, 1975, *Commedia dell'Arte*, acrylic on paper, 37 × 51
44. *Mermaid & Dwarf*, 1975, surrealist, collage on board, 91 × 117

Mural for Doric Villa, Regents Park 1976–78

45. *Rococo Monochrome Study*, 1975, cartoon, acrylic on paper, 27 × 33
46. *Entire Study 1:10 scale*, 1975, cartoon, acrylic on paper, *approx.* 27 × 60

47. *Main Wall 1:8 scale*, 1975, cartoon, acrylic on paper, 39 × 31
48. *Door Wall 1:8 scale*, 1975, cartoon, acrylic on paper, 39 × 31
49. *Stair Wall 1:8 scale*, 1975, cartoon, acrylic on paper, *approx.* 39 × 20
50. *Main Wall 1:5 scale*, 1975, cartoon, acrylic on paper, *approx.* 33 × 30
51. *Door Wall 1:5 scale*, 1975, cartoon, acrylic on paper, *approx.* 33 × 30
52. *Stair Wall 1:5 scale*, 1975, cartoon, acrylic on paper, *approx.* 33 × 26
53. *Front door 1:4 scale*, 1975, cartoon, acrylic on paper, *approx.* 48 × 28
54. *Main Wall 1:4 scale*, 1976, cartoon, acrylic on paper, 43 × 49
55. *Monochrome Stair Wall 1:4 scale*, 1976, cartoon, acrylic on paper, 50 × 34

56. *Quo Vadis?*, 1976, figure composition, acrylic on paper, 56 × 46
57. *Jean (White Sun Flowers)*, 1976, portrait, acrylic on paper, 32 × 46
58. *Victorian Beach*, 1976, still life, acrylic on paper, 25 × 31
59. *Fatal Allegations*, 1976, *Commedia dell'Arte*, acrylic on paper, 46 × 56
60. *Reflection in 'D'*, 1976, still life, collage on board, 120 × 90
61. *The Wind Fall*, 1976, still life, collage on board, 71 × 102
62. *Death in Venice*, 1976, surrealist, collage on board, 69 × 102
63. *Skull & Saddle*, 1976, still life, collage on board, 71 × 102
64. *Poet's Tomb*, 1977, illustration, acrylic on paper, 25 × 20
65. *Roman Extinguisher*, 1977, surrealist, acrylic on paper, 36 × 49

Hommage à Max Ernst, Montages of Victorian Engravings

66. *Witchcraft*, 1977, montage, engravings on paper, 13 × 18
67. *Still Life (Victorian)*, 1977, montage, engravings on paper, 13 × 18
68. *Pandora's Box*, 1978, montage, engravings on paper, 13 × 18
69. *The Bathing Machine*, 1978, montage, engravings on paper, 13 × 18
70. *Armadillo Experiment*, 1978, montage, engravings on paper, 13 × 18
71. *Air Attack*, 1978, montage, engravings on paper, 13 × 18

72. *The Sense of Touch*, 1979, figure composition, collage on board, 86 × 122
73. *Objects on Sand*, 1979, still life, oil on canvas, 91 × 71
74. *First Study for Clavichord*, 1979, cartoon, acrylic on paper, 23 × 33
75. *Painted Clavichord*, 1981, oil on wood, 38 × 123, height 75
76. *Glove Stretcher*, 1980, still life, acrylic on paper, 46 × 71
77. *Beach Toys*, 1980, still life, acrylic on paper, 40 × 30
78. *Pipes & Starfish*, 1980, still life, acrylic on paper, 36 × 53
79. *French Still Life with Pipe*, 1980, still life, acrylic on paper, 36 × 24
80. *French Still Life with Urn*, 1980, still life, acrylic on paper, 36 × 25
81. *Dream of Saint Ursula*, 1980, still life, acrylic on paper, 36 × 51
82. *Carpaccio's Dream*, 1980, still life, acrylic on paper, 70 × 50
83. *Grabs* (first version), 1980, surrealist, acrylic on paper, 41 × 53
84. *Grabs* (second version), 1980, surrealist, acrylic on paper, 41 × 56
85. *Radical Graduates*, 1980, surrealist, acrylic on paper, 36 × 53
86. *Vanity*, 1980, still life, acrylic on paper, 36 × 51
87. *Pulcinella on Parade*, 1979-80, *Commedia dell'Arte*, acrylic on paper, 38 × 51
88. *The Visitor*, 1980, figure composition, acrylic on paper, 56 × 41
89. *Crocodile Cicada*, 1980, surrealist, acrylic on paper, 53 × 38
90. *Classical Rock Pool*, 1980, still life, oil on canvas, 84 × 84
91. *These Are Pipes*, 1980, still life, acrylic on paper, 37 × 52
92. *Study for Decorated Obelisk*, 1980, cartoon, acrylic on paper, 35 × 52
93. *Decanter & Venetian Blinds*, 1980, still life, oil on canvas, 71 × 91
94. *Ampersand*, 1980, still life, acrylic on paper, 51 × 62
95. *Venetian Blinds & Bust*, 1980, still life, oil on canvas, 76 × 51
96. *Skull & Bottle*, 1981, still life, acrylic on paper, 45 × 29
97. *Acrobats*, 1981, *Commedia dell'Arte*, acrylic on paper, 53 × 42
98. *Flowers and Jug (Colours from Ashbrook)*, 1981, still life, acrylic on paper, 25 × 35
99. *Finzi & his Friends* (record sleeve), 1981, illustration, acrylic on paper, 31 × 31

Murals for Holland Villas Road, 1981–82

100. *Mural Study with Ballerina,* 1981, cartoon, acrylic on paper, 32 × 39
101. *Bathroom, 1st Study, Two Classical Figures & Temple*, 1981, cartoon, acrylic on paper, *approx.* 27 × 23
102. *Dancing Nymphs*, 1981, cartoon, acrylic on paper. 47 × 35
103. *Rough Sketch Nymphs*, 1981, cartoon, acrylic on paper, *approx.* 75 × 50
104. *Dancing Nymphs*, detail study LHS, 1981, cartoon, oil on canvas, 99 × 36
105. *Dancing Nymphs*, detail study RHS, 1981, cartoon, oil on canvas, *approx.* 40 × 30
106. *Dressing-Room with Venus*, 1:10 scale, 1981, cartoon, acrylic on paper, 31 × 35
107. *Dressing-Room with Urn*, 1:10 scale, 1981, cartoon, acrylic on paper, 46 × 61
108. *First Studies for Dressing-Room with Flowers*, 1:10 scale, 1981, cartoon, acrylic on paper, 31 × 55
109. *Dressing-Room with Obelisk & Palazzo*, 1:5 scale, 1982, cartoon, acrylic on paper, *approx.* 52 × 46
110. *Dressing-Room with Girl & Dog*, 1:5 scale, 1981, cartoon, acrylic on paper, 63 × 39
111. *Dressing-Room, Studies for Three Wardrobe Doors*,1:5 scale, 1981, cartoon, acrylic on paper, 52 × 32
112. *Dressing-Room with Dancer and Garland*,1:5 scale, 1981, cartoon, acrylic on paper, 52 × 36
113. *Dressing-Room, Study of Details* (same size), 1981, cartoon, acrylic on paper, *approx.* 61 × 40
114. *Dressing-Room, 'Piranesi' Frieze* (same size), 1981, cartoon, acrylic on paper, 33 × 71
115. *Hall, Nymph & Guinea Fowl*, 1:5 scale, 1981, cartoon, acrylic on paper, 54 × 30
116. *Hall, Winged Victory*, 1:5 scale, 1981, cartoon, acrylic on paper, 54 × 30
117. *Hall, Large Study*, 1982, cartoon, acrylic on paper, 86 × 56
118. *Hall, Window Study with Dog*, 1982, cartoon, acrylic on paper, 44 × 34
119. *Hall, Study for Overdoor*, 1982, cartoon, acrylic on paper, 29 × 42
120. *Hall, Study of Details* (same size), 1982, cartoon, acrylic on paper, 34 × 39

121. *Messer Pietro Mio, Triumph of Venus*, 1982, figure composition, acrylic on paper, 50 × 34
122. *Messer Pietro Mio, Triumph of Diana*, 1982, figure composition, acrylic on paper, 50 × 34

Murals for 24 Bruton Street, 1983–84

123. *Snake & Puppet Study*, 1983, cartoon, acrylic on paper, 55 × 44
124. *Volute & Leaf Insect Study*, 1983, cartoon, acrylic on paper, 55 × 44
125. *Rustic Arch & Jug Study*, 1983, cartoon, acrylic on paper, 55 × 44
126. *Vanity Sculpture Study*, 1983, cartoon, acrylic on paper, 55 × 44
127. *Shell Mantelpiece Study*, 1983, cartoon, acrylic on paper, 55 × 44

128. *Hanging Still Life*, 1983, still life, acrylic on paper, 33 × 51
129. *Roman Theatre*, 1983, surrealist, acrylic on paper, 61 × 43
130. *Stage Set Still Life*, 1983, still life, acrylic on paper, 33 × 53
131. *Guitarist*, 1983, Commedia dell'Arte, acrylic on paper, 33 × 24
132. *Study for Clavichord & Obelisk,* (same size), 1983, cartoon, acrylic on paper, 30 × 46
133. *Cat*, 1983, acrylic on paper, 34 × 26
134. *Metamorphoses: Tereus* (Blackford Opera), 1983, figure composition, acrylic on paper, *approx.* 42 × 35
135. *Metamorphoses: Erysichthon* (Blackford Opera), 1983, still life, acrylic on paper, 26 × 31
136. *J. M.* (Cartouche), 1984, illustration, acrylic on paper, *approx.* 20 × 20
137. *Mural Cartoon for 4 Kensington Gate, Flowers & Villa*, 1984, cartoon, acrylic on paper, 40 × 30
138. *Mural Cartoon for 4 Kensington Gate, Flowers & Shell*, 1984, cartoon, acrylic on paper, 40 × 30

Three-Dimensional Decorated Objects

139. *Wooden Marbled Obelisk Shelf*, c.1985, three-dimensional, acrylic on wood, 55 × 50
140. *Collaged Fibreglass Obelisk Shelf*, c.1985, three-dimensional, collage on fibreglass, 55 × 50
141. *Large Decorated 'Piranesi' Obelisk*, 1985, three-dimensional, oil on wood, 66 × 29
142. *Square Plan Yellow Marbled Obelisk*, 1985, three-dimensional, oil on wood, 50 × 21
143. *Ballfoot, Oblong Plan Classical Obelisk*, 1985, three-dimensional, oil on wood, 53 × 24

Mural for Greys Court, Henley, Oxfordshire, 1985, for Lady Brunner

144. *Main Wall*, 1985, cartoon, acrylic on paper, *approx.* 36 × 48

145. *Trophy, Wheel and Bonnet*, 1985–7, still life, acrylic on paper, 53 × 38
146. *Crab and Butterfly*, 1985, still life, acrylic on paper, *approx.* 26 × 32
147. *Dish Still Life with Hand*, 1985, still life, acrylic on canvas, *approx.* 24 × 36
148. *Crab and Volute*, 1985, still life, acrylic on paper, 50 × 72

149. *A Book of Tea for Crabtree & Evelyn*, 1986, illustration, acrylic on paper, 18 × 61
150. *Così Fan Tutte* (overmantle), 1986, figure composition, acrylic on canvas, 88 × 117
151. *Cartouche of Flowers*, 1986, still life, acrylic on paper, *approx.* 42 × 30
152. *Portrait of a Lady*, c.1986, portrait, acrylic on paper, 25 × 35
153. *Barley Roscoe*, c.1986, portrait, acrylic on paper, *approx.* 30 × 25
154. *Archaeological Fragments*, 1986, still life, acrylic on paper, 72 × 51

Mural panels for Bayswater flat, 1986

155. *Large Panel, study* (same size), 1986, cartoon, acrylic on paper, 82 × 30
156. *Tragic Mask, study* (same size),1986, cartoon, acrylic on paper, 50 × 30
157. *Small Egyptian, study* (same size), 1986, cartoon, acrylic on paper, 37 × 30

Murals for No. 1 Dean Street, 1986–87, for Guardian Royal Exchange

158. *Large Cartoon with Balustrade*, 1987, cartoon, acrylic on paper, 52 × 70
159. *Cartoon with Venus Sculpture*, 1987, cartoon, acrylic on paper, 47 × 29
160. *Cartoon with Seated Statue*, 1987, cartoon, acrylic on paper, 51 × 62

Mural for Britannia House (Doll's house 1:12 scale), 1991, music room

161. *Ceiling* (same size), 1987, cartoon, acrylic on paper, *approx.* 36 × 32
162. *Wall with Doors* (same size), 1987, cartoon, acrylic on paper, 38 × 27
163. *Wall with Obelisks* (same size), 1987, cartoon, acrylic on paper, 38 × 27

164. *Adam-Style Chimney Board* (for Mrs Hammerson), 1987, cartoon, acrylic on paper, 34 × 43
165. *Trophy, Helmet and Skull* (for Alexandra Palace), 1987, still life, acrylic on paper, 60 × 31
166. *Still Life with Torso & Gourds*, 1988, still life, acrylic on paper, 32 × 41
167. *Ostrich Pulcinella*, 1988, *Commedia dell'Arte*, acrylic on paper, *approx.* 25 × 40
168. *Marine Window*, 1988, surrealist, acrylic on paper. 33 × 40
169. *Fragmented Time*, 1988, surrealist, acrylic on paper, 38 × 28
170. *Jenny McAlpine*, 1988, portrait, acrylic on canvas, *approx.* 100 × 130
171. *Still Life with Cat*, c.1988, still life, acrylic on paper, *approx.* 50 × 65

Building Towers, Forming Gardens, The Barnabas Press, c.1989

172. *Cartouche. Enchanting Paths to Paradise*, 1989, illustration, acrylic on paper, 29 × 30
173. *Painshill*, 1989, illustration, acrylic on paper, 40 × 29
174. *Stourhead*, 1989, illustration, acrylic on paper, 40 × 29
175. *Fonthill Splendens*, 1989, illustration, acrylic on paper, 40 × 29
176. *Fonthill Abbey*, 1989, illustration, acrylic on paper, 40 × 29

177. *Still Life on Book*, 1989, still life, acrylic on canvas, 59 × 90
178. *Still Life at Lucca*, 1989, still life, acrylic on paper, 52 × 73
179. *Still Life on Dish with George I Medal*, 1989, still life, acrylic on canvas, 95 × 74

Mural for Norton House, Doncaster 1989/90

180. *Cartoon for Carpet*, 1990, cartoon, acrylic on paper, 38 × 57
181. *Cartoon with Venetian Villa & Dalmation*, 1992, cartoon, acrylic on paper, 58 × 41

Mural for Princes Gate, Knightsbridge, 1990, octagonal dining-room

182. *Wreath, Bust & Garden*, 1990, cartoon, acrylic on paper, 59 × 44
183. *Parrots & Urn*, 1990, cartoon, acrylic on paper, 59 × 44
184. *Shell & Urns*, 1990, cartoon, acrylic on paper, 59 × 44

185. *Katie Lying*, *c.*1990, figure composition, acrylic on paper, 51 × 34
186. *Katie Standing*, *c.*1990, figure composition, acrylic on paper, 52 × 35
187. *Viridissima Virga*, 1990, figure composition, acrylic on paper, 51 × 73

Murals for Regalian Project, Kensington Palace Gardens, 1991

188. *First Study for Regalian Project* (hall), 1989, cartoon, acrylic on paper, 36 × 36
189. *Art Deco Panel Study*, 1991, cartoon, acrylic on paper, 48 × 20
190. *Large Panel*, 1991, cartoon, acrylic on paper, 96 × 44

Perfect & Imperfect Enjoyments: Poems of the Earl of Rochester, The Folio Press, 1992

191. *The Restoration 1660*, 1992, illustration, acrylic on paper, 40 × 28
192. *A Satire on Charles II*, 1992, illustration, acrylic on paper, 40 × 28
193. *Upon his Drinking Bowl*, 1992, illustration, acrylic on paper, 40 × 28
194. *To my More than Meritorious Wife*, 1992, illustration, acrylic on paper, 40 × 28
195. *A Young Lady to her Ancient Lover*, 1992, illustration, acrylic on paper, 40 × 28
196. *A Satire on John Dryden*, 1992, illustration, acrylic on paper, 40 × 28
197. *Post Mortem Nihil Est*, 1992, illustration, acrylic on paper, 40 × 28
198. *Tail Piece*, 1992, illustration, acrylic on paper, 40 × 28

199. *Oliphant Chuckabutti Zoo*, 1992, *Commedia dell'Arte*, acrylic on paper, 58 × 43
200. *Portrait of Ingrid*, 1992, portrait, acrylic on paper, 41 × 28
201. *Crab Apples*, 1992, still life, acrylic on paper, *approx.* 36 × 28
202. *Regalian Cartoon with Racoon*, 1992, surrealist, acrylic on canvas, 92 × 88
203. *Lady with Goat*, 1992, figure composition, acrylic on paper, 45 × 57
204. *Masked Figures* (*Hommage à René Boyvin*) 1992, surrealist, acrylic on paper, 67 × 55
205. *Christmas Cover of Spectator*, 1991, illustration, acrylic on paper, 27 × 32
206. *Fonthill Abbey* (large version), 1992, figure composition, acrylic on paper, 63 × 48
207. *Painshill* (large version), 1992, landscape, acrylic on paper, 63 × 48
208. *Dubium Initium Sapientiae*, 1992, surrealist, acrylic on paper, 73 × 56
209. *Pulcinella Archaeologist*, 1992, *Commedia dell'Arte*, acrylic on paper, 72 × 51
210. *Scales & Pears* (small version), 1992, still life, acrylic on paper, 30 × 66
211. *Paper Hat Duochrome*, 1993, still life, acrylic on paper, 17 × 27
212. *Soldiers & Sow*, 1992, *Commedia dell'Arte*, acrylic on paper, 72 × 51
213. *Large Dish with Lemon*, 1993, still life, acrylic on canvas, 130 × 151
214. *Geographical Birthday Cartouche*, 1994, illustration, acrylic on paper, *approx.* 36 × 28
215. *Florentine Hog's Head*, 1994, figure composition, acrylic on paper, 30 × 38
216. *Scales & Pears* (large version), 1994, still life, acrylic on canvas, 60 × 132
217. *Obelisk Shelf with Green Bottle*, 1994, still life, acrylic on board, 35 × 50
218. *Swag & Jug. Still Life* (first version), 1994, still life, acrylic on board, 37 × 55
219. *Swag & Jug. Still Life* (second version), 1994, still life, acrylic on board, 37 × 55
220. *Rehearsal Trophy with Dancers*, 1995, figure composition, acrylic on canvas, 95 × 127
221. *Angels & Skull*, 1995, still life, acrylic on board, *approx.* 36 × 48
222. *Baroque Frieze* (for Bruton St), 1995, cartoon, acrylic on paper, *approx.* 44 × 74
223. *Three Volutes*, 1995, still life, acrylic on canvas, 78 × 117
224. *Clown with Chair*, 1995, *Commedia dell'Arte*, acrylic on paper, 62 × 46
225. *The Suitor*, 1995, *Commedia dell'Arte*, acrylic on paper, 48 × 60
226. *Cast & Bonnet*, 1995, still life, acrylic on paper, 96 × 72
227. *Italian Snake Charmer*, 1995, figure composition, acrylic on paper, 61 × 52
228. *Ancien Régime*, 1995, figure composition, acrylic on canvas, 99 × 135
229. *Obelisk Shelf with Tasso Medal*, 1995, still life, acrylic on board, 55 × 60
230. *Sea Horse & Domino*, 1995, still life, acrylic on canvas, 96 × 121
231. *Large Dish with Doll's Head*, 1995, still life, acrylic on canvas, 143 × 114

Metamorphoses, Ovid, The Folio Society, 1995

232. *Title Page*, 1995, illustration, ink on paper, 38 × 26
233. *Phaethon's Sisters*, 1995, illustration, acrylic on paper, 38 × 26
234. *Diana & Actaeon*, 1995, illustration, acrylic on paper, 38 × 26
235. *Salmacis & Hermaphroditus*, 1995, illustration, acrylic on paper, 38 × 26
236. *Atalanta & The Boar*, 1995, illustration, acrylic on paper, 38 × 26
237. *Orpheus & Eurydice*, 1995, illustration, acrylic on paper, 38 × 26
238. *The Marriage of Hippodame*, 1995, illustration, acrylic on paper, 38 × 26
239. *The Sacrifice of Polyxena*, 1995, illustration, acrylic on paper, 38 × 26

240. *Pomona's Garden*, 1995, illustration, acrylic on paper, 38 × 26
241. *Study for Ovid*, 1995, illustration, acrylic on paper, *approx.* 40 × 32
242. *Study for Diana & Acteon*, 1995, illustration, acrylic on paper, 38 × 26
243. *Study for Salmacis & Hermaphroditus*, 1995, illustration, acrylic on paper, *approx.* 33 × 18

244. *Foot & Artichoke*, 1996, still life, acrylic on board, 34 × 51
245. *Birthday Card for G. W.*, 1996, illustration, ink on paper, 17 × 22
246. *Jug of Feathers & Lemons*, 1996, still life, acrylic on board, 32 × 43
247. *Still life with Marble Foot*, 1996, still life, acrylic on board, 45 × 59
248. *Swag & Skull*, 1997, still life, acrylic on paper, 42 × 32
249. *Starfish & Doll's Arm*, 1997, still life, acrylic on paper, 41 × 30
250. *Venus & Shell*, 1997, still life, acrylic on board, 34 × 50
251. *Lucy in Straw Hat*, 1997, portrait, acrylic on board, 46 × 39
252. *Suitor & Regalian Trophy*, 1997, figure composition, acrylic on paper, 50 × 72
253. *Two Shakespeare Sketches*, 1997, illustration, ink on paper, 24 × 28

Forbidden Fruit, La Fontaine, The Harvill Press, 1998

254. *Joconde*, 1997, illustration, ink on paper, 22 × 13
255. *Cuckolded*, 1997, illustration, ink on paper, 22 × 13
256. *The Cradle*, 1997, illustration, ink on paper, 22 × 13
257. *Cherubino*, 1997, illustration, ink on paper, 22 × 13
258. *Forbidden Fruit*, 1997, illustration, ink on paper, 22 × 13
259. *Calendar*, 1997, illustration, ink on paper, 22 × 13
260. *Mercenary Mistress*, 1997, illustration, ink on paper, 22 × 13
261. *Eel Pâté*, 1997, illustration, ink on paper, 22 × 13
262. *Matron of Ephesus*, 1997, illustration, ink on paper, 22 × 13

263. *Sea Change*, 1998, surrealist, acrylic on board, 99 × 121
264. *Rococo Chair with Frock*, 1998, still life, acrylic on canvas, 134 × 92
265. *Angels, Lemons & Volute*, 1998, still life, acrylic on board, 82 × 115
266. *Still Life with Blue Vine Plate*, 1998, still life, acrylic on canvas, 94 × 71
267. *Venus, Candle & Bowl* (first version), 1998, still life, acrylic on canvas, 61 × 76
268. *Doll's Head & Spotted Shell*, 1998, still life, acrylic on paper, 42 × 58
269. *Shattered Head with Classical Fragments*, 1998, still life, acrylic on board, 55 × 64
270. *Obelisk, Arch & Fragments*, 1998, landscape, acrylic on paper, 49 × 34
271. *Matrons & Torso Fragment*, 1999, still life, acrylic on paper, 30 × 46
272. *Empty Tombs*, 1999, landscape, acrylic on paper, 50 × 35
273. *Aphrodisias*, 1999, landscape, acrylic on paper, 46 × 31
274. *Giant 'Egg & Dart' Fragment*, 1999, still life, acrylic on paper, 47 × 35
275. *Lady at Theatre*, 1999, figure composition, acrylic on board, 100 × 69
276. *Volutes at Ephesus*, 1999, still life, acrylic on board, *approx.* 30 × 19
277. *Relief Sculpture at Didyma*, 1999, acrylic on paper, 15 × 21
278. *Burmese Marionette*, 1999, still life, acrylic on canvas, 76 × 110
279. *Pulcinella Visits Egypt*, 1999, *Commedia dell'Arte*, acrylic on paper, 53 × 67
280. *Rock Face*, 1999, surrealist, acrylic on canvas, 97 × 121
281. *Venus, Candle & Bowl* (second version), 2000, still life, acrylic on canvas, 61 × 76

OPPOSITE: Fig. 174 A mural panel in a bathroom in Holland Villas Road, oil on canvas, *approx.* 188 × 140cm. 1982. The dancers were inspired by Charles Schenk's magnificent photographic studies: *Draperies in Action*, New York, 1902. I later heard that when the lady of the house saw the dancers she exclaimed, 'He has obviously never heard of Twiggy!'.

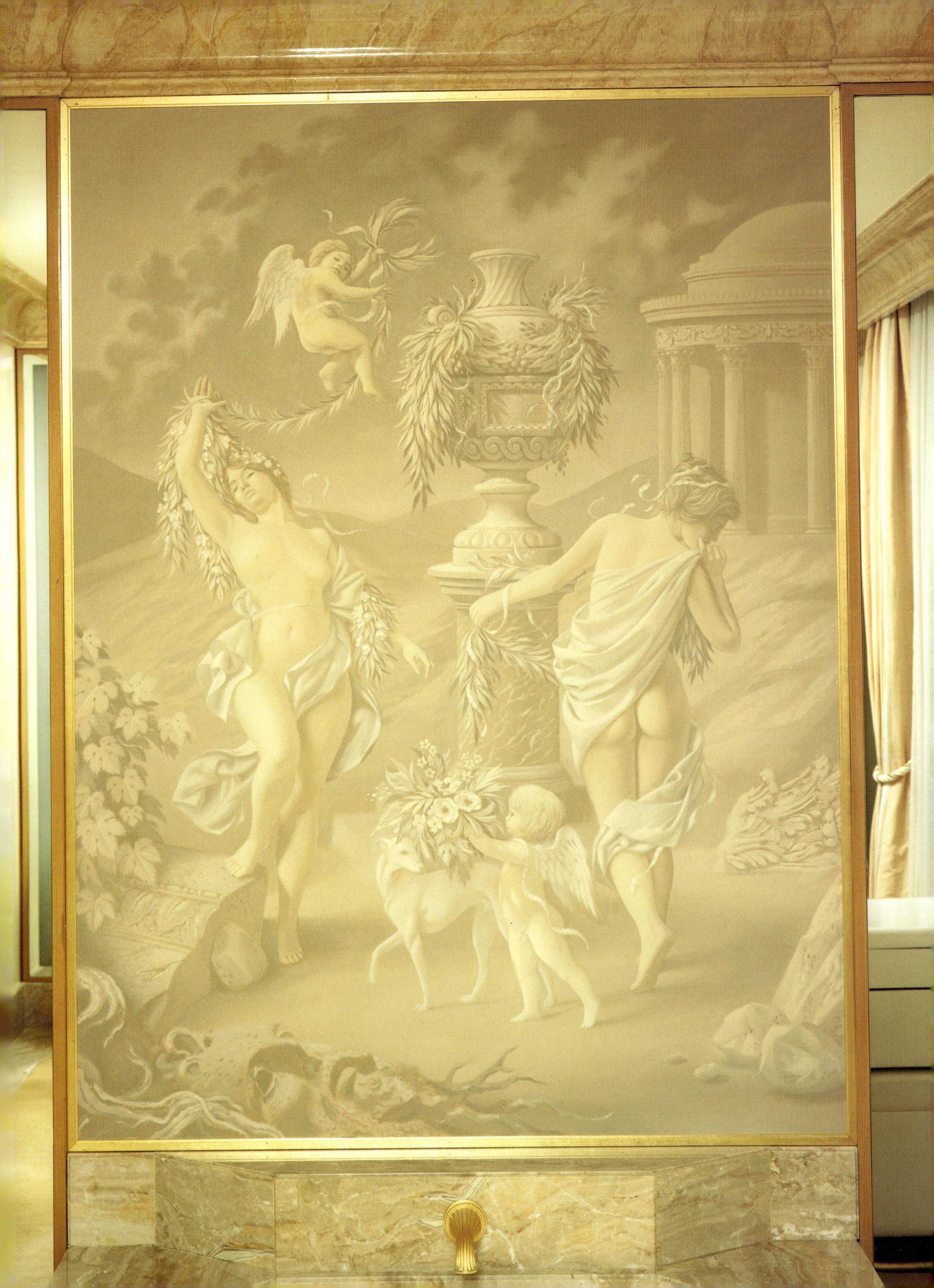

The limited edition consists of
one hundred and forty copies, signed and numbered: 1 to 140,
and ten copies: A to J, which are not for sale

It contains two wood engravings made in Italy in 1961:
A Winter Night and *The Dark Tower*
from *A Point of Departure* by Joy Finzi

The engravings are printed on mould-made acid free Zerkall paper
and are signed and numbered corresponding to the books

The limited edition is bound with a cloth spine
decorative printed boards and a slipcase by
The Fine Bindery, Wellingborough